THE ZONDERVAN 2021
PASTOR'S
ANNUAL

For a *FREE* downloadable copy of the book, please visit:
http://downloads.zondervan.com/zpa2021.

THE ZONDERVAN 2021
PASTOR'S ANNUAL

An Idea and Resource Book

T. T. CRABTREE

**ZONDERVAN
REFLECTIVE**

ZONDERVAN REFLECTIVE

The Zondervan 2021 Pastor's Annual
Copyright © 1980, 2000, 2020 by Zondervan

Requests for information should be addressed to:
Zondervan, *3900 Sparks Dr. SE, Grand Rapids, Michigan 49546*

Much of the contents of this book was previously published in *The Zondervan 2001 Pastor's Annual.*

ISBN 978-0-310-53666-6 (softcover)

ISBN 978-0-310-09964-2 (ebook)

Cover design: Angela Grit
Cover photo: © Anthony Heflin / Shutterstock
Interior design: Sue Vandenberg Koppenol

Printed in the United States of America

20 21 22 23 24 25 26 27 28 29 30 /LSC/ 15 14 13 12 11 10 9 8 7 6 5 4 3 2 1

CONTENTS

MISCELLANEOUS HELPS

Messages on the Lord's Supper

Messages for Children and Young People

Funeral Meditations

Weddings

Sentence Sermonettes

Indexes

CONTRIBUTING AUTHORS

Tom S. Brandon	AM	May 23
		June 27
		July 4, 11, 18, 25
		August 1, 8, 15, 22
Harold T. Bryson	PM	October 3, 10, 17, 24, 31
		November 7, 14, 21, 28
		December 5, 12, 19, 26
Hiram Campbell	AM	April 25
		May 2, 9, 16, 30
		June 6
James E. Carter	AM	August 29
		September 5, 12, 19
T. T. Crabtree		All messages besides those attributed to others
Harold T. Cummins	PM	April 4, 11, 18, 25
G. Nelson Duke	AM	October 3, 10, 17, 24
David R. Grant	PM	October 6, 13, 20, 27
		November 3, 10, 17, 24
		December 1, 8, 15, 22, 29
Robert L. Hamblin	AM	December 5, 12, 19, 26
James F. Heaton	PM	January 3, 10, 17, 24, 31
		February 7, 14, 21, 28
W. T. Holland	PM	July 4, 11, 18, 25
		August 1, 8, 15, 22, 29
		September 5, 12, 19, 26
David L. Jenkins	PM	May 5, 12, 19, 26
		June 2, 9, 16, 23, 30
		July 7, 14, 21, 28
Howard S. Kalb	PM	April 7, 14, 21, 28
		September 29
Jerold McBride	PM	March 7, 14, 21, 28
		May 2, 9, 16, 23, 30
		June 6, 13, 20, 27
Lowell D. Milburn	PM	September 1, 8, 15, 22
R. Travis Otey	AM	September 26
Charles Wade	AM	January 17
		November 7, 14, 21, 28
Fred M. Wood	AM	February 14, 21, 28
		March 7, 14, 21, 28
		April 4, 11, 28

PREFACE

Favorable comments from ministers who serve in many different types of churches suggest that the *Pastor's Annual* provides valuable assistance to many busy pastors as they seek to improve the quality, freshness, and variety of their pulpit ministry. To be of service to fellow pastors in their continuing quest to obey our Lord's command to Peter, "Feed my sheep," is a calling to which I respond with gratitude.

I pray that this issue of the *Pastor's Annual* will be blessed by our Lord in helping each pastor plan and produce a preaching program that will better meet the spiritual needs of his or her congregation.

This issue contains series of sermons by several contributing authors who have been effective contemporary preachers and successful pastors. Each author is listed with his sermons by date in the section titled "Contributing Authors." I accept responsibility for those sermons not listed there.

This issue of the *Pastor's Annual* is dedicated to the Lord with a prayer that he will bless these efforts to let the Holy Spirit lead us in preparing a planned preaching program for the year.

T. T. Crabtree
Springfield, Missouri

JANUARY

■ **Sunday Mornings**

Begin the year with Sunday morning messages that are evangelistic in objective and nature. "The Answer to Eternity's Most Important Questions" is the theme for this series of six messages.

■ **Sunday Evenings**

For Sunday evenings in January and February, use a nine-week series on the life and personality of Peter as he sought to be a faithful servant of Jesus Christ. The theme is "Peter's Pilgrimage of Faith."

■ **Wednesday Evenings**

Some things in life are optional while other things are essential. We will look at some essentials in a Wednesday evening series titled "Great Imperatives for Effective Living." On the last Wednesday evening of the month, we will change our focus a bit as we begin a series from Paul's letter to the Philippians called "Great Imperatives for Christian Living."

SUNDAY MORNING, JANUARY 3

Title: What It Means to Be Lost

Text: "As for you, you were dead in your transgressions and sins, in which you used to live when you followed the ways of this world and of the ruler of the kingdom of the air, the spirit who is now at work in those who are disobedient" (**Eph. 2:1–2 NIV**).

Scripture Reading: Ephesians 2:1–3

Hymns: "Since I Have Been Redeemed," Excell
"Love Divine, All Loves Excelling," Wesley
"Amazing Grace," Newton

Offertory Prayer: Our Father, you have given us all gifts, and we give to you this day the gift of ourselves. We thank you for life, for the strength to earn money, and for the motivation to return a portion of our money to you. Use these gifts in a way that brings glory to your name, strength to your cause, and power to your church. We give our lives to you, for you have given the greatest of all gifts to us, your Son Jesus Christ. In his name we pray. Amen.

Introduction

Sometimes we read in the newspaper or see on television that a mine has caved in and people are trapped in the tunnel. We feel something of the despair of their families as they grimly mutter, "They are lost! Lost!" "But," someone might say, "they are not lost. We know exactly where they are in the tunnel." "Yet," the reply comes back, "they are as lost as if they were a hundred miles underground. We cannot reach them. We know where they are, but they are lost."

This expresses the condition of those who are spiritually lost, without Christ and without salvation. We know where they are all right. But they are still lost without Christ.

For an answer to the query, "What does it mean to be lost?" there is no better place to turn than Ephesians 2.

I. To be lost is to be spiritually dead.

The lost person is cut off from the spiritual life and power that we find in Christ. Thus the condition of the lost person is death. Spiritual death is brought about by sin. Specific acts of sin are the result of the general habit of sin in one's life. These habitual sins kill all spiritual sensitivity.

In his famous sermon "Pay Day—Some Day," R. G. Lee tells of a man who called him one day, identifying himself as "the chief of the kangaroo court." At that time Lee was pastor of the First Baptist Church in New Orleans, Louisiana. The chief of the kangaroo court told Dr. Lee that all of that stuff he was preaching was nonsense, that God did not exist, and that what he described as sin was just good living. From time to time Lee received more telephone calls, some in the morning, some in the afternoon, some late at night, some at his church office, and some at home. But each of the calls from "the chief of the kangaroo court" taunted him and ridiculed him and his ideas of sin and judgment and God's accounting in life.

Then one day Lee received a call from the New Orleans Charity Hospital. The hospital official said a man at the hospital was about to die. He was out of his mind and raving, but he had asked for Dr. Lee. He had said something about being the chief of the kangaroo court. Immediately Dr. Lee rushed over. He was led to the man with whom he had talked on several occasions. He was the very picture of one in whom sin had evidently taken its toll. After he was introduced to Dr. Lee, he said, "The devil pays off all right—but he pays in counterfeit money . . . he pays in counterfeit money." And with these words he was gone to meet the God whom he had scoffed. He had lived long enough to give credit to what Scripture plainly teaches us: "The wages of sin is death" (Rom. 6:23 NIV).

II. To be lost is to be helplessly enslaved.

A. *Enslaved by the spirit of the age.* "You were dead in your transgressions and sins, in which you used to live when you followed the ways of this world" (Eph. 2:1–2 NIV). Think of things that characterize the spirit of our age or the ways of this world—greed, lust, pride, selfishness, unrestrained and undisciplined action.

B. *Enslaved by the power of Satan.* "You followed . . . the ruler of the kingdom of the air, the spirit who is now at work in those who are disobedient" (Eph. 2:2 NIV). The people of Paul's day believed that the air was filled with evil spirits. These spirits were ruled by the prince of the power of the air—the devil himself. In our day we have relegated the devil to cartoons and caricatures. But if we look closely at the world, we can see that the power of evil is still loose. Satan is directing the spirit of the age.

The German preacher Helmut Thielicke, in *How the World Began,* related an interesting experiment. Some of his students at the University of Hamburg volunteered at a camp for refugees from East Germany. Each afternoon they put on a puppet show. Dr. Thielicke played the part of the devil. He wielded a horrible, fiery red puppet in one hand and mustered up a menacing voice to represent all the terrible discords of hell. Then in tones brimming with sulfur, he advised the children to indulge in every conceivable naughtiness: never wash your feet at night; stick out your tongue at anybody you want to; drop banana skins on the street so people will slip on them. This sounds like a terrible message for children. But the results were enormous and generally recognized in the camp. The children suddenly began washing their feet at night and stopped sticking out their tongues. They actually shouted the devil puppet down with ear-splitting protests when he made his wicked suggestions. They would have absolutely no part with the devil.

Thielicke's puppet's temptation is different from our daily temptation at one significant point. Right from the start, Thielicke let it be known by the puppet's appearance and voice that the puppet represented the devil. Because of this, his suggestions could never succeed. In our experience, however, Satan works slyly.

C. *Enslaved by a spirit of rebellion.* By "those who are disobedient" (Eph. 2:2 NIV), Paul is referring to those whose lives are characterized by disobedience, the very essence of sin. From the time Adam and Eve disobeyed God in the garden of Eden until now, disobedience has been the heart of sin.

D. *Enslaved by our own desires.* The desires of the flesh and of the mind control the life. Flesh in the Bible and fleshly sins do not refer only to sexual sins. In Paul's list of sins of the flesh in Galatians 5:19–21, he includes with adultery and fornication other sins of idolatry, witchcraft, hatred, wrath, strife, envy, and so on. The flesh is the lower part of our nature; the flesh is that part of our nature that gives sin a point of attack.

III. To be lost is to be an object of wrath.

"We were by nature deserving of wrath" (Eph. 2:3 NIV). How vividly this expresses the fact that those who are lost and without Christ await the wrath of God and are objects of his wrath. God's wrath is not a whimsical thing. In the New Testament the wrath of God refers to his settled opposition to sin.

Part of God's wrath is revealed in the life of the lost person. Look to those whose lives have been lived in sin. They have become callous, hardened, and insensitive. God's wrath as a natural result of their sin has caused them to lose much of that which is finest and best in life.

But God's wrath also has a future aspect. The apostle Paul warned of our stubbornness and unrepentant hearts causing us to "[store] up wrath against [ourselves] for the day of God's wrath, when his righteous judgment will be revealed" (Rom. 2:5 NIV). The Bible confirms the judgment of God on our sin.

Conclusion

We have seen what it means to be lost, and thank God no one has to remain lost. Everyone can be saved. Ephesians 2:1–3 describes the condition of the lost. Verses 4–5, however, say, "But because of his great love for us, God, who is rich in mercy, made us alive with Christ even when we were dead in transgressions—it is by grace you have been saved" (NIV).

Charles H. Spurgeon never tired of telling the story of how he was saved. He had been trying to save himself by his own works. Then one rainy Sunday morning he wandered into a little chapel and sat down with the few worshipers who were there. That morning the minister preached on the text, "Look unto me, and be ye saved, all the ends of the earth" (Isa. 45:22). At the close of his sermon, he pointed his long, bony finger at Spurgeon and said, "Look! Look unto him, young man! Look unto Jesus, and you will be saved." That morning Spurgeon looked unto Jesus and was saved.

SUNDAY EVENING, JANUARY 3

Title: Preparation of Peter for Pentecost

Text: "But you shall receive power when the Holy Spirit has come upon you; and you shall be my witnesses in Jerusalem and in all Judea and Samaria and to the end of the earth" (**Acts 1:8 RSV**).

Scripture Reading: Acts 1:1–12

Introduction

For the next nine Sunday evenings, you are invited to consider what the Holy Spirit accomplished through Simon Peter from the time of Jesus' ascension until Peter's death.

Just before his ascension, Jesus gave his apostles this command: "Do not leave Jerusalem, but wait for the gift my Father promised, which you have heard me speak about. For John baptized with water, but in a few days you will be baptized with the Holy Spirit" (Acts 1:4–5 NIV). After Jesus' ascension, about 120 of his followers went to an upper room in Jerusalem to wait, as Jesus had commanded.

I. The preparation of Jesus' disciples (1:1–5).

A. *Jesus showed himself alive by many infallible proofs.* The disciples had come from doubt to certainty about Jesus' resurrection. They had seen the risen Lord.

B. *Jesus instructed his disciples.* He spoke to them of the things pertaining to the kingdom of God. In the four gospels we have a sample of his instruction. The sermons in Acts undoubtedly reflect Jesus' teaching during the forty days between his resurrection and ascension. During this period, Jesus reinterpreted their Holy Scriptures for them. For Cleopas and his companion, who did not know the meaning of the Scripture about the Messiah's resurrection, Jesus, on the way from Jerusalem to Emmaus, explained, "'O foolish men, and slow of heart to believe all that the prophets have spoken! Was it not necessary that the Christ should suffer these things and enter into his glory?' And beginning with Moses and all the prophets, he interpreted to them in all the scriptures the things concerning himself" (Luke 24:25–27 RSV).

Later that night Jesus appeared to the startled disciples in Jerusalem. He showed them his hands and feet, and he ate a piece of broiled fish and a honeycomb to assure them that he was no spirit or apparition. "Then he said to them, 'These are my words which I spoke to you, while I was still with you, that everything written about me in the law of Moses and the prophets and the psalms must be fulfilled.' Then he opened their minds to understand the scriptures, and said to them, 'Thus it is written, that the Christ should suffer and on the third day rise from the dead'" (Luke 24:44–46 RSV).

C. *Jesus gave them commandments.*

1. "Thus it is written . . . that repentance and forgiveness of sins should be preached in his name to all nations, beginning from Jerusalem. You are witnesses of these things" (Luke 24:46–48 RSV). The account in John 20 is very instructive. "Jesus said to them again, 'Peace be with you. As the Father has sent me, even so I send you'" (John 20:21 RSV).

2. Sometime between his resurrection and ascension, Jesus met the disciples by appointment at a mountain in Galilee. The angel at the tomb had instructed the women, "Do not be amazed; you seek Jesus of Nazareth, who was crucified. He has risen, he is not here; see the place where they laid him. But go, tell his disciples and Peter that he is going before you to Galilee; there you will see him, as he told you" (Mark 16:6–7 RSV).

This was probably the assembly of "above five hundred brethren" of whom Paul wrote in 1 Corinthians 15:6, and it was probably to them that the Lord delivered the Great Commission: "Now the eleven disciples went to Galilee, to the mountain to which Jesus had directed them. And when they saw him they worshiped him; but some doubted. And Jesus came and said to them, 'All authority in heaven and on earth has been given to me. Go therefore and make disciples of all nations, baptizing them in the name of the Father and of the Son and of the Holy Spirit, teaching them to observe all that I have commanded you; and lo, I am with you always, to the close of the age'" (Matt. 28:16–20 RSV).

3. At the end of the forty days after his resurrection, and just before his ascension, Jesus led his disciples to Mount Olivet. Instead of expressing interest in the coming of the Holy Spirit, who would lead them in witnessing to all nations, they asked, "Lord, will you at this time restore the kingdom to Israel?" (Acts 1:6 RSV). Since 63 BC Israel had been a province of Rome. It had achieved no real independence since the captivity about six centuries earlier. The restoration of the kingdom was considered part of the "sure mercies of David." Jesus replied, "It is not for you to know times or seasons which the Father has fixed by his own authority" (v. 7 RSV). There are some things we do not know or need to know. Times and seasons are with God. The duty of disciples then as now was to bear witness as Jesus commanded: "But you shall receive power when the Holy Spirit has come upon you; and you shall be my witnesses in Jerusalem and in all Judea and Samaria and to the end of the earth" (v. 8 RSV).

II. The ascension (1:9–12).

Jesus had accomplished on earth the work the Father had given him to do. "I have brought you glory on earth by finishing the work you gave me to do. And now, Father, glorify me in your presence with the glory I had with you before the world began" (John 17:4–5 NIV). Jesus had told his disciples, "It is for your good that I am going away" (John 16:7 NIV). He would go away that he might be nearer. Incarnate as Jesus, he was confined to a human body. As the Holy Spirit, he could return to dwell in all believers. "And when he had said this, as they were looking on, he was lifted up, and a cloud took him out of their sight" (Acts 1:9 RSV).

We are not to think that Jesus passed through infinite space. He passed from the sphere of the seen and the temporal to the sphere of the unseen and the eternal. He will be recognized by spiritual insight rather than by visual sight. We are not to think of Jesus as just out there somewhere. He is right here. Of course he is out there and here at the same time. Did he not say, "All authority in heaven and on earth has been given to me"? (Matt. 28:18 NIV).

If we humans, via television and the internet, can watch other humans walk on the moon, surely the risen Lord can be in heaven and on earth at the same time.

III. The promise of our Lord's return (1:10–11).

"While they were gazing into heaven as he went, behold, two men stood by them in white robes, and said, 'Men, of Galilee, why do you stand looking into heaven? This Jesus, who was taken up from you into heaven, will come in the same way as you saw him go into heaven'" (v. 11 RSV). "This Jesus" is the same person whom they had known in the days of his flesh. How encouraging! He "will come in the same way"—gloriously, mysteriously, but not necessarily to the same spot, or to live in human flesh, or to reign at earthly Jerusalem. Times and seasons are in God's hands, but the words of Jesus, especially Matthew 25:31 to the end of the chapter, seem to indicate that his second coming will end the gospel age. He is now present with believers in the person of the Holy Spirit, fulfilling his promises (Matt. 29:20; John 14:28).

Conclusion

The disciples had been assured that Jesus was alive. Jesus opened their eyes to the truths of their Scriptures so they could see the purpose for Jesus' crucifixion and resurrection. He then commanded them to bear witness to his death and resurrection to all people. But first he instructed them to go to an upper room in Jerusalem and wait (Acts 1:12–13). Why? Because Jesus had commanded, "Stay in the city, until you are clothed with power from on high" (Luke 24:49 RSV). They weren't to witness in their own authority and power, but in the authority and power of the Holy Spirit.

In a few days, at Pentecost, the Holy Spirit would inaugurate the gospel age by pouring out his power on the waiting disciples. Let us also wait before God. Let us not run ahead or lag behind the Holy Spirit, for the task of world evangelization is under his direction and by his power.

WEDNESDAY EVENING, JANUARY 6

Title: An Imperative Regarding the Negative and the Positive

Text: "Do not be conformed to this world but be transformed by the renewal of your mind, that you may prove what is the will of God, what is good and acceptable and perfect" **(Rom. 12:2 RSV)**.

Scripture Reading: Romans 12:1–2

Introduction

Let us rejoice that we find ourselves on Highway 2021 with all of its opportunities for ministry to others and service to our Lord. So that we might do a better job for our Lord, ourselves, and others, we are going to look at some of the great imperatives found in the writings of the apostle Paul as he wrote to the churches that were dear to his heart.

Paul's great challenge to the church at Rome provides us with an appropriate imperative with which to begin the new year. The imperatives in our text require that we give careful attention to the forces at work that affect our lives both negatively and positively. The negative imperative in our text calls attention to a great danger we all face—the peril of being contaminated by the environment in which we live. The positive imperative calls upon us to experience an inward spiritual transformation that produces a radical change in our conduct in the midst of this compromising environment in which we live.

I. The bold challenge to full commitment (Rom. 12:1).

Paul issues a challenge to all disciples of the Lord Jesus to present their bodies as a living sacrifice in service to God and others. Phillips translates this bold challenge: "With eyes wide open to the mercies of God, I beg you, my brothers, as an act of intelligent worship, to give him your bodies, as a living sacrifice, consecrated to him and acceptable by him." This is a pivotal verse. That which precedes is doctrinal, and that which follows is very practical. The first portion of the book deals with our beliefs, and the balance of the book deals with the expression of those beliefs in behavior.

II. An imperative regarding a great peril.

"Do not be conformed to this world" (Rom. 12:2 RSV). Phillips translates this warning in a powerful way: "Don't let the world around you squeeze you into its own mold." As the redeemed children of God, having been made new creatures in Christ Jesus (2 Cor. 5:17), we live in a world system that is under the dominion of the evil one (1 John 5:19). The sinful world in which we live is not passive and unconcerned. Evil is aggressive, and we must put forth effort to prevail against the squeezing, conforming power of the world system in which we live.

God calls us to be different. We are to be dead to sin and alive to God (Rom. 6:4, 11–14). Instead of responding affirmatively to temptations, we are to respond as dead persons. We must not permit either our evil nature within or the evil world about us to dominate us. We are to conduct ourselves as beloved children of God, walking in the light rather than in darkness (Eph. 5:3–14). Paul told the Colossians to put to death that which was earthly and evil in their nature (Col. 3:5–9) and in turn to put on the new nature and live as God's chosen ones (vv. 10–17).

III. An imperative regarding an exciting possibility.

"Be transformed by the renewal of your mind" (Rom. 12:2 RSV). Paul uses a Greek word here with which people today are familiar. It is the word *metamorphosis*, and it means to change the nature.

A farmer raised a field of cabbage but was unable to sell it. The cabbage went to waste in the field, and many cabbages were eaten by worms. Later the farmer's son noticed small yellow butterflies in the field where the cabbage had been raised. He learned that the worms had changed into butterflies. The technical name for that change is *metamorphosis.*

Paul was urging his readers to experience a remarkable transformation that is possible by a renewal of the mind that comes when one is born again and filled with the Holy Spirit. It is the work of the Holy Spirit using the Scriptures and a responsive heart to bring about inward mental and spiritual transformation that is manifested outwardly in a change in one's conduct.

If you would change your conduct, you must change your creed. If you would change your behavior, you must first of all change your beliefs. If you would become truly Christian in your conduct, you must become Christlike in your thinking. For only by a revolutionary change in your thoughts can you experience a revolutionary change in your conduct. The call to repentance is in reality a call to a complete change in one's thought patterns and decision-making processes with reference to God, to sin, to self, to things, and to others. How much change took place in your thinking about God, yourself, others, and things during the past year?

Paul challenged the Philippian Christians to have the mind of Christ (Phil. 2:5). Only as we let the Holy Spirit change our thinking and cause us to think like Christ can we experience the transformation that needs to take place in our lives.

Conclusion

The glorious end result of refusing to be conformed to the world and of experiencing inward mental and spiritual transformation is to prove in our own experience that the will of God is good and acceptable and perfect.

You can never really know that God's will is best for you and for others until you make this complete commitment of yourself to God's will as he reveals it to you. So with eyes wide open to the mercies of God, present yourself to him.

SUNDAY MORNING, JANUARY 10

Title: What It Means to Be Saved

Text: "And such were some of you: but ye are washed, but ye are sanctified, but ye are justified in the name of the Lord Jesus, and by the Spirit of our God" (**1 Cor. 6:11**).

Scripture Reading: 1 Corinthians 6:9–11

Hymns: "Saved, Saved," Scholfield
"Redeemed, How I Love to Proclaim It," Crosby
"All That Thrills My Soul," Harris

21

Offertory Prayer: Our Father, this is the day that you have made. We will rejoice and be glad in it. This is the day that we offer our gifts to you with joy. We are grateful to you for providing us with work and the strength to accomplish that work. We thank you for life, for salvation, for fellowship in the church, and for opportunities to serve others. Make us adequate for the tasks to which you have called us. Make us sensitive to the needs of those around us. And make us aware of your presence within us. We pray in the name of Christ our Savior. Amen.

Introduction

In Houston, Texas, during one of Billy Graham's evangelistic crusades, a man who owned a liquor store was saved. The next morning he put a sign on the front door that said, "Out of business." He was saved, and he would not carry on the same kind of business as before.

I read of another man who was saved in an evangelistic service. He was called "Old John," and he was notorious as the town drunk. Someone met him on the street the next morning and said, "Good morning, Old John." He said, "Who are you talking to? My name is not 'Old John.' I'm *new* John." He was born again, and a transformation had taken place in his life.

I also read about a man in a small Texas town who used to hitch his horse in front of the saloon each morning. One morning the saloon-keeper saw the man's horse hitched in front of the Methodist Church. The man was walking down the street, so the saloon-keeper called out, "Say, why is your horse hitched in front of the Methodist Church this morning?" The man turned and called back, "Well, last night I was converted in the revival meeting, and I've changed hitching posts." His life was no longer hitched to sin but to the Savior!

These three stories tell us something about what it means to be saved. To be saved means to change your way of life, to hitch yourself in faith to God so that his plan for your life can be accomplished.

Last Sunday we discussed what it means to be lost. Today we will consider what it means to be saved. In 1 Corinthians 6:9–11, Paul expressed quite well what it means to be saved. He told in verses 9–10 of the sins of the unrighteous. They are sins against self and against others. "And such *were* some of you," Paul said. "But ye *are*..." (emphasis added) continues the rest of the sentence, indicating that his readers had once lived in sin but were now transformed.

I. To be saved means to be cleansed from sin.

"But ye are washed." This word "but" is the strongest kind of adversative. It is used to show a clean break between what has gone before and what follows.

Cleansing from sin is the forgiveness of sins. When Christ saves us, he forgives our sins. Ephesians 1:7—"In him we have redemption through his blood, the forgiveness of sins, in accordance with the riches of God's grace" (NIV)—equates forgiveness with redemption. The first step in forgiveness

22

of sin is to realize our need for forgiveness. Reinhold Niebuhr said, "No cumulation of contradictory evidence seems to disturb modern man's good opinion of himself." This is our greatest hindrance to salvation: realizing that we really need it. Notice that of all those other awful categories of sin he said, "And such *were* some of you" (emphasis added). They *were* those things, but now their sins are forgiven.

How does this forgiveness come about? Revelation 1:5 refers to Jesus as the one who loved us and washed away our sins with his own blood. This is exactly how forgiveness and cleansing from sin come about.

A preacher said to a dying woman, "Have you made your peace with God?" "No," she said. "Do you realize," he said, "that you are dying and that soon you must go to face God and give an account of your life?" "Yes," the woman replied, "but I am not disturbed about that. I do not have to make my peace with God; Christ made that peace for me on Calvary nineteen hundred years ago. I am simply resting in the peace which he has already made" (Herschel Ford, *Simple Sermons on Great Christian Doctrines* [Grand Rapids: Zondervan, 1976], 76).

Christ has already made peace for us, which is the forgiveness of and cleansing from sin. We need only to enter into that peace through faith.

II. To be saved means to be set apart for service.

"But ye are sanctified." When we are saved, our sins are forgiven. But along with forgiveness comes sanctification, which means to separate, or to set apart. When God saves us, he sets us apart for his use. The verb tense for this word is the same as the tense for "washed." This means that sanctification is a decisive action that God has taken at one point. At the time of our faith and belief in Christ, God not only forgives our sins but also sets us apart for his service.

When America entered World War II, the nation's great automobile plants changed from peacetime production to wartime production. Instead of making automobiles, they began to make planes and tanks. In other words, they were set apart for a new type of work; the entire purpose of their machines was changed. And so it is that when a person is saved, the entire purpose of his or her life is changed.

Sanctification, then, is a definite act on the part of God at the time a person is saved. At that time the person is set apart for service to God. We can also consider sanctification as the process of growth that each Christian experiences. Sanctification is not only an act but also a process. We are to grow in grace.

III. To be saved means to be justified by God.

"But ye are justified." *Justification* is another term used by Paul to express our salvation. Even as God forgives and sets apart, he justifies those who have accepted Christ as personal Savior. This is a legal term used in a vital sense.

Justification basically means to show right or to pronounce right. But this definition fails to capture all that it entails. God does not merely pronounce us right; he makes us right. This is the very nature of salvation and the new birth. In justification God does for us what we cannot do for ourselves.

A. *Notice that it is sinners who are justified by God.* Recall the list of perverted personalities that Paul named in 1 Corinthians 6:9–10. These are the very people Paul said were now just and right through faith.

B. *This points us to another aspect of justification.* It is by faith. Paul contrasted justification by works and justification by faith. We are justified, made right before God, on the condition of our faith in him—not by anything we do. When Martin Luther was climbing the Scala Sancta, the sacred stairs, in Rome, kissing every step as was prescribed, he remembered the words of Scripture, "The just shall live by faith." He then stood up and walked back down the stairs. "The just shall live by faith!" then became the battle cry of the Reformation.

C. *Justification by faith is based on Christ's work for us.* Notice how we are washed, sanctified, and justified "in the name of the Lord Jesus, and by the Spirit of our God" (1 Cor. 6:11).

A preacher tried to explain to a miner that salvation is a free gift of God. The miner could not understand it in this way. One day the preacher accompanied him to the mines. They were preparing to descend several hundred feet by means of the company elevator when the preacher said to the miner, "How much will this cost me?" The miner replied, "It will cost you nothing." The preacher then said, "That is too cheap; I don't want to ride on anything that costs nothing." "Cheap!" exclaimed the miner. "This elevator cost $25,000—the company paid that much for it." "Oh," said the preacher, "I understand—it cost me nothing, but it did cost someone else a great price." Thus he was able to explain to the miner that salvation came to us in the same manner. It cost us nothing, but it did cost another great price—it cost Christ all that he had.

Conclusion

This is what it means to be saved. Forgiveness and sanctification and justification are all different aspects of the same act. This experience can be yours. Accept it by faith.

SUNDAY EVENING, JANUARY 10

Title: Peter Waiting on the Lord

Text: "And behold, I send the promise of my Father upon you; but stay in the city, until you are clothed with power from on high" (**Luke 24:49 RSV**).

Scripture Reading: Acts 1:12–26

Introduction

Luke, in closing his gospel, described Jesus' ascension this way: "And behold, I send the promise of my Father upon you; but stay in the city, until you are clothed with power from on high. Then he led them out as far as Bethany, and lifting up his hands he blessed them. While he blessed them, he parted from them. And they returned to Jerusalem with great joy" (Luke 24:49–52 RSV).

Jesus' followers had good reasons for their great joy. They had seen and heard the life, ministry, and teachings of Jesus, especially his teachings about the kingdom during the forty days since his resurrection. They were sure he was alive. They had experienced salvation and a divine call to make disciples of all nations. Further, Jesus had promised to be with them and to empower them for the task.

I. Jesus' followers did as Jesus commanded (1:12–13).

Jesus' followers did not know how Jesus would fulfill his promises, but they did as he had commanded. They serve as a good example for all believers. The Lord has not called us to understand him, but to follow him. His command was, "Stay in the city, until you are clothed with power from on high" (Luke 24:49 RSV). "Wait for the promise of the Father, which, he said, 'you heard from me'" (Acts 1:4 RSV).

A. *Where?* "Then they returned to Jerusalem from the mount called Olivet, which is near Jerusalem, a sabbath day's journey away; and when they had entered, they went up to the upper room" (Acts 1:12–13 RSV). This was probably the same upper room in which they had eaten the last Passover and in which Jesus had instituted the Lord's Supper.

B. *Who?* About 120 people were present. Where were the multitudes who ate the loaves and the fish? Where were the five hundred who had gathered on the mountain in Galilee? Eleven of the apostles were there; Judas had committed suicide. The apostles present were Peter, John, James, Andrew, Philip, Thomas, Bartholomew (also called Nathanael), Matthew (also called Levi), James son of Alphaeus, Simon the Zealot, and Judas the son of James (also called Thaddeus). Along with the women (who are not named) was Mary the mother of Jesus. Jesus' half brothers were among the disciples. They had not believed in him six months before: "Even his brothers did not believe in him" (John 7:5 RSV). Jesus had made a special appearance to James (1 Cor. 15:7), who became a leader in the church at Jerusalem (see Acts 15:13). Jesus' brother Jude was probably the author of the New Testament book that bears his name.

C. *What?* "All these with one accord devoted themselves to prayer" (Acts 1:14 RSV). Why pray when there was work to do? Jesus had so commanded. Many times Jesus had prayed before embarking on heavy responsibilities. For examples, see Mark 1:35–37 and Luke 6:12–16. Earlier Jesus had commanded, "Pray therefore the Lord of the harvest to send out laborers into his harvest" (Matt. 9:38 RSV). They were united in applying their strength to prayer. What an experience—a church united in a prayer effort!

II. Jesus' followers took time for the first church business meeting (1:15–26).

A. *The local church is part of God's plan.* Each Christian is responsible for obeying Jesus' commands, and Christians should cooperate in doing together what they cannot do separately. Here we witness something new and wonderful in the world—a church composed of saved people who have voluntarily covenanted together to do the Lord's will. Had Jesus given instructions about the church as part of his instructions about "the things pertaining to the kingdom of God" (Acts 1:3) during the preceding forty days? It is likely that he had. The apostles and other believers undoubtedly had the leadership of God.

B. Peter took the lead. That was Peter's way. Apparently it was also the people's will and in accord with God's plan.

C. Peter understood that the Scriptures were fulfilled by the death of Judas. He also understood that God wanted Judas's place among the twelve apostles to be filled. Acts 1:18–19 was probably a parenthesis by Luke. In verse 21 Peter quotes from Psalms 69:25 and 109:8.

  The requirements for an apostle, as set forth in Acts 1:21–22, are such that no person subsequent to the first century could fill them. Peter set forth the requirements, "and they put forward two, Joseph called Barsabbas, who was surnamed Justus, and Matthias" (Acts 1:23 RSV). Note that "they," the assembled church, appointed these two brethren. Peter did not appoint them. Both men were good men. The group resolved the choice by casting lots, and the lot fell on Matthias. The pure chance of the casting of the lot is removed by the church's earnest prayer and the superior qualifications of both men. There is no subsequent record of the use of this method. The New Testament churches advanced to the better way of voting democratically while seeking divine guidance.

Conclusion

God's delays are very difficult to understand. Why should the disciples wait ten days until Pentecost? Why should Moses spend forty years in the wilderness herding sheep? Why should Paul spend three years in Arabia? Why should Paul spend his last years in prison? Why does sickness often come to the most devout of God's servants when there is so much to do? Why wait?

1. *We must be obedient.* "Be thou faithful unto death, and I will give thee a crown of life" (Rev. 2:10). "Come ye after me, and I will make you

to become fishers of men" (Mark 1:17). Our responsibility is to obey. It is God's responsibility to make us fruitful.

2. *"We know that in everything God works for good with those who love him, who are called according to his purpose" (Rom. 8:28 RSV).* Sometimes we can see God's providential purpose. Moses, over a forty-year period, learned the wilderness over which he would lead the children of Israel. In Arabia Paul was able to get his theology straight. Paul's prison years gave him time to write his most profound epistles (Phil. 1:12–14). Paul's sickness humbled him and made him a more effective apostle (2 Cor. 12:7–10). Romans 8:28 is true whether we perceive it to be or not.

3. *Renewal of strength comes by waiting.* "But they that wait upon the LORD shall renew their strength; they shall mount up with wings as eagles; they shall run, and not be weary; and they shall walk, and not faint" (Isa. 40:31).

4. *Waiting before God humbles believers.* God often uses ordinary people and relatively unimportant situations to advance his kingdom. Charles Haddon Spurgeon was won to Christ in a small prayer meeting conducted by a layman on a rainy night. Dwight L. Moody was won by his Sunday school teacher. Andrew won his brother Peter. The lesson is that the victory is not by our own ability or strength but by God's Spirit and power. God's will is central. He will not suffer defeat. God plus one is a majority.

WEDNESDAY EVENING, JANUARY 13

Title: An Imperative Regarding Spiritual Competency

Text: "Do your best to present yourself to God as one approved, a workman who has no need to be ashamed, rightly handling the word of truth" **(2 Tim. 2:15 RSV).**

Introduction

The New International Version translates this text, "Do your best to present yourself to God as one approved, a workman who does not need to be ashamed and who correctly handles the word of truth." Phillips translates it, "For yourself, concentrate on winning God's approval, on being a workman with nothing to be ashamed of, and who knows how to use the word of truth to the best advantage."

While it is not necessary that one have a graduate degree from a school of theology before he or she can serve God effectively, it remains true that God places no premium on ignorance. In the words of our text, the apostle is urging upon Timothy and all of his readers the importance of presenting ourselves to our Father God as competent workers who are skilled in doing the work of God's kingdom.

Paul encouraged believers to present their bodies to God as living sacrifices. It is in our bodies that we are to honor and glorify him. It is in our bodies that we are to demonstrate both the wisdom and power of God. Paul affirmed this same concept in his first letter to the Corinthians, in which he declared that the body is the dwelling place of the Holy Spirit, and consequently it should not participate in immoral activities (1 Cor. 6:15–20).

The words of our text emphasize maturity, skill, and competency in the service of our Lord. Paul appealed to Timothy's sense of pride in personal accomplishment, "a workman who has no need to be ashamed." Have you ever seen a carpenter who was ashamed of his craftsmanship? Have you ever known a bricklayer who laid a crooked wall of brick? Have you ever known a woman who made a dress and was then ashamed to wear it? The apostle was encouraging Timothy to present himself to God and to do what was necessary to become a skilled worker who "rightly handles the word of truth."

We can do a number of very practical things to improve our spiritual competency in our ministry for our Lord. The King James Version translates this verse, "Study to show thyself approved unto God, a workman that needeth not to be ashamed, rightly dividing the word of truth." Competency requires study and practice. Only as we study can we be skilled. Let us focus attention on how we should study the Bible if we would rightly handle it so as to accomplish the purpose for which God intended it.

I. Let us read the Bible regularly.

We should spend time every day listening to God as he speaks to us through the Scriptures.

II. Let us read the Bible subjectively.

It is not enough that we read the Bible merely as a record of what happened in the ancient past. God can and will speak to us in the present if we will listen to him.

III. Let us read the Bible intelligently.

One must beware of reading the Bible as he or she would read some kind of crystal ball. We must follow certain guidelines as we study the Bible.

   A. *Let us try to understand what the Bible meant in its historical context.* This is when it was first recorded by man under the inspiration of the Holy Spirit.
   B. *Let us try to understand the language.* We need to understand the figures of speech and terminology the author was using to communicate divine truth.
   C. *Let us study the Bible in a logical manner, not merely searching for proof texts.* Let us examine each phrase and verse in its context. Let us study the paragraph in the light of the chapter, and the chapter in the light of the book, and each book in the context of the whole of Scriptures.

D. *Let us remember that the Bible is a record of God's self-revelation.* Only the Holy Spirit can unlock his secrets and reveal to us the great biblical truths of God.

IV. Let us read the Bible systematically.

A good pattern would be to read five chapters in the Old Testament every day and three chapters in the New Testament, reading straight through both the Old and New Testaments.

V. Let us read the Bible prayerfully.

Memorize and meditate on the great promises and the great warnings in Scripture.

VI. Let us read the Bible obediently.

We should study the Word so that we might learn about God, ourselves, and others. And as God reveals his truth to us, let us respond to it.

Conclusion

It is important that ministers interpret the Scriptures correctly and apply them properly. It is just as important that Sunday school teachers know how to handle the Word of God properly. And it is equally important that every Christian study to show himself or herself a worker who does not need to be ashamed and who uses the Word of God rightly. If we will study diligently and present ourselves joyfully to our precious Lord, it is highly unlikely that we will be ashamed of ourselves or of our lives when we stand before him.

SUNDAY MORNING, JANUARY 17

Title: How We Can Know God

Text: "All things have been delivered to me by my Father; and no one knows the Son except the Father, and no one knows the Father except the Son and any one to whom the Son chooses to reveal him" **(Matt. 11:27 RSV)**.

Scripture Reading: Matthew 11:25–30; Colossians 1:13–20

Hymns: "All Creatures of Our God and King," Francis of Assisi
"Fairest Lord Jesus," anonymous German hymn
"One Day," Chapman

Offertory Prayer: We begin now to anticipate the gift of your Son, O heavenly Father. To remind us that he is your gift to us and not our gift to ourselves, Jesus Christ, born of a virgin, reveals who you really are and what you really want from us. Our gifts are but a sign that all our life is given freely to you. Remind us that the greatest gift is your Son, and every gift we give is a way of remembering and being thankful. Amen.

Introduction

The majority of Americans believe in God, and many believe that Jesus Christ is the divine Son of God. This raises the question as to how we know there is a God.

I. We can know God by the mystery and majesty of creation (Matt. 11:25).

The mystery of the creative power is hidden from us. We cannot know the Creator or the meaning of his creation unless he reveals himself to us. We come to the majesty of creation with humility because we are faced with a reality of such scope and power that we know almost instinctively that its source is beyond human imagination or accidental happening. This way of knowing God is sometimes referred to as "general revelation" and is available to everyone (cf. Rom. 1:20–23, 25).

Robert Jastrow, an internationally known astronomer and authority on life in the cosmos, founded and directed NASA's Goddard Institute for Space Studies and served as a professor at both Columbia University and Dartmouth College. In his book *God and the Astronomers,* Jastrow claimed to be an agnostic in religious matters. His studies in astronomy, however, led him to believe that the universe had a beginning and that it will be impossible for scientists ever to discover exactly how that beginning came to be. Scientists have had great success in tracing the chain of cause and effect backward in time. But now, though they would like to pursue that inquiry farther back, "the barrier to further progress seems insurmountable. It is not a matter of another year, another decade of work, another measurement, or another theory; at this moment it seems as though science will never be able to raise the curtain on the mystery of Creation. For the scientist who has lived by his faith and power of reason, the story ends like a bad dream. He has scaled the mountains of ignorance; he is about to conquer the highest peak; as he pulls himself over the final rock, he is greeted by a band of theologians who have been sitting there for centuries" (Robert Jastrow, *God and the Astronomers* [New York: Norton, 1978], 115–16).

Jastrow believed the time of creation was some twenty billion years ago. Somewhere out in the great, dark vastness of the universe there just may have been a God who called it all into being. This is further evidence of the compelling nature of general revelation, which brings people to a shallow faith. It is not final, nor is it conclusive as regards Jesus Christ, but it is for many a place of beginning. Jesus calls the Father "Lord of heaven and earth." The mystery of creation is hidden from the wise but revealed to little children (Matt. 11:25).

II. We can know God by the mystery and majesty of Christ (Matt. 11:27).

Many people may be drawn to hope and beginning belief by the reality of creation, but redemption, reconciliation, and salvation are in Christ alone. Eugene Ionesco was the founder of the Theater of the Absurd. At the opening of the Salzburg Festival in 1972, he lamented, "The world has lost its bearings. Not that ideologies are lacking to give directions: only that they lead nowhere. . . . People are going round in circles in the cage of their planet because they have forgotten that they can look up to the sky. . . . Because all we want is to live, it has become impossible for us to live. Just look around you!" (quoted by Hans Küng in *On Being a Christian* [Garden City, NY: Doubleday, 1976], 57).

In this astounding time of scientific openness to the mystery of life and of human despair at the absurdity of life, how can we put a face on God? Jesus said, "No one knows the Father except the Son and any one to whom the Son chooses to reveal him" (v. 27 RSV). The apostle Paul called Jesus Christ "the image of the invisible God, the first-born of all creation. . . . For in him all the fulness of God was pleased to dwell" (Col. 1:15, 19 RSV). Jesus Christ revealed some very specific truths to us about the nature of the ultimate God.

A. *The birth of Jesus indicates that God was not afraid to enter fully into human life.* Carlyle Marney noted the danger that an incarnation represents. "Every incarnation risks a drowning! Either you will smother in the stuff of this present human existence, or you will know a triumph of the self through matter!" (Carlyle Marney, *Priests to Each Other* [Valley Forge, PA: Judson, 1974], 29). There is no escape, no deliverance that plucks us out. Jesus came to carry us through, dripping wet but not drowned!

B. *Our Lord Jesus taught us to call the mystery and majesty "Father."*

C. *In his life Jesus demonstrated how to live in a basic, trustful relationship with God.*

D. *In his death Jesus hung between heaven and earth, between God and man.* Crushed beneath our iniquities, Jesus died for us.

E. *Through Jesus' victory over death at the resurrection, he has invited us to the victorious life.* We know that death cannot rip us from the Father's hand.

F. *The promised return of Jesus to the earth reveals that God is not finished with this world or with our lives.*

Conclusion

Jesus Christ is unique, one of a kind, but he is willing to share life with all who will believe. He has given us eternal life "in order that he might be the first-born among many brethren" (Rom. 8:29 RSV). The heart of our Lord's appeal is simply this: you can know God by trusting him. In trusting him you will finally come to know him. Only in the life of the Son do we have any assurance that we can know God as he really is: God the Father, Lord of heaven and earth, Father of our Lord Jesus Christ, and Father to all who will turn to him in trusting faith.

SUNDAY EVENING, JANUARY 17

Title: Peter at Pentecost

Text: "But this is that which was spoken by the prophet Joel; and it shall come to pass in the last days, saith God, I will pour out of my Spirit upon all flesh" (**Acts 2:16–17**).

Scripture Reading: Acts 2:1–21

Introduction

"In my former book, Theophilus, I wrote about all that Jesus began to do and to teach until the day he was taken up to heaven" (Acts 1:1–2 NIV). The former treatise is the Gospel of Luke. In this gospel, Luke wrote of Jesus' ministry in the days of his flesh until his ascension. In Acts Luke was about to write of what Jesus continued to do and teach in the person of the Holy Spirit through his disciples.

I. The advent of Jesus and the advent of the Holy Spirit.

It is instructive to compare the coming of Jesus as Mary's baby at Bethlehem with the coming of the Holy Spirit at Pentecost as promised by the Father through Jesus (see Luke 24:49; John 16:7–16; Acts 1:4). Luke 1 records the events in preparation for the advent of the Messiah. Acts 1 records the events in preparation for the advent of the Holy Spirit. Luke 2 records the advent of Jesus for making salvation possible. Acts 2 records the advent of the Holy Spirit for the proclamation of salvation. Jesus made atonement for sin. The Holy Spirit applies the merits of Christ's atonement in the regeneration of sinners who believe on Jesus. The advent of Jesus was in humility. The advent of the Holy Spirit was in power to people who were already Christians. The advent of Jesus had been promised through the prophets. The advent of the Holy Spirit had been promised by the Father through Jesus. Jesus did not begin to be when he was born of Mary in Bethlehem. The Holy Spirit did not begin to be when he came at Pentecost. Jesus was incarnated once for all. The incarnation will not be repeated. The Holy Spirit inaugurated the new gospel age at Pentecost. It will not be repeated but will continue until Jesus comes again.

As we linger reverently around the manger in Bethlehem, so let us draw near to the upper room in Jerusalem.

II. The manifestation of the Holy Spirit (2:1–4).

A. *On the day of Pentecost.* Pentecost means "fifty days." It was one of the three great annual feasts of the Jews, the celebration of the completed grain harvest, and it came fifty days after Passover (cf. Ex. 23:16–17; Lev. 23:15–21; Deut. 16:9–17). It also celebrated the giving of the law at Sinai. Passover was an appropriate time for Jesus to die, for in his death he established the new Passover. "Christ our passover is sacrificed for us" (1 Cor. 5:7). Pentecost was an appropriate time for the Holy Spirit to commence his ministry within believers (cf. Jer. 31:31ff. and Heb. 8:8ff.).

B. *"They were all with one accord in one place" (Acts 2:1).* Has there ever been another church in which all the members were in one place harmoniously praying for God's promised blessing?

C. *Three miracles.*

1. "And suddenly there came a sound from heaven as of a rushing mighty wind, and it filled all the house where they were sitting" (Acts. 2:2). This was not wind, but a sound like wind. The word for wind and spirit (or ghost) is the same. At creation "the LORD God formed man of the dust of the ground, and breathed into his nostrils the breath of life; and man became a living soul" (Gen. 2:7). The Holy Spirit is the holy wind or holy breath that breathes new life into sinners when they are born again (cf. John 3:5–8; 20:22).

2. "They saw what seemed to be tongues of fire that separated and came to rest on each of them" (Acts 2:3 NIV). John the Baptist had prophesied that "He [the Messiah] shall baptize you with the Holy Ghost, and with fire" (Matt. 3:11). The fire that separates the dross from pure metal is a symbol of purity, separation, and judgment. The flames alighting on each believer signified that the Holy Spirit came on all believers without distinction. Whatever Peter and the other apostles received, the lowliest disciple also received.

3. "And they were all filled with the Holy Ghost, and began to speak with other tongues, as the Spirit gave them utterance" (Acts 2:4). There were present at Pentecost those from many nations who spoke many languages. When the disciples were filled with the Holy Spirit and spoke in other tongues as the Spirit enabled them, each one in the crowd heard the disciples speaking in his own language (see Acts 2:6–12).

4. These miracles attending the advent of the Holy Spirit confirmed his coming. In a similar way, the miracles at the birth of Jesus (the miraculous conception, the annunciation, the guiding star, the angelic chorus) had confirmed his advent.

Conclusion

Peter's explanation of Pentecost can be found in Acts 2:12–21. People who heard the disciples speaking in their languages were amazed and asked, "What meaneth this?" (v. 12). The irrational explanation of the skeptics that the disciples were drunk proved nothing. Peter dismissed it by saying that 9 a.m. was too early in the day for people to be drunk. Peter saw the occurrence as the fulfillment of a prophecy by Joel: "And it shall come to pass in the last days, saith God, I will pour out of my Spirit upon all flesh: and your sons and your daughters shall prophesy, and your young men shall see visions, and your old men shall dream dreams: and on my servants and on my handmaidens I will pour out in those days of my Spirit; and they shall prophesy" (vv. 17–18). He was quoting Joel 2:28–29. "This is that which was spoken by the prophet Joel," said Peter (Acts 2:16). The last days have now come—the days of the Messiah and gospel proclamation, the days in which disciples are to obey Christ's great commission. Peter probably did not know that these days would continue over many centuries.

The early Christians were experiencing the fulfillment of God's promise. God was pouring out his Spirit on all without distinction of age, gender, race, or professional standing. The time had come "that whosoever shall call on the name of the Lord shall be saved" (Acts 2:21). Peter does not explain the imagery in verses 19 and 20. The events have not been fulfilled literally and perhaps will not be, or perhaps they will be made clearer in the future.

But this is clear: in accord with the promise of the Father through Jesus, the Holy Spirit has come to abide through the last days until Jesus comes again. The Holy Spirit will guide and empower disciples to conduct a world mission enterprise in accord with Jesus' commands.

WEDNESDAY EVENING, JANUARY 20

Title: An Imperative Regarding Restoring the Fallen Brother

Text: "Brethren, if a man is overtaken in any trespass, you who are spiritual should restore him in a spirit of gentleness. Look to yourself, lest you too be tempted" **(Gal. 6:1 RSV).**

Scripture Reading: Galatians 6:1–10

Introduction

The church of the living God is often referred to as the household of God. A local congregation is a tangible expression of the household of faith. In the household of faith we are brothers and sisters, and we have mutual responsibilities to relate to one another as children of the Father God. The all-inclusive law that should prevail in the household of faith is the law of love.

As members of the household of faith, we are also servants of Jesus Christ. We have been given the mission of evangelizing the world. Perhaps the greatest handicap we have to overcome in leading the world to a knowledge of Christ is found in the failure of those who profess to be Christians. What is our individual and collective responsibility toward professing Christians who have fallen into sin and are failing to be good representatives of Jesus Christ? Are we making a proper response when we feel superior to fallen brothers and sisters? Is it proper for us to look down on them as failures and to compliment ourselves for our success? As we consider fallen brothers and sisters, are we to enter into a conspiracy of criticism, point out their faults and flaws, and chastise them?

The inspired apostle suggests that if we are true followers of Jesus Christ, if we are truly spiritual, that we have a major responsibility toward those who have fallen into sin. In our text he addresses us as "Brethren." As brothers and sisters, we are to love one another and be helpful to one another. Paul calls the brethren "you who are spiritual," meaning those who are indwelt by the Holy Spirit (Gal. 4:6), led by the Spirit (5:18), manifesting the fruit of the Spirit (5:22–23), and living by and walking in the Spirit (5:25). Every born-again Christian needs to face up to the challenge of caring for fallen brothers and sisters.

I. All of us stand in need of the ministry of restoration.

Let us be charitable with ourselves and others. Let us recognize that at one time or another each of us stands in need of the ministry of spiritual restoration. There are many reasons for this.

A. *We continue to live in and be a part of an unchanged human nature (cf. Gal. 5:16–21).* The new birth, great miracle that it is, does not eradicate or immobilize our fallen human nature. We continue to live in a sinful environment, and it is very easy to live for the flesh alone.

B. *The devil works continually to deceive, to defeat, and to destroy us (1 Peter 5:8).* Satan will lead us into sin unless we are constantly on the alert and walking in the power of the Holy Spirit.

C. *The church has not fully completed its responsibility for assisting new converts toward spiritual maturity.* Our Lord commissioned his church to evangelize, baptize, and catechize new disciples toward spiritual maturity (Matt. 28:18–20). Many churches have made the fatal mistake of leading a person to become a convert and then not leading that person on to maturity.

D. *Cares of the world and delight in riches lead us astray (Matt. 13:22).*

E. *An improper response to being hurt or disappointment in someone else can cause some of us to fall into an improper attitude and spirit that can lead us astray.* All of us have experienced this kind of a falling away from the high and holy will of God.

F. *Some need to be restored in love because they are depressed and ashamed of their past failures.* In the beautiful Twenty-Third Psalm, one of David's great statements about God is, "He restoreth my soul." This ministry of restoration is a continuous need in the family of God today.

II. We have a duty of love toward fallen brothers and sisters.

If we would engage in a ministry of restoration, we must give careful attention to both our attitudes and actions toward others.

A. *Our attitude toward fallen brothers and sisters.* We must be very careful lest we assume an attitude of self-righteousness that produces a harsh and critical spirit toward others. Sometimes it is much easier to be pharisaic than it is to be Christian. Our Lord was accused of being the friend of publicans and sinners, and he was. He had both the desire and the capacity to deal with sinners in a nonjudgmental manner that caused them to feel comfortable and accepted in his presence.

We need to recognize that fallen persons have a feeling of hurt within their hearts. Most likely they are disappointed in themselves and experience the shame of failure. Fallen brothers and sisters may be dealing with depression.

1. Let's put love to work on their behalf.
2. Let's practice forgiveness toward them.
3. Let's lift them up before God's throne of grace in prayer.
4. Let's encourage them to return to Christ.
5. Let's provide sympathetic help in their time of difficulty.

B. *Our actions on behalf of fallen brothers and sisters.*
1. Let's put forth a sincere effort to restore them to church attendance and to Christian fellowship.
2. Let's seek to encourage them to renew the process of spiritual growth and service.
3. Let's seek to restore them to activity and usefulness in the family of God and in the church of God.
4. Let's seek to restore them to harmony and understanding within the family of God.
5. Let's seek to restore them to meaningful activity and usefulness.
6. Let's be the love of God and the grace of God to them.

Conclusion

The words of our text reveal to us our personal responsibility toward our brothers and sisters in the household of faith who have been conquered by evil and defeated by sin. Phillips translates this verse: "Even if a man should be detected in some sin, my brothers, the spiritual ones among you should quietly set him back on the right path, not with any feeling of superiority but being yourselves on guard against temptation." It is unchristian for us to be critical of or indifferent to or to feel superior toward fallen brothers or sisters. Our text reveals God's will for his family. It also reveals a danger to which each of us is exposed. It reveals a duty to which love requires a response. And it reveals a need that is urgent and continuous. Let each of us respond to our obligations to other members of the household of faith.

SUNDAY MORNING, JANUARY 24

Title: Repentance in Salvation

Text: "Now after that John was put in prison, Jesus came into Galilee, preaching the gospel of the kingdom of God, and saying, The time is fulfilled, and the kingdom of God is at hand: repent ye, and believe the gospel" (**Mark 1:14–15**).

Scripture Reading: Mark 1:1–15

Hymns: "Out of My Bondage," Sleeper
"Savior, Like a Shepherd," Thrupp
"Lord, I'm Coming Home," Kirkpatrick

Offertory Prayer: Our Father, you have given us so much—life, health, love, and salvation. As we present our tithes and offerings to you, they seem small and insignificant compared to what you have given us. But they represent the dedication of our hearts to your will. Accept our gifts as you have accepted us. Please forgive our sins, strengthen us for the work before us, prepare us for this period of worship, and guide us with your Holy Spirit. We pray in Jesus' name and for his sake. Amen.

Introduction

I have heard that whenever the British navy makes a rope, a scarlet thread identifies it. A scarlet thread runs through the Bible also, identifying the message of salvation through faith in God. One element of salvation is the act of repentance. Before we can be saved from our sins, we must repent of those sins. This theme of repentance also runs through the Bible like a scarlet thread. Repentance is an absolute necessity in our Christian experience. The verses in the first chapter of Mark that tell of Jesus' early preaching in Galilee provide us with the two elements of salvation: repentance and faith. These acts are bound up together and cannot be separated. It is hard to say at what point repentance ends and faith begins.

We have seen what it means to be lost and what it means to be saved. Now let us consider today and next Sunday the conditions of salvation: repentance and faith.

I. Repentance in salvation involves a knowledge of sin.

The basic meaning of the Greek word for "repentance" is a changing of mind or a turning away. Thus repentance means that we must change our minds about sin and turn away from it. This begins with a knowledge of sin.

A. *Admission of sin.* Someone has said that the three hardest words for a person to say are "I have sinned." But this is exactly where we must start in repentance. We must admit to ourselves and to God that we have sinned and that we are unworthy. I once heard of a certain man's first step to grace. As he was shaving one morning, he looked at his face in the mirror and suddenly said, "You dirty rat!" And from that day he began to be a changed man. This is not an easy admission to make, for most of us have a pretty high opinion of ourselves. Nonetheless, this is where we must start in repentance. E. Y. Mullins said, "When we repent, we think God's thought about sin. We renounce it as Christ renounced it."

B. *Sin against God.* In the knowledge of sin, we not only see ourselves as sinners but also come to realize that all sin is against God. In his psalm of repentance, David cried out to God, "Against thee, thee only, have I sinned, and done this evil in thy sight" (Ps. 51:4). God has placed us here with a freedom of moral choice. And he has revealed to us his way of life. When we fail to do what is right, we fail God himself. We sin against him, and ultimately only he can forgive our sin.

II. Repentance in salvation involves sorrow for sin.

A. *As we realize that our sin is against God, we must have sorrow for that sin.* This is the very reason that repentance is necessary before we can be forgiven. If forgiveness were indiscriminately passed out without any regard for the person's sense of sin and need of forgiveness, it would be nothing but a light treatment of sin. Forgiveness is never mere toleration of sin. Toleration passes too easily into indifference. Forgiveness is the restoration of right relationships between God and people.

A distinction must be made between sorrow and mere remorse of conscience. You can go to any prison and find people who are sorry for what they have done and even sorrier that they got caught. But they are not so sorry that they would never do it again. Fear of punishment is not all that is involved in repentance. One can easily have great emotion because of sin and still not repent. Repentance carries an element of sorrow, sincere regret that leads people away from their sin and causes them to turn to God for forgiveness.

When John the Baptist preached to the people from the shores of the Jordan River, he demanded from them "fruits worthy of repentance" (Luke 3:8). And this is exactly what he meant. If we have repented of our sins, we must show it in the way we live.

B. *This is the repentance of complete committal of life to Christ.* One of the greatest stories in Christian literature is the story of Augustine. He was a lively young man, debonair and sophisticated. And like all the upper-crust young men of his generation, he had a mistress. His first mistress he kept for sixteen years. After he got tired of her, he got himself another one, and later, yet another. Now Augustine also liked to go to church on Sunday and hear Bishop Ambrose preach. Ambrose had the ability to lift a person out of himself to the point of thinking, *I want that*, and make him reach for spiritual things. So Augustine had a conflict with himself. He prayed, "O Lord, I want thee. I will give myself to thee." But in his mind there was a little parenthesis—he was not going to give up his mistress. So God didn't answer the prayer but the parenthesis. He did not give Augustine spiritual power. Finally, Augustine fought the battle through. One day he got down on his knees and prayed. He gave the Lord his whole self, including that parenthesis. And the minute he did, he received forgiveness.

III. Repentance in salvation involves turning from sin.

The third element in repentance involves the renunciation and repudiation of sin as an act of will. When we realize that we have sinned, and when we become sorry for that sin, we turn away from our sin and turn to God. Repentance is not complete in just knowing that we are sinners. Neither is repentance complete in feeling sorrow or remorse for our sin. It becomes complete when as an act of will we repudiate our sin and turn from it. All three elements are necessary for repentance: knowledge of sin, sorrow for sin, and turning from sin.

The requirements of true repentance indicate that the decision to turn away from sin is not simply an intellectual change of mind. The mind includes the whole moral nature of an individual. When we repent of our sin, our whole life is reoriented with Jesus Christ as the center.

Nor is repentance a once-and-for-all act. The Christian life is a life of repentance. The initial act of repentance when we first trust Christ as Savior is just the beginning of a life of repentance.

Repentance, then, is an act of grace whereby we realize our sin, experience sorrow for that sin, and turn to God in faith. It is a change of mind toward sin as well as a change of action. It involves the emotions, the intellect, and the will.

At one time during the Civil War, Captain Smith of "Stonewall" Jackson's staff was at Robert E. Lee's headquarters. The great Southern leader said to Captain Smith, "Tell General Jackson that the first time he rides in this direction, I will be glad to see him on a matter of no great importance."

When Captain Smith delivered the message, Jackson replied, "I will go tomorrow morning at six o'clock, and I wish you to accompany me."

The next morning when Captain Smith awoke, a snowstorm was raging. So he naturally assumed that General Jackson would postpone the journey to see General Lee. In about an hour, however, he was roused from his sleep by an orderly, who said that Jackson had already had his breakfast and was preparing to leave for General Lee's headquarters. Captain Smith hurriedly dressed, climbed in the saddle, and galloped off with General Jackson. They faced the blowing wind and snow for eight miles and came to Lee's headquarters just as he was finishing breakfast.

Seeing Jackson, Lee expressed surprise and asked why he had come during the storm.

Jackson replied, "You said that you wished to see me."

Then General Lee said, "But I told Captain Smith to tell you that it was a matter of no great importance and could await your convenience. I had no idea of bringing you out in such weather as this."

Then Jackson said, "General Lee's slightest wish is a supreme command to me, and I always take pleasure in prompt obedience."

Here was obedience to a command of little consequence. But God has issued a command of eternal consequence. "Now [God] commands all men everywhere to repent" (Luke 17:30 RSV). Jesus said, "Unless you repent you will all likewise perish" (Luke 13:3 RSV). This is God's wish for us. And it should be a supreme command that we take pleasure in following.

Conclusion

Repentance involves knowledge of our sin, sorrow for that sin, and turning away from that sin to God. The turning away from sin is faith. Repentance and faith belong together. As you now repent of your sins, will you not also turn to God in faith to accept his forgiveness and his offer of salvation?

SUNDAY EVENING, JANUARY 24

Title: Power of the Holy Spirit in Peter's Sermon

Text: "Therefore let all the house of Israel know assuredly, that God hath made that same Jesus, whom ye have crucified, both Lord and Christ" **(Acts 2:36)**.

Scripture Reading: Acts 2:21–40

Introduction

Peter preached the first sermon of the gospel age in Jerusalem on the day of Pentecost. His listeners had been amazed by the miracles they had seen, especially that of speaking in tongues.

Before his ascension Jesus had promised, "Ye shall be baptized with the Holy Ghost not many days hence" (Acts 1:5), and "Ye shall receive power, after that the Holy Ghost is come upon you" (Acts 1:8). The Lord's promise was fulfilled on the day of Pentecost when believers were filled with the Holy Spirit and yielded to him control of their minds and wills.

Pentecost, in the primary sense that the Holy Spirit came to begin the gospel age, will not be repeated. It does not need to be repeated any more than Jesus needs to be incarnated again. The Holy Spirit is here. He abides in the heart of every believer. "Any one who does not have the Spirit of Christ does not belong to him" (Rom. 8:9 RSV). The degree to which a person allows the Holy Spirit to direct and empower his or her life depends somewhat on that person's voluntary dedication. Otherwise, Paul would not have commanded, "Be filled with the Spirit" (Eph. 5:18). The tense indicates that the Holy Spirit is to fill our lives continually.

I. Peter's sermon: Jesus whom you crucified is the Messiah (2:22–36).

    A. *Jesus was "a man approved of God among you by miracles and wonders and signs" (v. 22).*

    B. *God raised him from the dead (vv. 23–36).*

        1. Peter affirmed that Jesus' resurrection was in accord with David's prophecy in Psalm 16:8–10. These words could not apply to David, because he did see corruption and his place of burial was known to all.

2. Added confirmation that Jesus is alive was the evidence of the power of the Holy Spirit who was promised by Jesus. His ascension to power fulfills David's prediction in Psalm 110. "The LORD [Jehovah] said unto my Lord [the Messiah], Sit thou on my right hand, until I make thy foes thy footstool" (Acts 2:34–35). Recall that on Tuesday before his crucifixion, Jesus had silenced his enemies by appealing to this same Scripture passage (see Matt. 22:41–46).

II. The Holy Spirit convicts people of sin.

A. *Peter's sermon convicted his listeners.* He accused them of murder. "Therefore let all the house of Israel know assuredly, that God hath made that same Jesus, whom ye have crucified, both Lord and Christ" (Acts 2:36). By crucifying Jesus, they had placed themselves in antagonism to God. They had shouted, "Crucify him!" God said, "Exalt him."

B. *The Holy Spirit convicted them of sin.* "They were pricked in their heart" (v. 37). Jesus had said that the Holy Spirit would come to convict the world of sin because of their relation to himself (see John 16:7–11). Sin is anything contrary to God's will. These people came to see that in their enmity to Jesus they were sinning against God. In anguish of soul they cried out, "What shall we do?" (Acts 2:37). What can we do to get right with God? How do those who find themselves in antagonism to God get right?

III. Peter's answer (2:38–40).

A. *"Repent" (v. 38).* The word has been weakened in translation by its association with penance. The word means "change one's mind" or "change one's attitude." In other words, we are to change our manner of life from what it is now to accord with what God wants it to be. Specifically, we are to change our mind with reference to Jesus. God says that Jesus is Lord and Christ. Anything less than making Jesus Lord of our lives falls short of repentance.

Repentance is more than reformation. A person may quit cursing, drinking, stealing, abusing others, and so on, and still fall short of repentance. Repentance is the decision to turn from all sin with God's help.

Repentance from sin and faith in Jesus go hand in hand. We cannot believe in Christ for salvation unless we turn from sin. We cannot repent of sin unless we believe in Christ, because if we fall short of accepting Jesus Christ as Lord and Savior, we are still sinning the greatest of all sins. A soldier described his conversion experience: "I was marching in the army of Satan. I heard a new Commander, the Lord Jesus, say, 'About face.' I turned my back on the old commander. When the new Commander said, 'Forward march,' I marched!"

Turning our back on the old commander is repentance. Marching with the new Commander is faith.

Other Scripture verses make it plain that a change of life (by repentance and faith) is the sole condition of acceptance with God (see Matt. 21:32; Luke 12:3; 24:47; John 3:16, 36; 5:24; Acts 3:19; 16:30–31; 20:21).

B. *"And be baptized every one of you in the name of Jesus Christ for the remission of sins" (v. 38).* There is a break in thought between "repent" and "be baptized" that is not retained in the translation. The number changes from plural to singular, and the person from second to third. The meaning is: "Let every one of you who has repented be baptized in the name of Jesus Christ." One who has repented and believed is to be baptized on the authority and command of Jesus, as in Matthew 28:19–20, *for* the remission of sins. "For" in the Greek, as in English, is ambiguous. For example, "He went to town for bread, for I sent him." The first "for" expresses purpose; the second "for" expresses cause. "Be baptized . . . for the remission of sins" does not mean in order to get remission; it means because of the remission of sins, we receive when we repent. Baptism is a symbol of the reality (see Rom. 6:1–6).

C. *"Ye shall receive the gift of the Holy Ghost" (v. 38).* This is the Holy Spirit himself who abides in the heart of every believer.

D. *"Under the leadership and power of the Holy Spirit, we are to save ourselves from this corrupt generation" (v. 40).*

Conclusion

The promise of salvation is for all time to all people who answer God's call to salvation by "repentance toward God, and faith toward our Lord Jesus Christ" (Acts 20:21).

Let us repent for salvation and be baptized in accord with Jesus' command because of the remission of our sins. Let us give the Holy Spirit free control to consecrate us to Christ and to keep us from worldliness.

WEDNESDAY EVENING, JANUARY 27

Title: The Shape of Our Christian Citizenship

Text: "Only let your manner of life be worthy of the gospel of Christ" **(Phil. 1:27 RSV).**

Scripture Reading: Philippians 1:27–30

Introduction

Paul shared many thrilling truths in his letter to his beloved church at Philippi. The letter to the Philippians is a letter of gratitude and joy that reveals the love of the apostle for this congregation. It records repeated expressions of the congregation's love and support of the apostle in his missionary ministries. With genuine love and wisdom and with great optimism, the apostle gave some imperatives to these friends in the family of God. And as he spoke to them, he speaks to us today.

Philippi was a Roman colony, and its citizens enjoyed the privilege of being Roman citizens. They enjoyed legal rights there as if they lived on Roman soil near the capital of the Roman Empire. Paul reminded these believers on two different occasions that their real citizenship was heavenly (Phil. 1:27; 3:20). Paul was not suggesting that they ignore the obligations of earthly citizenship, but he challenged them to recognize their unique relationship with God and his kingdom work. He challenged them to live in the pagan city of Philippi as citizens of the holy and higher kingdom of God.

As he neared the end of his letter, Paul sent greetings to the saints in Caesar's household. This may have served as a challenge to those in Philippi to be faithful and devoted servants of Jesus Christ (Phil. 4:22), for if one could live for Christ in Caesar's household, it follows that one could live for Christ in Philippi or in any modern city.

Our response to God must take many different forms according to the pressures and the needs we encounter. It is interesting to note the manner in which Paul hoped his readers would conduct themselves as citizens of the kingdom of God.

I. He would have them stand firm in one spirit with one mind (Phil. 1:27).

The threat of divisiveness or disunity has always threatened the church's witness. This is true today, and it was true in the early days of the Christian movement.

We need to recognize that there are many handicaps or hindrances to maintaining a unity of mind and spirit.

1. *The immaturity of God's family can cause disunity.*
2. *The individuality of persons can often create disunity.*
3. *Honest differences of opinion can sometimes be very divisive.*
4. *Physical and emotional fatigue can often create disunity.*
5. *We must recognize that our enemy the devil is always seeking to divide the people of God so that he might conquer them.*

The apostle Paul was urging the church in Philippi to take steps toward unity within the body in order that they might reflect God's grace and goodness in their city.

II. He would have them strive together in a united effort.

   A. *We must strive together side by side for the sake of the gospel.* Jesus' followers should work together like dedicated and disciplined athletes on a winning team. We should cooperate in redemptive activity like the members of a choir singing in perfect harmony. We should seek to avoid any discord lest we cast reflection on the message we proclaim.

B. *We must strive together to protect the purity of our faith.* Truth has always been attacked by error. Some people try to mix error with truth. Thus we must strive together to protect the purity of our message.

C. *We must strive together side by side in proclaiming the good news in our personal world.*

III. He would have them stand firm against opposition.

In Paul's world, preaching a message of a crucified but risen Savior was not a popular thing to do. Because of the multiplicity of idols and shrines, many with vested interests opposed any religion that served as a competitor for the status quo. Bravery, with a refusal to surrender to fear, was an essential for success in the face of opposition to the gospel message. Likewise, we must not rush off like a terrified horse when we are confronted by those who oppose our Christian message.

IV. He encouraged them to be willing to suffer for the sake of Christ (v. 29).

In some parts of the modern world it is popular and socially acceptable for one to be a professing Christian. Such was not the case in Philippi, nor is it true in many parts of today's world. Many contemporary followers of Jesus Christ have never faced up to the fact that the cross is the symbol of our faith and our commitment to God's will. If we would be true followers of Jesus Christ, we must be willing to suffer as he suffered and as others have suffered for their faith.

Conclusion

What is the shape of your Christian life in the modern world? As those who seek for a city whose builder and maker is God, we must demonstrate the characteristics of heavenly citizenship in the here and now. Philippi was a Roman colony, and the citizens of Rome were encouraged to dress like Romans, act like Romans, think like Romans, speak like Romans, and never forget that they *were* Romans.

Paul encouraged the saints at Philippi to dress, act, think, and speak in a way that would be worthy of Jesus Christ. Let us strive with the help of the Holy Spirit to be good citizens of the kingdom of God in our community now.

SUNDAY MORNING, JANUARY 31

Title: Faith in Salvation

Text: "Now the just shall live by faith: but if any man draw back, my soul shall have no pleasure in him. But we are not of them who draw back unto perdition; but of them that believe to the saving of the soul" (**Heb. 10:38**).

Scripture Reading: Mark 1:14–15

Hymns: "Have Faith in God," McKinney
         "Faith Is the Victory," Yates
         "How Firm a Foundation," Rippon

Offertory Prayer: Our Father, we thank you for all your blessings in life. We are grateful for your mercy and grace. Help us, O Father, to understand and appreciate the real meaning of faith. May we live in faith all our lives. Part of this faith is to trust you for the material things of life as we practice the stewardship of your material blessings. As people of faith, may we also be good stewards in faith. Accept these gifts, we pray. Forgive us our sins, we plead. And strengthen us for all of life as we receive inspiration for noble living from this time of worship. We pray this in Jesus' name and for his sake. Amen.

Introduction

The classic biblical definition of faith is found in Hebrews 11:1: "Now faith is the substance of things hoped for, the evidence of things not seen." The Greek word translated "substance" had a technical meaning in the business world of the first century; it referred to one's property or effects. This is seen in the story of a woman named Dionysia. She is described as "a woman of set jaw and grim determination." It seems that she had lost a case in the local court over a piece of land to which she laid claim. Not satisfied with the decision of the lower court, she determined to take her case to a higher court in Alexandria. She sent her slave to that city with the legal documents safely enclosed in a stone box. On the way the slave lost his life in a fire that destroyed the inn where he had stayed for the night. For two thousand years the sand of the desert covered the ruins of the inn, the charred bones of the slave, and the stone box. Archaeologists uncovered these remains. In the box they found the legal documents. They read the note that Dionysia wrote to the judge in Alexandria. "In order that my lord the judge may know that my appeal is just, I attach my *hypostasis*." She designated that which was attached to her note by the Greek word translated "substance" in Hebrews 11:1. The attached document was translated and found to be the title deed to the piece of land she claimed as her own possession, the evidence of her ownership (Kenneth W. Wuest, *Bypaths in the Greek New Testament for the English Reader* [Grand Rapids: Eerdmans, 1940], 18–19).

This is faith—our title deed to salvation in Christ and the mercy and grace of God. The thing for which we earnestly hope is salvation. Faith is the title deed to that great hope, that great reality—the salvation of our souls.

I. Faith in salvation has a definite object.

When we begin to examine the faith that saves, we notice that this is not just a vague thing that reaches out to nothing. It is faith in a definite object—Jesus Christ.

A. *Our faith must be in Christ, not the church.* Many people have faith that the church will save them. But the church itself cannot save.

B. *Our faith must be in Christ, not the Bible.* The Bible is God's Word. It brings us to Christ, but it cannot save us. It simply tells us how God has provided our salvation. Only faith in Christ brings salvation.

C. *Our faith must be in Christ, not our good deeds.* Do you remember the conversation that Jesus had with Nicodemus? Nicodemus was a good man; perhaps there was none better among his contemporary Jews. But Jesus told him, "Ye must be born again" (John 3:7).

II. Faith in salvation has a complete trust.

What is faith? In its simplest terms, faith is complete trust. When we trust Christ as Savior, when we have faith in him, it means that we completely trust him to cleanse us, forgive our sins, and save us for now and eternity.

Norman Vincent Peale illustrated this sort of trust in Christ by an incident in his life. He had addressed a group of two thousand students at the Naval Air College in Pensacola, Florida. Because he had to return to New York without loss of time, his hosts provided for his return in a plane piloted by a navy captain. He said that it was the first time he had been the sole passenger in a plane, and he had a wonderful time.

When they left Pensacola the skies were blue and cloudless. Everything was favorable. But later on en route, the captain told him that he had been advised that New York was heavily overcast. "As a matter of fact," he said, "we'll have to go in on instruments."

"Well, Captain," Peale said, "Why don't we land at Philadelphia or somewhere else? It will be all right with me. I like Philadelphia."

"I thought you wanted to go to New York," the pilot said.

"Yes, that's where I want to go," Peale answered.

"Okay," replied the pilot. "New York is where we are going."

As they approached the city, the pilot informed Peale, "We're going down now." He directed his attention to the instruments and began explaining all the indications. Peale had never followed the procedures so closely. They went down, down, down. Finally, when it seemed they could not go much farther without crashing into the ground, he saw flashing water and a sandy beach that seemed only a hundred feet or so below them. Then the lights of the runway—illuminated in the middle of the day—were before them and they came right up to the ramp. The landing was beautiful. Peale was filled with admiration. He exclaimed, "Captain, that was a marvelous landing! That must have required a great deal of skill."

"Well," admitted the pilot, "I've been doing this for a long time, and I ought to have developed some proficiency. But if you think it was a good landing, I would say that while it did require a degree of skill, the primary thing it took was faith."

"Faith?"

"Definitely. On the instrument board I have instruments. And when I'm flying in an overcast, I have to have faith in these instruments. I know they work; I've used them before; I know what they will do. They're constantly tested; I know they may be counted upon; I have implicit faith in them. If I didn't have that faith, I might say to myself, 'Well, maybe this instrument isn't exactly right—so I'd better do this—make this variation—or this.' And that could have tragic consequences. But I do have implicit faith in my instruments, and that is what brought us in through this overcast to a safe landing" (Norman Vincent Peale, *How to Get Answers That Really Answer* [n.p.: n.d.], 3–5).

This is the kind of faith we must have in Christ as Savior. Faith in salvation has a complete trust.

III. Faith in salvation has a distinct consequence.

A. *One consequence is that God forgives our sin.* Right at the time we turn to him in faith, confessing our sins to him and trusting in him to forgive us, our sins are forgiven and we are saved.

B. *Another consequence of faith is submitting to Christ as Lord.* Whenever a person becomes a Christian, Christ becomes the Lord of his or her life and soul.

C. *But the direct consequence is that we live a life of faith.* Faith in Christ for salvation is not just the faith of a moment. It is faith for a lifetime.

A blind man in a downtown area had a seeing-eye dog. He held the dog's leash, and the dog guided him through crowds of people, directed him through traffic, took him about his business, and returned him to his home. As the man followed the dog, he showed complete faith in the dog. In complete trust we accept Christ as our Savior, committing our life to him and living the life of faith.

Conclusion

The faith that saves is this complete committal of our life to Christ. He is the object of our faith.

SUNDAY EVENING, JANUARY 31

Title: Peter and the Church at Jerusalem

Text: "Then they that gladly received his word were baptized: and the same day there were added unto them about three thousand souls. And they continued stedfastly in the apostles' doctrine and fellowship, and in breaking of bread, and in prayers" (**Acts 2:41–42**).

Scripture Reading: Acts 2:41–47; 4:31–37

Introduction

Peter closed his sermon at Pentecost with an exhortation (1) to repent, (2) to be baptized in the name of Jesus Christ, and (3) to stay separated from a crooked generation. The results were tremendous; three thousand people made a public response. Afterward they did two things.

I. "They that gladly received his word were baptized" (2:41).

What word? The word that Peter had preached about Jesus. Peter had said, "God hath made that same Jesus, whom ye have crucified, both Lord and Christ" (2:36). Those who believed in Jesus were baptized. This is what Jesus had commanded in the Great Commission: "Therefore go and make disciples of all nations, baptizing them in the name of the Father and of the Son and of the Holy Spirit" (Matt. 28:19 NIV). People become disciples when they receive forgiveness of sin and the gift of the Holy Spirit. Baptism is a way by which those who have become disciples confess that Christ died and rose again for them and that they have died to sin and are living a new life in Christ (see Rom. 6:3–6).

II. These baptized believers continued steadfastly.

Conversion is the beginning of the Christian life. A newborn baby is expected to grow. Those who are newly saved are babies in Christ no matter what their age may be.

A. *They continued steadfastly in the apostles' doctrine.* This would consist primarily in the Old Testament as Jesus had interpreted it for them and in the reports of what Jesus did and said as narrated by the apostles who were eyewitnesses. A good understanding of the apostles' teaching can be obtained from the sermons in Acts (especially those of Peter) and the records that were later written down as the Gospels.

B. *They continued steadfastly in fellowship.* Fellowship means sharing or participation. Under the leadership of the Holy Spirit, the new believers continued to have services every day. Multitudes from many nations who had come for Pentecost had now become disciples and remained in Jerusalem. "All the believers were together and had everything in common. They sold property and possessions to give to anyone who had need" (Acts 2:44–45 NIV). This was not communism. No one was forced to sell their possessions. Not everyone parted with their possessions. The tenses make it clear that as the need arose, believers prompted by the Holy Spirit voluntarily brought their goods for distribution.

The stewardship principle that all belongs to God and that as possessors we are to administer for him is eternally valid. The specific practice of not working and having services continually was only temporary. If continued it would have reduced all Christians to poverty. Normally the giving away of all of one's possessions would be a renunciation of responsible stewardship.

Joseph Barnabas (of whom we shall hear later as the missionary companion of Paul) sold his land and brought the money to the apostles for distribution (Acts 4:36–37).

C. *They continued steadfastly in breaking of bread and in prayer.* "Breaking of bread" seems to be a term for observing the Lord's Supper as Jesus had commanded his disciples to do (see Matt. 26:26–30; 1 Cor. 11:23–29). For a time the disciples continued to worship in the Jewish temples. They probably continued to keep the appointed times for prayer (see Acts 2:46–47). For example, "Peter and John went up together into the temple at the hour of prayer, being the ninth hour" (Acts 3:1). Even later, Paul, the missionary to the Gentiles, usually began his ministry in the Jewish synagogue. This was an appropriate procedure from our Christian viewpoint.

Conclusion

The essentials of a great growing church today are the same as those for the church at Jerusalem.

They preached Jesus as Lord.
They were filled with the Holy Spirit.
They preached repentance and faith as the conditions of salvation.
The observed the ordinances, baptism and the Lord's Supper,
   as symbols.
They participated in worship and witness.
They gave liberally of their possessions.
They faced persecution gladly for the sake of the name of Jesus.
They worshiped in the temple and visited in homes.
They were a democracy under God.
They did not condone sin in the members.

God can bless a church like that.

Suggested Preaching Program for the Month of
FEBRUARY

■ **Sunday Mornings**

On the first Sunday of the month, wrap up the series "The Answer to Eternity's Most Important Questions." On the second Sunday, begin a series on Jesus' seven sayings from the cross, which will take you through Palm Sunday. The title of this series is "Christ Speaks from the Cross."

■ **Sunday Evenings**

Complete the series "Peter's Pilgrimage of Faith."

■ **Wednesday Evenings**

Continue with a series of messages based on Paul's letter to the Philippians, giving attention to the "Great Imperatives for Christian Living."

Wednesday Evening, February 3

Title: The Command to Cooperate

Text: "Therefore, my beloved, as you have always obeyed, so now, not only as in my presence but much more in my absence, work out your own salvation with fear and trembling; for God is at work in you both to will and to work for his good pleasure" **(Phil. 2:12–13 RSV)**.

Introduction

As disciples of Jesus Christ, we need to give joyous attention to the great imperatives that fell from the lips of the apostle Paul. This veteran soldier of the cross, this great missionary leader, this warmhearted pastor was seeking not only to glorify God, but to point out those human responses that were essential for spiritual growth and effectiveness in witnessing.

In the words of our text, Paul was encouraging the disciples at Philippi to cooperate with God as he carried on a good work within them.

I. God's good work began in conversion (Phil. 1:6).

The church in Philippi had heard the good news of God's love as revealed in the life, death, and resurrection of Jesus Christ. They recognized what they needed to do to receive the gift of new life. Paul told them that the conversion experience is but the beginning of the human response to God, and it is but the initiation of God's great redemptive work on our behalf.

II. God's good work in us continues as we cooperate (Phil. 2:12–13).

Paul was not declaring that the believers in Philippi had to work their way to heaven. The salvation of the soul is not the result of the good works of even a sincere and devout person (Eph. 2:8–9; Titus 3:5). Instead, Paul was affirming that if they would experience God's full salvation from the downward pull of a fallen nature, they had to cooperate with God as he worked within them.

Modern translations can help us to see that for which the apostle was pleading. The New International Version reads, "Therefore, my dear friends, as you have always obeyed—not only in my presence, but now much more in my absence—continue to work out your salvation with fear and trembling, for it is God who works in you to will and to act in order to fulfill his good purpose."

A. *If we would work with God, we should make much of his Book.* God will communicate his will to us through the pages of the Bible.
B. *If we would work with God, we must find our way into the closet of prayer.* Prayer is the means by which we communicate with God, but even more important, it is the means by which he communicates with us.
C. *If we would work with God, we must let the church be the church in our lives.* It is through the local expression of God's family that we experience his presence and his love. It is through the church that we receive encouragement and correction and comfort.
D. *If we would work with God, we must be responsive to the Holy Spirit.* He is seeking day by day not only to strengthen us, but to use us in witnessing to unsaved people around us.

III. God's good work in us will be completed when the Lord returns (Phil. 3:20–21).

Our salvation begins in conversion and continues through consecration. It will finally be consummated when Christ returns from heaven for his own. In conversion we are saved from the penalty of sin. As we cooperate with Christ, we are saved from the power and practice of sin. When the Lord returns, we will be saved from the very presence of sin.

Conclusion

Our citizenship is in heaven. As disciples of Jesus, we are pilgrims here. This world is not our home; we are only passing through. As citizens of the kingdom of heaven, we must live out that citizenship in an environment that is not conducive to spiritual growth. It is in this present world that we must let our manner of life be worthy of the gospel of Jesus Christ (Phil. 1:27). This is a personal challenge to each of us.

SUNDAY MORNING, FEBRUARY 7

Title: The Call to Come and the Call to Go

Text: "And he appointed twelve, to be with him, and to be sent out to preach and have authority to cast out demons" **(Mark 3:14–15 RSV)**.

Scripture Reading: Mark 3:13–19

Hymns: "Praise Him! Praise Him!" Crosby
           "All Hail the Power of Jesus' Name," Perronet
           "What a Wonderful Saviour!" Hoffman

Offertory Prayer: Holy Father, we accept this day as a day that you have made. We rejoice and are glad in it. We bow down and worship before you. We rise up to praise you and go forth to proclaim your greatness and goodness to others. We come today bringing our tithes and offerings that we might not only invest in, but be involved in, your redemptive work of sharing the good news of your love to all humankind. Bless this congregation of believers. Bless each one who gives to your work. Accept these gifts and bless them to your honor and glory. In Jesus' name. Amen.

Introduction

A popular hymn has placed words in our mouths as we think in terms of coming to Jesus Christ:

> Just as I am, without one plea
> But that Thy blood was shed for me,
> And that Thou biddest me come to Thee,
> O Lamb of God, I come! I come!
> —*Ron and Patricia Owens*

We can respond to the words of the poets by coming to Jesus just as we are and by encouraging others to come just as they are. But we cannot come to Jesus and *remain* exactly as we are. He produces radical changes in those who come to him and experience his transforming presence.

Jesus' transforming power is demonstrated most dramatically in the changes that came about in the disciples, who later became apostles. In the days following Jesus' ascension, they were brave and courageous proclaimers of a message that brought upon them the hostility of both political and religious leaders. Luke declared, "Now when they saw the boldness of Peter and John, and perceived that they were uneducated, common men, they wondered; and they recognized that they had been with Jesus" (Acts 4:13 RSV).

An apostle must first be a disciple, and not all disciples become apostles. A disciple is a listener, a learner, a follower. Twelve of Jesus' disciples became his apostles. The word translated *apostle* means "one sent forth." Thus an apostle was a representative of another who went on a mission. Apostles have some parallels with our modern ambassadors. In 1 Corinthians 12 Paul spoke of apostles as being the gifts of the Spirit to the church. We cannot limit this term to the original Twelve. Anyone who goes forth on a mission, being led by the Holy Spirit, is in reality an apostle with a message.

It is interesting in the account of the calling of the Twelve that Jesus appointed them "to be with him, and to be sent out to preach." Experiencing the new birth is only a starting point. If we would become the servants, the helpers, the apostles of Jesus Christ, we must "be with him."

The disciples became apostles. The disciples who sincerely worshiped Jesus Christ and stayed with him went forth to be his witnesses. These twelve men, originally so helpless and so insignificant, became the helpers of Christ, of God, and of the church. These men who became known as apostles were originally receivers. They were self-seekers who had a vested interest in following Christ. But by being with him, they were changed into givers. They started their pilgrimage as reservoirs and ended their pilgrimage as streams or artesian wells. They went from being spectators to participants and eventually partners of the Lord Jesus.

Jesus Christ calls us to be with him before he sends us out to be his blessing to others.

I. Jesus calls all to come.

A. *He invites us to him that we might experience the cleansing of forgiveness.* Through his death on the cross, Jesus dealt with our sin problem. He offers to us forgiveness that is free, full, and forever. Every person needs to be clean before God.

B. *He invites us to enter into a family relationship with God (John 1:11–12).* No one likes to be an outsider. No one enjoys being alienated and experiencing loneliness. Jesus Christ came in order that all people might enter into God's family. He wants everyone to experience the sense of belonging that comes to those who are members of God's family.

C. *He invites us to come to him for fullness of life (John 10:10).* Jesus intends that we experience something more than birth into God's family or enrollment in his school. He wants us to experience wholeness.

II. Jesus calls all to companionship.

After inviting people to become believers and disciples, Jesus selected and called them into a companionship in which they might become apostles. We are to respond to him as Lord and Teacher and Shepherd and Friend. Before the original disciples could become apostles, it was necessary that they "be with him."

A. *Only by being with Jesus could the disciples get acquainted with God.* Later Jesus was to say, "He who has seen me has seen the Father" (John 14:9 RSV). Jesus came to introduce God to people and people to God. He came to manifest the character and purpose of God. He wanted his disciples to be with him so they could truly become acquainted with God.

1. It takes time to get acquainted with someone.
2. We must listen to someone to get acquainted with him.

3. We must carefully watch someone to get deeply acquainted with him.

These disciples desperately needed to get acquainted with the God whom Jesus Christ was revealing. To experience this acquaintance they had to be with Jesus. How long have you been with Jesus? To what degree are you watching and listening to God in order that you might come to a greater acquaintance with him?

B. *Only by being with Jesus can we learn how to live by faith.*
   1. We have to learn to trust God.
   2. Many of us want to trust in ourselves or in circumstances. We want to walk by sight and common sense.
   3. Many of us want to plot our own course and then let God okay it. We want to jump off the cliff and depend on God to rescue us.
   4. Jesus teaches us that God is good and wise, that God is at work for good in all things and that he is always reliable, and that God does not always work according to a human timetable. Jesus helps us know that God will always show us what is right.

C. *Only by being with Jesus can we learn the way of love.* Jesus wanted to teach his disciples to love God supremely and to love others with the same measure they loved themselves.

Most of us live self-centered, selfish lives. We confuse lust with love. Jesus taught and demonstrated the way of love. He always had a persistent, unbreakable spirit of goodwill toward others and an unflinching desire for constructive action on their behalf. The security and development of others was always uppermost in his mind. By his example, as well as by his teachings, Jesus showed his disciples what it meant to live by the principle of love. They could learn this only when they were with him.

How much time do you spend with Jesus? Are you in the process of learning to live by the principle of love?

D. *Only by being with Jesus could his disciples learn the importance of absolute obedience.* Jesus was obedient to his Father and sought at all times to carry out God's will in his life—even to the point of dying on a cross. He sought to instill within his disciples the desire to so love God that they would always be obedient to his commands, for he knew that the evangelization of the world would be dependent on their obedience. When a person dies to self, he or she will be raised back to life again. This is a principle that remains true for us today.

Conclusion

Have you come to know Jesus Christ through the forgiveness of your sins? Have you come to know God as Father and his family as brothers and sisters? Have you spent time with Jesus in order that he might place his mark upon your mind and heart so that others can see his presence in your life?

It was after considerable teaching and growth that "the disciples were for the first time called Christians" (Acts 11:26 RSV). In Antioch they became Christians as they let Jesus change them into his own image.

God needs you; others need what God can do through you. Determine that you will be with him so that he can make an apostle out of a disciple, using your life as the raw material.

SUNDAY EVENING, FEBRUARY 7

Title: Peter and the Church Face Opposition

Text: "Then Peter and the other apostles answered and said, We ought to obey God rather than men" **(Acts 5:29)**.

Scripture Reading: Acts 4:1–30; 5:17–42

Introduction

Christians, by the very fact that they are Christians, are a standing reproach to evil. "For every one who does evil hates the light, and does not come to the light, lest his deeds should be exposed" (John 3:20 RSV). Jesus said, "If the world hate you, ye know that it hated me before it hated you. If ye were of the world, the world would love his own: but because ye are not of the world, but I have chosen you out of the world, therefore the world hateth you. Remember the word that I said unto you, The servant is not greater than his lord. If they have persecuted me, they will also persecute you; if they have kept my saying, they will keep yours also" (John 15:18–20). Jesus warned the disciples, "In the world ye shall have tribulation: but be of good cheer; I have overcome the world" (John 16:33). Our Lord's final beatitude promises great reward for the disciples who suffer persecution for righteousness' sake (see Matt. 5:10–12).

I. Opposition by the authorities (Acts 4:1–4).

A. *Peter and John preached to the people "in the portico called Solomon's" (Acts 3:11 RSV).* Peter affirmed that the God of Abraham, Isaac, and Jacob, the God of our fathers, glorified his Son Jesus in the healing of the lame man. Peter charged the people and their rulers with the death of the Prince of Life when they shouted for Pilate to release a murderer and crucify Jesus.

B. *Peter and John were arrested by the authorities and thrown in prison for the night.* The group who arrested them were "the priests, and the captain of the temple, and the Sadducees" (4:1). The priests were probably the high priests. The captain was the officer in charge of the temple area. The Sadducees were the powerful politico-religious party who dominated the council, or the Sanhedrin, which was the seventy-member ruling body of the Jewish nation. They compromised with the Roman conquerors.

55

C. *The authorities arrested Peter and John for preaching the resurrection of Jesus.* The Sadducees probably questioned their authority to teach in the temple as they had that of Jesus a few weeks earlier (see Matt. 21:23). They were also troubled by the popularity of this movement with the people.

II. On trial before the Sanhedrin the next day (Acts 4:5).

A. *The Sanhedrin before whom Peter and John were brought to trial was mostly the same body that had condemned Jesus.* They were all there: rulers, the official representatives of the people; elders, older men of influence and position; scribes, copiers of the Scriptures who became expert interpreters; Annas, the former high priest whom the Romans had replaced with his son-in-law, Caiaphas; John, the son of Annas; Alexander, whose relative is unknown; and other kindred of the high priest.

   They led off the inquiry by asking, probably scornfully, "By what power, or by what name, have ye done this?" (4:7). How could men such as yourselves who have had no rabbinical training perform this healing?

B. Peter, filled with the Holy Spirit, spoke boldly (4:8–12).
   1. Jesus fulfilled his promises (Matt. 10:16–20; Luke 21:12–25).
   2. Peter preached to the Sanhedrin the same sermon he had been preaching to the people in Solomon's portico of the temple.

C. *The Sanhedrin made a decision.* They were amazed by the boldness of Peter and John. They knew these men had been with Jesus and could testify that it was really he who was alive. They could not deny the miracle. By a great leap of illogic they determined to do by law and by force what they could not do by reason (4:18).

III. The response of Peter and John (Acts 4:19).

A. *"But Peter and John answered and said unto them, Whether it be right in the sight of God to hearken unto you more than unto God, judge ye. For we cannot but speak the things which we have seen and heard"* (4:19–20). This was but one of many occasions when a government has sought to legislate religion. The Sanhedrin was saying in effect, "Keep still and we will not harass you." But Peter and John could not keep still. Truth must be proclaimed. Experience is a divine imperative. No law can silence the gospel.

B. *The Sanhedrin threatened them and let them go.* "And being let go, they went to their own company, and reported all that the chief priests and elders had said unto them" (4:23). Christian fellowship is wonderful. How praying Christians must have encouraged John and Peter! Their prayer in Acts 4:24–30 is rather remarkable. They did not pray to be spared from persecution. They prayed that with boldness they might bear their testimony.

Sometime later, while the apostles were preaching in the temple, the Sadducees arrested them (see Acts 5:17–42). On this latter occasion the officers beat them, commanded that they not speak in the name of Jesus, and let them go. "And they departed from the presence of the council, rejoicing that they were counted worthy to suffer shame for his name. And daily in the temple, and in every house, they ceased not to teach and preach Jesus Christ" (vv. 41–42).

Conclusion

No person or group of persons, ecclesiastical or civil, has any right to command a person to do something contrary to God's will. Religion is a personal concern between each person and God. "So then every one of us shall give account of himself to God" (Rom. 14:12). When government stays in its appointed sphere, there is no conflict between obligation to government and obligation to God. Jesus' great word "Render to Caesar the things that are Caesar's, and to God the things that are God's" implies that one ought to be able to be a good Christian and a good citizen at the same time. Whenever government steps beyond its bounds and commands disobedience to God, Christians can do nothing other than reply, "We ought to obey God rather than men" (Acts 5:29).

WEDNESDAY EVENING, FEBRUARY 10

Title: An Imperative Regarding Grumbling

Text: "Do all things without grumbling or questioning, that you may be blameless and innocent, children of God without blemish in the midst of a crooked and perverse generation, among whom you shine as lights in the world" (**Phil 2:14–15 RSV**).

Scripture Reading: Philippians 2:12–18

Introduction

In the midst of a number of great affirmations and challenges to the Philippians, Paul gave voice to a negative imperative. It comes through loud and clear that the saints would not bring glory to God or happiness to themselves if they joined the griping and complaining committee. "Do all things without grumbling or questioning" (RSV) is the apostolic counsel.

To properly understand the significance of this imperative regarding grumbling, we need to examine the context. Paul was speaking to his beloved brothers and sisters in Christ. In fact, some of them were his sons and daughters in Christ. He wished for them the highest and the best the Father God had for them. He desired the personal satisfaction of seeing them fulfill God's purpose for them. This would be a source of joy to the apostle not only during his life, but also in the day when Jesus Christ comes to receive and reward his followers. In this passage let us notice the work of God within us, and let us consider the response that we should make to him.

I. The good work of God within us.

This verse contains the good news of God's personal presence in the heart of the believer as an individual and within the fellowship of the church as a collective body. "God is at work in you" (Phil. 2:13 RSV). This is good news letting us know that our great and eternal God is not an unmoved, unconcerned creator. He is the God who has come in the person of the Holy Spirit to dwell within us and to work his good work within us. Paul had spoken about the beginning of this good work (Phil 1:6). He also spoke of the consummation of God's good work at some undated time in the future (Phil. 3:20–21). In the meantime, God is at work to deliver us from the inward corruption of a sinful nature and from the contaminating effect of the crooked and perverse world in which we live.

A. *God works within us to help us choose the right (v. 13).*
B. *God energizes us to do the good and the right (v. 13).*
C. *God wants us to be blameless in the midst of a sinful world.* It is his will that we show ourselves to be unmixed and unadulterated.
D. *God wants us to be without fault or flaw in the midst of a sinful world.* As we manifest these characteristics, we prove ourselves and give evidence to our contemporaries that we are indeed the children of God.
E. *God wants us to shine in the darkness (v. 15).* Our light points others to the way of God (v. 15).
F. *God wants us to hold forth the word of light to those in spiritual darkness (v. 16).*

Our Father God is interested in doing more for us than merely giving us a ticket to heaven and saving us from an eternity in hell. It is his good will that we demonstrate the traits of our heavenly citizenship in the present. He wants us to guide others away from the life of no faith that leads to ruin and eternal separation from God.

II. The proper human response to God's good work.

How will we respond as individuals and as a body of believers to the good work of God within us? Paul makes some very positive suggestions.

A. *First of all, he suggests that we be obedient (2:12).* Jesus affirmed that we give proof of our genuine discipleship by being obedient to the commandment of love (John 13:34–35). He also declared, "You are my friends if you do what I command you" (John 15:14 RSV). There is no substitute for obedience. It is impossible for God to accomplish his purpose in us or through us if we do not respond to him with loving, joyful obedience.
B. *We must be willing to cooperate with God as he works within us.* Responding in joy and excitement and loyalty, we must work with God as he works

58

within us. Our reason for working with God should not be because otherwise we will miss heaven. Paul was not teaching that we must work our way to heaven. He was insisting that we must work with God to avoid failure in our lives and in our witness.

C. *Paul commanded that we avoid a grumbling and complaining attitude.* The pilgrimage of Israel from Egypt to the promised land provides the background for this suggestion. A study of the Old Testament reveals that Moses had a complaining attitude at times. The people of Israel have a consistent performance record of grumbling and griping and finding fault, not only with God, but with Moses and Aaron. Grumbling and faultfinding often indicate the following:

1. Intellectual rebellion against God.
2. Moral rebellion.
3. The absence of faith.
4. The absence of love for God and others.
5. The absence of wisdom. Grumbling does not accomplish anything good at work or at home. Christians accomplish nothing positive by complaining about their circumstances.
6. The absence of concern for others.

Conclusion

The pathway of grumbling and faultfinding is the pathway to failure and disappointment. We are to be without rebuke in the midst of a crooked and perverse world. We cannot find ourselves in that desired state if we give ourselves to grumbling.

Are you a grumbler? Are you a faultfinder? Do you complain toward God? Do you gripe about your family situation or whine about your fellow church members?

Grumbling is a human fault to which all of us must plead some degree of guilt. Let us recognize that grumbling is not only foolish but is also sinful. Let us forsake this negative attitude and abrasive habit so that God can accomplish his good purpose within us.

SUNDAY MORNING, FEBRUARY 14

Title: Deal Kindly with an Erring One

Text: "Then said Jesus, Father, forgive them; for they know not what they do" (Luke 23:34).

Scripture Reading: Luke 23:27–38

Hymns: "Depth of Mercy! Can There Be," Wesley

"Though Your Sins Be as Scarlet," Crosby

"Softly and Tenderly Jesus Is Calling," Thompson

Offertory Prayer: Our Father, we are grateful for your constant care and for the assurance that you love us in spite of our unworthiness and sin. Even as your love is poured into our hearts by the Holy Spirit whom you have given to us, may we spread your love by a spirit that reflects the compassion of our Savior. May our offering reflect our love for all people everywhere, especially those who have never heard the message of Jesus Christ. We dedicate our money to your service, but even more than that, we ask that you will use us personally in sharing the good news through effective witnessing. We pray in Jesus' name. Amen.

Introduction

A man who was not able to speak was once asked to define *forgiveness*. He took a pencil and wrote, "It is the beautiful fragrance a flower yields when trampled upon." This is what an unknown poet had in mind when he or she wrote the following:

> The sandal tree perfumes, when riven,
> The ax that laid it low;
> Let man who hopes to be forgiven
> Forgive and bless his foe.

Words are like windows! They let us see into the speaker's mind and heart. The first recorded phrase that we have of Jesus from the cross is a prayer to his Father to forgive those who put him there. This first of the seven words from the cross shows us that the Savior knew what he was doing when he died on Calvary. Three of these sayings were addressed to God, and four to people. Though they were spoken at different times and for various purposes, there is an unmistakable unity. This first one, in a sense, was the foundation for the other six, for unless Jesus had possessed a forgiving spirit toward those who crucified him, he never could have been the world's Savior.

I. The worst moment in history.

Whatever other tragedies the world has witnessed, none even closely approximates this ghastly scene. The best man who ever lived was killed like a common criminal. When Clovis, king of the Franks, was converted to Christianity, he still had many crude ideas that needed refining. One day as he heard someone reading the story of how Jesus was crucified, he raised his sword and said, "If I and my Frankish army had been there, they would not have done that to him." Men who were not even worthy to be in the same world with Jesus dared to condemn him. Others equally sinful implemented the decision and executed him. What a caricature of justice!

II. God overrules human ignorance and sin.

Paul wrote to Timothy, "Great is the mystery of godliness" (1 Tim. 3:16). How true! Nowhere is this better illustrated than when God took the cruelest thing humankind ever did and channeled it into his redemptive purpose. Centuries earlier one of Israel's greatest prophets said concerning the coming Suffering Servant, "It pleased the Lord to bruise him" (Isa. 53:10). This certainly does not mean that God took delight in Jesus' sufferings; rather, it means that Jesus' death had God's approval because it was in accordance with his eternal will. The Savior who died on Calvary in history was slain in the heart of God from the foundation of the world.

God took human hatred and used it to demonstrate divine love. He is in the process of doing this even today. Jesus has been paradoxically called the one who was "far too good to be saved," but he is also the one who "did something by dying." On Calvary's hill that fateful day, there were three deaths and three kinds of deaths. One man died *in sin* because he rejected divine love. The other thief died pardoned *from sin* because at the last hour he pleaded for mercy. The one on the middle cross died *for sin* because he was the only one who could.

Death came to the unrepentant sinner, as one writer put it, "like the world's last wind, dark and sterile and hopeless." But to Jesus death came "in a sudden shaft of light as the sun striking its way . . . to etch out the shadows." During those six hours that Jesus hung on the cross, his eyes revealed a great, even though a brooding, glory. Few people could see the light of that glory, but it was there. The sinless was made sin in order that sinners might be made sinless.

III. But this is not universalism.

Let's remember what the gospel teaches. For people to be saved, they must repent of their sins and place their faith in the Savior. Thus, when Jesus cried to the Father with an exhortation to "forgive them for they know not what they do," he was not calling on God to save these people against their will. As omnipotent as our God is, he has limited himself by humankind's free will. God's love for the world does not mean that he will save the world. It only means that he has provided the way in which the world can be saved.

What is forgiveness? In the sense of salvation, it is an action that releases us from the guilt and consequences of our unrighteous acts and attitudes. This requires repentance on the part of those who wish to be forgiven. Paul used the word *justification* to describe the state of those who have begun the Christian life. These individuals have been pardoned from the guilt of their unregenerate hearts. Since the primary meaning of the word *forgive* is "to remove," we often speak of being justified once, when we begin the Christian life. But our sins are forgiven regularly as we pray to God and ask for forgiveness. Forgiveness removes the sin that mars our daily fellowship with him. This may be, in a sense, an oversimplification, but basically this is the distinction between forgiveness and justification.

Forgiveness can mean something else. It can be a "forthgiving" of oneself in renewed feelings of friendliness and renewed activity of friendly purpose.

In this sense, one seeks to restore "soul union" between the one who wronged and the one who was wronged. This is why we must forgive to understand God's forgiveness. Those who have never forgiven another do not truly understand what takes place when God, for Christ's sake, forgives them.

Jesus presented God as a father who meets the prodigal son with the offer of forgiveness. He practiced this in his ministry many times. Thus, when Jesus asked God to forgive them, he was doing the very thing he taught his followers to do: "Love your enemies . . . and pray for them which despitefully use you, and persecute you" (Matt. 5:44).

Implicit in the prayer from the cross was the request that God would lead his enemies to be sorry for this terrible sin, sorry enough to repent and turn to the Savior. It is possible that some of the very people who had a part in the crucifixion later accepted Jesus as Lord and Savior.

Conclusion

Do you have a forgiving spirit? General Oglethorpe is reported to have heard John Wesley preach a sermon on forgiveness. The general said, "I can never forgive." Wesley replied, "Then sir, I hope you never sin."

Nineteenth-century preacher Thomas De Witt Talmage said concerning those who fail to show compassion and forgiveness, "I lay down as a rule, without any exception, that those people who have the most faults themselves are the most merciless in their watching of others. From the scalp of the head to the soles of the feet they are full of jealousness and hypercriticism. They find their lives hunting for muskrats and mud turtles instead of hunting for rocky mountain creatures and soaring eagles."

> Deal kindly with an erring one
> Oh, do not thou forget,
> However darkly stained by sin,
> He is thy brother yet.
>
> Forget not often thou hast sinned
> And sinful yet must be,
> Deal kindly with the erring one
> As God hast dealt with thee.
>
> —*Julia Abigail Fletcher Carney*

One further word needs to be said about forgiveness. Are you a forgiven person? One becomes a Christian only by experiencing the forgiveness of God through what Jesus Christ did on the cross in atonement and perfected in his resurrection from the grave. The prayer of Jesus was not for God to wink at the sin of ignorance, nor was it a request for a blanket pardon for the sin of his murderers. Neither was it a request for God to thrust forgiveness on those who did not want it. His prayer was a request that condemnation of those who killed him be held in abeyance until they might know the true meaning of what they were doing and repent. God has done that for you if you have not yet been saved. He has not canceled the consequences of your guilt, but he has postponed the consequences so that you might have time to receive Christ as your Savior. Will you do it?

SUNDAY EVENING, FEBRUARY 14

Title: Peter and the Apostles Recommend Election of Deacons

Text: "Therefore, brethren, pick out from among you seven men of good repute, full of the Spirit and of wisdom, whom we may appoint to this duty. But we will devote ourselves to prayer and to the ministry of the word" **(Acts 6:3–4 RSV)**.

Scripture Reading: Acts 6:1–7; Philippians 1:1; 1 Timothy 3

Introduction

What kind of church do you want your church to be? The first church at Jerusalem had many qualities worthy of emulation: the people were filled with the Holy Spirit; they assembled regularly; they prayed; they preached a good gospel; they were good stewards of their possessions; they triumphed over persecution.

Not all, however, were good. Judas, their treasurer, had been a thief, and he committed suicide. Ananias and Sapphira lied about their giving and were struck dead by God. The church did not grasp the meaning of missions beyond their own city and race, and it took much persecution to teach them that lesson.

The Jerusalem church had grown rapidly. The 120 in the upper room gained three thousand more at Pentecost (Acts 2:41). "In those days when the number of disciples was increasing, the Hellenistic Jews among them complained against the Hebraic Jews because their widows were being overlooked in the daily distribution of food" (Acts 6:1 NIV). The solution to this problem led to the selection of seven men who were elected as deacons.

I. The problem.

As recorded in Acts 2:43–47 and 4:32–37, the emergency of vast numbers of people without employment who remained in Jerusalem for worship services every day was met by the Jerusalem church through an unusual application of stewardship. Believers as led by the Holy Spirit sold farms, houses, and other valuables, then brought the proceeds to the apostles for distribution to meet the need. The Greek-speaking Jews complained that their widows were not being treated as well as the Hebrew-speaking widows.

II. The solution.

A. *The apostles thought about it.* This is a first step in the solution of any problem. As a wise philosophy professor often advised, "Brood over it; you might hatch out something." They must have prayed about it and sought the leadership of the Holy Spirit.

B. *The apostles recommended that the church (the multitude of disciples) choose seven men for this deacon service.* They were to choose men with the following characteristics:

    1. "Of good repute." They were not only to be men of good character but also of good reputation.

    2. "Full of the Spirit." Deacon service is important service. Deacons are servants of the Lord first and then servants of the church.

    3. "Full of . . . wisdom." They were to be men of practical wisdom.

C. *The church chose the deacons.* The apostles' recommendation pleased the church, and they chose seven men. What method the church used to make the selection, Luke does not record. The men chosen all had Greek names, which indicates thoughtful consideration. We may assume that the choice was prayerful.

D. *The church ordained the deacons.* "Whom they set before the apostles: and when they had prayed, they laid their hands on them" (Acts 6:6). It is not clear whether the whole church or just the apostles laid their hands on the deacons. The laying on of hands was a symbolic way of praying for God's blessings. Matthew 19:13 records that parents brought their little children to Jesus "that he should put his hands on them, and pray." The laying on of hands probably also signified their belief that God, as it were, had laid his hands on these men for this service. Paul was one of the presbytery who laid hands on Timothy (1 Tim. 4:14; 2 Tim. 1:6). We suppose this was when he was ordained to the ministry. When Barnabas and Saul were called for missionary service, the church at Antioch "prayed, and laid their hands on them" (Acts 13:3).

III. The office of deacon.

A. *The deacons were elected to release the apostles from serving tables so they were free for praying and ministering the Word.* The apostles did not have any successors.

B. *Pastors and deacons are both the servants of Christ and the servants of the church.* Pastors are called to leave their secular vocations and devote full time to the ministry as a vocation. Deacons can remain in their secular vocations. The relationship is illustrated by the deacon's son, who said to the pastor's son, "Your father gets paid for being good, but my father is good for nothing."

    Pastors and deacons are to cooperate. They should be (and usually are) good friends.

Conclusion

Were the first deacons to serve for life or just for the specific task for which elected? We do not know. By the time Paul wrote Philippians, they were recognized with the bishops as officers of the church (see Phil. 1:1). In 1 Timothy 3 Paul listed the qualifications for both bishops and deacons. He assumed that a church would have both.

It is a great honor to be elected a deacon, but deacons are not elected to honor themselves but to honor Christ (1 Tim. 3:13).

WEDNESDAY EVENING, FEBRUARY 17

Title: An Imperative Regarding False Teachers

Text: Look out for the dogs, look out for the evil-workers, look out for those who mutilate the flesh. **(Phil. 3:2 RSV)**

Scripture Reading: Philippians 3:2–11

Introduction

In this imperative concerning false teachers, the apostle Paul warned the beloved congregation in Philippi against the peril of being misled in their faith. In the verses that follow the text, we gain the impression that these false teachers were the Judaizers—those who believed that Gentiles must become Jews in order to be Christians.

The Judaizers found it exceedingly difficult to believe that the Gentiles were included in God's great redemptive purpose. They would have preferred to restrict Christianity to Jewish listeners, and they resisted every outreach effort that was extended toward non-Jews. The Judaizers were seemingly unable to see that their traditions placed restrictions on the love and mercy of God. They were legalistic and literalistic in their interpretations of the Old Testament. They were blind to the changes that the preaching of the gospel and the work of the Holy Spirit were bringing about in the hearts and lives of Gentile believers.

In this warning concerning the necessity of being on guard against false teachers, Paul feared that the Philippian congregation would be subjected to the same kind of perils that he dealt with in his letter to the Galatians. The Galatians had responded to the gospel by faith. Later they were confused and misled by these Judaizers, who caused them to fall away from the way of grace. They added to faith the works of the law as essentials for salvation.

I. A warning against legalism.

From verse 3 and following, we draw the conclusion that Paul was informing his converts in Philippi to be on their guard. They needed to oppose those who insisted that the proper observance of external religious ceremonies, along with ancestral relationships, gave them a position of privilege in God's sight.

Paul went into great detail to demonstrate that he no longer put his faith and trust in the things on which he previously had based his hope for a right relationship with God. He no longer put faith in his religious self-discipline or achievements as a basis for acceptance before the Father God (Phil. 3:7–10). Paul encouraged the Philippian congregation to trust in Jesus Christ plus nothing for a righteousness that comes through faith (Phil. 3:9).

II. A warning against false teachings.

In the closing verses of Philippians 3, Paul warned believers against listening to and following those who separate creed from conduct and behavior from belief. The false teachers in this passage may be the Gnostics, who believed that people found acceptance before God on the basis of a superior knowledge. This was communicated to them by those who were initiated into the secrets of the knowledge of God. The Gnostics believed that matter is essentially evil and that the Creator God is so exalted and so far removed from humankind that he is unconcerned about human conduct.

These false teachers denied the true humanity of Jesus Christ and in so doing also denied his divinity. The end result was complete license in conduct. Paul warns his beloved Philippians against the belief that there is no relationship between the condition of the soul and the life that one lives.

Conclusion

There are many false teachers in the world today. Some of them are very sophisticated. We need to beware lest religious teachers lead us astray from the truth of God's Word. We need to be cautious lest we are led away from the path of proper conduct by what we see on television or in videos. We need to be on guard lest we are led astray by the customs and the traditions of our culture that are often accepted as the law and the gospel.

Perhaps the finest way to prevent ourselves from being misled is to make a total commitment to Jesus Christ as heaven's infallible teacher as well as Lord and Savior. Let's listen to him as he speaks to us with authority concerning God, others, and things that are of eternal value.

SUNDAY MORNING, FEBRUARY 21

Title: God Can Save Anyone Anywhere Anytime

Text: "And Jesus said unto him, Verily I say unto thee, To day shalt thou be with me in paradise" **(Luke 23:43)**.

Scripture Reading: Luke 23:39–43

Hymns: "When I Survey the Wondrous Cross," Watts
"Pass Me Not, O Gentle Saviour," Crosby
"The Nail-Scarred Hand," McKinney

Offertory Prayer: Our Father, we thank you for the beauty of this world. We are grateful for the light of the sun, the wind on our faces, the color of the flowers, and for all the lovely things that enrich our lives. We thank you for all the world that you have made. Sin has entered it, and because of that, we need a Savior. You have provided that Savior in Jesus Christ. We bring our gifts that the message of Christ may be proclaimed to those who do not know him. Some of our money will be used here at this church. Some will be used at other places, even at the uttermost part of the world. May we, your people and the sheep of your pasture, not only enter into your gates with thanksgiving and into your courts with praise, but also have thankful hearts and give cheerfully of our means that those without a Savior may hear the gospel and find eternal life. We pray in Jesus' name. Amen.

Introduction

Since Jesus came into the world to identify himself with sinners, it was quite appropriate that he should die between two of the worst. No doubt, those who placed him there did so with malice, intending to add insult to the injurious death they had imposed upon him. Again, however, as on other occasions, God used the wrath of humans to glorify himself. Jesus had the opportunity to demonstrate to the world his great grace and mercy even in the last hours of his life upon earth.

I. Last words are significant.

Some of the most fascinating quotations in anthologies are those of the final words people spoke while on earth. A famous atheist is reported to have said on his deathbed, "About to take a fearful leap into the dark." On the other hand, the final testimony of one of America's greatest evangelists was, "Earth is receding; heaven is opening; God is calling!"

The two thieves, with their last words, reveal a great contrast between two types of people. One continued to reject Jesus until the very last, mocking him by demanding with a sneer that he prove his power with a miraculous act. The other man, however, must have understood the spiritual nature of Jesus' message and ministry, for he requested a part in Christ's kingdom. Surely this thief was not referring to any political organization that he thought Christ would establish by overthrowing the Roman government. His request "Remember me when thou comest into thy kingdom" (v. 42) spoke of a life beyond.

II. Deathbed salvation is possible.

Can one be saved after years of sinning? Of course, for this is what God's grace is! Such a transaction should be analyzed discreetly. A wise pastor said to a young ministerial student, "I believe in deathbed confessions. I believe one can be saved in his last moments. I've seen several, and I must admit that I'm always a bit nervous about them, wondering if the confession was absolutely genuine. But I know that deathbed confessions are valid and accepted by God."

No doubt about this one! Jesus verified the sincerity of the thief's confession. The request was more than the asking of a favor. This man was saying, in essence, "I'm sorry for my sins. I accept you for who you say you are. In this last brief period of my life, I want to go on record that I identify with you and all that you stand for. Where I have erred, please forgive me. I throw myself entirely upon your mercy. Let me be a part of you during these remaining moments on earth and let me share with you where you go." This is all any of us can do, regardless of how young or how old we may be. No one is saved by piling up good works in order to obligate God to declare him or her righteous. Even the best persons on earth are sinners, and their righteousness is like "filthy rags" in God's sight.

III. We can know that we are saved.

Have you ever heard someone say, "I hope I'm a Christian" or "I'm try-ing to be a Christian"? Such statements sound very humble, but they are completely unscriptural. The Bible makes it clear how one is saved: "Confess with your lips that Jesus is Lord and believe in your heart that God raised him from the dead" (Rom. 10:9 RSV). When you have done this, you are saved. You may or may not feel a sudden surge of emotions. The feeling is not the fact nor even the proof. The authority for our salvation rests upon what God's Word says to us. A feeling may come immediately or gradually, but the fact of the new life occurs instantaneously. Beyond the shadow of a doubt, we can know that our names are written in the Lamb's Book of Life. To say that you are certain of your salvation is not boasting but is rather accepting that God does what he says he will do.

God put our sins on Jesus' back when Jesus died on the cross. God is so completely satisfied with the substitutionary death of his Son for our sins that he will eternally remain so and will never again take up judgment against us. In the resurrection of Christ, God vindicated everything that Jesus did and gave all authority to him. When we receive the Savior in simple faith, we can say with assurance, "I'm saved and I know it." How marvelous is this assurance.

Conclusion

Although the thief was saved at the twelfth hour, he was saved! Someone spoke of it as "literally blundering into paradise." This is not, however, a fair description. We all "blunder" into heaven, because we must come simply as sinners, throwing ourselves upon the grace of God. True, this man was one who had wasted his life, but in a sense we all do the same thing until we come to the Savior. Many years ago Ambrose, one of the early Christian preachers, said, "How much richer was Christ's grace than the malefactor's prayer!" A modern writer expressed it, "Christ swept the man into the full embrace of God's love."

One fact worth noting is that it was not the words of Jesus that led the man to repentance and faith. Jesus did not address the thief at all until the thief spoke to him. The convicting work of the Holy Spirit had already been done before the man uttered a word. The sinlessness of Jesus, his refusal to utter a word of harshness, his magnanimity in the face of cruel treatment—these were the things the Holy Spirit used to bring the thief to his prayer for forgiveness.

Yet when Jesus did speak, he added greatly to the impression he had already made on the man. He spoke of the unseen world as a place with which he was already familiar. Jesus assured the thief that he was as influential in that world as the thief considered him to be. When this sinner laid on Jesus the guilt of his sin, the weight of his soul, and his concern for eternity, Jesus accepted the burden and brought assurance to him. He can do the same for anyone, anywhere, anytime. He can do it for you!

SUNDAY EVENING, FEBRUARY 21

Title: God Pricks Peter's Prejudice

Text: "And Peter opened his mouth and said: 'Truly I perceive that God shows no partiality, but in every nation any one who fears him and does what is right is acceptable to him'" **(Acts 10:34–35 RSV)**.

Scripture Reading: Acts 10:1–11:18

Introduction

Simon Peter was steeped in the prejudice of the Jews against the Gentiles. On the wall of partition in the temple at Jerusalem was written, "Let no Gentile go beyond this point on peril of death." Peter explained his scruples to Cornelius, "You are well aware that it is against our law for a Jew to associate with or visit a Gentile" (Acts 10:28 NIV). The Samaritan woman explained to Jesus the prevailing practice when she said, "For the Jews have no dealings with the Samaritans" (John 4:9).

At Pentecost Peter had preached, "For the promise is unto you, and to your children, and to all that are afar off, even as many as the Lord our God shall call" (Acts 2:39). But he seemed to have thought that the Gentiles must first become Jews before they could become Christians.

In spite of the Great Commission and the impact of John 10:16, "Other sheep I have, which are not of this fold: them also I must bring, and they shall hear my voice; and there shall be one fold, and one shepherd," the disciples had preached "to none but unto the Jews only" (Acts 11:19).

I. The dawning of new truth.

    A. *Cornelius's vision (10:1–8).* Cornelius was a devout, prayerful, generous Gentile soldier who commanded a hundred men at Caesarea. An angel told him in a vision to send men to Peter, who was lodging with Simon the tanner in Joppa. Cornelius selected a devout soldier and two household servants and sent them to Joppa.

    B. *Peter's vision (10:9–18).* The following day at noon while waiting for his meal, Peter fell into a trance. He saw the heavens open and a great sheet like a ship's sail "let down by four corners upon the earth. In it were all kinds of animals and reptiles and birds of the air" (vv. 11–12 RSV).

Peter had been reared to observe the distinction of clean and unclean foods (see Lev. 11). He had never eaten anything that was ceremonially unclean. When the voice he recognized as the Lord's said, "Rise, Peter; kill and eat" (v. 13 RSV), he could not overcome his prejudice to do it. The Lord's reply, "What God has cleansed, you must not call common" (v. 15 RSV), was an enigma to him. The vision was repeated three times for emphasis. While Peter was thoroughly perplexed about its meaning, the visitors from Cornelius arrived.

C. *Peter met the messengers from Cornelius (10:17–23)*. Encouraged by assurance from the Holy Spirit, Peter went down to meet them. They explained their mission. "So he called them in to be his guests" (v. 23 RSV). If he actually invited them to stay under the same roof with himself and his Jewish host, this was a departure from his rearing.

D. *Peter went to Cornelius in Caesarea (10:23–32)*. When Peter left the next morning for Caesarea, he had a few Jewish brethren accompany him. This showed discerning foresight. He would need them as witnesses.

Cornelius had gathered together a large group of his relatives and close friends. "When Peter entered, Cornelius met him and fell down at his feet and worshiped him. But Peter lifted him up, saying, 'Stand up; I too am a man'" (vv. 25–26 RSV).

Cornelius recounted how the Lord had led him to send for Peter. "Now therefore," he said, "we are all here present in the sight of God, to hear all that you have been commanded by the Lord" (v. 33 RSV). Peter opened his mouth to preach, and a truth that was new to him came forth: "Truly I perceive that God shows no partiality, but in every nation any one who fears him and does what is right is acceptable to him" (vv. 34–35 RSV).

Peter had basically one sermon. He had preached it at Pentecost to the people in the temple, to the Sanhedrin, and now he preached it to Cornelius and his friends. Peter concluded his sermon with these words, "To him all the prophets bear witness that every one who believes in him receives forgiveness of sins through his name" (v. 43 RSV). Now the words "every one" took on additional meaning. When Peter formerly had said, "every one," his prejudice had limited the word to Jews and proselytes. Now "every one" really did include everyone. To Peter's surprise, the Holy Spirit manifested approval of the acceptance of the Gentiles much as he had done at Pentecost.

Could anyone object because of their race to baptizing persons who glorified God? The Jewish believers did not object, so Peter commanded the Gentile believers to be baptized in the name of the Lord.

II. Controversy at Jerusalem over the new departure (11:1–18).

   A. *The accusation (vv. 1–3).* The report of what had been done reached Jerusalem. When Peter returned to Jerusalem, the Jewish Christians, who were as prejudiced as Peter had been, "criticized him, saying, 'Why did you go to uncircumcised men and eat with them?'" (vv. 2–3 RSV).

   B. *Peter's defense (11:4–17).* Peter told the story carefully from beginning to end. He concluded, "If then God gave the same gift to them as he gave to us when we believed in the Lord Jesus Christ, who was I that I could withstand God?" (v. 17 RSV).

   However, the issue had not been settled for everyone. Some admitted this as a special case but did not accept the principle. The Judaizers were to make great trouble for the missionaries.

Conclusion

   Important issues are involved here.

   1. *The dignity of human personality.* No person is common. God loves all people. The gospel is for all. Everyone is precious in God's sight.
   2. *God has no respect of persons.* God has respect *for* people but not of people. He is not partial. The Jew is no better than the Gentile.
   3. *Salvation is for everyone on the same basis.* That basis is not circumcision nor baptism, but belief in Jesus Christ (see John 3:16; Acts 10:43; Gal. 3:25–29; 5:6).

WEDNESDAY EVENING, FEBRUARY 24

Title: Rejoice in the Lord

Text: "Rejoice in the Lord always; again I will say, Rejoice" **(Phil 4:4 RSV)**.

Scripture Reading: Philippians 4:1–7

Introduction

   Paul, from a prison cell, wrote this epistle of joy to the members of a congregation in another city where he had been imprisoned. After having been beaten with many stripes, Paul and Silas were able to experience the joy of worship in the midst of unfavorable circumstances (Acts 16:25–26).

   It is rather surprising to find an exhortation to rejoice in the Lord coming from one who was a prisoner for his faith. Yet Paul repeatedly urged the believers in Philippi to rejoice. In this imperative he reveals to us the source of joy, and he encourages us to respond to this source of joy. He is recommending a positive mental attitude characterized by optimism and hope amid circumstances that may not be favorable.

The Philippian believers needed this exhortation, and we need it today. We have something to rejoice over and be glad in. Jesus desired that his disciples experience fullness of joy (John 16:24; 17:13).

The world needs a religion of joy. Many people live in defeat and despair because they search for joy and happiness in the wrong places. Paul did not say, "Rejoice in your health." One's health can fail. Paul did not say, "Rejoice in your wealth." You may not have wealth, and even if you did, you could lose it. Paul did not say, "Rejoice in your friends." Your friends may disappoint you. Paul did not say, "Rejoice in your family." One's family can be a source of unhappiness. Rather, Paul said, "Rejoice in the *Lord* always; again I will say, Rejoice." He encourages us to make a spiritual inventory of that which gives life meaning and purpose. He urges us to truly value that which is valuable and to find our greatest satisfaction in our relationship with God.

I. Let us rejoice in the Lord's person.

The God and Father of our Lord Jesus Christ is a moral God. He is a God of integrity who is characterized by righteousness and dependability. He never makes a mistake and will never conduct himself in such a way as to disappoint us, for he is a God of holiness and love. Let us rejoice that he is the kind of God he is.

II. Let us rejoice in the Lord's purposes.

All of God's purposes toward us are purposes of love, and he deals with us according to his perfect wisdom. He knows our past, our present, and our future. No evil is in him and no selfishness is in his purposes toward us. God's will is that none of us should perish, but that all of us should experience life in its fullness.

III. Let us rejoice in the Lord's promises.

The Bible is a book that contains many promises from the Father God to his children. We need to discover these promises and respond to them in faith and obedience. By his promises he uplifts us and enriches us.

IV. Let us rejoice in the Lord's power.

Our God is no weakling. He is the creator God and the sustaining Lord. He provides all good things for us. In his strength we can resist evil and can become what he wants us to be and achieve what he wants us to do. Let us rejoice in God's inexhaustible spiritual power, which is available to all who seek and serve him.

V. Let us rejoice in the Lord's abiding presence.

Our Lord promised his disciples that he would be with them at all times, in all circumstances, to the very end of the age (Matt. 28:20). He is the God who has promised never to leave us or forsake us. It is impossible for us to drift beyond the range of his loving care (Ps. 139).

VI. Let us rejoice in the Lord's provisions.

God has provided for the forgiveness of all our sins in the past, and he provides for our deepest needs in the present. Further, he promises to provide a home at the end of the way (John 14:1–3).

Conclusion

Many things in life can cause us to become downcast, disappointed, and discouraged. We must beware lest we search for happiness and joy in the wrong places. When the Lord is the basis for our hopes for the future, we will find the source of unending joy.

Paul said, "Rejoice in the Lord always; again I will say, Rejoice." As you rejoice in the Lord, you will find life to be more meaningful. And you will find life to be more productive as you seek to minister to others.

SUNDAY MORNING, FEBRUARY 28

Title: Never Forget Life's Duties

Text: "When Jesus saw his mother, and the disciple whom he loved standing near, he said to his mother, 'Woman, behold, your son!' Then he said to the disciple, 'Behold, your mother!'" **(John 19:26–27 RSV)**.

Scripture Reading: John 19:25–27

Hymns: "In Christ There Is No East or West," Oxenham
"Where Cross the Crowded Ways of Life," North
"Hark, the Voice of Jesus Calling," March

Offertory Prayer: Our Father, we are grateful for another day, another gift of time. Help us not to put off until tomorrow the things we should be doing today. Help us to do every task, face every duty, and shoulder every responsibility without delay, never allowing anything to be half-finished nor any task undone. Help us to realize that high on our priority list should be the stewardship of our material possessions. As we bring them this morning, may we find joy in this part of the service. Bless all those who will be touched for God and for good because of our gifts today. We pray in Jesus' name. Amen.

Introduction

One of the great mysteries of Christianity is the relationship of Mary, the mother of Jesus, to her first and greatest Son. She knew more than anyone else that he was virgin-born. All others, even her husband, had to take it on faith. On the night of the Savior's birth and in the days that followed, many strange and wonderful things happened. Mary "kept all these things, and pondered them in her heart" (Luke 2:19).

How often Mary must have wanted to tell all she knew but opted to exercise discretion. To bear a burden and not be able to tell of it is difficult.

73

But what about knowing great things concerning your son and not being able to tell others? Wouldn't that be an almost impossible task?

Yet in approximately three years, Mary saw the mission of Jesus take a turn that, in all likelihood, she had never expected, the opposite of all for which she had hoped. At one time she seems to have joined his brothers in the conclusion that her firstborn was taking the wrong road on the way to his divinely decreed mission. And now, at his crucifixion, she must have seen the further deterioration of the messiahship and what seemed to be the utter collapse of the mission.

What was Mary going to get out of it? Only some kind words from her Son as he said to John, "Behold thy mother!" Is this all, or is there more? We know there was a resurrection. How much she understood at that moment we cannot be certain. But we do know that her fears, frustrations, and disappointments received a glorious reversal when her Son arose as the ever-living Lord.

I. Jesus tremendously elevated womanhood.

In the Jewish world of the Old Testament, a woman was but a piece of merchandise. Although in certain places the Mosaic law protected women, they had far fewer rights than men. But when Jesus came, he immediately identified himself with the downcast and the outcast, including women who had been made second-class or even third-class citizens. Jesus went so far as to say that prostitutes would enter the kingdom of God before the legalistic Pharisees. This was not because he condoned immorality or overlooked sexual impurity, but because he realized that it was the overbearing attitude of the religious hypocrites of the day that had put women down and made them only chattel in the economy.

Do you remember the story of the Samaritan woman at the well as recorded by John in chapter 4 of his gospel? John tells us that the disciples marveled to find their Master talking with a woman (v. 27), yet none of them asked why he did it. That brief comment of John, whom we should remember was one of the disciples present on the scene, shows how Jesus has changed the world.

Women today should stop and ask themselves some questions. Who made it fit and decent for a man of God to stop and talk with you? Who has thrown a zone of mercy and protection around your children? Who has lifted you and transformed you from being man's plaything to becoming man's beloved companion? Who has elevated you from being man's chattel and property to becoming his friend, his equal, his inspirer? Who obliterated the mark of slavery from your face? Who put on your brow the halo of chivalry and tenderness? Who has changed your position in society so much that instead of it being a marvel today that a man of God talked with a woman, the real marvel is that there ever was a day when men did marvel that a man of God talked with a woman. Modern women should do as another New Testament woman did—bring an alabaster box filled with precious and very costly ointment, break it, and pour it with love and gratitude on the head of Jesus, and wash his feet with tears of love. Such an attitude would be quite appropriate, because only in lands where the message of Jesus Christ has come has womanhood been elevated to a true and deserved position in life.

II. Yet even Christian America has been slow to learn.

In spite of the gospel's progress in human relationships, it took a long time for our country, founded on Christian principles, to recognize that women are loved equally by God and are also children of God when born again by his Spirit. Did you know that no woman ever protested legally against her husband's infidelity in America until 1801? Did you know that only three cases in which a wife took the initiative in a suit for divorce are recorded up until 1840? Did you know that a woman was admitted to the Harvard Medical School in 1850 and then forced out? Did you know that Charles Fox in 1797 said, "It has never been suggested in all theories and projects of the most absurd speculation that it would be advisable to extend the elective suffrage to the female sex"?

Yet Jesus cared for women. He saw the grief of his mother and made provision for her. With tenderness he told John to care for her. In that hour of unutterable agony, Jesus saw not only the weak men but the weeping women, especially the one who had cared so much for him. He knew the fading of hope in her had brought desolation to her heart. He realized that her faith was imperfect and her understanding was inadequate, but he also remembered her tender care and solicitude for him. He refused to adopt the traditional attitude of society. He was the "pioneer of faith" in many ways, especially in attitudes toward women. How slow we have been to catch up with Jesus and let his mind be in us!

III. Do the duty nearest.

Too many of us want to immunize ourselves from the dreary obligations of everyday responsibility by dreaming wistfully of what we would do if we had greater fields of service in which to labor. Years ago a teenage girl adopted a sort of "better-than-thou" attitude toward her peer group because she had "surrendered to missions" and meant to be a foreign missionary someday. A wise, full-time religious worker, visiting her church for a study week, said to her, "Honey, the most important thing in your life is not that you are going to be a foreign missionary someday, but that in your youth organization, the group of which you're captain has charge of the program next Sunday night. If you cannot be a good group captain now, it's very doubtful that you will be a good missionary, or a missionary at all, when you're twenty-five years old."

Jesus saw the duty nearest to him and did it! He made provision for his mother. He laid upon John the responsibility of caring for her. He was dying to atone for the sins of the world, but he would not hide behind that great mission to escape the drudgery of the small details. In *Gaspar Becerra*, Henry

Wadsworth Longfellow told of the artist who was seeking to carve an image of the Virgin Mary, using precious wood that had been brought from a distant Eastern isle. Day and night he toiled, but to no avail. He then slept and had a vision telling him to shape from the burning brand of oak "the thought that stirs within thee!" He awoke and carved the image from glowing wood on the hearth nearby. Longfellow concluded by saying,

> O thou sculptor, painter, poet!
> Take this lesson to thy heart:
> That is best which lies nearest;
> Shape from that thy work of art.

Conclusion

Although this third word from the cross seems, in some way, to have less inspiration for our spiritual lives than any of the others, in reality perhaps it has the most! If each of us were only willing to do our job quietly yet efficiently, not worrying about who received the credit, great things could be accomplished for the Master. Longfellow expressed this thought:

> Nothing useless is, or low!
> Each thing in its place is best
> And what seems but idle show
> Strengthens and supports the rest.

SUNDAY EVENING, FEBRUARY 28

Title: Peter and Paul

Text: "We believe it is through the grace of our Lord Jesus that we are saved, just as they are" (**Acts 15:11 NIV**).

Scripture Reading: Acts 15:1–34; Galatians 2:1–15

Introduction

There is no record of any meeting of Peter and Paul before Paul's conversion. From Paul's account in Galatians 1:15–24 and Luke's account in Acts 9:19–30, it seems that three years after Paul's conversion (which time he had spent in Damascus and Arabia), Paul went up to Jerusalem, where he spent fifteen days with Peter. The disciples were afraid of him at first because of his reputation as a persecutor of believers. Barnabas, however, championed his cause, and Paul preached boldly in the name of Jesus. Later, when Paul's enemies were about to kill him, the disciples helped him escape to his early home in Tarsus by way of Caesarea. This visit was before Peter's experience with Cornelius.

The persecution that arose at the death of Stephen (one of the seven deacons and the first Christian martyr) scattered the Christians. When some of the Greek-speaking Jews preached to the Gentiles in Antioch, Syria, a great number believed. The church at Jerusalem heard about this and sent Barnabas to investigate. He saw that it was a work of the Lord, so he sent to Tarsus for Paul to come and help. They continued with a profitable ministry at Antioch. From there Barnabas and Paul, with John Mark as their helper, went on the first missionary journey. John Mark soon turned back, but Paul and Barnabas went on and had great success. When they returned to Antioch, "and had gathered the church together, they rehearsed all that God had done with them, and how he had opened the door of faith unto the Gentiles. And there they abode long time with the disciples" (Acts 14:27–28).

I. Peter stood with Paul at the Jerusalem conference (Acts 15:1–35).

A. *The demands of the Judaizers (Acts 15:1–2).* Some Jewish Christians in the church at Jerusalem believed that a Gentile must be circumcised and become a Jew before he could be a Christian. They were doubtless sincere in arguing that Jesus was circumcised and that he had not come to destroy one jot of the law (Matt. 5:17–19). The case of Cornelius they thought was exceptional. Without any authority from the church at Jerusalem (Acts 15:25), these men came to Antioch in Syria and dogmatically asserted, "Except ye be circumcised after the manner of Moses, ye cannot be saved" (v. 1).

Paul and Barnabas had preached, "Be it known unto you therefore, men and brethren, that through this man is preached unto you the forgiveness of sins: and by him all that believe are justified from all things" (Acts 13:38–39).

The issue was clearly drawn. If salvation depends on circumcision or any other ceremony, it is not of grace by faith.

B. *The deputation to Jerusalem (Acts 15:2–3; Gal. 2:1–3).* The church at Antioch sent Barnabas and Paul and other Christians to confer with the apostles and elders at Jerusalem.

All along the way through Phoenicia and Samaria, Paul and Barnabas continued to tell about the conversion of the Gentiles and what God had done through them on their missionary journey.

C. *Reception by the Jerusalem church (Acts 15:4–5).* The church, the apostles, and the elders received them cordially. At the public meeting, some of the believers who had been Pharisees interrupted, saying that "it was needful to circumcise them [the Gentile converts], and to command them to keep the law of Moses" (v. 5). Apparently the apostles and elders had not expected this to come up in a public meeting, so the church meeting was dismissed. Then the apostles and elders met with the visitors.

D. *A conference of leaders (Acts 15:6; Gal. 2:1–10).* In this conference all of the apostles and elders stood with Paul. James, Peter (Cephas), and John extended their support. They urged Paul and Barnabas to

77

continue their mission to the heathen. After the private meeting in Acts 15:6, the church seems to have assembled for the conference beginning in Acts 15:7.

E. *Open church conference (Acts 15:7–29).* Opportunity for full discussion was given. After all had spoken, Peter told the story of how God had led him to preach to the Gentile Cornelius and his household. God had authenticated their salvation by giving them the Holy Spirit just as he had done at Pentecost. He had saved them by faith. Peter put himself and his influence on the side of Paul and Barnabas as he concluded, "We believe it is through the grace of our Lord Jesus that we [Jewish Christians] are saved, just as they [Gentile Christians] are" (v. 11 NIV).

James, half brother of our Lord, spoke last. He agreed with Peter. He showed how the salvation of the Gentiles agreed with prophecy and proposed complete liberty for Gentile Christians. He suggested some concessions to Jewish feelings that did not violate the principle.

The church adopted the resolution. They chose Judas, called Barsabbas, not otherwise known, and Silas, who later became Paul's traveling companion on the second missionary journey, to carry the letter announcing the good news.

II. Paul rebuked Peter publicly (Gal. 2:11–16).

After the Jerusalem conference, Peter went to Antioch and seemed for a time to have acted consistently with his Christian convictions in that he ate with the Gentiles. Then certain men from Jerusalem who held to the old prejudices in which they and Peter had been reared came to Antioch. Peter was evidently influenced by them and separated himself from the Gentiles.

Paul saw that this new practice of Peter was utterly inconsistent with the truth of the gospel (v. 14), and so he boldly withstood Peter to his face before them all (v. 11). In effect, Paul asked Peter, "If you, a Jew, have ceased to trust in your Jewish ceremonies for salvation, but have been saved, not as a Jew but as a person, by personal faith in Jesus, why then do you ask a Gentile who has been saved, not as a Gentile but as a person, by personal faith, to practice customs that you have abandoned?" (vv. 14–15, author's paraphrase).

Conclusion

Paul won the argument, but more importantly, he won Peter and Barnabas to a more consistent Christian practice.

Salvation by grace through faith apart from ceremony is right, not because the Jerusalem conference affirmed it, but because it is essential Christianity, just as is also respect for persons.

Paul's boldness in standing for the truth is worthy of our emulation.

MARCH

■ **Sunday Mornings**

Continue "Christ Speaks from the Cross," a series on Jesus' seven sayings from the cross.

■ **Sunday Evenings**

The suggested theme for Sunday evenings this month is "Questions People Ask about the Holy Spirit."

■ **Wednesday Evenings**

"Invitations to the Heart" is the title of a series of messages from the Psalms. Response to these invitations will help renew the church and bring joy to the hearts of believers.

WEDNESDAY EVENING, MARCH 3

Title: Let Us Sing to the Lord

Text: "It is a good thing to give thanks unto the LORD, and to sing praises unto thy name, O most High" **(Ps. 92:1)**.

Scripture Reading: Psalms 92:1–4

Introduction

Some say that three books are necessary for advancing the kingdom of God—the Bible, the hymnbook, and the pocketbook. Especially important are the Bible and the hymnbook. The Bible is the record of God's self-disclosure to our hearts and lives, while the hymnal is a revelation of the noblest thoughts and intents of the human heart and of its emotional response to God in worship and prayer.

I. Sacred music has always been connected with worship.

When the psalmist calls upon us to join our hearts together with him in singing to the Lord, he is encouraging us to do what Moses had done after the crossing of the Red Sea (Ex. 15), what Solomon would do when the temple was dedicated (2 Chron. 5:12), what the angels would do when they announced the birth of Christ (Luke 2:9–14), and what we will do when we get to heaven.

II. The ministry of sacred music.

The psalmist is not alone in challenging people to join in praise to God. We find the apostle Paul saying to the church at Ephesus, "[Address] one another in psalms and hymns and spiritual songs, singing and making melody to the Lord with all your heart, always and for everything giving thanks in the name of our Lord Jesus Christ to God the Father" (Eph. 5:19–20 RSV).

A. *We should join our hearts together in singing psalms and hymns and spiritual songs.* This is the noblest medium for the ascription of praise to God. Singing aids us in our worship.

B. *The singing of hymns and spiritual songs with joy in the heart moves the unsaved to trust Jesus Christ as Savior.*
1. There have been no great revivals apart from much singing.
2. A songless church is a powerless church.
3. The singing of gospel songs is an important part of an evangelistic service in which the church is trying to win the lost to faith in Jesus Christ.

C. *The singing of hymns and spiritual songs produces a unity of spirit, mind, and purpose among the people of God.* Singing contributes immeasurably to the fellowship of the church.

D. *The singing of hymns and spiritual songs creates a martial spirit among the people of God, encouraging them to march against sin and evil.*

E. *The singing of hymns and spiritual songs serves as a medium for learning great scriptural truths about God.*

III. Let us join together in singing to the Lord.

The psalmist said, "I will sing to the LORD all my life; I will sing praise to my God as long as I live" (Ps. 104:33 NIV). We can sing about God's greatness and power. We can sing about God's goodness and mercy. We can sing with the joy of those who have been forgiven. We can sing because death has been defeated. We can sing because immortality is a reality through the risen Christ.

Conclusion

We may not be able to sing with great expertise, but at least all of us can make a joyful song to the Lord. We can rejoice that our God is the God who puts a song in the heart.

SUNDAY MORNING, MARCH 7

Title: The Road to Duty Is Lonely

Text: "My God, my God, why hast thou forsaken me?" **(Matt. 27:46)**.

Scripture Reading: Matthew 27:34–50

Hymns: "Pass Me Not, O Gentle Savior," Crosby
"I Will Not Forget Thee," Gabriel
"O Love That Wilt Not Let Me Go," Matheson

Offertory Prayer: Our Father, we are grateful for the disciplines of life that make us strong. We pray that we will never ask for easy times, but rather seek to be strong people. We thank you for the infirmities that oppress us, for the doubts that perplex us, and for the sorrows that crush us. Help us never to forget that the adversities of life strengthen the fiber of our souls. Grant that above all things we may be faithful. In our living and our giving, in our praying and paying, in our spending and our sending, may we reflect the Spirit of Christ and be good stewards of all that you have given us. We pray in Jesus' name and for his sake. Amen.

Introduction

All conscious human beings have what is called a "pain threshold." When we pass beyond this threshold, we enter into the realm of delirium, and no cool hand can reach us. How far had Jesus gone at the time he cried out today's Scripture text from the cross? He may have been on the border, but he was still conscious enough to reach back into the Old Testament and pull out a quotation from one of his favorite psalms to express his innermost feelings. By quoting this psalm that was so related to God's purpose in history, he was in all probability also giving witness to people that he was the Messiah.

The words Jesus spoke came near the conclusion of the six hours he suffered on the cross. His enemies had already quoted from this psalm when they said, "He trusts in God. Let God rescue him now if he wants him" (Matt. 27:43 NIV; see Ps. 22:8). Perhaps Jesus was refuting their words with his quotation that had unique application to the situation at hand.

What was happening at Calvary? Jesus was treading the lonesome road to bring forgiveness to humankind. Some things we can share with others, but some duties in life must be faced alone. In Gethsemane Jesus had suffered just such an experience. Now he was facing it again.

I. In one sense, God never leaves us.

Scripture verses abound to teach us that God is always keeping watch over his own. God always remains with his own during their darkest times.

All of us can remember an experience in our life when everyone forsook us but God. How wonderful to know that no matter what comes, we as Christians can call upon the eternal God, knowing that he is our refuge and strength.

One of the greatest heresies possible is to believe that God forsakes his own. Do God's will, and he will be with you to the end! We don't have to wait until we die to be in God's presence, for we can be confident that when we seek to please him here on earth, he is present with us.

II. But Jesus' case was different.

One of the most profound mysteries, perhaps the greatest, in the world is the relationship of the human to the divine in our Savior. As a human being, Jesus suffered; and we must never for one moment forget this fact of Jesus' life. Although the Father was with him in times of loneliness and heartache, as in the garden of Gethsemane, when he prayed, "Do you think I cannot call on my Father, and he will at once put at my disposal more than twelve legions of angels?" (Matt. 26:53 NIV), this case was different. Jesus had come to pay the supreme price for human sin. No theologian can fully explain why it was necessary for Jesus to die in order for humans to live. This is because we cannot fully understand the divine nature. But God willed that humans must be saved from their sin by a divine substitute, Jesus Christ. Paul said that in this way God becomes both just and the justifier of those who put their faith in him (Rom. 3:26). Jesus gave his life as a ransom for many. He was the Lamb of God, the perfect sacrifice, bearing the sin debt of the world. For him to be an effective substitute for our guilt, he had to bear our sins alone. Even God had to "turn his back" on his only Son, as Jesus became the curse in order for us to be set free from the curse.

III. Whatever the cost, remain faithful.

Throughout all of Jesus' ministry, he was tempted to turn aside from his goal because of hardships. His friends did not want to see him die. Peter rebuked him when he spoke of his coming death. His own soul trembled when the cup of affliction was put into his hand. Nevertheless, Jesus set his face as flint to go to Jerusalem. He endured the pain of the cross without uttering a word of complaint.

Doing our duty means difficulty and often danger. Effort, restraint, sacrifice, and discipline form the package. Standing for our principles in order to reach the goal requires great patience. Often we must begin again and forgive those who do not even want forgiveness enough to repent. Dedication is the price in any realm of endeavor.

Most important, we cannot do our duty unless we love. Jesus went to the cross for the world's eternal redemption because he loved. Loneliness was present every step of the road, but there was no other way!

Conclusion

Nothing worthwhile comes easy! But the reward is worth the toil. We do not have to wait until we get to heaven to begin reaping the harvest from the seed we have sown. One of the highest rewards for our toil is not what we get for it but what we become by it.

If the road of Christians as they pursue their duty is lonely, much more so that of sinners. They must repent, and that, too, is a lonesome road. But it is also a glorious one.

SUNDAY EVENING, MARCH 7

Title: Who Is the Holy Spirit?

Text: "And it came to pass, that, while Apollos was at Corinth, Paul having passed through the upper coasts came to Ephesus: and finding certain disciples, he said unto them, Have ye received the Holy Ghost since ye believed? And they said unto him, We have not so much as heard whether there be any Holy Ghost" **(Acts 19:1–2)**.

Scripture Reading: Acts 19:1–6

Introduction

Have you ever met the Holy Spirit? Do you know who he is? Can you share with others the truths you know about him? Can you tell others where he lives or what he does or what he is like? If you can't, then do not feel that you are alone, for there are many other sincere Christians who cannot answer the question "Who is the Holy Spirit?"

In fact, some conscientious Christians in Ephesus whom Paul had met did not even know the Holy Spirit existed. These men were believers, yet they were not complete believers. That is, they had received the message of John and had been baptized by him, but they were unaware of the Holy Spirit. The great difference between the preaching of John the Baptist and the preaching of Jesus Christ is that John's preaching was a pronouncement of judgment. The preaching of Jesus Christ was the declaration of good news.

Yet John's preaching was an essential stage, because in any Christian experience, two steps must be taken.

1. *We can't live as we should.* First, we realize our inability to live as we should. As we are making this step, we often try to do better but inevitably fail to do so because we have only our own strength on which to draw.

2. *Sin can be removed.* The second step is when we come to discover that only through the grace of Jesus Christ can the just desert of sin be removed. As we take this step, we discover the joyful fact that only by the work of the Holy Spirit can we ever live as we should.

The believers at Ephesus were aware of their need to live a better life, but they were not aware of the power of the Holy Spirit to enable them to do so. Their experience demonstrates the truth that without the Holy Spirit we cannot please God. We will have an incomplete Christianity. Even after seeing our sins and the need to repent, we cannot change apart from the Holy Spirit. Thus it is vitally important that we, like the believers at Ephesus, find the answer to the question "Who is the Holy Spirit?"

I. The Holy Spirit is a person.

John 16:13 says, "Howbeit when *he*, the Spirit of truth, is come, *he* will guide you into all truth: for *he* shall not speak of *himself*; but whatsoever *he* shall hear, that shall *he* speak: and *he* will show you things to come" (emphasis added). The Holy Spirit is neither an impersonal force nor a mere influence; rather, he possesses a full and distinct personality. A person has been defined as one who when speaking says *I*; when spoken to is called *you*; and when spoken of is called *him* or *her*.

A. *Personal pronouns are used in relation to the Holy Spirit (see John 16:13).*
B. *The Holy Spirit has qualities of a person, such as knowledge (1 Cor. 12:8), love (Rom. 15:30), and will (1 Cor. 12:11).*
C. *The Holy Spirit acts like a person.* He searches the deep things of God (1 Cor. 2:10). Also, the Holy Spirit speaks (Acts 13:2), intercedes (Rom. 8:26), testifies (John 15:26), teaches (John 14:26), guides (Acts 16:6), and commands and appoints (Acts 20:28).
D. *The Holy Spirit can be treated like a person.* By this the Scripture means that he can be grieved and rebelled against. Isaiah made reference to this fact in 63:10. Paul also spoke of this in Ephesians 4:30. Hebrews 10:29 informs us that the Holy Spirit can be insulted. Furthermore, the Holy Spirit can be lied to (Acts 5:3).

The Bible always pictures the Holy Spirit as a person and never as an impersonal force. Therefore, as a person the Holy Spirit relates to us—he understands, he feels for us, and he is our divine Friend and Helper.

II. The Holy Spirit is God.

The Holy Spirit is none less than God himself because:

A. *The Holy Spirit possesses divine attributes.* The Holy Spirit is omnipresent. The psalmist illustrates this in Psalm 139:7–10 by pointing out that there is nowhere we can go to flee the Lord's presence. Even if we were to ascend into heaven, make our bed in hell, or go to the most extreme parts of the sea, we could never go beyond God's presence. The Holy Spirit also possesses eternity, which only God possesses. He is called "the eternal Spirit" in Hebrews 9:14. The Holy Spirit is omniscient and was described as such by Paul in 1 Corinthians 2:11 when he said, "No one knows the thoughts of God except the Spirit of God" (NIV). The Holy Spirit further is omnipotent, or all-powerful (see Luke 1:35).
B. *Divine works are ascribed to the Holy Spirit.* Some of these works are creation (Gen. 1:2), the giving of life (John 6:63), and prophecy (2 Peter 1:21).
C. *The Holy Spirit is made equal with God the Father and the Son.* In the Great Commission we are told to go, teach, and baptize in the name of the Father, Son, and Holy Spirit (Matt. 28:19). Also, he is made equal with God the Father and the Son in the apostolic benediction recorded in 2 Corinthians 13:14.
D. *The Spirit is called God and Lord.* In Acts 5:3–4 Simon Peter asked Ananias, "Why hath Satan filled thine heart to lie to the Holy Spirit? . . . Thou hast not lied unto men, but unto *God*" (emphasis added).

III. The Holy Spirit is God's agent on earth.

In John 14:16–17 Jesus promised that he would pray to the heavenly Father, and that the Father would send the Holy Spirit, who would abide with us forever. The power of God may be thought of in three ways in relation to the Trinity. It is founded in the Father, revealed through the Son, and activated by the Holy Spirit. From the beginning of time until now, the Holy Spirit has been God's active agent for whatever work God has to do.

A. *The Holy Spirit is God's agent on earth in the creation of the world.* We are told in Genesis 1:2 that the Holy Spirit brought order into the universe when he moved upon the face of the waters. We are further told in Job 26:13 that the Holy Spirit garnished the heavens. Psalm 104:30 tells us that he renews the face of the earth, and Job 33:4 informs us that the Holy Spirit gives life to human beings.

B. *The Holy Spirit is God's agent on earth in the ministry of Christ.* Matthew 1:30 informs us that Jesus was conceived in Mary "of the Holy Spirit." Furthermore, the Holy Spirit was active in the development of Christ as he "grew and became strong" and "was filled with wisdom," for "the grace of God was on him" (Luke 2:40 NIV).

In Christ's official consecration at his baptism, we are told of "the Spirit of God descending like a dove and lighting upon him" (Matt. 3:16). Following this, the Holy Spirit was active in Christ's ministry during the temptation experience in the wilderness (Matt. 4:1).

Luke's account informs us in Luke 4:18–19 that the Spirit of the Lord was upon Jesus Christ during his preaching and healing ministries. Also, Paul said in Romans 8:11 that the Holy Spirit "raised up Christ from the dead."

C. *The Holy Spirit is God's agent on earth in the creation of Holy Scripture.* The Holy Spirit revealed certain truths to individuals, which they in turn recorded as sacred Scripture. Revelation 1:10 gives us such an illustration. John wrote, "I was in the Spirit on the Lord's day, and heard behind me a great voice." Also, the Holy Spirit inspired the Scriptures in an even more direct way. Through revelation he gave new truth that unaided reason could not discover, but through inspiration he transmitted both old and new truths. We are told that all Scripture is given by inspiration of God (2 Tim. 3:16). And in John 14:26 we are assured by Christ that the Holy Spirit would bring all things to our remembrance. Surely part of the inspiration of the Scripture was the Holy Spirit bringing to the remembrance of the writers certain truths and experiences that they might be included as part of sacred Scripture.

The Holy Spirit is active in relation to the Bible through illumination. Illumination relates to our ability to comprehend the truths that have been revealed and inspired. Paul said in Ephesians 1:17 that we have been given "the spirit of wisdom and revelation."

D. *The Holy Spirit is God's agent on earth in the work of the church.* The Holy Spirit initially empowered the church in Acts 1:8. He was involved in the expansion of the church in Acts 2:1–4. And he is seen in 1 Corinthians 12:4–11 as equipping the church.

Conclusion

Who is the Holy Spirit?

1. He is a person—and thus one who cares for you.
2. He is deity—and thus one who can help you.
3. He is God's agent on earth—and thus one who can save you.

Listen to the Holy Spirit as he extends the last invitation of the Bible. "The Spirit and the bride say, Come. And let him that heareth say, Come. And let him that is athirst come. And whosoever will, let him take the water of life freely" (Rev. 22:17).

WEDNESDAY EVENING, MARCH 10

Title: Giving Thanks to God

Text: "Let us come into his presence with thanksgiving; let us make a joyful noise to him with songs of praise!" **(Ps. 95:2 RSV)**.

Scripture Reading: Psalm 92:1–4

Introduction

The psalmist said, "It is good to give thanks to the LORD, to sing praises to thy name, O Most High" (92:1 RSV).

1. *Our being thankful pleases the Lord.* He does not actually need our thanks or our love, but we can be sure that his heart rejoices when we offer thanks for his goodness and kindness to us.
2. *Being thankful is good for us.* When we take time to review all the good things God has done for us, our hearts are filled with joy and our faith is increased. Thus we can be optimistic as we face the future.
3. *Our being thankful is good for those around us.* Hearing our expressions of thanksgiving to God may be the means of others coming to have faith in him. We should praise God so that others will be attracted to him. Certainly we cannot be a very good witness to God's grace if we have no gratitude in our hearts that expresses itself in thanksgiving.
4. *Our being thankful is good for those beyond our acquaintance.* The influence of a grateful heart moves out as a benevolent influence upon others. Many people can be blessed if we follow the invitation of the psalmist and give thanksgiving to God.

I. Let us give thanks to God for his character.

The Bible reveals God to be personal, powerful, and always present. The Bible reveals our God to be a righteous God characterized by integrity and justice. The Bible reveals God to be trustworthy, reliable, and merciful. We should always, in every situation, thank and praise God for being the kind of God he is.

II. Let us give thanks to God for the church.

Through the church God blessed many of us with Christian parents. Through the church he gave us the good news of his love. Through the church he has provided us with teachers and worthy examples to follow. He has also provided us with invaluable friends and made us part of a great family in the church. Even though the church is imperfect, let us thank our Father God for it.

III. Let us give thanks to God for our country.

Around the world all people should discover those things about their nation and their government for which they can give thanks to God.

IV. Let us give thanks to God for our family.

The Bible teaches us that we are to honor and respect our parents. We are to obey them in the Lord. After they become aged, we are to provide for them.

Those who have been fortunate enough to be reared in a Christian home should be eternally grateful to God for this wonderful blessing.

Many of us can be thankful for a Christian companion who has been God's blessing to us in marriage.

Many of us can be thankful to God for Christian children.

V. Let us give thanks to God for personal blessings.

Each of us has received unique gifts, some of which are evident to all, but many of which are private and personal. It is good for us to thank God for these unique blessings.

Conclusion

Being thankful does not happen automatically; being thankful is a learned habit. The psalmist would encourage all of us to develop the habit of coming into the Lord's presence with thanksgiving. He would also encourage us to go out into the community and express our thanks to God to others.

SUNDAY MORNING, MARCH 14

Title: Jesus Thirsted So That We May Drink

Text: "Jesus . . . saith, I thirst" **(John 19:28)**.

Scripture Reading: John 19:23–29

Hymns: "The Old Rugged Cross," Bennard
"Alas, and Did My Savior Bleed," Watts
"When I Survey the Wondrous Cross," Watts

Offertory Prayer: Our Father, help us never to forget that no morning wears to evening without some heart breaking. Comfort those whose happy days and sunshine have turned perhaps even suddenly to the midnight of a broken heart. Bless those who are sad. Take away the ache of their loneliness. May those who are worried find a peace of mind that comes when they realize that your Word promises they will never be tested beyond what they can bear. Help those who are tempted. Give them grace to resist temptation. And warn those who are carelessly walking the razor's edge of temptation. Teach those who have not yet learned the joys of tithing what a blessing giving back to you what is yours will be to their own lives. May those who know this joy seek to be good witnesses of this truth even as of the truth that Jesus Christ saves from sin. Bless our gifts this morning to your glory. In Jesus' name we pray. Amen.

Introduction

Of all the things Jesus suffered, the fact of his thirst seems most inconsistent. At the beginning of his ministry, he began his conversation with a Samaritan woman by asking her for a drink (John 4:7). He used his request as a means of talking with her about his kingdom and to give her living water. Those who drink of this eternal water will never thirst again.

How significant that Jesus began his ministry by asking for water, and now ends it by asking for water. Meanwhile, he used thirst as a theme in many instances. What a great common denominator thirst is for both the body and the soul.

I. Jesus suffered many things.

How terrible were Jesus' enemies! During his ministry they surrounded him with jibes, and at the cross they continued to taunt him. During his trial he did not open his mouth, but on the cross his sufferings were so great he had to speak. See how humanity shone forth in the Savior! He was all God, but he was also all man!

Although Jesus' cry, "I thirst," seems mild when compared to the other brutalities inflicted upon him, in reality it may have been the greatest. To die of thirst is one of the cruelest deaths. Do you recall times when you have been extremely thirsty? It is one of the emptiest feelings a person can have; we seem helpless.

At the beginning of Jesus' ministry, he hungered and was tempted by Satan. At the end he was thirsty. The devil used every possible means to defeat the Savior by making him take a shortcut to his messiahship. But Jesus would not yield. We do find, however, that he cried out in this last struggle. His bodily anguish needed to find expression. Our physical needs may be forgotten temporarily during a crisis of spiritual conflict, but they always assert themselves with great insistence near the close. Jesus suffered! And he did so for our sins.

II. Jesus did not dodge duty.

In answer to Jesus' plea, the soldiers gave him vinegar to drink. When we first read this, we are tempted to suppose that because of the unnatural type of drink they offered, the men intended to insult Jesus. We thus rank it among the taunts and sufferings Jesus endured at the crucifixion. A closer look at oriental historical customs, however, shows us that vinegar was the common drink of the Roman army and was most likely to be at hand at the moment.

We read elsewhere that Jesus was offered a different drink but refused it. He was offered a medicated potion, wine mingled with myrrh, to deaden his pain. Jesus refused to meet death in a state of stupefaction. Jesus refused because he would conquer sin not through the flesh but through the Spirit. Had he escaped from pain and suffering through some kind of medication, he would not have borne our sins completely. The vinegar or sour wine he received was merely a refreshing draught and did not in any way deaden the pain or make him suffer less for our sins.

III. Calvary was not a pretty place.

The Christmas story is beautiful, but not so the message of the cross. The story of Jesus' crucifixion is ugly and painful. It is easy to say, "Let us now go even unto Bethlehem," but it is not so enticing to stand at the foot of the cross and hear the Savior cry. Psalm 69 is certainly a foreshadowing of this dreadful event. Jesus identified with it. When he quoted it, he was saying that he himself was the very heartbeat of this ancient Hebrew hymn. Jesus identified himself with all the hope Israel ever had in a Messiah. His cry became a sigh in a dry and thirsty land.

Have you ever seen how truly ugly all Jesus' suffering is and how we should shudder afresh every time we read the story? Because Jesus suffered, millions have been blessed with personal salvation and strength for everyday living. Even in his cry for thirst, we see him bearing our sins in his own body on the cross.

"I thirst," was the only cry of physical weakness Jesus uttered, but there is something most sincere and attractive about one who is not ashamed to voice his weakness and pain. Jesus' action gives us the key to his saviorhood. He was afflicted in all our afflictions. The cross was ugly and painful. People would gladly banish it from their thinking if they could. Calvary remains as the time of sin's victory, yet sin's defeat; of God's defeat, yet God's victory, for God's Son defeated sin once and for all by dying in humankind's place and rising from the dead.

Conclusion

Do you thirst? Do you desire to be someone better than you are? If so, God can meet that need. To the Samaritan woman, Jesus said, "But whosoever drinketh of the water that I shall give him shall never thirst; but the water that I shall give him shall be in him a well of water springing up into everlasting life" (John 4:14). This is the gift of eternal life. When we have met the Master, surrendered to him, and been mastered by him, our lives will be different. We will no longer thirst, for our needs will have been met and God's Spirit will have moved into our hearts.

The message of the cross is that Christ can quench thirst because he once thirsted. He can make alive because he conquered death. We must remember, however, that the Christian life is not an abundance of material things but rather a realization of spiritual things. When Jesus brought the woman at the well face-to-face with her sin, she tried to change the question: Which mountain should people worship on, Mount Gerizim with the Samaritans or Mount Zion with the Jews? Jesus reminded her that the hour was coming when people would worship at neither mountain. He reminded her that "God is a Spirit: and they that worship him must worship him in spirit and in truth" (John 4:24). When he declared to her that he was the Messiah, she received him and went off to town to tell others of her great discovery. You, too, will experience this joy if you will surrender to him who has the water of eternal life.

SUNDAY EVENING, MARCH 14

Title: Why Study the Holy Spirit?

Text: But the Comforter, which is the Holy Ghost, whom the Father will send in my name, he shall teach you all things, and bring all things to your remembrance, whatsoever I have said unto you. **(John 14:26)**

Introduction

In our sophisticated age of scientific investigation and factual reporting, why should we take time to study the Holy Spirit? When Christ has commanded us to look on the fields that are white unto harvest, how can we justify spending time in such a study? When there are so many souls to be saved, so many lives to be salvaged, and so much work to be done, why should we take time to study the Holy Spirit?

Perhaps the attitude these questions express explains many of the meaningless activities and unproductive efforts of our lives and our churches. We have the sails, but we lack the wind. We have the desire, but we lack the drive. When we take an honest look at ourselves, our church, and our world, we will see why we should take time to study the Holy Spirit.

I. Because we are totally dependent on him.

Some people think like this: When there are so many miles to be traveled, when there is so much to be done when we get there, and when we have gotten such a late start, why should we take time to stop for gas? Yet the answer is quite obvious, isn't it? We are totally dependent on the gas. Without fuel, the miles will not be traveled, the work will not be done, and the destination will not be reached!

That is exactly the meaning of Zechariah 4:6 in regard to the Holy Spirit: "Not by might, nor by power, but by my spirit, saith the LORD of hosts."

A. *We are dependent on the Holy Spirit for the salvation of ourselves and others.* Jesus said, "That which is born of the flesh is flesh; and that which is born of the Spirit is spirit" (John 3:6). Then he said that we should not be shocked by the fact that we must be born again. Our need for forgiveness and God's power to forgive are brought together by faith. This concept can be illustrated like this: A lightbulb may have all the ability to burn, but it cannot burn, though electricity runs to the switch, until that switch has been thrown. In this analogy, faith is symbolized by the switch. When the faith switch is thrown, our need for forgiveness and God's power to forgive are brought together. And the power that brings them together is the Holy Spirit. Or, in the words of Jesus, we are "born" of the Holy Spirit.

When Jesus said, "That which is born of the flesh is flesh," he was simply saying that we are flesh and that our power is limited to what flesh can do. By ourselves we cannot be other than defeated and frustrated. This we know all too well. But when the Holy Spirit is allowed entrance into our lives the moment we accept Jesus, the Holy Spirit can do for a defeated life what we could never do.

To be born again is to be changed in a way that can only be described as rebirth. The change comes when we allow Jesus into our hearts. Then we are forgiven of our past and armed by the Spirit for the future. We become citizens of the kingdom and children of God, and we enter into eternal life because we have been "born of the Spirit."

B. *We are dependent on the Holy Spirit for our growth as Christians.* Paul encourages us to be confident that the Holy Spirit who started the good work of salvation in us will keep on performing it until the day Jesus returns (Phil. 1:6). In other words, our growth, or sanctification, is simply the continuation of what the Holy Spirit did for us at the moment of salvation. It is the result of allowing the Holy Spirit freedom to appropriate salvation in all areas of our lives. Such sanctification becomes both an act and a process. It is an act in that at the moment of salvation we enter the kingdom of God. It is a process in that as we grow spiritually, areas of our lives become increasingly committed to God's will.

C. *We are dependent on the Holy Spirit for our understanding of the Bible's message.* In John 16:13 Christ assures us that the Holy Spirit will guide us into all truth. The Bible is not just another book and therefore cannot be approached or understood as any other book. It is more than words printed on a page. It is the Word of God; therefore, to be understood, it requires the Spirit of God. That is why each time we read the Bible we should pray, "Open thou mine eyes, that I may behold wondrous things out of thy law" (Ps. 119:18). Paul reminds us in 1 Corinthians 2:14, "But the natural man receiveth not the things of the Spirit of God: for they are foolishness unto him: neither can he know them, because they are spiritually discerned."

An airplane that is lost in a storm may be seeking to find its direction. It has a good receiver, and the control tower is transmitting a strong signal. But only when the pilot tunes to the right frequency will he pick up the signal and get back on course.

We are lost and cannot find our way. We have a good mind and a keen ability to decipher God's truths, and God is transmitting his truths day after day. The Holy Spirit tunes us to the right frequency so that we can hear the message and stay on course. Without the work of the Holy Spirit, we become like those whom Jesus described as having ears yet not hearing.

D. *We are dependent on the Holy Spirit for the ability to lead others to Christ.* Perhaps nowhere is this truth spelled out more clearly than in Acts 1:8, where Jesus said that we receive power only after the Holy Spirit comes upon us. Then and only then, he said, will we be witnesses to him wherever we go. Nothing will ever happen apart from the Holy Spirit's working in us as his witnesses and in those with whom we share our witness. We will be nothing more than "religion salespeople." But as we allow the Holy Spirit to lead us to the right person and give us the right words to say, we will return as did the Spirit-empowered disciples, with joy, saying, "Lord, even the devils are subject unto us through thy name" (Luke 10:17).

E. *We are dependent on the Holy Spirit for effective prayer.* Romans 8:26 informs us that the Holy Spirit will help us with our inability to know how to pray. When we really don't know what to pray for, or even how we should pray, the Holy Spirit will intercede on our behalf.

Often our desires are not what they ought to be. Or it may be that we don't express them in the right way, or they are misdirected. As we wait on the Lord, the Holy Spirit can come and take our desires that are too deep or too intense for us to express. He can express them in the language of God.

II. Because God has said so much about the Holy Spirit.

The second verse in the Bible speaks of the Holy Spirit as the one who "moved upon the face of the waters" (Gen. 1:2). The closing section of the Bible (Rev. 22:17) speaks of the Holy Spirit as the one who invites us to come and drink the water of life freely. Everything that falls between Genesis 1:2 and Revelation 22:17, whether it be the creation story, God's working through Israel, the birth of Christ, the establishment of the church, or the glorious revelation of Christ at the end of time, all is the work of the Holy Spirit.

God has much to say about the Holy Spirit in the Old Testament. In fact, the Holy Spirit is mentioned 378 times in the Old Testament. In the New

Testament he is mentioned 335 times. Certainly a total of 713 references to the Holy Spirit in God's Word will convince us of the worthiness of our study.

III. Because today's problems cannot be solved without the Holy Spirit.

It is humanly impossible to convict people of sin so that they will turn to Christ. Jesus recognized this and told us in John 16:8 that the Holy Spirit would convict the world of sin. When God's Holy Spirit convicts a person of sin, that sin may be hidden to the eyes of others, but the Holy Spirit is sounding an alarm within that person. If the Holy Spirit were taken out of the world, there would be no sense of right and wrong, no conscience, no sorrow for evil done, and no force to hold back Satan's power. Without the Holy Spirit, you could not say to a Christian, "He who is in you is greater than he who is in the world."

We must never forget that we do not wrestle against mere human beings, flesh and blood, but rather against supernatural powers of darkness and all kinds of wicked forces in high places (Eph. 6:12). Apart from the presence of the Holy Spirit, these forces could not be restrained. There would be no hope for the world.

Conclusion

Come, Holy Spirit, heav'nly Dove,
With all thy quick'ning pow'rs;
Kindle a flame of sacred love
In these cold hearts of ours.

O raise our thoughts from things below,
From vanities and toys;
Then shall we with fresh courage go
To reach eternal joys.

—*Isaac Watts*

WEDNESDAY EVENING, MARCH 17

Title: Let Us Worship and Bow Down

Text: "O come, let us worship and bow down, let us kneel before the LORD, our Maker!" **(Ps. 95:6 RSV)**.

Scripture Reading: Psalm 95:1–7

Introduction

Have you ever received an invitation to a special musical program in a church? Have you ever received an invitation to become a part of a Bible study group? Have you ever received an invitation to attend a series of evangelistic services? In reality, all of these were an invitation to worship.

The psalmist spoke to one and all in the words of our text, extending to us an invitation to respond to the Lord with reverence and worship.

I. Let us bow down and worship the Lord because of who he is.

The psalmist spoke of the Lord being our Maker, or Creator. The Lord Jesus, before whom we are to bow, is the fulfillment of Old Testament prophecy. He is the eternal God who clothed himself in human flesh and came to dwell here on earth among us. We should worship him because of who he is.

II. Let us worship him because of what he dared to do.

A. *Our Lord dared to clothe himself in human flesh.* He was not content to remain as the eternal all-powerful God. Though invisible and intangible, he chose to become visible, tangible, and audible.

B. *Our Lord loved the unlovely and showed mercy to them.* This caused him trouble and pain, but he gave himself to the lepers, the sick, the prostitutes, the outcasts, the publicans, and the Gentiles.

C. *Our Lord took upon himself the burden of our sin.* Jesus took our guilt and shame upon himself and died to save a sinful, wayward race.

D. *Our Lord entered the realm of death on our behalf.*

III. Let us worship him because of what he accomplished on our behalf.

A. *Jesus conquered death for us.*

B. *Jesus revealed the reality of immortality.*

C. *Jesus exalted women to the position they were meant to have.*

D. *Jesus liberated the slaves of the world.*

E. *Jesus uplifts the human spirit.* He is unalterably opposed to every effort or system that degrades or dehumanizes humankind.

IV. Let us bow down and worship him because of what he wants to do.

A. *Jesus wants to give each person the gift of eternal life.* He wants to bring people into a loving relationship with him.

B. *Jesus wants to use each person in redemptive service.* He wants people to minister to and help others.

Conclusion

With joy, love, and a desire to be completely obedient, let us bow down and worship him. Worship is an activity of the soul. It is our personal response to God. Let us worship him in spirit and in truth.

SUNDAY MORNING, MARCH 21

Title: God's Plan Is Now Complete

Text: "When Jesus had received the vinegar, he said, 'It is finished'; and he bowed his head and gave up his spirit" (**John 19:30 RSV**).

Scripture Reading: John 19:25–30

Hymns: "There Is a Green Hill Far Away," Alexander
"In the Cross of Christ I Glory," Bowring
"Man of Sorrows, What a Name," Bliss

Offertory Prayer: Our Father, you have told us that to whom much has been given, much is required. We are indeed a favored people! Millions of people went to bed hungry last night. Millions more are barely able to eke out an existence. But the worst thing is that there are even more millions of people who do not know Jesus Christ as Savior. Some of them live in lands of poverty, but others live in places of affluence. We bring our gifts to you this morning. Use them to support your work at this church and in all places where they will be sent. As we have entered into the labors of others, we pray that others will enter into our labors as we give our money to tell the story of Jesus. We give for our local church field and for all people everywhere who need to hear the good news. We pray this in Jesus' name. Amen.

Introduction

At least twice in Jesus' ministry he must have cried wildly and exultantly. One occasion came at the beginning of his ministry and the other at the close. When he finished with the third temptation in the wilderness, he shouted, "Get thee behind me, Satan" (Luke 4:8), indicating that he was through listening to the tempter. Now at the close of his ministry, Jesus once more shouted. This time the cry was likewise wild and exultant: "It is finished!" Both cries followed prolonged periods of distress. The first cry followed forty days of hunger and temptation. The other followed many hours of haunting misery and excruciating suffering. Both times Jesus proclaimed his identity with something and somebody. Both times he testified in the presence of God that he could withstand all the assault that the satanic forces of evil might bring against him. No pressure was great enough to make Jesus surrender his determination to be God's suffering servant and sinless sin bearer.

Few people can finish a job completely. At best we are but stammerers when we try to speak about God and weaklings when we try to do anything in his name. But Jesus was different! He never stumbled, mumbled, or grumbled. He kept his eye on God his Father. He would not turn back or be turned back; he was determined to complete the task God brought him into the world to perform. His victorious cry, "It is finished!" reveals three things worth taking to heart.

I. The sufferings of Jesus are now finished.

Many years before Jesus' crucifixion, one of Israel's great prophets had said in anticipation of Calvary, "It was the will of the LORD to bruise him; he has put him to grief; when he makes himself an offering for sin, he shall see his offspring, he shall prolong his days; the will of the LORD shall prosper in his hand" (Isa. 53:10 RSV). The suffering of God's Son was in full accordance

95

with God's eternal purpose. Because we are human, we cannot fathom the divine mind. We only know that God chose the substitutionary atonement of his Son as the way of redeeming humankind from sin. When Jesus hung on the cross for six hours, he bore in his own body all that we deserve to suffer for our sins throughout eternity. The thought is too profound for us to comprehend! It is the Lord's doing, and it must remain wonderful in our eyes!

Jesus' sufferings did not begin on Calvary; he was persecuted at every stage in his life. The Pharisees constantly dogged his tracks, seeking every opportunity to find him guilty of violating some small part of the Mosaic law. Often the worst suffering is not physical torture but mental anguish. Jesus was hated by the religious leaders of his day. He was too orthodox for the liberal Sadducees and he was too liberated from the technical demands of the law for the overbearing Pharisees. Though this latter group resided chiefly in Jerusalem, they followed him to Galilee during his marvelous eighteen-month ministry when he was so popular. They tried to make his life miserable by constantly nit-picking everything he did to meet the human need of the underprivileged people in that area.

The greatest suffering was, however, in Gethsemane and on Calvary. So intensely did he feel the weight of the world on him as he prayed that he cried out to God, "Let this cup pass from me" (Matt. 26:39). Jesus' sufferings in Pilate's hall were both physical and mental. He was handed over to cruel executioners who beat him with thongs laced with pieces of bone or lead. This was physical suffering to the utmost! Then they placed a crown of thorns on his head and a purple robe around him. In some ways this must have hurt more than the scourging. Finally, Jesus endured indescribable suffering as he was nailed to the cross. Matthew merely said, "And they crucified him" (Matt. 27:35). But what depth is contained in that simple phrase!

Now all the suffering was over. Jesus was beyond the reach of his enemies. No longer could they taunt him or throw insults at him. He had paid the price for our sins and no one could hurt him anymore.

II. The prophecies of Jesus' life and death are finished.

Beginning in the garden of Eden and continuing until the last chapter in the last book of the Old Testament, we have what has been called the "messianic strain." God made himself known in many ways through revelation and inspiration, but the Old Testament is primarily a "drama of redemption." Every book has something to say of God's eternal purpose in the world. Some of the prophecies are direct statements clearly predicting the coming of certain events that became realities in the life, death, and resurrection of Jesus. Others are in symbols, but they are, nonetheless, God's divine word of assurance to Old Testament people that his redemptive purpose would not be defeated.

In the Sermon on the Mount, Jesus said that he did not come to abolish the Law or the Prophets, but to fulfill them (Matt. 5:17). Christians in the first century had no New Testament. They found Jesus in the Jewish Scriptures.

Philip was asked by the Ethiopian eunuch the meaning of an Old Testament prophecy (Isa. 53:7–8). The New Testament says that he "began at the same scripture, and preached unto him Jesus" (Acts 8:35).

In conversation with Nicodemus, Jesus reached back into the Old Testament for a beautiful parallel between the history of Israel and his own ministry, saying that "as Moses lifted up the serpent in the wilderness, even so must the Son of man be lifted up" (John 3:14). The symbolic teaching of the Passover, Day of Atonement, and all guilt offerings were fulfilled when Jesus died. The curtain separating the Holy Place from the Holy of Holies was torn in two when Jesus died. No longer does the high priest go behind the curtain. Jesus is our High Priest, and every believer has unlimited access to come boldly before the throne of grace to find help in time of need.

Every prophecy, every type, every ceremony, every ritual, every foreshadowing of the coming Messiah's life and death for our sin has been fulfilled. It is finished!

III. The plan of salvation is now finished.

All that was necessary for the atonement of humankind's sin had now been accomplished. Of course, the resurrection had to follow, but the price had been paid. The raising up of Jesus was the Father's work. The Son had paid the price.

History records the linking of the great railway system across the United States. One group began in the East and built the tracks westward. The other group began in California and built eastward. A great day came when the two tracks met. Governors from two states attended the gala occasion. A gold spike was nailed at the last to commemorate the event. Someone spontaneously shouted, "It is finished!" What was finished? A "through way" had been provided. People could go from the East to the West, crossing the nation on rail. But when Jesus shouted, "It is finished!" an even greater "through way" had been established. People could now go all the way from earth to heaven through the Savior, who gave his life as a ransom for sin.

Conclusion

This was perhaps the greatest shout from the cross, for Jesus had completed the work God had sent him to do. From now on the responsibility is on us. Have you received the atonement and applied it personally to your life? Jesus died for all, but not all will be saved—only those who come to him by faith. Have you come? If not, will you come today?

SUNDAY EVENING, MARCH 21

Title: What Are the Gifts of the Spirit?

Text: "Each one should use whatever gift he has received to serve others, faithfully administering God's grace in its various forms" (**1 Peter 4:10 NIV**).

Scripture Reading: 1 Peter 4:8–11 (see also Romans 12:1–8; 1 Corinthians 12–14; Ephesians 4:1–16)

Introduction

What are the gifts of the Spirit, and how can you tell which one you have? To find the answer to these questions, you need your Bible in hand, because you need to know what the Bible says about this matter and not what I say or what any other person says.

Christ has said in his Word, "Ye shall know the truth, and the truth shall make you free" (John 8:32). And to the extent that you and I are able to grasp the truth, we will move into the freedom that God wants us to enjoy. To the extent that we have to depend on human experiences that change from moment to moment, we will be locked into the bondage of the subjectivism of human experience. Thus we want to get our teeth into something solid in God's Word. Four passages in the New Testament deal specifically with the gifts of the Spirit—Romans 12:1–8; 1 Corinthians 12–14; Ephesians 4:1–16; and 1 Peter 4:10–11.

We will focus our study on these four passages, moving from one to the other as we find the answers to the questions "What are the gifts of the Spirit, and how can you tell which one you have?"

I. What are the gifts of the Spirit?

You will notice in each of these passages the superiority of the *fruit* of the Spirit over the *gifts* of the Spirit. For instance, 1 Peter 4:8 said, "Above all, love each other deeply" (NIV) (the first fruit of the Spirit listed in Galatians 5:22). Each of these passages emphasizes the necessity of having the fruit of the Spirit in order to have the proper attitude for demonstrating the gifts of the Spirit. If you ever get that turned around, you are in trouble. Then Peter gave one of the most obvious avenues for displaying the gifts of the Spirit, namely, "Offer hospitality to one another" (1 Peter 4:9 NIV).

Peter said as much in 1 Peter 4:10 about the gifts of the Spirit as Paul said in an entire chapter, so let's look at verse 10 very closely: "Each of you should use whatever gift you have received to serve others" (NIV). Everyone in the body of Christ is a "gifted" person. There is not a special class of people in the church who are the "gifted ones." This is taught again and again in these four passages.

Notice the tense of the verb—"have received." Not "will receive" or "may receive," but "have received." How many have received a gift? Everyone. Thus a gift is not something I am seeking. Why? I already have it. I don't seek something I already have. Paul did, however, say that we are to "eagerly desire" the gifts of the Spirit, "especially prophecy" (1 Cor. 12:31; 14:1, 39 NIV).

What logical conclusion can we draw from this? If everyone has received, we must have received our particular gift or gifts at the moment of our new birth. Just as we received our natural talents when we were physically born, so we received our gifts of the Spirit when we were spiritually born again.

That does not mean that we immediately began to develop our gift any more than we immediately began to develop our talent. Some people live their whole lives and never discover their talent, and some discover it late in life, such as Grandma Moses, the aged artist. Some Christians never take seriously the Holy Spirit in their lives and thus never become aware of or develop and use the gift the Holy Spirit has given them.

Peter said, "Each of you should use whatever *gift* you have received" (NIV, emphasis added). What is the obvious meaning of "gift"? A gift is not something you earn; a gift is free to the recipient. Therefore your particular gift of the Spirit is given to you free, just as salvation was. Remember, salvation is a "gift of God: Not of works, lest any man should boast" (Eph. 2:8–9). You do not receive a gift of the Spirit because of your spiritual standing or your deep prayer life. Thus you cannot boast or be prideful about it.

Peter said that we are to use our gifts to serve others, "as faithful stewards of God's grace in its various forms" (4:10 NIV). We aren't to covet someone else's gift but are to minister with the gift God has given us. He does not expect us to minister what he has not given us, so be what you are. If God has made you a "foot" in the body of Christ, be a foot; if a "hand," be a hand, and so on (1 Cor. 12).

We are to use our gifts to "serve others" (4:10 NIV). Some people say they want this gift or that gift because it means so much to them or it does so much for them. They miss the whole point. The gifts of the Spirit are not given to be used for oneself, but for ministering to others. We are merely stewards of God's gifts; we do not own them. A time will come when all stewards must give an account to God of how we used our gifts of the Spirit.

There are many gifts of the Spirit. We can learn about additional gifts in other passages. In Romans 12:6–8 Paul lists seven gifts of the Spirit.

A. *Prophecy (Rom. 12:6)*. Prophecy, or preaching, involves a message that is directed to a group of people. It is the gift to communicate God's Word effectively. It is not "foretelling," but "forthtelling."

B. *Ministry (Rom. 12:7)*. This gift is certainly not limited to deacons, but ordaining someone to the deaconship would certainly say, "We recognize that this person has this particular gift of the Spirit." Ministry is the God-given ability to show Christ's love in practical service to others.

C. *Teaching (Rom. 12:7)*. The message of Christ not only needs to be proclaimed; it also needs to be explained.

D. *Exhortation (Rom. 12:8)*. Teaching is normally done with a group; exhortation is normally done on a one-to-one basis, as a counselor would do. Exhortation should have a dominant note, and that note should be encouragement. It aims not at dangling someone over the flames of hell, but at spurring him or her on to the joy of life in Christ.

E. *Giving (Rom. 12:8)*. This is a wonderful gift that comes with many blessings. When people turn this gift loose in their lives, God increases his blessing to them so they can have more with which to practice this gift.

F. *Ruling (Rom. 12:8).* This gift is closely related to, if not the same as, "governments" mentioned in 1 Corinthians 12:28. Ruling means to occupy a leading place. "Governments" literally means those who steer a ship through the rocks and reefs to the harbor. Some people carry out the administration of the church.

G. *Showing mercy (Rom. 12:8).* It is possible to forgive a person in such a manner that the very act of forgiveness is an insult. Paul said the Holy Spirit gives the gift of showing mercy "with cheerfulness."

First Corinthians 12:8–10 mentions eight more gifts of the Spirit.

H. *Wisdom (1 Cor. 12:8). Sophia*—the highest kind of wisdom. It comes not so much from the mind as from communion with God.

I. *Knowledge (1 Cor. 12:8). Gnosis*—practical thinking. This is the knowledge that knows what to do in any given situation. It is the practical application of wisdom to human life.

J. *Faith (1 Cor. 12:9).* This refers not to the faith that saves, but to the faith that accomplishes great exploits for God. For example, Noah and the flood, David and Goliath. These people are not smarter, nor do they necessarily work harder. They have the gift of faith that enables them to attempt the near impossible!

K. *Healing (1 Cor. 12:9).* This is power to cure diseases by means of medicines, surgery, or prayer and faith. We cannot limit healing to any one method, for the method is not the important issue.

L. *Working of miracles (1 Cor. 12:10).* A supernatural power given to some to do great deeds. It was especially needed in the first century to confirm the claims of the gospel. William Barclay suggests that this gift was often used in healing a disturbed mind. It could have expressed itself in exorcism—the casting out of demons both real and imagined.

M. *Discerning of spirits (1 Cor. 12:10).* This is the gift of the protector in the church. This gift keeps people from following phonies. It is the ability to discern a false spirit from a true spirit. In Acts 5, Peter discerned the false spirit of Ananias and Sapphira.

N. *Kinds of tongues (1 Cor. 12:10). Thayer's Greek-English Lexicon of the New Testament* defines the word *glosson* as: "1) The organ of speech," and "2) The language used by a particular people in distinction from that of other nations." W. E. Vine, in *Expository Dictionary of New Testament Words,* said, "The supernatural gift of speaking in another language without its having been learned." This gift in the early part of the first century was helpful in communicating the gospel quickly to nationalities that otherwise could not have heard it.

O. *Interpretation of tongues (1 Cor. 12:10).* The ability, whether learned or supernaturally given, to translate into the language of the listeners what the speaker was saying in another language.

II. How can you tell which gift you have?

"Now there are diversities of gifts, but the same Spirit. And there are differences of administrations, but the same Lord" (1 Cor. 12:4–5).

Since there are many gifts of the Spirit ("diversities of gifts"), how can we know which gift we have so we can begin to use and develop it? First Corinthians 12:11 says the Holy Spirit "apportions to each one individually as he wills" (RSV).

A. *Four steps are suggested by Dr. Earl Radmacher.*
    1. Your preparation. You must learn the truth. "Ye shall know the truth, and the truth shall make you free" (John 8:32). You must know:
        a. The kind of God the God of gifts is. "No good thing will he withhold from them that walk uprightly" (Ps. 84:11). God wants you to discover your gift. It is not his will that it be hidden from you.
        b. What the gifts are.
    2. Your position. This is a recognition of your position in the body of Christ. "So we, being many, are one body in Christ, and every one members of one another" (Rom. 12:15). You are an important member of the body of Christ.
    3. Your practice. You must begin practicing what you believe may be your gift. For example, if you are teaching, and the first Sunday you have twelve pupils, the second Sunday eight, the third four, and the fourth two, you have one of two problems. (1) You did not prepare well, or (2) you do not have the gift of teaching, but you do have some other equally important gift.
    4. Your participation. Remember that you are a participant along with others. You are not in isolation but in relation with others. "In whom ye also are builded together" (Eph. 2:22). As we participate in practicing our gifts in the church, we should ask, "How am I coming across to others? How do they read me?" Their evaluation and response may confirm your gift or cause you to consider another gift.
B. *Three questions to ask.*
    1. Do I enjoy using my gift? Does this bring happiness and satisfaction to me? Am I comfortable doing this? God does not force square pegs into round holes. He does not expect us to use what we do not have.
    2. Do others enjoy my doing it? It may well be that I enjoy doing something that others do not enjoy me doing.
    3. Does God bless my doing it? Simply because God does not bless my doing a certain thing does not mean that God is displeased with me. It may simply mean that I do not have the gift for doing what I am trying to do. So I should not feel rejected by God. I should seek to discover what my gift really is.

Conclusion

You have a gift—a very important gift. It may be different than mine. But I need you, I respect you, and I thank God for both you and your gift.

"Each one should use whatever gift he has received to serve others, faithfully administering God's grace in its various forms" (1 Peter 4:10 NIV).

WEDNESDAY EVENING, MARCH 24

Title: Let Us Praise the Lord

Text: "Praise the LORD! O give thanks to the LORD, for he is good; for his steadfast love endures for ever!" **(Ps. 106:1 RSV)**.

Scripture Reading: Psalm 117:1–2

Introduction

The book of Psalms contains poetic praises of the God of Israel by those who had devout and grateful hearts. We are repeatedly invited to join with them in giving praise to God. It is a good thing to give praise to God, for our hearts are encouraged when we remind ourselves of God's goodness, greatness, and faithfulness. We also encourage the faith and faithfulness of other members of God's family. And finally, when we praise God, we encourage unbelievers to give serious thought to putting faith in Jesus Christ as Lord and Savior.

I. Let us praise the Lord for the perfection of his person.

The psalmist said, "O give thanks to the LORD, for he is good." Satan tries to convince us at times that God is not good, that God does not love us, and that God cannot be trusted. We need to be cautious lest we listen to his subtle suggestions. Our God never makes a mistake, for he is perfect in character. He is a moral God, a God of integrity who can be trusted. He is reliable and trustworthy. Let us praise him for being that kind of God.

II. Let us praise the Lord for his purposes.

God's purposes are always gracious. He cares for us. This is declared most beautifully in that verse that has been called "the little Bible": "For God so loved the world that he gave his only Son, that whoever believes in him should not perish but have eternal life" (John 3:16 RSV). Jesus declared, "I came that they might have life, and have it abundantly" (John 10:10 RSV).

III. Let us praise the Lord for his precious promises.

The Bible contains many of God's promises to us. Like Abraham, we should cling to God's promises. We should move forward in life as well as in death, trusting in God's ability and power to keep his promises (Rom. 4:2–21).

IV. Let us praise the Lord for his power.

Our Lord has the power to do anything that is consistent with his character. God has placed some limitations on his power in that he will not compel us to become his children. Neither will he force us to do his will against our will. His power is available to us to do all that we must do to accomplish his will and to face life with its difficulties and disappointments (Phil. 4:13).

V. Let us praise the Lord for his abiding presence.

The psalmist was greatly comforted by faith in the abiding presence of the Lord of Hosts (Ps. 46:7). Our Lord promised to be with his followers to the end of the age (Matt. 28:20).

VI. Let us praise the Lord for his future provisions.

It was only normal that the apostles were distressed because the Lord would soon depart from them. Later they were greatly comforted by his promise that he would prepare a place for them in the future (John 14:1–4).

Conclusion

How long has it been since you praised the Lord? Count your blessings one by one. Do not remain silent. Give voice to the gratitude of your heart. Praising the Lord will bring his blessings to you. Praising the Lord will strengthen the family of God. Praising the Lord will encourage others to trust Jesus Christ as Savior.

SUNDAY MORNING, MARCH 28

Title: Trust God with Yourself

Text: "Then Jesus, crying with a loud voice, said, 'Father, into thy hands I commit my spirit!' And having said this he breathed his last" **(Luke 23:46 RSV)**.

Scripture Reading: Luke 23:39–49

Hymns: "When We Walk with the Lord," Sammis
"At the Cross," Watts
"Alas, and Did My Saviour Bleed," Watts

Offertory Prayer: Our Father, we come to magnify you on this Palm Sunday, but we also come with a sense of need. We want to know you more so that we may enter more fully into a more meaningful and purposeful life. Give us not only the desire to serve you more faithfully, but the power to perform the things that we earnestly wish to do. A part of our service is the bringing of our tithes and offerings that the work of your kingdom may be advanced. Bless us as we give. We pray in Jesus' name. Amen.

Introduction

Never did people look upon a scene more ghastly, both in physical horror and in moral atrocity, than when the Sinless One was put to death by brutality and bigotry. To the world, the death of Christ spoke of utter defeat.

Realistically, however, this event combined with Jesus' resurrection brought forth the greatest victory the world has ever seen.

These last words of Jesus are perhaps interpreted by some as a parting wrench of pain. Actually, they were not only a prayer of relief at the mercy offered by death, but also a cry of joyful victory that Jesus had endured to the end and completely fulfilled his redemptive mission.

I. Most, perhaps all, people die as they live.

A. *The last words people speak on this earth are significant.* Those people who have been skeptical or critical will probably think, if not say aloud, the famous words of Hobbes, "I am going to take a leap in the dark; I commit my body to the worms and my spirit to the great Perhaps." Those who have been constant seekers after greater understanding and truth will probably say with the great scholar Goethe, "More light, more light." Those who have lived as John Wesley, dedicated to Christ and committed to his will, can say with that great minister, "The best of all, God is with us."

B. *Jesus' last words were especially significant.* When Jesus was about to commit himself to the Father, he reached back into the Old Testament and found a quotation from the book of poetry that has succored many people both before and after he lived. The psalmist spoke divinely inspired words in the midst of tumult and danger as he recognized that God was merciful and faithful, able to protect and deliver.

As Jesus hung on the cross in anguish, he called out those words as his last act of surrender to God, yet his cry had a different meaning than that of the psalmist. The psalmist longed to be preserved from death, while Jesus asked to be preserved through death unto everlasting life. Although Jesus used the words of the ancient prayer, he made them his own. He had lived the perfect life; now he was dying the perfect death. He transformed the psalmist's prayer into one of tender confidence by substituting the word "Father" for the psalmist's expression "O LORD God of truth" (Ps. 31:5). Both prayed to the same person, of course, but Jesus could call him "Father" in a way that was not possible for any other person.

II. Only in God can we find security.

A. *The illusion that security can be found in worldly pursuits drives people to do foolish things.* We sacrifice our freedom, surrender our initiative, compromise our ideals, and often waste our opportunities by wandering off after something we believe will make us immune to any contingency that threatens us. A foreign ambassador warned some time ago for us to be on guard against trying to establish a society that confuses comfort and civilization. As a nation and as individuals, we may attempt to save our lives and end up losing them by forgetting that strength of character, national and personal, is forged only in the furnace of discipline. Hard work must precede success. Suffering and pain must come before true peace can be realized. A Spanish mystic of another generation prayed, "May God deny you peace but give you glory." Where then is true security to be found? Only in God! And only in revelation of God brought to us by Jesus Christ.

B. *Jesus found his security in God.* Jesus had found his earthly security in doing God's will. Now he found his security at death in the same place. We never find true fulfillment until we surrender ourselves to the Father's purpose. Augustine wrote, "Thou hast made us for Thyself, and we are restless until we rest in Thee."

Many years ago an American minister visited a mission hospital and was asked by the doctor, "Would you like to see a major operation?" The operation lasted for seven hours. Intense heat and ether fumes were so overbearing that the minister had to go outside to refresh himself. At the conclusion he said, "Doctor, is this an average day?" The surgeon smiled. Perspiration stood on his brow while his hands trembled with fatigue. The minister asked, "How much would you be paid for an operation like this in America?" The doctor named the going rate for such an operation. The minister then asked, "How much do you get for it here?" The doctor looked at the poor woman who had been wheeled into the operating room clutching only a copper coin, begging him to save her life. He said, "Her gratitude and my Master's smile." He then added, "But that is worth more to me than all the money the world could give."

We find our security, peace, joy, and everything worthwhile by trusting in God's perfect will for our lives.

III. The first step.

One must start at the beginning! No one becomes a Christian by piling up good works on the altar. The first step is to trust the Lord with our eternal destiny by receiving Jesus Christ as Savior. The death of Christ on Calvary was God's redemptive plan consummated on earth. The weight of our sins drove nails into Jesus' hands and feet. The resurrection completed the divine drama! As Jesus commended his spirit into the hands of his Father and then expired, so we enter into the Christian life by dying to self. Paul said, "I am crucified with Christ: nevertheless I live; yet not I, but Christ liveth in me: and the life which I now live in the flesh I live by the faith of the Son of God, who loved me, and gave himself for me" (Gal. 2:20).

If we want to know the joy that the Savior knew in his victorious cry at death, we must make the complete commitment he made. We must literally wager our life on the fact that God not only loves us but has provided for our needs in the death of Christ on Calvary and will remove the guilt of our sin when we surrender ourselves to him. Nothing else is sufficient! Nothing else is necessary! Do it today!

Conclusion

How wonderful to see a person possessing the quiet confidence of a life resting in the providence of God! Pilate did not have that confidence. He had allowed Jesus to be condemned when he could have saved him. The Sanhedrin did not have that peace. They were disorganized and confused. Judas did not have that peace. He had already gone out and hanged himself. The frantic mob lacked that peace. The frightened band of disciples could not claim it. Only Jesus could, for only he had committed himself completely into the hands of his Father.

Are you willing to trust yourself to the Savior? It is the wisest thing, the safest thing, and the most needed thing you could ever do. Fanny Crosby wrote,

> Thou the spring of all my comfort,
> More than life to me,
> Whom have I on earth beside Thee?
> Whom in heaven but Thee?

Indeed, if Jesus Christ cannot be trusted with our soul's salvation and our life's joy, who can be?

SUNDAY EVENING, MARCH 28

Title: How Can I Be Filled with the Holy Spirit?

Text: "And be not drunk on wine, wherein is excess; but be filled with the Spirit" (Eph. 5:18).

Introduction

A famous oil field is known as the Yates Pool. During the Depression this field was a sheep ranch owned by a Mr. Yates. Yates was unable to make enough money from the ranch to pay the principal and interest on the mortgage and was therefore in danger of losing his ranch. With little money for clothes or food, his family had to live on government subsidy.

Day after day Yates was troubled about how he would be able to pay his bills. A seismographic crew from an oil company came into the area and told Mr. Yates that there might be oil on his land. They asked him for permission to drill a wildcat well, and he signed a lease.

At 1,115 feet a huge oil reserve was discovered. The first well came in at 80,000 barrels a day, and many other wells produced more than twice as much. Thirty years after the discovery, a government test of one of the wells showed that it could still produce 125,000 barrels of oil a day. And Mr. Yates owned it all! Since the day he purchased the land he had held the oil and mineral rights, yet he had lived on relief—a multimillionaire living in poverty! What was the problem? He did not know the oil was there. He owned it, but he did not possess it.

The moment we become children of God through faith in Christ we become heirs of God, and all of his resources are made available to us. Everything we need to live a joyous life of Christian victory is ours in the person of the Holy Spirit who lives within us. But many Christians do not understand how to draw upon the resources of the Holy Spirit. As a result, they live in spiritual poverty, not knowing or experiencing the great riches and resources that are already theirs through the Holy Spirit. Like Mr. Yates before the oil discovery, many Christians own but do not possess the riches that are already theirs.

So that we might draw upon the vast reservoir of the Holy Spirit, let us answer some questions people ask about being filled with the Holy Spirit.

I. What is "being filled with the Holy Spirit"?

A. *It is a birthright to be claimed.* "The Spirit himself testifies with our spirit that we are God's children. Now if we are children, then we are heirs—heirs of God and co-heirs with Christ" (Rom. 8:16–17 NIV). Part of your inheritance is the fullness of the Holy Spirit. Because you are a born-again Christian, it is your birthright to be filled with the Holy Spirit just as Peter was filled, as Stephen was filled, and as 120 men and women were filled in the upper room. What have you done with your birthright? Have you claimed it?

B. *It is a command to be obeyed.* "Be filled with the Spirit" (Eph. 5:18). Some people may think, *It's optional whether I claim my birthright or not; no doubt it's a good thing for some people to be filled with the Spirit, but I don't need to be.* Let us learn, however, that "Be filled with the Spirit" is a command to be obeyed. You will notice in Ephesians 5:18 a double command: a negative, "Be not drunk," and a positive, "Be filled." The positive command is as authoritative as the negative, and it was binding on just as many of those Ephesian Christians as was the negative command. And what was true for those believers is equally true for all believers today.

C. *It is a commitment to be made.* "Present your bodies a living sacrifice, holy, acceptable unto God" (Rom. 12:1). To be filled with the Spirit is to be filled with Christ. If we are filled with the Spirit, we are in Christ. We are walking in the light as he is in the light, and the blood of Jesus Christ will cleanse and keep on cleansing us from all sin. To be "filled" with Christ means to be controlled by Christ—not as a robot, but as one who is led and empowered by the Spirit.

Eight years had passed since the conversion of the people at Ephesus until Paul commanded them in Ephesians 5:18 to "be filled with the Spirit." This has been the experience of many of us. Quite unintentionally we operated for years without really giving the Holy

Spirit the control he needs to have in our lives. Our goals were good and noble, but they were just that—*our* goals. Then one day we realized there just had to be more than we had discovered.

II. Why should I be filled with the Holy Spirit?

There are three reasons why you need to be filled with the Holy Spirit.

A. *God's will is that you be filled (John 14:16–17).*
B. *I have some problems that can be solved only by the Holy Spirit.* The paraphrase of Romans 7:18–19 and 24–25 in *The Living Bible* reads as follows: "I know I am rotten through and through so far as my old sinful nature is concerned. No matter which way I turn I can't make myself do right. I want to but I can't. When I want to do good, I don't; and when I try not to do wrong, I do it anyway. . . . Oh, what a terrible predicament I'm in! Who will free me from my slavery to this deadly lower nature? Thank God! It has been done by Jesus Christ our Lord. He has set me free."

Some of the obvious problems I may have that can only be solved by the Holy Spirit include a secret spirit of pride, a love of human praise, anger or impatience, self-will, carnal fear, a jealous disposition, unbelief, formality, and deadness. These are some of the traits that generally indicate a carnal heart and thus the need to be filled with the Spirit.

C. *I want to experience the greatest joy and effectiveness possible in my Christian life.* "I am come that they might have life, and that they might have it more abundantly" (John 10:10).

It is not unusual to hear someone say, "I have never surrendered my life to Christ because I am afraid of what he will do to me." Does that sound like a loving Father? These people do not understand how much God loves them and how much freedom and joy he will give them. Christians who allow the Holy Spirit to fill them experience a new dimension of peace and effectiveness.

III. How can I be filled with the Holy Spirit?

We must not confuse being filled with the Spirit with the gift of the Spirit. If we do not see a clear-cut difference between these two, we can never have an intelligent grasp of what being filled with the Spirit means.

In AD 56 these Ephesian Christians had received the gift of the Spirit (Acts 19); and then, eight years later when writing from prison in Rome, Paul told them to be filled with the Spirit. If the gift and being filled were the same, there would have been no need for Paul to write. The gift of the Spirit comes at conversion (Acts 2:38); being filled with the Spirit comes at consecration (Rom. 6:13). They may be close together or years apart.

A. *Self-examination.* "But let a man examine himself" (1 Cor. 11:28). Above all else, we must be honest with ourselves. We must not ignore or attempt to hide from ourselves any of our sins. We must ask ourselves,

"What are those things in my life that prevent the Holy Spirit from being able to fill me?"

B. *Confession of all known sin.* "If we confess our sins, he is faithful and just to forgive us our sins, and to cleanse us from all unrighteousness" (1 John 1:9). After examining ourselves in the light of God's Word, we should confess all sin brought to mind by the Holy Spirit. Until we start calling our pride, anger, complacency, and bitterness "sin," we will never have the filling of the Holy Spirit. However, when we recognize these deficiencies as sin and confess them to God, he will "cleanse us from all unrighteousness."

C. *Submission of ourselves completely to God.* "But yield yourselves unto God, as those that are alive from the dead, and your members as instruments of righteousness unto God" (Rom. 6:13). To be filled with the Holy Spirit, we must make ourselves completely available to God to do anything the Holy Spirit wants us to do. If there is anything in our lives that we are unwilling to do, then we are resisting God, and this always limits God's Spirit.

D. *Ask to be filled.* "If ye then, being evil, know how to give good gifts unto your children: how much more shall your heavenly Father give the Holy Spirit to them that ask him?" (Luke 11:13). Any suggestion that we wait or tarry or labor is a human suggestion. Only the disciples were told to wait, and the reason was that the day of Pentecost had not yet come. Since that day, God's children have only had to ask for his filling to experience it.

E. *Believe you are filled.* "Jesus said unto him, If thou canst believe, all things are possible to him that believeth" (Mark 9:23). For many Christians, the battle is won or lost right here. Believing we are filled with the Spirit is merely taking God at his word, and that is the only absolute this world has.

IV. How can I know I have been filled with the Holy Spirit?

A. *Because of the promise of God's Word.* "Therefore I say unto you, What things soever ye desire, when ye pray, believe that ye receive them, and ye shall have them" (Mark 11:24).

B. *Because of the fruit of the Spirit.* "By their fruit you will recognize them" (Matt. 7:20 NIV). Galatians 5:22–23 lists the fruit of the Spirit: love, joy, peace, forbearance, kindness, goodness, faithfulness, gentleness, and self-control.

C. *Because you will have both the power and the desire to witness.* "You shall receive power when the Holy Spirit has come upon you; and you shall be my witnesses in Jerusalem and in all Judea and Samaria and to the end of the earth" (Acts 1:8 RSV).

D. *Because the Holy Spirit will glorify Christ through you. "He shall glorify me" (John 16:14).*

109

Conclusion

When can I be filled with the Holy Spirit? Now! Examine yourself. Confess your known sins. Submit yourself unreservedly to Christ, then simply ask to be filled and believe that you are filled.

Why not trust the Holy Spirit with your life? This is not a once-for-all experience. It is an experience we will repeat every day, but it must begin sometime. Why not let that time be now?

> Take my life, and let it be
> Consecrated, Lord, to Thee.
> Take my hands and let them move
> At the impulse of Thy love.
> At the impulse of Thy love.
>
> Take my feet, and let them be
> Swift and beautiful for Thee,
> Take my voice and let me sing
> Always, only, for my King.
> Always, only, for my King.
>
> Take my lips and let them be
> Filled with messages for Thee,
> Take my silver and my gold—
> Not a mite would I withhold.
> Not a mite would I withhold.
>
> Take my love, my God, I pour
> At Thy feet its treasure store;
> Take myself and I will be
> Ever, only, all for Thee,
> Ever, only, all for Thee.

—*Frances R. Havergal*

WEDNESDAY EVENING, MARCH 31

Title: Let Us Rejoice and Be Glad

Text: "This is the day which the LORD has made; let us rejoice and be glad in it" **(Ps. 118:24 RSV)**.

Scripture Reading: Philippians 4:4–7

Introduction

The psalmist encourages all of us to rejoice and be glad. This is not only good religion but good psychology.

I. Let us rejoice in the present.

"This is the day which the LORD has made." Someone has said that there are three days on everybody's calendar: yesterday, today, and tomorrow. The most important day on our calendar is today. Yesterday is gone into the tomb of time. To live in yesterday is to waste today and rob tomorrow. To live in tomorrow may cause a person not to come to grips with the present. We must see that tomorrow is wrapped in what we do today.

We need to recognize the importance of the present. Today is the only day of which we can be sure. We must beware lest we accept the philosophy "Let us eat, drink, and be merry, for tomorrow we may die." On the other hand, we should celebrate the present to the fullest and live responsibly, for tomorrow may never come.

II. Let us accept this day as the gift of God.

The psalmist would encourage us to see every day as a gift from God to us. Today is neither accidental nor incidental. God wants to be in the midst of this day with us. He wants to help us make it into a useful, productive day that will enable us to have pleasant memories of it when tomorrow comes.

Let us be grateful for this day, for in it we have the opportunity to worship, work, and witness. Let us rejoice in this day, for in it we have the opportunity both to give and to receive.

III. Joy is important to God.

It is interesting to note our Lord's emphasis on joy. There was joy at the announcement of his birth. Because of the joy that was set before him, he was able to endure even the shame of the cross (Heb. 12:2). In the parable of the talents, the servants who were rewarded were permitted to enter into the joy of their master (Matt. 25:21). Our Lord spoke of joy in the presence of angels when a sinner repents (Luke 15:7, 10, 32).

Conclusion

Let us rejoice and be glad in God's love for us. Let us rejoice in the privilege of being sons and daughters of God. Let us rejoice and be glad because of the privilege of serving our Lord. Let us rejoice in the assurance of an eternal home in the future. Let us rejoice and be glad today in anticipation of rewards for our faithfulness when we meet our Savior.

APRIL

■ **Sunday Mornings**

Begin a new series titled "The Living Christ" on Easter morning and continue it through the third Sunday of the month. Then, in the days leading up to Mother's Day and continuing through Father's Day, use the theme "Strengthening Christian Marriage and Family Living."

■ **Sunday Evenings**

For Sunday mornings this month, use the theme "Listening to the Voices of the World." These messages have been supplied by a dynamic missionary to Kenya. The emphasis is on sharing the good news of Christ.

■ **Wednesday Evenings**

"Great Words from the Bible" is the theme for study and meditation this month.

SUNDAY MORNING, APRIL 4

Title: Hell's Most Horrible Hypothesis

Text: "If Christ be not risen . . ." (**1 Cor. 15:14**).

Scripture Reading: 1 Corinthians 15:10–20

Hymns: "He Lives," Ackley
"Christ the Lord Is Risen Today," Wesley
"The Strife Is O'er," Pott

Offertory Prayer: Our Father, only your Son can pour healing balm into our sore and wounded hearts. Only his love has preserved in us the faith that alone comforts and sustains us in dark hours. We pray that the blessed promise of the Spirit's presence, together with the hope of resurrection and eternal life, will enable us to bear the heartaches and sorrows that we know will come along our life's journey. On this Easter Sunday morning, may the presence of the risen and living Savior enable us to say with a trusting heart, "Thy will be done." Keep us ever faithful to your Word. Accept these tithes and offerings that we bring as part of our dedication to you. Help us use these gifts wisely and make them effective in proclaiming the gospel of Jesus Christ in our church, our community, and even to the ends of the earth. We pray in Jesus' name. Amen.

Introduction

One of Paul's greatest strategies was to anticipate the argument of his opponent and then answer it. To the Romans he wrote, "Shall we continue in sin, that grace may abound? God forbid. How shall we, that are dead to sin, live any longer therein?" (Rom. 6:1–2). To the Galatians he wrote, "Is the law then against the promises of God? God forbid: for if there had been a law given which could have given life, verily righteousness should have been by the law" (Gal. 3:21). Writing to the Corinthians, Paul anticipated an argument that, had it been valid, would have destroyed the foundation of the Christian faith. Some in that sophisticated city were saying there was no such thing as a resurrection from the dead. This was, of course, one of the cardinal differences between the Pharisees and the Sadducees. The former held tenaciously to the supernatural and thus accepted the fact of a resurrection. The Sadducees, borrowing their worldly wisdom from the Greeks, had "thrown in the towel" and given up any hope for a life to come.

With his keen logical mind, Paul saw that if there was no such thing as a resurrection of the dead, then the glorious news that Christ is alive must be labeled as false and untrustworthy. What would that do to the Christian faith? The worst possible thing!

For the sake of discussion, Paul posed an assumption to the Corinthian Christians. What if the worst possible thing that can be said about Jesus is true? Let's look at it! One authority defines a hypothesis as "a tentative assumption made in order to draw out and test its logical . . . consequences." Paul presented the most horrible hypothesis that hell could ever manufacture in order to set the scene for an examination of the consequences, thus testing the validity of such a claim.

I. Our personal faith and witnessing is meaningless—if Christ is not risen.

Think for a moment of the great preachers who have lived through the centuries—Spurgeon in London, Moody in America, David Livingstone in Africa, Kagawa in Japan, Morrison in China, Carey in India, Niemoeller in Germany. All of these men were fools, duped by their own egos, wasting their lives. In more recent years, Billy Graham's crusades were and now Franklin Graham festivals are not only a waste of time and money, but a propagation of false doctrine. These terrible things are true unless the historical fact of the resurrection is true.

Every effort that we have made to win the lost to Christ has been only foolishness and vanity unless Christ arose from the dead. We have received no true forgiveness because the price for our redemption has not been paid. For, you see, the resurrection of Christ was the one event by which God placed his approval on the atonement. Our loved ones who have gone on before are not asleep in Christ but have gone out into a dark and empty nothingness. We are of all people most miserable if Christ is not risen.

II. But wait a moment.

The horrible dream is not true! The nightmare is ended! Christ is risen! The grave could not contain him. The enemies of Christ could not prevent

God's acting in power. Some who crucified him seem to have had more faith in his resurrection than some of his followers. They said, "Command therefore that the sepulchre be made sure until the third day, lest his disciples come by night, and steal him away, and say unto the people, He is risen from the dead: so the last error shall be worse than the first" (Matt. 27:64). Why did they do this? Perhaps not so much that they feared the disciples, but they were afraid Jesus was actually telling the truth and had power to perform his words!

Jesus did arise! Two scholars who were devout skeptics determined to destroy Christianity by research. One chose the conversion of Paul and the other the resurrection of Jesus. After months of honest study and investigation, each confessed he had become a Christian. The one who investigated the resurrection of Jesus said, "All the evidence vindicates the claim. No doubt about it, Jesus arose."

The purpose of this message is not to prove but to proclaim. Others have proved. Read their works, study the evidence, but then remember one thing: you cannot be saved by believing with your head. You must accept the truth with your heart, which means full commitment to the resurrected Christ.

III. Do you have the "burning heart"?

Luke recorded the conversation between Jesus and two disciples on the Emmaus road. At first they did not recognize Jesus, but later, after he had revealed himself to them and then disappeared, they said to each other, "Did not our heart burn within us, while he talked with us by the way, and while he opened to us the scriptures?" (Luke 24:32). When the resurrection is accepted by faith, a power comes into our lives that is possible no other way. It is this "burning heart" that sends missionaries across the sea and that inspires men and women to "count all things but loss" for service in God's kingdom. Christianity is founded on the resurrection of Christ. Unless he arose, we have no motive for going into all the world and preaching the gospel.

Jesus did arise! The evidence is irrefutable. His death on the cross was a public event known to everyone. Paul said to King Agrippa, "This thing was not done in a corner" (Acts 26:26). In a short time, the news of Jesus' death and resurrection spread over the known world. Do you have this burning heart? If so, you can say with the unknown person who wrote the following:

> Fear not to take your place
> With Jesus on the throne,
> And bid the powers of hell and earth
> His sovereign scepter own.
>
> Your full redemption's rights
> With holy boldness claim,
> And to its utmost fulness prove
> The power of Jesus' name.

Even those who have been skeptical of religion feel a tug when a crisis comes. Although Thomas Huxley was a skeptic for years, when his four-year-old son died, he wrote to Charles Kingsley, "As I stood beside the coffin of my little son the other day . . . the minister read . . . 'If the dead rise not . . . let us eat and drink for tomorrow we die.' . . . I cannot tell you how inexpressively this shocked me. . . . Why the very ape's no better." The burning heart is a reality! When we face the issue of life and death, the flame is fanned. If we will accept the fact of the resurrection and receive as personal Savior the one who arose, the flame can burst forth into a dynamic fire.

Conclusion

The hypothesis is not true! The satanic forces have done their best to persuade the world, but the evidence is irrefutable. Earth's blackest day, Calvary, and earth's brightest day, the resurrection, were just three days apart. Jesus went for a short time into the realm of death that he might come back forever as Lord of life.

An author who traveled in the East tells of a night in the desert. There was no sign of inhabited land, only desert sand. That night a man slipped out of the camp and returned the next morning with a fresh green blade of rice. During those three days and nights that Jesus was in the tomb, the land was desolate. Jesus slipped out into the dark black night and brought back the fresh green of life eternal. This was no accident! God acted in history! Death took hold of the manhood of Jesus and killed him. God took hold of death, and death died! Christ is the firstfruits of those who sleep. Because he has arisen, we, too, will arise with new and glorious bodies!

> Seek ye the Lord?
> Search not the cold and empty tomb;
> He is not linked with night and gloom;
> He is not bound by death and strife:
> His name is Light and Love and Life!
> He lives; Is risen; Go find ye then
> The Living Lord—in the hearts of men!
>
> —*M. Ethel Anderson*

Hell's most horrible hypothesis fails the test of experience and validity. The resurrection is true! Jesus is alive! Go tell it on the mountain!

SUNDAY EVENING, APRIL 4

Title: Quiet Voices

Text: "There are, it may be, so many kinds of voices in the world, and none of them is without signification" (**1 Cor. 14:10**).

Scripture Reading: Romans 10:12–17

Introduction

In every age there have been significant voices in the world. In our age these voices can be heard as we read the newspaper, listen to the radio, watch television, or even when we think of the world's condition. The Bible also has much to say about voices. Sometimes the sounds we hear when we listen to the voices of the Bible or to the voices around us may be pleasant. These voices may be like music or like waves of the sea or like falling rain. But some of these voices may be unpleasant sounds—arguing, crying, or screams of anguish.

When the Bible speaks of voices, it may be speaking of the voice of John—one crying in the wilderness, or of Jesus crying with a loud voice, or of a prophet's voice, or of Peter's or Paul's voice. Our text tells us that there are many kinds of voices in the world.

I. The voice of human need.

A. *Much of human need is physical.* Millions of people are desperate for physical help—the hungry, the naked, the sick, the abused, the oppressed, the imprisoned. For example, something as senseless as illiteracy can make people silent victims. Around the world as many as a quarter of all people cannot read or write. Many of the illiterate in third-world nations are virtually slaves. They are in debt most of their lives and find it difficult to pull out of the mire. Such people are forever driven—hungry, diseased, afraid, unhappy. But some are grimly determined to rise out of their condition. The voice of their own human need cries out to us.

B. *If we listen we can also hear the voice of spiritual need.* These are the people who are searching for help, the ones who hunger for fellowship. They are looking for an answer to the cause of life and suffering and even death. Some are guilt-laden. They are disrupted by the loss of self-respect, always on the defensive, disturbed and confused, seemingly unable to rebuild their lives. Some time ago a man took his own life. Beside him was this note: "When man has lost God, then there isn't much to live for." We hear the voice of spiritual need.

Within other people there are tiny civil wars going on. These people seem possessed of hostility, pent up and ready to explode. They harbor feelings of anger, bitterness, or selfishness, with little or no time for God.

With millions of physically and spiritually needy people all around us, we must as Christians hear their voices. This is the voice of human need. Let us heed it.

II. The voice of a sinful world.

A voice is calling us to bring a message of release, freedom, and redemption from sin. The Lord's Prayer shows the necessity of our sins being forgiven (Luke 11:4). This implies, just as Jesus said, that the world is a servant of sin (John 8:34). All are under sin (Rom. 3:9). Paul spoke of the law of sin and death (Rom. 8:2) but was quick to admit that sin dwelt in him and that unforgiven sin would pay its wages—death.

And so the world today seems to shout again and again regarding our Savior, "Crucify him! Crucify him!" The sinful world goes on searching in sinful pleasure, in money, in materialism, but fear and frustration remain. The inner civil wars bring despair. As the world continues in its sinful way, there is a loss of fellowship with God. There is darkness and death. A former Buddhist priest who had been saved testified, "I have come out of darkness and sin." But one who had not been saved by Christ, an old Indian, said as he lay dying, "It is so dark. Won't someone come and tell me how to die?" These then are some of the voices of a sinful world. Let us heed God's voice as we consider world mission responsibilities.

III. The voice of the Christian faith.

A. *Into the confusion of sinful living and human need comes the voice of the Christian faith.* This is the voice of our Savior himself, as it were, the voice of God. And above the jungle of confusion, we hear the call of faith.

   1. Only our Christian faith can give an adequate picture of humanity. It is our faith that tells us of sin and this proneness to hate and war. But it is from that picture that something worthwhile can arise if we have God's help.

   2. Only our Christian faith can give us an adequate picture of God. He is not remote; rather, he is the one who took action about the human rebellion. He came in Christ.

   3. Only our Christian faith brings humankind and God together.

B. *Notice how the voice of the Christian faith was heard by a man named Africa.* A mother named her child Africa. Later in life Africa was sick with tuberculosis. He was illiterate at that time and lost. But Africa found a mission hospital and stayed there for six months and was cured. As he was leaving, Africa said in Swahili, *"Afante sana* ['Thanks very much']. As I leave, I can say, here I have heard the voice of Christ, and I am saved. Here because a doctor helped me—a Christian doctor—I am well. And because a Christian friend cared and helped me, I can read. So I leave this hospital a man amazingly happy because I have seen the faith of Christ and heard his voice. I know the difference the Christian faith makes."

Conclusion

The voices in the world speak to us in their own quiet way. And so perhaps we have been able to hear these quiet voices—the voice of human need, the voice of a sinful world, and the voice of the Christian faith. But could it be that we have not really heard? Or perhaps in our hearing we have not really cared. We must seek to be responsive. We must be willing to see the faces of the people of the world and hear their voices. Then we must respond with love and caring.

The Christian response for some who have heard these voices will be this: "Yes, I will care. I will pray, give, feel, learn, share." In other cases the Christian response will be, "Yes, I'll go. I'll go to a friend. I'll share my Christian faith. It is not possible for me to reach around the world, but I'll find one lonely child or one needy person or one lost person. And I'll wipe the tears of that one or share the loving Christ with that one who is near."

Perhaps there are some who can now say, "Here am I, Lord. Send me wherever you wish, anywhere in the world. I will follow you wherever you lead." Perhaps you can say, "I see, Lord, and I care, and I am available to share. I surrender. I give my life to you to serve wherever you need me." Perhaps you are able to say, "I now choose your will instead of mine in everything I do for the rest of my life." Have you made a decision today regarding these matters? Share it. Share it with our church. As we close our service now, share your inner decision with our church and receive prayerful, loving, caring support.

WEDNESDAY EVENING, APRIL 7

Title: Apostasy

Text: "And then many will fall away, and betray one another, and hate one another. And many false prophets will arise and lead many astray" **(Matt. 24:10–11 RSV).**

Scripture Reading: 2 Thessalonians 2:2–3

Introduction

The Greek word for "apostasy" means a falling away, a withdrawal. The word is used twice in the New Testament, and it means the abandonment of the faith.

Forsaking the Lord was the recurring sin of the chosen people, especially in their contracts with idolatrous nations. The tendency to apostasy appeared in their earliest history and remained with them to the end of their national existence.

When men or women repudiate their marriage vows, when political leaders give up their party, when soldiers desert the army, when preachers forsake their calling, we make much of it and stand ready to criticize and condemn. But what about the religious apostates?

Apostasy, falling away, withdrawal, is widespread in the church today. Jesus said about the last days, "Because wickedness is multiplied, most men's love will grow cold" (Matt. 24:12 RSV). Paul said, "Let no one deceive you in any way; for that day will not come, unless the rebellion comes first" (2 Thess. 2:3 RSV).

I. What are some causes of apostasy?

A. *Lack of a genuine conversion causes apostasy.* Many people drop out of church or fall away from the faith because they lack a genuine Christian experience of grace. These people may have joined the church because others were joining or for social or business reasons.

B. *Lack of biblical instruction causes apostasy.* It is entirely possible that those professing faith in Christ did not have any instruction concerning the privileges and responsibilities of believers. Without proper instruction these people may drift away from and become indifferent toward the church.

C. *Persecution causes apostasy (Matt. 24:9–10).*

D. *False teachers cause apostasy (Matt. 24:11).*

E. *Worldliness causes apostasy (2 Tim. 4:10).*

F. *Forsaking spiritual living causes apostasy (Heb. 10:25–31).*

G. *Personality conflicts cause apostasy.* Often people are so constituted that they cannot work and get along with others; they are overly sensitive, have their feelings hurt too easily, and soon withdraw from all participation. They decide to quit.

II. What are some losses caused by apostasy?

A. *The loss of personal faith.*

B. *The loss of assurance.*

C. *The loss of fellowship with God's people.*

D. *The loss of joy.* Those who fall away from Christ become empty and useless. Life for them has no real meaning. They are robbed of a useful life of service for the Savior.

III. What are some cures for apostasy?

A. *Complete dedication to Jesus Christ (Rom. 12:1–2; Heb. 12:1–2).*

B. *Bible reading (Ps. 119:30; Matt. 22:29; Rom. 15:4; 2 Tim. 3:16–17).*

C. *Prayer (1 Chron. 16:11; Ps. 55:17; Dan. 6:10; Luke 18:1).*

D. *Fellowship with God's people (Prov. 13:20; Matt. 18:20; 2 Cor. 6:14).*

E. *Witnessing for Christ (Ps. 107:2; Matt. 4:19; Acts 1:8; 5:20; 18:9–10).*

F. *Obedience (Matt. 12:50; John 7:17; Rom. 14:12–13; 1 John 2:6).*

Conclusion

The Bible speaks of many who became apostates. Ahab, a king of Israel, was influenced by Jezebel to desert the true religion of Jehovah and turn to idolatry. King Saul became covetous and jealous, and this turned his heart away from the Lord. Demas deserted the cause and left Paul because he loved the world more than the cause of Christ. John the apostle wrote, "They went out from us, but they were not of us; for if they had been of us, they would no doubt have continued with us" (1 John 2:19).

SUNDAY MORNING, APRIL 11

Title: How Much Do You Love Jesus?

Text: "Simon, son of John, do you love me more than these?" **(John 21:15 RSV)**.

Scripture Reading: John 21:1–17

Hymns: "More Love to Thee, O Christ," Prentiss
"My Jesus, I Love Thee," Featherstone
"I Love Thee," Anonymous

Offertory Prayer: Our Father, we pray that your indwelling Holy Spirit will purge sin from us. Help us never to give first-class loyalty to second-class things. Enable us to see as you see, to judge as you judge, and to choose as you choose. May we have high on our list of priorities the needs of a lost world, not only here at home, but to the ends of the earth. Use the money that we bring this morning to spread the gospel to all people no matter who they are or where they are. We pray this in Jesus' name. Amen.

Introduction

The Sea of Galilee is one of the most beautiful places in the world. Even today you can board a ship at Tiberias, take the short trip to Capernaum, and feel that you are living in biblical times. The angel had promised on the resurrection morning that Jesus would meet his disciples in Galilee. That promise had been fulfilled, at least for seven of the disciples, who had been fishing all night without success until Jesus came.

Breakfast was over! Jesus had provided everything, as he always does when we have a need. He had told his disciples where to cast their nets for fish, had prepared a fire of coals on which to cook the fish, and, from some source, had secured bread.

Jesus focused the "after breakfast" conversation on one thing. In one sense, he was speaking to all the group even though he directed his words to Simon Peter. Scholars have had a problem with the grammatical construction of Jesus' question to Peter. Exactly what did Jesus mean by the expression, "Do you love me more than these?" Three suggestions have been made.

I. "Do you love me more than your fellow disciples do?"

A short time before Jesus was arrested in the garden of Gethsemane, Simon Peter had boasted that his loyalty was greater than that of his peers. As they went out to the Mount of Olives after observing the first memorial supper, Jesus said to the group, "All ye shall be offended because of me this night: for it is written, I will smite the shepherd, and the sheep of the flock shall be scattered abroad" (Matt. 26:31).

Peter answered first, as he usually did, saying, "Though all men shall be offended because of thee, yet will I never be offended" (26:33). Perhaps

Peter did not mean to boast but was rather seeking to assure the Savior of his loyalty. But that's not the way it came across! Without realizing what he was saying, Peter was letting the others know that even though their faith may be weak, he would never fail to trust his Master completely and serve him without compromise or disloyalty.

This question comes to us in our day. How strong is your love when compared or contrasted with the love of other Christians? Of course, let it be said immediately that we are not in competition with our fellow Christians as to who is the best servant of Jesus. Such an attitude is entirely unchristian if it causes us to develop a critical spirit toward others and a comparison of faults and virtues. This can make us almost pharisaical in our approach to Christian consecration. Yet the question is worth asking! Are you only a nominal Christian? Or are you known among your friends as one whose loyalty to Jesus is far above the minimal standard?

Almost every church has at least two groups of people. First, there are those who merely belong. Perhaps they are saved, but they are not showing by their fruits any evidence of a deep love for Jesus. They more or less hang on for the ride but cannot be depended on to witness or serve in any effective way. On the other hand, there is the inner circle, the nucleus, that bears the load. Which group are you in?

II. "Do you love me more than you love other people?"

There were six others with Jesus and Peter. What about Simon's love for Jesus as compared with his love for his fellow friends?

Peter must have been a man of influence, for he was the one Jesus chose to be the leader of the Twelve. That influence was demonstrated when one day he said to his friends, "I go a-fishing." They replied, "We also go with thee" (John 21:3). No doubt, Peter enjoyed his leadership of the group. All of them may have become disillusioned. They probably had not seen Jesus since his second appearance in the upper room when he had revealed himself to Thomas in such an expressive way. Jesus had accepted the challenge of showing the scars left by the nails and allowing Thomas to thrust his hand into the side that had been wounded. Perhaps the disciples had asked themselves, "Was it all real, or was it some sort of dream we had?"

Peter's decision to go fishing was more than getting away for a few hours; he was ready to return to his old job. Now Jesus came and showed Peter once again his divine person and his need for Peter to be a part of his redemptive plan. But Jesus said that Peter needed to love him more than he loved his friends. Even if Peter's friends deserted him, he must determine to follow Jesus.

Some questions come to us. What do you love the most? The applause of the crowd or the approval of the Savior? Will peer pressure cause you to compromise your faith? Is there a price tag on your dedication? One great Christian hymn writer told how, as a young man, he faced the decision of drinking an alcoholic beverage at a party. He watched others, whom he thought to be strong Christians, drink freely. He realized he must make a decision when the offer came to him. He chose one young lady nearby as his model and said to himself, "Whatever she does, I will do." She smiled sweetly and turned her glass upside down when the host came to her. After that, it was easy for him to refuse to drink. He later married that fine girl, and they served the Lord faithfully for many years. But suppose she had yielded; would this have been an excuse for him? We must love Jesus more than we love anyone else. And we must never allow another person to come between us and our Savior.

III. "Do you love me more than these 'things' that are near you?"

The most likely interpretation of our text is that Jesus pointed to the fishing nets and other equipment used in the trade as he asked Peter, "Do you love me more than these?" The real test of a Christian is when he or she is confronted with the matter of personal priorities. The problem of "things" and making a living is always with us!

Nowhere does the Bible condemn anyone for striving to earn the necessities of life for oneself and one's family. Only when this labor gets out of hand and becomes top priority does it become wrong. Paul said, "If any one does not provide for his relatives, and especially for his own family, he has disowned the faith and is worse than an unbeliever" (1 Tim. 5:8). The Bible warns us, however, about majoring on the material things of life.

One of our greatest spiritual needs today is, in the words of a modern writer, "to defy the tyranny of the tangible." What are the "real things" in life? Are they those that can be seen and handled? No! These things can fade away in a moment. But you cannot tear away the spiritual truths or concepts behind them. You can burn a book, but you can't burn an idea. You can destroy a bridge, but you can't destroy the concept of a bridge. What is the true cause of an automobile? Is it the assembly with all its automated machines? No, you must look deeper into the personal purposes of the manufacturers and the buying public. How we need to be liberated from the enslaving power of things!

What do you love the most? Things or spiritual principles? Answer that question realistically and you will give a correct evaluation of yourself as a Christian. Years ago I heard an outstanding preacher make a statement I have never forgotten. He said, in contrasting Abraham and Lot, that Abraham was the kind of man who, if his business interfered with his religion, gave up his business, while Lot was the kind of man who, if his religion interfered with his business, gave up his religion. Do you love Jesus more than the "things" that are constantly around you in daily living?

Conclusion

The three questions are self-explanatory. No application or summary is needed. Rather, we need to look at ourselves realistically and face honestly the question of our love for Jesus. After all has been said and done, the true motivation for service is love. If we love, we serve. If we do not love, we do not serve. If we are not serving, it is because we do not love Jesus enough. The answer for more dedication on the part of Christians is for each of us to have a greater devotion to the living Savior.

Jesus said, "No man, having put his hand to the plough, and looking back, is fit for the kingdom of God" (Luke 9:62). It requires no strength of character to quit, to give up your faith, to renounce your allegiance to Christ and his church. Anybody can quit. Are you an apostate? Have you given up living for Christ?

SUNDAY EVENING, APRIL 11

Title: Quiet Miracles

Text: "Now when he was in Jerusalem at the passover, in the feast day, many believed in his name, when they saw the miracles which he did" **(John 2:23)**.

Scripture Reading: Matthew 9:1–8

Introduction

Quiet miracles happen every day. Nature itself proclaims a miracle each season as mighty changes take place—from bare branches to buds, from flowers to fruits. A transformation takes place that changes the world from winter to spring. Likewise, from a smile, a loving word, and a touch, a distressed heart can go from cold despair to hope. These quiet miracles illustrate God's power. And we hear of God's quiet miracles in reports from mission fields around the world.

In today's Scripture reading from Matthew 9, we see Jesus performing the quiet miracle of forgiveness and linking it to the quiet miracle of physical healing as the paralyzed man is given strength.

I. Quiet miracles glorify God (John 11:1–4, 40–45).

A. *In this miracle of raising Lazarus, something tremendous happened.* Jesus saw Lazarus's death as an opportunity for the glory of God to be seen (v. 4). In that quiet moment when Lazarus came forth from the grave, many believed and gave God the glory (v. 45).

B. *Likewise, something tremendous is happening in Africa today.* In various parts of Africa, from Nigeria to Kenya, from Tanzania to South Africa, we hear stories of God at work. For several years we learned how to spread the Christian gospel among the Maasai people of East Africa. God showed his mighty power in a quiet but miraculous way. For more than a century the Maasai people had for the most part resisted the gospel. But in recent years great opportunities were opened to Christian missionaries. An example of this is in a small village called

Ilmamen. A Maasai elder told a missionary, "We sat under the trees to watch you and listen to your message. Later we came to look in at the church window. Now today you see us inside, believing, accepting, receiving the Christ with the message you bring." This is a quiet miracle among the Maasai people.

Another example involves a man named Wanbua who came to Christ as a young adult after watching Christian films on the life of Christ. Slowly, in the quietness of viewing those films, his life was changed. Wanbua went on to graduate from the University of Nairobi and today is an outstanding Christian. In fact, he began a Christian church in his own home that has outgrown his home and become a fully functioning Christian congregation.

II. Quiet miracles illustrate God's power.

"Then all the multitude kept silence, and gave audience to Barnabas and Paul, declaring what miracles and wonders God had wrought among the Gentiles by them" (Acts 15:12).

A. *The Holy Spirit had brought Paul and Barnabas to make their report.* They told the fascinating story of their labors among the Gentiles. They reiterated the miracles, signs, and wonders that God had wrought. It was as if they were saying, "Let us give you examples of how we have seen the power of God change wicked people into holy people solely by the matchless grace bestowed in Jesus Christ." And so they gave example after example just as returning missionaries do when they come back from their fields of labor. In their excitement, missionaries tell of the marvelous miracles of new birth, of how the grace of God has changed wicked men and women into godly people.

B. *We read frequently in Acts of quiet miracles illustrating God's power.* The records of Paul's work during those years clearly illustrate his absolute dependence on the quiet, miraculous power of God and God's plan. God's plan for Paul included three things:
   1. To evangelize Asia, the richest providence in the Roman Empire.
   2. To instruct the churches and encourage them to grow in Christian maturity.
   3. To strategize for further missionary advances.
      In each step of these plans, Paul depended completely on God's quiet, miraculous power.

C. *God's power was seen in recent times when missionaries and national Christians were seeking land in eastern Africa.* They needed land where they could build a training center for African pastors and lay leaders. They sought for many months until finally an African chief, who was also a Christian pastor, was able to help them find a three-acre plot of land where a Bible training center has now been built. A most interesting feature of this search for land was when a Muslim, one who normally would not desire Christian influence, stepped forth to say, "I will make my land available to the Christians." Yes, this was truly a quiet miracle illustrating God's power.

III. Quiet miracles produce faith.

"And many other signs truly did Jesus in the presence of his disciples, which are not written in this book: But these are written, that ye might believe that Jesus is the Christ, the Son of God; and that believing ye might have life through his name" (John 20:30–31).

A. *Many of these unrecorded miracles and signs of Christ must have been quiet miracles.* John knew that one purpose of Christ's miracles was to produce faith (v. 31).

B. *The Holy Spirit is bringing young people across the world to the Christian faith.* As an example of this, two young Indian women came to know of Christ and slowly, quietly accepted his grace in their lives. Today one of these women, a former Hindu, teaches the Bible to children in London. Because of God's great work in her life, she shares the Christian message with many, many children and adult friends alike. The other young Christian has concluded her training in the United States and is serving as a missionary to her own people in India. These women are modern examples of quiet miracles.

Conclusion

"A Miracle Will Happen Here," a song by Richard Baker (Dallas: Christian Doe Music Publications, 1972), tells us that God is still in the business of doing quiet miracles.

WEDNESDAY EVENING, APRIL 14

Title: Hypocrisy

Text: "Woe unto you, scribes and Pharisees, hypocrites! for ye make clean the outside of the cup and of the platter, but within they are full of extortion and excess. Thou blind Pharisee, cleanse first that which is within the cup and platter, that the outside of them may be clean also" **(Matt. 23:25–26).**

Scripture Reading: Matthew 23:13–33

Introduction

The word *hypocrisy* is repulsive to honest, sincere Christians. Nothing about hypocrites appeals to us. The word *hypocrite* means playing a part as an actor on stage. Hypocrites are those who act out a part, who feign to be what they are not. Some hypocrites play-act when it comes to living a Christian life. They have a form of godliness but deny the power thereof (2 Tim. 3:5). They wear masks to hide their true identity, and they appear better than they actually are. They assume an appearance of piety and virtue they do not possess.

Jesus called hypocrites "whited-washed tombs, which look beautiful on the outside but on the inside are full of the bones of the dead and everything unclean" (Matt. 23:27 NIV). According to Jesus, hypocrites appear righteous to others but are merely play-acting and are full of deceit. Hypocrites, according to Jesus, are pretenders, wolves dressed in sheep's clothing. Jesus gravely condemned hypocrisy, saying, "Woe unto you, scribes and Pharisees, hypocrites!"

How does one become a hypocrite?

I. Giving to be seen by others makes one a hypocrite (Matt. 6:1–4).

In his Sermon on the Mount, Jesus condemned pious hypocrites. Giving to be seen by others is rigorously denounced. In spite of this warning of condemnation, some people today would blow a horn and sound a trumpet, calling attention to their generous giving. Jesus warned his disciples against such a practice. This kind of giving has no reward from the Father in heaven.

What about modern-day churches that publish their giving records? Are they bordering on hypocrisy? Giving has become competitive among churches.

Are you giving to be seen by others? Or do you give because you love the Lord and want to be a good steward of what he has given you?

II. Praying to be seen by others makes one a hypocrite (Matt. 6:5–15).

Certain individuals in the days of Jesus made it a practice to pray in the synagogue and on the streets to be seen and heard by others. Jesus called them hypocrites, for their chief purpose was to be seen by others. All their piety was for show. They wanted others to refer to them as religious and spiritual. Since public applause was their motive, that was the only reward they received. The Father is not moved by petitions like these. Jesus told us to go apart and pray to the Father in private, and he will reward us openly.

III. Fasting to be seen by others makes one a hypocrite (Matt. 6:6–18).

Jesus condemned fasting as practiced by some. He referred to those who disfigured their faces, put on some strange garb of mourning, and paraded before the public, striving to make an impression. Jesus said they were wearing masks, playing a part, flaunting a false piety. Their inward character was concealed behind a camouflage of artificial holiness. Such fasting is insincere, and the Father does not approve of it.

IV. Hunting for a mote makes one a hypocrite (Matt. 7:1–4).

Jesus identified and condemned those who hunt for specks as hypocrites. Who were the speck hunters in his day, and who are the speck hunters in our day? How can we identify these speck hunters, the self-appointed faultfinders in our midst? Jesus identified them as spiritual surgeons, asking to operate on those who had a little speck in their eyes. These spiritual surgeons desperately needed to have their planks removed before they sought to remove the specks in other people's eyes.

Such critics, spiritual surgeons with planks in their eyes, are those who are so imperfect that they find a twisted comfort in criticizing others. Their vision is so blurred, their outlook so distorted, their minds so perverted, their motives so insincere, that when they look at others, they see themselves. They practice without license.

Are you a speck hunter? Are you a criticizer? If so, go to the Great Physician for a major operation on your heart. Go to the school of Christian graces. Take courses in empathy, sympathy, and brotherly love. When you have done this, you might be able to help your weaker brother or sister stand up for the Lord!

Conclusion

Are you playing church? Are you playing a part? Are you wearing a mask? If so, you are a hypocrite. Only Jesus can help you. Hypocrisy is a terrible thing. Let us not become hypocrites, play-actors, mask-wearers. Let us be like Jesus, who is "the same yesterday, and to day, and for ever" (Heb. 13:8).

SUNDAY MORNING, APRIL 18

Title: Until Jesus Comes, Be Witnesses

Text: "But ye shall receive power, after that the Holy Ghost is come upon you: and ye shall be witnesses unto me both in Jerusalem, and in all Judaea, and in Samaria, and unto the uttermost part of the earth" (**Acts 1:8**).

Scripture Reading: Acts 1:6–12

Hymns: "I Know That My Redeemer Liveth," Pounds
"We'll Work Till Jesus Comes," Mills
"What If It Were Today?" Morris

Offertory Prayer: Our Father, you have invited us to come boldly to your throne of grace. We thank you for this glorious privilege. We come now with hearts of gratitude to offer our gifts to you. Use them to extend your kingdom in the hearts of people everywhere. Grant that we may be faithful in every area of life, so that through our lives as well as our gifts, people will come to know Jesus. We pray in his name. Amen.

Introduction

Jesus' earthly ministry was now complete! He was born of a virgin, lived a blameless life, died a vicarious death, and arose from the grave with a glorified body. He had been on earth for forty days since his resurrection "speaking of the things pertaining to the kingdom of God" (Acts 1:3). He was now ready to return to heaven. The Mount of Olives, just outside the eastern wall of Jerusalem, served as an ideal location from which to view God's City of Peace. Jesus chose it as the place from which to give his final promise to come again and for his ascension into heaven.

The disciples were curious about the future. When asked about a coming kingdom, Jesus pushed that into the background to give an urgent command for his followers, in that day and every day, to major on telling the world about the Savior. He used the word *witness*, which is from another noun meaning "martyr." In the days of Jesus, and those that followed soon after, to be a Christian witness could mean death. In certain parts of the world, it is still dangerous to proclaim the message of Christ. In fact, to be a genuine witness is not easy in any civilization. Certain requirements are necessary. Let us look at three of them.

I. A witness must know something.

Go to a courtroom and look at a witness on the stand. What is the first requirement? A witness must be certain of the facts, else there is no need for him to appear in court. If the witness says, when asked a question, "I think—" immediately the opposing attorney will arise and say, "I object, Your Honor! We are not interested in what this witness thinks. We're only interested in what he knows." The judge will then sustain the objection.

What is the first qualification for a witness of Jesus Christ? He or she must know something! Paul certainly did. He said, "I know whom I have believed" (2 Tim. 1:12) A great Christian of another generation was asked on his eighty-sixth birthday how he felt toward the next life now that he had reached such an advanced age. He replied, "I have naturally been thinking much of that during recent years. I have stood in the shadow of bereavement many times and sought to comfort sorrowing hearts. Now in my declining days, I can say, I am not half so sure what the future life is as I was forty years ago. But I'm twice as sure that it is." How true! As we grow older, the details of heaven—that is, what type of place it will be—are not nearly as important as the certainty we have that "[our] Father's house has many rooms" (John 14:2 NIV). We can have a steadfast hope of a home in heaven if we know Jesus Christ as our personal Savior.

What about your knowledge of the Savior? A good witness must know something!

II. A witness must say something.

Every once in a while we read of a witness coming along years after a crime who has a testimony that frees a prisoner from jail. If this person had been a witness at the trial, the prisoner never would have been convicted. This person knew facts but didn't tell them! As a result, the prisoner was convicted unjustly.

To know about Jesus and fail to tell others is criminal! What if somebody knew the remedy for cancer or AIDS and kept quiet? No logical argument nor eloquent persuasive oratory can turn the world upside down; only the simple testimony that Jesus is Savior and Lord can do that. Many stories have been told of tragedies in people's lives because of undelivered messages. The greatest tragedy, however, is that many people have never been saved simply because a Christian failed to speak the proper words at the proper time.

Our failure to ask someone if he or she would like to become a Christian may be the only reason that person does not become saved. John D. Rockefeller Sr. played golf with a dear friend of his in the insurance business. One day the friend heard that Rockefeller had taken out a life insurance policy for one million dollars. When he saw the wealthy man, he asked, "Why didn't you let me write the insurance policy for you?" Rockefeller replied, "Why didn't you ask me to let you?" Many people never become Christians simply because good people who know Jesus as Savior and could testify concerning him simply fail to tell a lost friend about Jesus.

III. A good witness must be something.

A famous skeptic who was called the spiritual father of Nazism nearly became a Christian at one time. While he was trying to make the decision, he decided to live among Christian people to see what Christians were like. He is reported to have said, "These Christians will have to look a lot more redeemed before I believe in it." Gandhi attended a Christian school and was disillusioned. He is believed to have said, "I would have been a Christian if it had not been for Christians." Of course we cannot always accept at full face value such statements from non-Christians as the true reason for their failure to receive Christ. But there is enough truth in such an indictment to make us examine our way of life.

In the courtroom a witness may know something and say something, but if the opposing attorney has evidence that the witness is not a person of integrity, the attorney can present the facts to the court and make an impassioned plea to throw out the testimony. Likewise, all of our verbose vocalizings will be like "sounding brass or a tinkling cymbal" unless our lives are consistent with our testimony.

Conclusion

The first call is for us to become Christians! Until we have been born again, we begin at no beginning and work toward no end. If you are not a Christian, become one today!

New birth, however, is but the first step of the Christian life. In the ultimate sense, our Christian experience includes the totality of our relationship and fellowship with Jesus from the moment we receive him as Savior until the day we receive our resurrected body at his second coming. If you are a Christian, be a witness. Seek to be wise as you testify, but do not fail to let others know, both through lip and life, that Jesus is your all in all. Many things make us grow, but the fruit of a Christian in the most real sense is another Christian!

SUNDAY EVENING, APRIL 18

Title: Quiet Growth

Text: "The number of the disciples multiplied in Jerusalem greatly" (**Acts 6:7**).

Scripture Reading: Matthew 13:31–32; Revelation 7:9–12

Introduction

"I am preaching to a dying church," said a seminary student to his professor. "What should I do?" The professor began his answer with questions. "Is it God's will for this church to die?" "Do you believe that God can enable your church to grow?"

We are living in an age when some churches are weakening and dying. Yet God wills church growth, and he can make growth possible. From Latin America, Africa, and elsewhere in the world, reports are coming in of dramatic conversions to Christ. The church is rapidly growing in numbers and in spiritual strength.

This message invites you to share in the thrill of seeing God adding to the church daily those who are being saved (Acts 2:47). As God gave quiet growth to the first-century churches, and as he continues to bless his church with growth all over the world, so he desires to give growth in our church also. The Lord of the harvest invites you and me to actively participate with him in this quiet growth.

I. Quiet growth—God gave it in the first century.

A. *Jesus spoke of the kingdom of heaven as a tiny seed slowly, quietly, miraculously growing (Matt. 13:31–32).* Luke tells us that "the number of the disciples multiplied in Jerusalem greatly" (Acts 6:7). "The word of God grew and multiplied" (Acts 12:24). And one day, standing before the throne, we will see a great multitude that no one can number (Rev. 7:9).

B. *Jesus used harvest language in his teaching.* He said, "See how the fields are already white for harvest" (John 4:35 RSV). This harvest will produce a multinational Christian fellowship. The people of God may be Samaritan, Greek, Roman, Jew, or Gentile, but they will be sealed in one body by the gift of the same Spirit (Acts 11:15–17). So Luke's recording of about three thousand souls converted at Pentecost (Acts 2:41) points to the quiet growth and grand harvest. Listen to the continuing record of the quiet growth that God gave in the first-century churches: "More than ever believers were added to the Lord, multitudes both of men and women" (Acts 5:14 RSV). In Samaria "the multitudes with one accord gave heed" (Acts 8:6 RSV). "All the residents of Lydda and Sharon . . . turned to the Lord" (Acts 9:35 RSV). In Antioch "a large company was added to the Lord" (Acts 11:24 RSV). So there was quiet growth given by God in the first century.

II. Quiet growth—God continues it today.

A. *The same Savior and the same Holy Spirit make the church grow today.* God did not die; nor does he sleep. His power is making things happen all around the world today. One missionary from Kenya talks about quiet growth. "We have grown from six to sixty churches in seven years. We believe that the soundest way to bring people to Christ and toward spiritual maturity is to start many, many small churches as rapidly as possible. We have found that there are five necessary steps in starting a church.

"First: prayerful probe of needy areas and the tracing of the distribution of people. Combining New Testament distribution with visitation.

"Second: the teaching of church extension principles to pastors and lay leaders. We stress the Holy Spirit bringing the harvest.

"Third: the setting of reachable but measurable goals and subgoals. For example, every believer seeking to win one person to Christ every month, and every church starting a new church every year.

"Fourth: providing limited but adequate funds. We help each church to some small degree with a simple building.

"Fifth: we implant the conviction that small is beautiful. Christ shook the world with eleven faithful men."

B. *Among one tribe on the coast of Africa more than four thousand converts were won to Christ and over one hundred new churches started in less than two years.* Five teams, each composed of one elder and one seminary student, began visiting the villages. When the team entered the village, they would find a family willing to let them teach. They would then teach adults the fundamentals of the faith for five days. At the end of the week, an invitation would be given to accept Christ. Those responding were baptized and formed into a congregation. Then each team moved on to the next village. Two more teams were added. Finally, phase two began, each village receiving follow-up work. The next phase was a mobile Bible school originally conducted by teachers from the seminary.

C. *In all this we see God giving quiet growth.* Yes, churches can grow, and churches are growing as millions turn to Christ, thousands of churches expand, and other new thousands of churches are planted. God continues silent growth today.

III. Quiet growth—God invites us to participate in this growth.

A. *God can do some amazing things with one congregation, or even with one person.* One unlikely person who was invited by the Lord to participate in quiet growth was Bruno Frigoli. Bruno had been a bodyguard to Mussolini, and after years of hiding, he was born again as a new man full of love. Bruno became an ardent Bible student totally committed to Christ. The Lord invited Bruno to participate in his plan of quiet growth among the Aymara people of Bolivia. What can God do with one person? When Bruno began his ministry among the Aymaras in 1968, there were only 20 churches of his denomination in Brazil. At the end of 1972 there were 104 churches. At the end of 1974 there were 300 churches. By 1980 there were more than 600 churches. The Bolivian revival became a South American revival, reaching into nineteen South American nations.

B. *God's quiet growth includes personal growth in the fruit of the Spirit.* "But the fruit of the Spirit is love, joy, peace, longsuffering, gentleness, goodness, faith, meekness, temperance: against such there is no law" (Gal. 5:22–23). Growth in Christian graces is a privilege and a duty of God's children. The Lord of the harvest also invites us to take part in growth by personally reaching out to the world.

Conclusion

To your life and to the life of our church, let us apply thoroughly these principles of quiet growth.

1. Quiet growth requires spiritually dynamic leaders.
2. Quiet growth requires serious prayer by individuals and groups.
3. Quiet growth requires home Bible studies with non-Christians.
4. Quiet growth includes house-to-house evangelistic visitation.

Growth is God's alone to give. We cannot impart life to any plant. But you and I must be obedient to God by sowing the seed, watering the plants, and cultivating the field. We must do this in such a careful manner that growth of the church of Jesus Christ will result.

WEDNESDAY EVENING, APRIL 21

Title: Take Heed

Text: "Therefore we ought to give the more earnest heed to the things which we have heard, lest at any time we should let them slip" **(Heb. 2:1)**.

Scripture Reading: Hebrews 1:1–2:4

Introduction

In tonight's text, "*heed*" means to pay careful attention to and is the opposite of disregard for God's Word. The writer of Hebrews tells us that Christ is superior to prophets and angels, and because the revelation of God in Christ is superior, we ought to give earnest heed to the things we have heard. Because Jesus is the final and supreme revelation of God, we are to give special attention to God's message as it is revealed in Christ.

Using this passage as a guide, let us consider some things that deserve our careful attention.

I. Take heed to the doctrine taught by others.

"Take heed, beware of the leaven of the Pharisees, and of the leaven of Herod" (Mark 8:15).

It was necessary for Jesus to issue this warning because his disciples had come out of a pharisaic atmosphere and they would meet the Pharisees again and again. He combined the warning concerning the Pharisees with a warning concerning Herod. The leaven of the Pharisees was bad theology, and the leaven of Herod was bad politics. Christians need to beware of unspiritual and irreligious teaching. We also need to beware of ungodly blindness that insists on signs to show God and truth.

II. Take heed that no one deceives you about Christ.

"Take heed that no man deceive you. For many shall come in my name, saying, I am Christ; and shall deceive many" (Matt. 24:4–5). It is amazing how successful some deceivers have been through the ages with eschatological programs and teachings about the second coming of our Lord. Many have claimed to be what Jesus is, the Christ, or Messiah. Let us beware of those who seek to lead us astray.

III. Take heed to God's Word.

"We have also a more sure word of prophecy; whereunto ye do well that ye take heed, as unto a light that shineth in a dark place, until the day dawn, and the day star arise in your hearts" (2 Peter 1:19).

133

The phrase "a more sure word of prophecy" has reference to all the messianic prophecies. The transfiguration scene confirmed the messianic prophecies and made clear the deity of Jesus Christ as God's beloved Son. What Peter saw with his eyes and heard with his ears does not equal the affirmation of the glory and deity of Christ that is presented in God's Word. Eyes and ears may deceive us, but there is no doubt of the truth and certainty of God's Word.

We constantly need to focus our minds on God's prophetic Word concerning our blessed Lord!

IV. Take heed to what you hear about responsibility.

"Take heed what ye hear: with what measure ye mete, it shall be measured to you: and unto you that hear shall more be given. For he that hath, to him shall be given: and he that hath not, from him shall be taken even that which he hath" (Mark 4:24–25).

We need to take heed to what we hear and how we hear. Some things should not be heard, for they blacken the mind and heart. What is worth hearing should be heard rightly and heeded. Let us hear attentively with understanding. Let us rightly use words of truth. To use the truth selfishly is to lose it. To share the truth with others is to gain more truth. For, as Jesus said, "Give, and it shall be given unto you" (Luke 6:38).

V. Take heed to yourself.

"And take heed to yourselves, lest at any time your hearts be overcharged with surfeiting, and drunkenness, and cares of this life, and so that day come upon you unawares" (Luke 21:34).

Jesus issued this blanket warning to his disciples and others who would follow them. They should guard their hearts against being weighed down with dissipation, drunkenness, and the anxieties of life. They need to ward off anything that would prevent them from watching constantly for the Lord's return. Sinful living and earthly cares dim the sense of hope and expectancy for the Lord's return, and this loss of expectancy leads to sinful living.

Conclusion

Paul said to the Corinthians, "Let every man take heed how he buildeth thereupon" (1 Cor. 3:10). We must build on the right foundation. We do not need to lay a new one, but only build on the foundation already laid. Let us carry out the plans of the original Architect. Let us heed the original design. Let us be what Christ wants us to be!

SUNDAY MORNING, APRIL 25

Title: Marriage—by God's Appointment

Text: "He who finds a wife finds a good thing, and obtains favor from the LORD" (Prov. 18:22 RSV).

Scripture Reading: Genesis 2:20–25; Proverbs 18:22; Ephesians 5:30–33; Hebrews 13:4

Hymns: "Christian Hearts, in Love United," von Zinzendorf
          "Leaning on the Everlasting Arms," Hoffman
          "Make Me a Channel of Blessing," Smyth

Offertory Prayer: We are thankful to you, heavenly Father, for your overwhelming love. We thank you for your Son, Jesus Christ. Thank you for the example of love that Jesus has expressed to the church. You have given this to us as a type of love we are to exhibit within our homes. May we be faithful in this endeavor. Accept our offerings as a partial expression of that godly love. In Jesus' name we pray. Amen.

Introduction

All young people must make three major decisions. They must confront the issue of who or what is to master their lives. They must decide on their missions and/or vocations. They must consider whether they will marry and, if so, choose lifelong mates. Their salvation is dependent on their decision regarding the master of their lives. Their society is contingent on their mission and purpose. Their personal lives are directly affected by their choice of marriage partners.

Marriage holds a vital position in the life of an individual, but it is not God's will for every person to be married (1 Cor. 7:7). Each person must seek God's will regarding this important issue. Those who marry outside the will of God face unnecessary hardships.

In the consideration of marriage from God's perspective, let us make note of the spiritual vim, vigor, and vitality found within the marital union.

I. God's vim in marriage.

The word *vim* comes from the Latin word *vis*, which means "to empower." In regard to marriage, this concept deals with the beginning, or the empowering, of marriage. Blessed is the couple who allow God to initiate marriage.

  A. *God's purpose.* God has a plan for every person's life. This includes your marital status. It is wise to seek God's purpose and plan for your life even before you start seeking a marriage partner. Many problems are solved before they arise if you know what you are going to do for a vocation before you consider marriage.

  B. *God's person.* The heavenly Father is aware of the different personalities and needs of all humankind. God has a profound concept of marriage. If the Lord is allowed to have his way, each person will be led to marry the person who is most suitable. This is the basic key to marital compatibility.

  C. *God's procedure.* If a marriage is to be a testimony for the Lord Jesus Christ, those considering marriage should be sure that the wedding ceremony is conducted in accordance with God's procedures. Secret ceremonies, elopements, and "shot-gun" weddings all cast shadows on the Christian witness.

II. God's vigor in marriage.

The word *vigor* comes from a Latin word meaning "to prosper." God did not develop marriage as a form of punishment for wayward people. Rather, he desires people "to prosper," or to enjoy the state of matrimony. God's plan calls for a vigorous marriage. Three factors are involved if a couple is to enjoy marriage.

    A. *God's goals in marriage.* The wise couple sets specific goals for their marriage. It must be more than a simple hit-or-miss effort. They should set goals for spiritual growth, educational advancement, financial security, and social involvement. These goals give a sense of direction and aid the couple in finding satisfaction in their marriage.

    B. *Good behavior.* The high moral code of the Bible is aimed at strengthening the soul. When people become involved in immorality, their inner self is greatly weakened. They become insecure and defensive. Their sin causes many problems to come into their lives.

    C. *Routine living.* Most people enjoy occasional excitement, but the happiest marriages are centered around wholesome routines of life. There are enough unexpected events to keep the family excited (or upset) without deliberately causing them. Though a family takes a vacation to get out of life's ruts, security and enjoyment can be found in life's routines.

III. God's vitality in marriage.

The word *vitality* comes from the Latin word *vitalis*, which means "to perpetuate." The Scriptures discourage the breaking of the marriage contract. A number of safeguards can bind the marital unit.

    A. *Good habits.* As a wholesome routine offers security to the family, so good habits serve as cement for the marriage. Regular church attendance is an essential activity for the family. Times of worship are extremely valuable in centering a marriage on Jesus Christ. Other habits that will help the family are tithing, serving through the local church, and being involved in wholesome community activities.

    B. *Godly love.* There is no substitute for godly love in a family. An exciting, youthful love may exist between a husband and wife, but there should always be a deeper godly love between family members. This type of love is simply a reflection of God's love for us, and it binds the family together.

    C. *Growth.* The family unit and every member in it should be in a continuing growth process. Life must not become stagnant. Growth in spiritual, physical, financial, and social matters must be a part of the routine of marriage and will give the family a sense of accomplishment.

Conclusion

God's design for marriage is likened to Christ's relationship to the church. It has structure, purpose, leadership, and continuity. It is a serious yet enjoyable experience.

SUNDAY EVENING, APRIL 25

Title: Quiet Lessons

Text: "In the farthest corners of the earth the glorious acts of God shall startle everyone. The dawn and sunset shout for joy!" **(Ps. 65:8 TLB)**.

Scripture Reading: 2 Corinthians 4:6–18

Note to pastor: This sermon outline is intentionally shortened. It is suggested that you include your local evangelistic and mission concerns within or at the conclusion of the sermon.

Introduction

Today God is trying to teach his people some very important lessons. His teaching method is not forceful or obtrusive. Instead, God wants to teach us quiet lessons. He seeks willing, teachable, responsible students. Both from the Bible and from contemporary life, God's Spirit presses these quiet lessons upon us. Let us listen to God's instruction in the following lessons.

I. There is a world to be won.

The psalmist spoke of this lesson: "Ask of me, and I will make the nations your heritage" (Ps. 2:8 RSV). In Psalm 65:8 we read of "the farthest corners of the earth" (TLB) where God's amazing acts are done. But there is a race against evil going on in the world, and time is running out. Christians must respond more faithfully to Christ's command to win the world: "Go therefore and make disciples of all nations" (Matt. 28:19 RSV). We must continue to declare Christ's love and his lordship everywhere he is not known, for there is a world to be won.

II. God is putting light in dark places.

"The people which sat in darkness saw great light" (Matt. 4:16). All over the world new congregations are sprouting up and growing. Surely this is God putting light in dark places.

III. We must depend on the Holy Spirit.

The Holy Spirit is ready to empower us, to do the humanly impossible (Acts 1:8). He is ready to guide this church into just those activities that will lead great numbers to respond to Christ. The power of God's Spirit will accomplish his purpose with signs, wonders, and miracles.

IV. Most of what God wants to do is done through his church.

Jesus said, "I will build my church" (Matt. 16:18). In Ephesians 5:25 we read that Christ loved the church and gave himself for it. The church with all its weaknesses is still the fellowship of the Holy Spirit, the school of Christ, and the people of God. Let us not criticize or tear down Christ's church. Instead, let's stay in it and change it if necessary. Improve the church so that it increasingly wins people to the Master and effectively matures the believers.

Note to pastor: Under points V through VIII, use some of the following Scripture passages and develop them along lines most suited to your local evangelistic mission needs.

V. God can bring victory out of defeat (I Chron. 29:11–12; I John 5:4).

VI. Our helplessness is God's opportunity (Ps. 68:35; 2 Cor. 12:10).

VII. God never gives up on anyone—should we (I Cor. 15:58; Gal. 6:9; Heb. 12:3)?

VIII. God knows the way, and he has the power (Ps. 62:11; Luke 1:37; Rom. 4:20–21).

Conclusion

These are some of the quiet yet vital lessons for life that God is trying to teach us. Are we willing to become teachable? William Carey, Baptist missionary to India, said, "Attempt great things for God and expect great things from God." Have we recently attempted any great things for God? We are in a spiritual war. Let us get prepared for this war. Let us use the Spirit's gift to each of us as we seek new ways in these new days to be effective soldiers of Christ. With these quiet lessons learned, let us step forth in faith.

WEDNESDAY EVENING, APRIL 28

Title: Forgiveness

Text: "If we confess our sins, he is faithful and just to forgive us our sins, and to cleanse us from all unrighteousness" (1 John 1:9).

Scripture Reading: Matthew 6:9–15

Introduction

Forgiveness is easy to talk about but difficult to practice. George Herbert said, "He who cannot forgive others breaks the bridge over which he must pass." Lawrence Sterne said, "Only the brave know how to forgive; it is the

most refined and generous pitch of virtue human nature can arrive at."
Jean Paul Richter said, "Humanity is never so beautiful as when praying for
forgiveness, or else when forgiving another." And Frederick William Robertson
said, "We win by tenderness; we conquer by forgiveness."

But our foremost authority on forgiveness, Jesus Christ, said centuries
earlier, "If ye forgive men their trespasses, your heavenly Father will also
forgive you: but if ye forgive not men their trespasses, neither will your Father
forgive your trespasses" (Matt. 6:14–15).

What is forgiveness? The word *forgiveness* means to pardon, to remit,
to absolve from blame, to cease to feel resentment against an offender on
account of a wrong done, to abandon a claim against a debtor. Forgiveness in
the Bible, however, is much more. Forgiveness involves restoring a personal
relationship that has been interrupted. The apostle John said, "If we confess
our sins, he is faithful and just to forgive us our sins, and to cleanse us from
all unrighteousness" (1 John 1:9).

I. Forgiveness is conditioned on repentance of sins and faith in Jesus Christ.

Two conditions must be fulfilled before forgiveness can be granted:
repentance and faith. Only Christ is invested with the authority to forgive.
When one complies with the conditions of forgiveness, Christ promises to
issue forgiveness.

II. Forgiveness is based on the death of Jesus Christ.

The very fact that Jesus offers forgiveness on the conditions of repentance
and faith does not do away with the necessity of atonement. The law demands
that sin be punished. Even God cannot and does not forgive sin apart from
the sacrifice Christ made. He assumed our guilt and paid the penalty in full.
For without the shedding of blood there is no remission of sin. Every altar
and every sacrifice made on the altar signifies this.

Paul said, "For he hath made him to be sin for us, who knew no sin; that
we might be made the righteousness of God in him" (2 Cor. 5:21). "For Christ
is the end of the law for righteousness to every one that believeth" (Rom.
10:4). Forgiveness can only be exercised by Christ because he died for our sins.

III. Forgiveness is limited.

Some passages in the New Testament seem to limit forgiveness. These
passages are those in which Jesus discussed the unpardonable sin (Matt.
12:31–32; Mark 3:28–30; Luke 12:10). The sin against the Holy Spirit cannot be
forgiven because it brings eternal damnation, the loss of moral discrimination,
indifference to one's own condition, and hostility toward the Lord.

IV. Forgiveness is the spirit of a Christian.

The Bible tells us to exercise forgiveness toward those who offend us or
trespass against us. Of course we cannot remove the guilt of sin. Peter once

asked Jesus, "Lord, how oft shall my brother sin against me, and I forgive him? till seven times? Jesus saith unto him, I say not unto thee, Until seven times; but, Until seventy times seven" (Matt. 18:21–22). Peter was certain that seven, being a biblical number, would be enough, but Jesus said "seventy times seven." That is 490 times. Most Christians would lose patience before they reached the number seven, to say nothing of seventy times seven.

The value of forgiveness is manifested in one's Christian spirit. We all know how miserable it is to hold ill will or a grudge against someone. Jesus can free us from such a spirit and make us happy. Joy and an unforgiving spirit cannot live together.

V. Forgiveness brings blessed results.

What are some of the things forgiveness produces or brings to the believer?

A. *Forgiveness awakens love for God.*
B. *Forgiveness brings peace of mind.*
C. *Forgiveness removes the cause of alienation, removes mistrust.*
D. *Forgiveness gives us insight into the character of our Lord.*

Conclusion

Let us be forgiving people. The oft-repeated saying, "I can forgive, but I cannot forget," is only a half-truth. God said, "For I will forgive their iniquity, and I will remember their sin no more" (Jer. 31:34). You and I are not infallible or all-wise, but we can climb to the heights where we cease to feel resentment in our hearts toward anyone. It is not easy, but it is possible because our Lord has forgiven us. Vengeance belongs to the Lord. As Judge of the earth, he will recompense a just reward to all. We would do well to be forgiving and leave the vengeance to him!

MAY

■ **Sunday Mornings**

Throughout May and continuing through Father's Day, use messages with the theme "Strengthening Christian Marriage and Family Living."

■ **Sunday Evenings**

The Sunday evening sermons for May and June are taken from the Sermon on the Mount. The series theme is "Listening to Heaven's Infallible Teacher."

■ **Wednesday Evenings**

Begin a series from the book of James with the theme "The Practical Expression of Our Faith in Daily Living."

SUNDAY MORNING, MAY 2

Title: The Functioning Family

Text: "If it seem evil unto you to serve the LORD, choose you this day whom ye will serve; whether the gods which your fathers served that were on the other side of the flood, or the gods of the Amorites, in whose land ye dwell: but as for me and my house, we will serve the LORD" **(Josh. 24:15).**

Scripture Reading: Joshua 24:14–15; Psalm 133:1; Ecclesiastes 9:9

Hymns: "Have No Fear, Little Flock," Jillson
"Savior, Like a Shepherd Lead Us," Thrupp
"Turn Your Eyes upon Jesus," Lemmel

Offertory Prayer: Our Father in heaven, our hearts are filled with gratitude that you have allowed us to become members of your eternal family. Give us wisdom that our earthly families may reflect your eternal values. Give us insight that our response to this offering will be an indication that these eternal values are being expressed through us. In Jesus' name we pray. Amen.

Introduction

The word *family* comes from the Latin word *famulus*, which means "servant." A family may be defined as a social unit bound together by a legal marriage contract. The family may or may not include children. A cold definition does not express the expected and desired experiences of happy family living. For a family to fulfill its true intent, it must be a unit functioning for

141

the benefit of all involved. A true functioning family will have Christ at its center, and its members will form interrelationships of service to one another. Let us look at ways a Christian family should function.

I. Physical

A family unit should meet the physical needs of all its members. Marriage should not be entered into until the physical needs of all concerned have a potential of being met.

- A. *Needs.* The head of the family is responsible for seeing that each member has sufficient food, clothing, and shelter. The apostle Paul gave his godly wisdom on this matter in 1 Timothy 5:8.
- B. *Health.* Happiness may bring about good health, whereas sadness or bitterness may cause ill health. The Christian family should establish an attitude that will aid in good health. Also, the home has the responsibility for healthy habits, maintenance of medical care, and proper treatment when illness comes.
- C. *Recreation.* It is a joy to see family units involved in recreational activities. Children's minds are deeply influenced by moments of fun and relaxation they experience with their parents. Thus a wise parent will make sure to provide many such experiences.
- D. *Work.* Some people are capable workers, whereas others have never really learned how to work. A major function of the home life is to teach each member the art and the satisfaction of work. Work should not be pictured as a despised task, but rather as a purposeful activity aiding the family and the society.

II. Mental.

No institution affects the mentality of an individual as much as the home. One of the greatest gifts a person receives from nature is his or her mind. The home is the place where this mind is to be motivated to reach its greatest potential.

- A. *Attitude.* A positive mental approach to life always has at its basis a good mental attitude. Two factors are basic to a good attitude.
  1. Parents must love themselves and each other, and then they must project this love into the life of their child.
  2. A sense of belonging must be built into every family member.
- B. *Purpose.* A person with a good mental attitude is a person with a sense of purpose. True purpose comes when we align ourselves with God's will. This gives us a sense of direction as well as a feeling of accomplishment.
- C. *Finances.* Finances are an important consideration. Financial security is most definitely a state of mind. Each family member should have a true evaluation of money and its use. Money must never be an improper

priority in the family's lifestyle. Also, the concept of money should be related to giving a full measure of work when receiving payment.

D. *Study.* Our society has become a "spoon-fed" generation of instant knowledge. Instead of reading and studying to secure a deeper and more wholesome education, the individual is tempted to feed on a dish of popular journalism that is easily funneled into the home. The family should be the place where genuine study and learning are taught and practiced.

III. Spiritual.

The spiritual nature of a person is more important than his or her physical or mental attributes. When this life ceases, the spiritual nature will continue. An eternal existence is directly affected by the circumstances of this life as they relate to a person's spiritual being.

A. *Conversion.* The most important spiritual experience is that of the "new birth." The most thorough system of soul winning is one in which an entire generation is won to Jesus Christ by every family unit winning its own to salvation. Parents can have no greater joy than to win their own child to Jesus Christ.

B. *Church.* Almost any husband and wife may have a child, but a loving environment is necessary to nourish that child. So it is spiritually. An individual may be born again outside of the ministry of the local church, but regular involvement in the church is important for spiritual nurture and growth. After all, Jesus established the local church because he saw a need for it. Who has the authority to counteract his wisdom and action? The local church and its programs are necessary for Christian growth.

C. *Consecration.* The home is an excellent place to teach the priority that Jesus should have in the life of the individual. Dedication to Christ should follow conversion. Salvation brings new desires that will find expression when the individual is consecrated to God's will.

D. *Devotion.* The way for a family to keep the dedication of its members current is to have daily devotions. Time should be set aside for worship as part of the family's daily routine.

Conclusion

The family is the most influential social factor in the life of the individual. Is Christ glorified by the actions and attitudes you find when you look at your home?

SUNDAY EVENING, MAY 2

Title: The Salt of the Earth

Text: "You are the salt of the earth. But if the salt loses its saltiness, how can it be made salty again? It is no longer good for anything, except to be thrown out and trampled by men" (**Matt. 5:13 NIV**).

Introduction

Without question the Sermon on the Mount as recorded in Matthew 5–7 has been more widely discussed than any other writing of equal length. Many Bible scholars believe that the best-known fact about Jesus is that he gave the Sermon on the Mount.

Following the Beatitudes, Jesus offers a series of teachings that, if incorporated in our lives, would revolutionize our very existence. In Matthew 5:13 Jesus makes the pointed statement, "You are the salt of the earth" (NIV). In this statement Jesus has given to us an expression that has become one of the finest compliments that can be paid to any individual. When we wish to underscore the worth of an individual, we might say, "He is the salt of the earth!" This shows the influence that Christians are to have on society.

I. The source of influence.

"You are the salt of the earth." Christ seems to be stating quite clearly that the source of our influence is found in the persons we are! He said, "You *are* salt," not "You *have* salt" or "You *dispense* salt." Only as Christians *are* salt in their lives and character can they exercise the influence of salt in their society.

None of us exert influence on other people by our words if what we say is not backed up by what we are. It is the influence of our personality that will produce changes in others. The purity of our private lives has everything to do with the purity of our public influence. Centuries ago the Romans contended that salt was the purest of all things because it came from the purest of all elements, the sun and the sea. Thus, if Christians are to be the salt of the earth, they must be an example of purity. Christians who want to be spiritually influential must hold high standards of purity in speech, conduct, thought, and action.

The presence of salt cannot be ignored. It is a positive influence. If it is present, we cannot fail to recognize its presence. If it is absent, we miss it. Where the salt of the earth is in the form of Christian influence, people will be aware of it. It will not always be welcome, but it will be recognized. But unless Christians are pure, they cannot exercise the power of Christian influence.

II. The sphere of influence.

Christ said, "You are the salt of the earth." Since we are the salt of the earth, where are we to unloose our preserving and purifying powers? The answer is found in the word "earth." That is, we are to exercise our influence in the here and now, in the community in which we live, in the face of the needs that confront us. It is our business to serve as the salt of the earth in the city in which we live. It is our business to see that our community is clean, that it is a wholesome environment in which young people will have the best possible chance to grow and develop. Salt does its most effective work by being brought in direct contact with the substance on which it is to work. And so we are not to withdraw ourselves from the world, but as the apostle James said, we are to stay "unspotted from the world" (James 1:27).

Salt has been a preservative throughout the ages. In ancient times salt was used whenever something was to be preserved. Without the presence of those reflecting the character of Jesus Christ, civilization will self-destruct. Humankind does not become increasingly pure but tends to become increasingly impure. The presence of Christians in society is an absolute necessity if that society is to be saved from disintegration. As Christians we are called on to be the preservative in our society. We must be those who by our presence defeat corruption and make it easier for others to do good.

Salt has a flavoring influence. Without salt, food has little if any flavor. So Christ is saying that the Christian is to life what salt is to food. We are to lend flavor to life. The tragedy is that so many people have assumed that to be Christian is to have no flavor in life. They have wrongly concluded that Christianity removes flavor from life.

After Constantine had embraced Christianity as the religion of the Roman Empire, there came to the throne another emperor, Julian. He wished to go back to the old gods. His reason was that Christians were hollow-eyed and pale-cheeked individuals who had no ambition or joy. Julian saw Christians as void of any color or flavor.

Oliver Wendell Holmes is quoted as saying that he might have entered the ministry if certain clergymen he had known had not acted so much like undertakers. It is reported that Robert Louis Stevenson once entered in his diary with real delight, "I have been to church today and I'm not depressed!"

People need to discover the joy and radiance of the Christian faith. In a world that is so depressed and seems to have lost the luster of life, we as Christians are charged with the joyous responsibility of being the salt of the earth, adding flavor to life.

III. The sacrifice of influence.

"But if the salt loses its saltiness. . . ." When Jesus referred to his disciples as salt, they were without question highly complimented. They had not realized prior to this how important they were. But Christ did not call them salt in order to send them on an ego trip. He desired to impress them with a solemn warning—they could lose their saltiness. That is, they could sacrifice their influence.

Salt, pure sodium chloride as we know it, does not lose its saltiness. But the Palestinians got their salt from the Dead Sea, and that salt was not pure. It was mixed with other minerals that often affected its flavor. In time it could become tasteless. When this happened, it was good for nothing but "to be thrown out and trampled." So the disciples were given a solemn warning.

They were to preserve their society or be pulverized by it. None of us are immune to losing our own savor. If Christians are not fulfilling their purpose as the salt of the earth, they are on their way to disaster.

The final word of caution that Jesus sounded concerning the end of salt that has lost its saltiness—that it would be thrown out and trampled—indicates that neither God nor people have any use for it. We may ask, "Where are the churches of Asia Minor, of Antioch, of Constantinople, and of Alexandria?" They are trodden underfoot! Over the entrance of a Damascan mosque you can read the half-obliterated inscription, "Thy Kingdom, O Christ, Is an Everlasting Kingdom." But above this faded inscription are these words in bold letters: "There is no god but Allah and Mohammed is his prophet." The salt lost its savor.

Conclusion

Is it possible to restore lost savor, to regain sacrificed influence? Yes, it is! Christians who have lost their savor can win it back by going again to the source from which they received it. God placed no obstacles in the way of a penitent returning to the fountain of all power and purity. When the influence has been sacrificed, there is only one thing to do. We must repent and return to our first love. When this is done, we will once more be "the salt of the earth."

WEDNESDAY EVENING, MAY 5

Title: When Temptation Comes

Text: Consider it pure joy, my brothers, whenever you face trials of many kinds, because you know that the testing of your faith develops perseverance. **(James 1:2–3 NIV)**

Scripture Reading: James 1:1–4

Introduction

The author of the epistle of James is unique, along with his brother Jude, among all the writers of the Bible, for these two men were half brothers of our Lord Jesus Christ. Though apparently neither of these men was convinced that Jesus was the Son of God until after his resurrection, it appears that James's spiritual growth and acceptance among the Christians was phenomenal. For soon none among the followers of Christ was better known, and none more respected, than James. He was recognized as the bishop or leader of the first organized church in Jerusalem. We will notice as we study this epistle that James used more nearly than any other writer the very words of Jesus. He also reproduced more perfectly the spirit of the Old Testament Scriptures that he had studied as a boy in the synagogue school with Jesus.

Those to whom James addressed his letter were Jews. He called them "the twelve tribes in the Dispersion" (James 1:1 RSV), his fellow Jews who were scattered in various parts of the Roman world. They had accepted Christ as the Messiah, and James wrote from Jerusalem to urge them to live according to their Christian profession. The purpose of his letter is extremely practical. He attempted to correct the errors of these believers and to admonish them for their failures. James did not endeavor to teach doctrine in his epistle. Rather, his aim was to stimulate true and effective Christian living. On this foundation he urged his readers to build the necessary superstructure of consistent works. We might say, then, that the theme of James's epistle is "Christian wisdom," or practical knowledge—truth applied to life. It shows how Christians must live in times of temptation, trial, and persecution. He demanded reality in one's practice of Christianity; he rebuked all pretense and self-deception. He insisted that faith will be tested by works and that character will correspond to profession.

I. Note first the greeting with which James opened his letter.

A. *He began with a description of himself: "a servant of God and of the Lord Jesus Christ."* The word he used for servant is *doulos*, or bondslave, one who has been deprived of his personal freedom and is an instrument in the hands of his master. *Doulos* comes from a Greek word meaning "to bind." Thus a believer should be bound to his Master. Also, the slave did not have the concerns that free persons have about clothing, lodging, or food (see Matt. 6:31–33).

B. *He did not use the customary Christian greeting that Paul and others used in introducing their epistles.* He used the simple word *chairein*, which is the verb "to rejoice." Its deeper meaning is "to be satisfied." His first message to the persecuted believers scattered throughout the world was to rejoice in whatever state they found themselves, knowing that their lives were guided not by accident but by the providence of God.

II. James spoke of the proper attitude Christians should take when they find themselves surrounded by various temptations and trials (1:2–3).

A. *He told believers to get the most out of every experience God permits to come into their lives—the unpleasant as well as the pleasant.* Joy under all circumstances should be the main characteristic of the Christian life.

B. *He did not say that all trials and temptations are joyous experiences.* The joy comes when the victory is won, when the lesson is learned. Never do we appreciate the sunshine as much as we do after a long stretch of dreary, rainy weather.

C. *What are these "trials of many kinds"?* When James spoke of "facing" these temptations, the verb he used means "to fall upon," as one would stumble over some unseen or unnoticed obstacle. Thus these are trials that Christians more or less bump into in the normal course of everyday life. But God will give his people discernment to recognize them.

D. *"The testing of your faith develops perseverance."* The more a tree is blasted by strong winds, the deeper into the earth it sends its roots. The kind of patience James said will result from our trials is that which provides the ability to stand fast under pressure.

III. Our goal as a result of overcoming temptations (1:4).

A. *When we are able to accept the trials and testings of life in the way God intended, three things happen.*
1. We will become "mature"—God will bring to a successful completion what he started.
2. We will be "complete"—this patience, this unswerving constancy that develops in our lives, will remove imperfections and weaknesses.
3. We will ultimately "not lack anything."

B. *We must let patience do its work in our lives.* Our stubbornness can raise a barrier between us and spiritual growth and maturity.

Conclusion

When we as Christians learn that God has provided resources to help us overcome temptation, failure will become less and less the norm and more and more the exception in our lives.

SUNDAY MORNING, MAY 9

Title: Mother—a Basic Need of Life

Text: "Husbands, love your wives, even as Christ also loved the church, and gave himself for it. Children, obey your parents in the Lord: for this is right. Honour thy father and mother; which is the first commandment with promise" **(Eph. 5:25; 6:1–2).**

Scripture Reading: Ephesians 5:25–6:3

Hymns: "Faith of Our Mothers," Faber
"God of Grace and God of Glory," Fosdick
"O Blessed Day of Motherhood," McGregor

Offertory Prayer: Our heavenly Father, as we approach this hour of offering and sacrifice, we dare not forget the hour of our own beloved mother's sacrifice that we might have physical life. Nor can we forget the hour of our beloved Savior's sacrifice that we might have eternal life. May our giving be with a comparable spirit of love and sacrifice. In Christ's name we pray. Amen.

Introduction

The climax of God's creative activities was the presentation of humankind. The natural system that God selected to populate the earth was that of union between husband and wife. The father is essential to plant the seed in order for children to be created, but the mother is the basic unit for conceiving, developing, and giving birth to a child.

Hearts are almost universally sentimental when reference is made to a mother. Because of her unique role in producing the family, a mother has her own particular needs. And the family and society have special needs that a mother can meet.

I. A mother's needs.

The role of a mother is not easy to fulfill. Many factors outside the home influence children, so it is necessary for a mother to make certain efforts if she is to be successful in rearing her children.

A. *A mother needs to have society on her mind.* A mother must be aware of the evils facing her children when they are not under her immediate care, and she must warn her children of these evils. Care must be taken so that none of these dangers invade the intimacy of the home.

On the other hand, since children's attitudes are forged by their mother, a mother must also be aware of the good that exists in the world and instill in her children a desire for this good in their lives.

B. *A mother needs to have God in her heart.* A mother plagued by guilt will be a ghost in the lives of her children. Therefore a mother owes it to her family to have a clear conscience and a soul set free by salvation through Jesus Christ. Then she may guide her beloved children to genuine life in him. The most peaceful spot on earth is the path in the center of God's will. The wise mother desires this reality for herself and her family.

C. *A mother needs to have a husband by her side.* A mother must have the true friendship of her husband. They must work side by side to make the home a nurturing environment for their children.

D. *A mother needs to have children under her guidance.* The Bible requires that children obey and respect their parents. A basic need of the mother is for her children to love and obey her. A rebellious child will force a mother to a premature grave.

The basic needs for successful motherhood are met by God, by the yielded spirit of the mother, by the loving heart of the husband, and by the obedient mind of the child.

II. A mother is needed.

God ordained a basic place for motherhood within the structure of our society. We cannot do without her. Those who have tried to do so have suffered the consequences.

A. *A mother is needed by a sick society.* Motherhood is a symbol of righteousness and concern. When there is a degrading of this concept, society becomes sick. When a mother exemplifies biblical standards of holiness, society is healed.

B. *A mother is needed by her children.* Children have lofty feelings of pride about their parents. Although no parent can be perfect, a mother owes it to herself and her children to strive to maintain a proper life.

C. *A mother is needed by her husband.* Her husband needs her to assist in the rearing of their children. Mothers should foster a true spirit of maternal love so as to truly minister to their child and to be a source of strength to her husband.

D. *A mother is needed by the church.* The local church has an awesome dependency on mothers. A mother learns biblical truths and shares them with her family and friends. Her time and talent are used in the many functions of the congregation. Her children follow in her footsteps.

Conclusion

God has placed a mother in the life of every person, yet some circumstances may not allow certain people to benefit from a mother's tender concern. But blessed is that mother who shares the truth and life of God with the children he has placed within her care.

SUNDAY EVENING, MAY 9

Title: The Light of the World

Text: "You are the light of the world. A city set on a hill cannot be hid" **(Matt. 5:14 RSV)**.

Scripture Reading: Matthew 5:14–16

Introduction

It may well be that Jesus' greatest compliment to a Christian is, "You are the light of the world." In this statement Jesus commands us to be nothing less than what he himself claimed to be. Jesus said, "As long as I am in the world, I am the light of the world" (John 9:5). Thus, when Jesus asks us as his followers to be the light of the world, he is asking us to be nothing less than what he is.

Jesus is saying that we are important people. We think of important people as those who are well known or who have prominent positions, for example, the apostle Paul, the reformer Martin Luther, and the general and president George Washington. Yet as Jesus gave his Sermon on the Mount, he spoke with people whose names we do not know—ordinary individuals—and called them "the light of the world." Jesus was telling them that they were important, that they mattered in God's kingdom. Today Christ says to you and me, "You are important; you are the light of the world." In this passage in Matthew we find an exclamation (v. 14), an illustration (v. 15), and an application (v. 16).

I. An exclamation.

I have a feeling that Jesus did not say passively, "You are the light of the world." Rather, I am convinced that he emphatically exclaimed, "You are the light of the world!" It is absolutely astounding that Jesus would know us for what we are and yet say that we are "the light of the world."

It is significant that Jesus said, "You *are* the light of the world." When I started out in ministry, I thought the most important thing was preparing sermons. Sermons were important to me, perhaps the most important thing I did. In those early days, I served one church for five years, during which I preached more than six hundred sermons. If I went back to that church today and asked the people to give me a list of ten sermons that I preached in those five years, I doubt if any of them could list more than one or two. On the other hand, all the people would be able to tell me how I lived, the spirit I had, and the impression my life made on them. I now have come to realize that ministers give the greatest sermon by the lives they lead rather than by the words they deliver.

Jesus did not say, "In time you will bring the light," nor did he say, "Someday you will become the light." He said, "You are the light." It is not by things we say or deeds we do, but by the people we are that we can be the light of the world.

One evening when Robert Louis Stevenson was a child, he stood at the window watching an old lamplighter at work. The lamplighter made his way down the street lighting one lamp after another. This process fascinated young Stevenson. Thinking that his quietness meant that he was up to some mischief, his maid called out to him, "What are you doing, Robert?" He answered, "I'm watching a man making holes in the darkness!" What an exclamation! "You are the light of the world!" When Jesus said that we are the light of the world, what did he mean? The meaning is made clear in his illustration in verse 15.

II. An illustration.

In verse 15 Jesus said that a person does not put a candle under a basket, but on a candlestick, so that it can give light to all in the house. Christ said at least three things about the light the Christian's life is to radiate.

A. *A light is to be seen.* The average house in Palestine was very dark with perhaps only one window. A little lamp would be lit so that people might see their way around the darkened house. Once the lamp went out, it was not easy to rekindle it, for there were no matches as we have today. So the little lamp would be left burning hour after hour. When the family left the house, for safety's sake, they would take the lamp from its stand and put it under an earthen bushel. When they returned, they would put it back on the stand, since the primary purpose of the lamp was to be seen, not hidden.

So Jesus said that Christianity is to be seen. Your Christianity should be perfectly visible to all. No one should have to ask you, "Are you a Christian?" The very life you live is a light to be seen.

B. *A light is to guide.* As an airplane approaches a landing strip, the pilot sees a line of lights that mark the path the plane must take. So the Christian's life must make clear to others the way to Christ. In other words, a Christian must be an example. Our world needs guiding lights. Your life and mine are to be that kind of light.

C. *A light is to warn.* When a light is flashing at a railroad crossing, it is a warning that a train is approaching. Sometimes it is a Christian's duty to warn others. If our warnings are given not in condemnation but in love, they will be effective.

Jesus has a disturbing habit of making perfectly clear what he expects us to do in regard to his teachings. Such was the case here, where he made a pointed application of this lesson.

III. An application.

In verse 16 Jesus said, "Let your light so shine before men, that they may see your good works and give glory to your Father who is in heaven" (RSV). With this statement Jesus shifts our attention from the character of Christians to their conduct.

A. *A plea.* Verse 16 begins with a plea: "Let your light so shine before men." This is an earnest plea that we live our lives so that others will be attracted to Christ. But how are we to shine? Clovis Chapell said that this analogy makes at least four suggestions.

1. We are to shine naturally. Just as it is the nature of a bird to sing, it should be the nature of a Christian to shine before others. Our radiance should have a beautiful spontaneity.

2. We are to shine sacrificially. Light is always costly. Whenever we see a light, we can be assured that something is being consumed. Energy is being expended. As a candle burns, it is growing shorter. As a lamp burns, it consumes not only the oil, but also the wick. When Jesus came as the Light of the World, his shining was at a great cost. If we are to shine as lights of the world, we must consider ourselves expendable. We must be willing to sacrifice a bit of ourselves each day we live.

3. We are to shine openly. If we are to shine before others, we must shine openly. We are never to be ashamed of our relationship with Jesus Christ.

4. We are to shine right where we are. If I am not willing to shine where I am, I will not shine at all. I don't know where you are today. It may be in a conspicuous place, a place of high social position, or it may be in a place no one notices. But wherever you are, you are to shine in that place. You are not there by accident but by divine appointment. And Jesus said, "You are the light of the world."

B. *A pattern.* In verse 16 Jesus said, "Let your light so shine before men, that they may see your good works." It is quite clear that we are to shine, but the question is how. Jesus said here that we are to shine through good works. The word "good" means not only virtuous, but also beautiful and attractive. There must never be a hint of hardness or austerity in the goodness of our lives. Ours must be a goodness that attracts people to Christ. There is a charm in Christian goodness that makes it an appealing thing to all who see it.

C. *A purpose.* Jesus said we are to shine before others so they will see our good works and glorify our Father in heaven. Never is our shining meant to draw attention to ourselves.

A group of people who had been in a prayer meeting all night saw Dwight L. Moody early in the morning. He asked them what they had been doing. They said, "Mr. Moody, we have been in an all-night prayer meeting. Can't you see how our faces shine?" Moody replied, "Moses wist not that his face did shine." The point was well made. The goodness that is conscious of itself and draws attention to itself is not the kind of goodness of which Jesus spoke. Christians are never to think of what they have done or whether it has reflected favorably on them. They must seek to draw the eyes of people not to themselves but to God.

Conclusion

A Christian doctor in China had built an efficient hospital through many years of hard work. When the communist wing of the national army swept northward, they looted this hospital and left it in shambles. The work of countless years went down the drain. This was not an easy thing to forgive or to forget. But undaunted, the Christian doctor followed the army and attended to its sick.

When General Chiang Kai-shek saw this, he asked, "What makes this doctor tend to the sick and wounded when these very men destroyed his hospital?" His wife, who was herself a Christian, replied, "It is his Christianity." General Chiang Kai-shek said, "Then I must become a Christian too." The doctor was a major influence that led the general to become a Christian even when a strong anti-Christian movement was sweeping his nation.

The Christian doctor lived as "the light of the world." And so can you and I. God never asks us to be what he will not equip us to be. We can be "the light of the world"!

WEDNESDAY EVENING, MAY 12

Title: Candidates for the Crown of Life

Text: "Blessed is the man that endureth temptation: for when he is tried, he shall receive the crown of life, which the Lord hath promised to them that love him" **(James 1:12)**.

Scripture Reading: James 1:5–12

Introduction

When we began our study of James's epistle last Wednesday evening, we discovered that he plunged immediately, after the briefest possible introduction, into his theme, which had to do with how Christians are to cope with trials, temptations, and persecution.

In James 1:5 it appears that James was changing direction altogether. This is not the case, however. He was simply striking the central note of his letter. He was going to tell his readers how to meet these temptations when they come.

I. James mentioned three vital needs for dealing with trials (1:5–8).

A. *First, we need wisdom.* "If any of you lack wisdom . . ." (v. 5). Why is wisdom a necessary ingredient? If Christians are to see their trials in a true light and make proper use of them, they must understand them. This is often impossible with human capabilities alone. To James, wisdom was more than knowledge or intelligence. It was a moral and spiritual quality based on the fear of the Lord, which is the essence of a practical faith. This wisdom of which James spoke was considered by the Hebrews to be an attribute of God and later became identified with the very Spirit of God. There is every possibility, then, that James was equating wisdom with the indwelling Holy Spirit. He may have been saying that the more we allow God's Spirit to fill us, the more of God's wisdom we will have.

B. *Second, we need prayer.* "If any of you lack wisdom, let him ask of God" (v. 5). James said that if we are conscious of a lack of wisdom in our lives, we should pray to God, and God will supply it. Next James listed four encouragements to prayer.

    1. God "giveth to all men." It is God's disposition to give.

    2. God "giveth to all men liberally." God gives generously.

    3. God "upbraideth not." God gives without reproach.

    4. "And it shall be given him." Here is the note of absolute certainty! Thus, in all of this James was saying for us to come with assurance and confidence to the throne of grace.

C. *Third, we need faith.* "But let him ask in faith, nothing wavering" (v. 6). We are to ask for wisdom with a trust in God that our request will be granted according to God's divine will. Note, too, that James warned that there is to be no "wavering" when we ask in faith. We are not to vacillate between faith and unbelief, between trust and distrust, when we pray. A person who prays like this, said James, is as unstable as the surge of a storm-tossed sea.

II. James listed some specific examples of trials (1:9–11).

A. *He spoke first of "the brother of low degree," or the test of poverty (v. 9), referring to Christians who live in humble circumstances.* The word "low" does not

154

refer to spiritual condition, but to earthly status. Such people were numerous in the early church, and James exhorted them to "rejoice," to rise above their outward poverty and the depression so often connected with it. The poor, said James, are to realize that they truly are exalted spiritually as new creations in Christ Jesus, as bearers of the divine image and partakers of the divine nature.

B. *He then spoke of "the rich," for whom prosperity is a kind of test (v. 10).* These people are not to glory in what they have come to possess materially but in the fact that they are "made low." That is, they must come to realize that they cannot be proud of their material wealth, understanding that all worldly glory is perishable and that true wealth consists of things that are eternal.

III. James described the reward for faithfully enduring temptation (1:12).

This reward is twofold.

A. *First, it involves the possession of an inner "blessedness."* "Blessed is the man that endureth temptation." "Blessed" in the New Testament means "favored" and speaks of a kind of joy that is unaffected by outward circumstances. James was not saying that the "blessedness" comes in the actual trial itself, but in the way in which the Christian receives and endures the test. The Christian who emerges from such a trial strengthened is indeed blessed.

B. *Second, such a believer will "receive the crown of life."* In the Greek world, crowns were given to athletes who were victorious in the games. They were also given to citizens who distinguished themselves in some community service. So the crown among the Greeks was either a prize of victory or a badge of honor. The Christian who properly endures the trials of life has exceedingly great joy and a royalty the highest earthly potentate has never realized apart from Christ! It is the crown of life—that is, the crown that consists of life, abundant and overflowing.

Conclusion

The poet William Cowper wrote these memorable lines:

> Ye fearful saints, fresh courage take;
> The clouds ye so much dread
> Are big with mercy, and shall break
> In blessings on your head.

> Judge not the Lord by feeble sense,
> But trust Him for His grace;
> Behind a frowning providence
> He hides a smiling face.

SUNDAY MORNING, MAY 16

Title: Children—God's Probe

Text: "Sons are a heritage from the LORD, the fruit of the womb a reward. Like arrows in the hand of a warrior are the sons of one's youth. Happy is the man who has his quiver full of them!" **(Ps. 127:3–5 RSV)**.

Scripture Reading: Psalm 127:1–5; Proverbs 22:6; Ephesians 6:1–4

Hymns: "Showers of Blessings," Nathan
          "My Lord Is Near Me All the Time," Gaultney
          "In Loving-Kindness Jesus Came," Gabriel

Offertory Prayer: As we pray to you as our heavenly Father, we are aware that you have accepted us as your own dear children. We praise your name for this great privilege made available to us through the sacrifice of your Son. May we make tangible recognition of your ownership on our lives as we give freely of our tithes and offerings. In Jesus' name we pray. Amen.

Introduction

God's infinite wisdom decrees that some families should be blessed with children while others should be blessed without them. When parents experience extreme rebellion or hardship in the life of a child, they may question the wisdom of ever having had children, whereas those without children may wonder why God did not allow them to be blessed with children. God has all wisdom, but humankind has finite wisdom. Therefore people should accept God's plan for their lives by faith without any doubting whatsoever.

Those whom God has selected to be parents have found that children are used of God to probe the depth of the parents' Christian experiences. Just how serious are parents regarding their dedication to morality? How have parents arranged their priorities? What values do they place on money, time, and recreation?

Parents have a basic responsibility to guide and direct their children through the difficult mazes of life. In the final analysis, children's lives will be determined by their own choices in these critical matters.

I. The development of children.

The role of the parent diminishes while the task of the child intensifies in the process of development. Conflicts arise between parents and children at several critical points. Sometimes parents are hesitant about releasing responsibilities that should be taken up by their child in the developmental process. On the other hand, a child may seek responsibilities for which he or she is not prepared. These are all normal problems that must be recognized and dealt with as they arise.

A. *Birth and infancy*. Infants are not born in accordance with their own will. Rather, parents bear a child because it is their desire. Since this is a fact, parents must keep in mind that the rearing of a child is their responsibility, not the responsibility of a relative, friend, institution, or social agency.

B. *Education*. The future of a child's responsiveness to the larger world is dependent on his or her formal education. From preschool through college, wise parents guide their offspring from one point of advancement to the next. Experienced parents are able to protect their child from many pitfalls.

C. *Puberty*. Nature has a way of placing potential problems on children before they are ready to cope with them. So it is with puberty. Children's bodies develop into potential adulthood while their minds may still be immature. Thus it is essential that parents have the right attitude about sex and are willing to face the realities of life with their child.

D. *Teens*. The turbulence of teenage years may appear to be difficult for parents, but that is because their child is going through an adjustment period. The patience, wisdom, love, and ability of the parents may be placed under deep stress. Parents must maintain their authority and leadership during this period.

E. *Young adults*. Young adults also need their parents' guidance. There comes a time when it is normal for children to leave home and establish their own family unit. Parents should guide their young adults through this period with much love and wisdom.

II. The decisions by children.

The role of parents in the life of their child is awesome, but the child must assume responsibility for making decisions. Parents do not have the privilege or the power to make inner decisions for their child; therefore the child must make personal choices for himself or herself. The life of the child is directed by personal decisions—right or wrong.

A. *Concerning salvation*. Parents may serve as an excellent example with their Christian life. They may be involved in the church and try to win their child to Jesus Christ. But the actual choice of salvation is left up to the child.

B. *Concerning education*. Wise parents see value in education. Understanding their child's personality and abilities my enable them to help guide their child to a potential career. They may associate themselves with institutions of learning. They may offer to finance all the costs of education. But if the child does not have an inner desire and motivation, the parents' time and money will be wasted.

C. *Concerning society.* For parents to be concerned about their child's friends is natural. Are they moral? Do they have a good or bad influence on their child? Parents may move their family into a good neighborhood, provide excellent schools, and attend an active church, but children will seek out their own friends.

D. *Concerning morality.* Most parents are concerned about their child's development of sexual awareness. Illicit and perverted sex have been made popular through the entertainment media. Parents must be consistent in teaching and exemplifying God's principles concerning sex. But the final decision as to how to handle the matter is up to the child.

III. Directions for children.

Though the home is very dependent on the school and the church for guidance in the child's life, parents are still the key. There is no alternative. Parents must retain their leadership in their child's life.

A. *Personal worth.* A child may be graded on a false scale in the educational system. A child may be misinterpreted within the church program. No one knows that child like the parents. Therefore it is necessary for parents to drill a sense of personal worth into the heart of their child. Though other institutions may attempt to do so, the family unit is the ideal place for a child to get the feeling that he or she belongs.

B. *Example.* A child learns by example. The best, or the worst, example in the world is the parent. How many times are parents reminded that their child is following in their footsteps? A child needs a real hero to imitate. Blessed is the parent who is willing to pay the price to be a child's hero.

C. *Teaching.* The education of a child should not be left totally to an institution outside the home. There are too many teaching aids available for parents to neglect the valuable task of teaching their own child. A child's needs will probe the priority system of the parents at a critical time.

D. *Guidance.* Authority is a must in the life of a child. It is a responsibility that should be shared by the mother and the father. If parents do not fulfill their role in this matter, then legal and social authorities may have to do what the parents would not do.

Conclusion

Children are valuable to our society and our churches. God uses a child in the home to strengthen its weak points. Parents must be alert to the problems and seek to correct them. Above all, the sustaining power of God is needed for parents to be successful.

SUNDAY EVENING, MAY 16

Title: A Reliable Guide for Successful Living

Text: "Think not that I am come to destroy the law, or the prophets: I am not come to destroy, but to fulfil" **(Matt. 5:17).**

Scripture Reading: Matthew 5:17–20

Introduction

Success in life is no accident; it does not just happen. We must intend to live successfully, but even strong intentions are not enough. We need a reliable guide that we can safely follow. Such a guide is offered in this portion of the Sermon on the Mount. Christ contended that the law is nothing less than a reliable guide for successful living.

I. The meaning of the law (Matt. 5:17, 20).

When Jesus spoke of the law as a reliable guide for successful living, he was not referring to the burdensome additions the scribes had added. Rather, he was speaking of the heart and essence of the law itself.

Jesus simplified what others had complicated when he made love central to the law. In so doing, Jesus reduced the 613 laws of the scribes to the law of love for one's Lord and one's neighbor. In doing this, he retained the real meaning of the law, which was reverence for God and respect for others. In this sense Jesus offered the law as a reliable guide for successful living.

In explaining the meaning of the law in verses 17 and 20, Jesus stated a fact, realized a fulfillment, and refuted a fiction.

> A. *A fact stated (v. 17).* Jesus said, "Think not that I am come to destroy the law, or the prophets." Two occasions are recorded in the Gospels in which Jesus warned people not to misjudge. The first is this occasion, and the other is when he used this same construction: "Think not that I am come to send peace on earth" (Matt. 10:34). On both occasions he was issuing a disclaimer to popular beliefs concerning him.
>
> Here Jesus disclaimed that he was a mere deconstructionist. No one was ever sent of God to do nothing but to destroy. To destroy requires little intelligence or compassion. The most unschooled person can destroy more in an hour than a great artist can create in a score of years. Therefore Jesus stood as one who would fulfill rather than destroy the law.
>
> In this statement Jesus avoided two dangers. First, he avoided the danger that he was a negative God. Second, he avoided the danger of having no standards or expectations for his followers.
>
> A great many people still think of Christ as a great destroyer. Their religious life appears to be one of simply giving up things.

Renunciation seems to be their motto. Such people forsake their passions, deny their tastes, punish their bodies, and isolate themselves from the better things of life. Here Jesus was saying that he did not come to preach the renunciation of such things, but rather the consecration of them.

Christ was no anarchist. Christ clearly avoided taking a position that would cause anyone to say, "Christ is the end of the law; now I can do whatever I please." All duties, all responsibilities, and all demands are not gone. We need the law for successful living—not the kind of burdensome laws the Pharisees and scribes created, but rather the law that Christ came to fulfill.

B. *A fulfillment realized (v. 17).* Jesus contended that he came not to destroy but to fulfill the law. To "fulfill" means to "express" the law. Jesus came to save the law from its oral distortions, to clarify its purpose, and to redefine its application. For example, when a young person completes high school and enters college, she does not destroy all that she has learned in her earlier years. As she enters college, she is endeavoring to carry the already-acquired knowledge further toward completion. In this way Christ fulfills the law. The old law was good, but it was not perfect. It had value, but it was not complete. Had this not been the case then, there would have been no need for Christ's ministry. The question is, how then did Christ fulfill the law?

1. Jesus fulfilled the law in his own person. Jesus dramatized in his own life what it means to revere God. That reverence did not consist in laboriously following rules and regulations. It expressed itself not in sacrifice but in mercy; its pattern was not legalism but love.

2. Jesus fulfilled the law by giving it inward meaning. Prior to the coming of Christ, the law related primarily to the externals of life. It concerned itself chiefly with conduct. Jesus took us to a deeper meaning of the law than simply the external actions of people. He realized that people are not always known by their actions. To know people as they really are, we must visit the inner chambers of their thoughts and imagination.

3. Jesus fulfilled the law by giving it a positive application. Jesus made the law constructive. For years the dominant theme of the law was "Thou shalt not." By the time the rabbis had superimposed their own meaning on the laws, there were so many things a person was not allowed to do that little time was left for positive thinking. Jesus changed this dramatically. He turned our attention, not so much to what we are *not* to do, as to what we *are* to do. Jesus seemed to define goodness, not so much in terms of abstaining from vices, as in obtaining virtues.

C. *A fiction refuted (v. 20).* It seems as though Jesus is asking us to do the impossible. He challenges us to exceed the righteousness of the Pharisees and scribes. In reality the Pharisees had an extremely high standard of righteousness. Why would Jesus issue such a challenge? He did so because, in their commitment to the law, the Pharisees had made the law purely external and mechanical. It lacked the inner dynamic of a religion of heart and soul. A common fiction accepted as fact was that righteousness consisted of keeping the mechanics of the law. Christ clearly denied this thinking.

In the Old Testament we find great and universal principles by which we are to live. In contrast we find very few rules and regulations. For instance, the Ten Commandments provide us with great principles, out of which we must find our own rules for life. The maze of rules and regulations with which Jesus had to contend is illustrated by an eight-hundred-page book called the Mishnah that the scribes had written interpreting the Ten Commandments. As though this volume were not enough, later Jewish scholars busied themselves making commentaries explaining the Mishnah. Today we know these commentaries as the Talmud. They consist of twelve printed volumes! And this all started with ten simple guidelines for successful living!

II. The immutability of the law (Matt. 5:18).

Here Jesus said that if heaven and earth pass away, not even a small jot or tittle of the law will pass away until it has all been fulfilled. Since situation ethics and moral relativity are the theme of many self-styled freethinkers, this statement of Christ must come to them as quite a shock.

The smallest letter, the jot, was like an apostrophe. The smallest part of a letter, the tittle, was a small projection on the foot of a letter. Christ is saying the law is so sacred that not even the smallest detail of it will ever pass away—it is immutable! The Ten Commandments are the permanent stuff on which our relation to God is built. And if we are to experience successful living, we must adopt these as our guide. There are several reasons why the law is immutable.

A. *The law is immutable because God does not change.* Malachi 3:6 quotes God as saying, "I am the LORD, I change not." Why should God change? He is perfect. He made us, and as our maker he alone knows best how we can live successfully. Therefore he gives us his laws, not to limit or restrict us, but to free us to become the best we are capable of being.

B. *The law is immutable because humankind does not change.* "Can the Ethiopian change his skin, or the leopard his spots? then may ye also do good, that are accustomed to do evil" (Jer. 13:23). A nationally known television newscaster once concluded a commentary on public scandals by quoting an ancient philosopher who said, "We need never to be surprised at what a man does if we will remember what a man is." We are reminded that human nature still requires a clearly defined, reliable guide for successful living.

C. *The law is immutable because right and wrong do not change.* Psalm 19:7 and 8 say, "The law of the Lord is perfect," and "The statutes of the Lord are right." Henry Ward Beecher once said that the law is valuable, not because it is law but because it is right.

Right and wrong do not change. The Roman Empire fell not because it was overwhelmed from without but because it decayed from within. Today's society is following that same pattern, yet God's guide for moral recovery is still the immutable law he gave us millenniums ago.

III. The measure of the law (Matt. 5:19).

Jesus said that we are measured by the law—we do not measure the law. We must remember that we sit *under the judgment* of the law; we do not sit *in judgment of* the law. We—not the law—are on trial. History documents the fact that no person can "break" the law, for the law still stands. Rather, people are broken as they violate the law.

A. *The law measures us on the basis of what we do (v. 19).* Jesus warned us against the so-called breaking of the law and of influencing anyone else to break it. Our astronauts need an external unchanging point of reference in their flights in outer space. That unchanging point of reference is some star or other heavenly body. They cannot rely on feelings or even the most sophisticated electronic equipment. Feelings and equipment can malfunction. Stars and heavenly bodies will not change. Likewise, the law serves as a reliable point of reference from which we get the direction and proper course for our lives. The law is the only reliable measure for what we do.

B. *The law measures us on the basis of what we teach (v. 19).* Jesus further warned us against teaching or in any other way influencing people to violate the law. It is bad indeed to do wrong, but it is even worse if we also lead others to do wrong by what we teach.

C. *The law measures us on the basis of what we are.* What we do and what we teach reveals what we are. And we are called to be the salt of the earth and the light of the world. How we handle the Word of God and his commandments reveals the genuineness of our Christian character.

Conclusion

The circuit-riding preachers in the old West would swim their horses across the rivers. When they were crossing an overflowing river, if they watched the swirling water around them, they could become dizzy, fall into the water, and be swept away by the current. On the other hand, if they kept their eyes fixed on a tree or rock or hill on the other side of the stream, they could ride through safely.

In the storms of life, it is the law of God that gives us calm and safety and balance. As we fix our eyes, not on the swirling water around us, but on God's eternal laws, we, too, shall ford the rivers of this life undisturbed by the water around us.

WEDNESDAY EVENING, MAY 19

Title: Swift to Hear, Slow to Speak

Text: "Wherefore, my beloved brethren, let every man be swift to hear, slow to speak, slow to wrath: for the wrath of man worketh not the righteousness of God" (James 1:19–20).

Scripture Reading: James 1:13–21

Introduction

The most difficult problem people have in regard to sin is to confess that they are wrong, that they are guilty. If you were to visit a jail and ask prisoners why they are there, you would get all kinds of answers. Some would say, "I didn't do anything; it was the people with me. I just happened to get caught!" Another would say, "I didn't have a fair trial!" Still another would say, "The judge made a mistake; someone else is guilty, and I'm paying for his crime!"

Remember how Adam, when he yielded to temptation in the garden of Eden, turned to God and said, "The woman whom thou gavest to be with me, she gave me of the tree, and I did eat" (Gen. 3:12). Then when Eve was confronted with her sin, she replied, "The serpent beguiled me, and I did eat" (3:13).

What is the problem? All of these excuses are given by people in order to exonerate themselves. The hardest thing in the world for a person to say is, "I'm guilty; I'm suffering the consequences of my own sin." So James began this section of his letter by discussing a problem that was current in his day as well as ours: Who is to blame for our sin?

I. First, James told us where to place the blame for temptation (1:13–16).

A. *James referred to temptation in the sense of outward trials—troubles and afflictions of all kinds (vv. 2–12).* First he used the noun form—"temptation"—the thing, the object, even the person who could be the source of our fall. But here the word becomes a verb—"tempted"—suggesting an act, or action. He was talking about an inward enticement to commit sin, to do evil. Of course there is a connection between the two. Outward trials are often the occasion for inward temptation to do evil. When one fails to stand successfully in the face of outward trials, the result may be a stirring up of evil impulses and desires and ultimately the committing of open sin against God.

B. *Who is responsible when temptation comes?* Is God implicated in any way at all? God does send trials. Scriptural evidence supports this fact (see Gen. 22:1; Deut. 8:2; 2 Chron. 32:31). But is God answerable for the evil effect these trials produce when we refuse to allow them to serve their intended purposes in our lives? James was both positive and conclusive when he said, "Let no man say when he is tempted, I am tempted of God: for God cannot be tempted with evil, neither tempteth he any man" (v. 13).

C. *James resolved the problem: "But every man is tempted, when he is drawn away of his own lust, and enticed" (v. 14).* Those who yield to temptation have no one to blame but themselves! In verse 15 James showed how our lustful desires produce actual sins. When a person surrenders to lust, conception takes place, and lust gives birth to sin. Sin has its roots in human nature, and humans must bear full responsibility for their evil deeds.

II. James proceeded to talk about the true character of God (1:17–18).

James did not attempt to give a deep, theological description of God. Rather, in two short sentences, he drew back the curtain and gave us a beautiful statement about God.

A. *He said that God is a beneficent God.* He is a heavenly Father who longs to do good and beautiful things for his children. In the previous verses, James had approached God from the negative standpoint, telling us that God is not the author of evil in our lives. Here he became strongly positive: "Every good gift and every perfect gift is from above" (v. 17).

B. *He said that God is immutable—unchangeable (v. 17).* James had already said that a person is often as unstable and unpredictable as the wind-tossed waves of the sea (v. 6). But he said that there is never a moment of variation with God. James used two terms from astronomy to make his point. "Variation" and "shadow of turning" were used by the ancients to describe the movement of the heavenly bodies. People do not always interpret God's actions as good, but James said there is no variance in his goodness. So what is God like? He is the beneficent giver, the unchangeable lover, and the purposeful Creator.

III. James said when to be quick and when to be slow (1:19–21).

A. *"Let every man be swift to hear, slow to speak, slow to wrath: for the wrath of man worketh not the righteousness of God" (v. 19).* What did James mean by this? He was talking about a person's readiness or eagerness to listen to God's Word. Listening is not the easiest thing a person does.

Thus James may have been referring to the attitude of reverent and quiet attention to the Word of God. This may also relate to what James said later about those who were so eager to be teachers that they had no time to be students! In other words, they could not "hear" God adequately because they were so quick to speak, to give their opinion about everything (see Eccl. 5:2).

B. *James made four key points (v. 21).*
   1. Our duty is to receive the Word of God.
   2. First we must "lay apart all filthiness."
   3. We must perform this duty with meekness.
   4. Our incentive is that God's Word can save our souls.

Conclusion

The chief glory of God's Word is that it has the ability to save our souls. We are saved when we repent of our sins and receive Jesus Christ as Lord and Savior of our lives. We are being saved as we allow God's Word, activated within us by the Holy Spirit, to bring about spiritual growth and the development of godly character.

SUNDAY MORNING, MAY 23

Title: Trouble and Triumph in the Home

Text: "He that troubleth his own house shall inherit the wind: and the fool shall be servant to the wise of heart" **(Prov. 11:29).**

Scripture Reading: Proverbs 11

Hymns: "All Hail the Power of Jesus' Name," Perronet
"Yield Not to Temptation," Palmer
"Amazing Grace," Newton

Offertory Prayer: Heavenly Father, we receive your love into our hearts this moment and return that love to you with thanksgiving in our hearts and praise on our lips. We also return it to you by giving our tithes and offerings to be used for the needs of others in the world. Thank you for the privilege of giving and for the joy of seeing you abundantly provide for our needs. Release those who are selfish and stingy from that kind of bondage. Grant that our hearts may be clean and pure as we place our offerings on your altar. In the name of him who is Lord of all, we pray. Amen.

Introduction

Our text is an unusual proverb that has a warning against troubling one's home. It is a message to all members of a household and is a plea for true harmony and happiness in the home. When we create disturbances in the home, we can expect to lose everything or, in other words, to inherit the wind.

There is no more needed message in America than the one concerning the home. Someone has said that what is wrong with America begins and ends with the family. But I hasten to say that there is hope for homes that find spiritual direction. Let us look at both the troubles and triumphs of the home today.

I. Troubles in the home.

What troubles the home today?

A. *The home is troubled by the relative morals of the times.* Popular ideas going around are "What I do is nobody's business except mine" and "Anything goes as long as no one gets hurt." These ideas are based on the philosophy that there are no absolutes in life, that all of life is relative. It is openly declared today that lies, adultery, fornication, theft, promise-breaking, and killing are sometimes permissible, depending on the situation. But let us remember the words of Galatians 6:7: "A man reaps what he sows" (NIV).

B. *The home is troubled by social pressures, as seen in financial stresses, moral needs, and social demands.* If permitted, social pressures will create disturbances in the home. Conformity to society is a powerful force.

C. *The home is troubled by moral inconsistencies.* Parents often have a double standard for what is permissible for themselves and their children. But children see the sins of their parents and are apt to copy them. What parents are surely is reflected in their children.

D. *The home is troubled by spiritual indifference, as seen in the crumbling foundations of faith and in the uprooting of spiritual relationships.* Studies in human behavior say that formal religion is one of the strongest influences of a happy home. Where husbands and wives actively participate in the life of a church, they tend to have lasting marriages. It takes much more than just a "church connection," however, for a home to know triumph. What will make our homes victorious?

II. Triumphs in the home.

A. *The home needs leadership.* God has willed that parents are the leaders in the home. Deuteronomy 6:4–9 is a command to parents to lead their children in the worship of God and the teaching of the Word in the home. God's Word is to be kept in our hearts, taught and talked about, and remembered in our daily lives. God's Word to children is in the fifth commandment, "Honour thy father and thy mother" (Ex. 20:12). These two ideas relating to parents and children dwell side by side in life. They create harmonious relations in the home.

B. *The home needs love.*

    1. Love between husbands and wives, as seen in Ephesians 5:22–23. This is God's kind of love—real, deep, and meaningful.

2. Love that transforms a home from frustration and fussing to harmony and a healthy spirit.
3. Love that communicates itself, rather than nursing itself and the wrongs done to it.
4. Love that practices faithfulness to the marriage vows made at the marriage altar.
5. Love that expresses itself in the Christlike spirit of respect and thoughtfulness in the home.
6. Love that forgives one another. This is the key to solving many family conflicts.
7. Love that is positive-minded, that strives to be an answer rather than a problem.
8. Love that is growing, realizing that none of us are full-grown. God is not finished with us yet, so let us not only be patient with him, but also with ourselves and with one another.
9. Love that shares with others in all relationships.

III. The home needs a Lord.

Most of all, the home needs a Lord, Jesus Christ, to whom the family can look for direction and power. Just as he gives abundant life to individuals, he does also to families. He gives us direction and shares his presence with us daily.

In Acts 16 a man in deep spiritual need sought help for his life spiritually. He was saved, and in the experience he made Christ Lord of his home. Is Jesus Christ Lord of your life? Is he Lord of your family?

Conclusion

Life's crises are too many and too deep to try to live without leadership, love, and Christ's lordship in your home. Will you open your heart to his triumphs? Anything less means trouble.

SUNDAY EVENING, MAY 23

Title: Believe and Behave

Text: "I say unto you, That whosoever is angry with his brother without a cause shall be in danger of the judgment" **(Matt. 5:22)**.

Scripture Reading: Matthew 5:21–48

Introduction

Perhaps the greatest demands of all the teachings of Jesus are found in this segment of the Sermon on the Mount. In the preceding four verses, Jesus declared that the law—not the burdensome laws of the scribes, but the law of God based on the two great principles of reverence for God and respect for others—is a reliable guide for successful living.

Now Jesus demonstrated how respect for others affects our behavior. He expects those of us who believe to behave! Jesus made it quite clear that Christianity is no easy "do-as-you-please" religion. In love and yet in firmness he said that if we dare bear his name, we are to believe and behave!

That Christianity is not simply a private affair between you and God is seen in that all the areas Jesus mentioned deal with your relationship to other people. Jesus said there are five problems with others that we will not have when we believe and behave.

I. The problem of anger (Matt. 5:21–26).

Jesus contended that outward conformity to the old law that forbids killing is not sufficient. He taught that we will be judged according to the inward desires of our hearts.

Quite clearly the ancient law said, "Thou shall not kill." But Jesus forbids even the attitude of anger against others. The King James Version says that a man is condemned who is angry with his brother "without a cause" (v. 22). It is significant that the words "without a cause" are not found in any of the ancient manuscripts. Jesus' statement is actually a total prohibition against anger in any form. It is not enough, according to Christian standards, simply to refrain from striking a person. Christianity requires that we not even desire to strike a person, and that we not harbor ill feelings against a brother.

A. *The danger of anger (v. 22).* The word *danger* appears three times in this one verse, obviously underscoring the danger of anger. Even a casual familiarity with Scripture gives knowledge of the occasion on which our Lord went into the temple and saw a man whose hand was deformed. Mark 3:5 records that when Jesus looked at those who opposed his healing, he did so "with anger." The apostle Paul said, "Be ye angry and sin not" (Eph. 4:26). From these two references it is obvious that anger is not always condemned in the Bible. God has given us the ability to feel anger, but he expects us to use it constructively.

We should notice in this passage in Matthew that Jesus was not speaking about anger concerning a situation but about anger directed toward individuals. It seems that what Jesus was forbidding here is selfish and vindictive anger. The word *raca* can hardly be translated because it describes a tone of voice more than content or meaning. Jesus forbids the use of this word because it displays a spirit of arrogance and contemptuous anger. He said that one who is guilty of this is liable to the judgment of God.

Jesus also forbids the use of the word *fool.* This word was used to cast aspersions on the moral character of another person. Jesus forbids us to destroy another person's name and reputation. To persist in doing so is to be liable to the severest judgment of all, the judgment of the fires of hell itself.

B. *The defeat of anger (vv. 23–26).* Jesus painted the picture of a worshiper standing before the altar. There comes to the worshipers mind the fact that someone is angry at him, or perhaps that he is angry at someone else. Should he complete his act of worship and then go solve his problem, or should he solve the problem first? Jesus contended that we should discontinue worship, go to our brother or sister, make things right, and then return to a meaningful worship experience.

Jesus was clearly saying that Christians should take the initiative in reconciliation. Such reconciliation will never come by wishful thinking or even by prayer alone. The sooner we take this initiative in asking and granting forgiveness, the better and the easier it is. The longer we wait, the more fixed becomes the attitude of resentment and anger. Therefore, Jesus said, "First be reconciled to thy brother" (v. 24).

Also in this passage Jesus was saying that Christian reconciliation is a prerequisite to fellowship with God. Whenever we hold grudges and attitudes of anger toward others, we become estranged from God. The admonition is first to be reconciled to our brother or sister and then come and offer our gift to God.

II. The problem of adultery (Matt. 27–28).

Any act that damages everyone concerned can never lead to a happy or Christlike life. In the matter of adultery, everybody involved loses. Never is there a happy ending to an affair, whether that affair be extramarital or premarital. Therefore Jesus attacked this problem head-on. He asserted that if you believe as you should, you will behave as you should in your personal morals.

A. *The root of adultery (v. 28).* Just as Jesus did in the case of murder, he distinguished between the deed and the disposition. The law condemns the act of adultery; Jesus condemned the attitude of adultery.

We can conclude that the attitude he condemned is the lustful look. But the lustful look is not the passing thought, nor a physical desire, nor a glance. If we take the law of Moses literally, a man on a desert island could never be guilty of adultery. But according to the teachings of Christ, he could if he persisted in his lustful attitude toward women. In his imagination he could treat a woman as a passing pleasure rather than as a person. A woman does not need to be physically present for him to commit adultery with her in his heart. Thus Jesus dealt with the root of the problem of adultery, which is a matter of the heart.

B. *The remedy for adultery (vv. 29–32).* Jesus seemed to offer two remedies. First, there is personal purity. It is true that amputation of an arm may remove thievery, but it does not remove the heart of the thief.

The goal Jesus was advocating was not mutilation of the body but purity of morals.

The second remedy Jesus offered was respect for marriage. Divorce was a husband's prerogative in the old Jewish law. Without recourse to courts or outward advice, he could terminate the marriage whenever he chose. All he had to do was serve a written document of divorce to his wife.

The original intention of the bill of divorcement was to protect and define a woman's rights. But Jesus said that a person who believes and behaves should go one step further. He will respect marriage as the divine institution God intended it to be.

In our application of this principle of Jesus, we must be careful not to become pharisaical in our attitude. Surely, if God will forgive those who lie, steal, or commit adultery and repent, he will forgive those who have made a mistake in their marriage.

III. The problem of dishonesty (Matt. 5:33–37).

A. *The problem of dishonesty is compounded by empty oaths (vv. 34–36)*. The Jews were notorious for dividing oaths into two classes—those that were absolutely binding and those that were not binding. For instance, an oath that contained the name of God was binding, but an oath that omitted the name of God was not binding. Those who were not familiar with this form of trickery could believe a person's oath when that oath meant absolutely nothing.

In light of this, Jesus did not forbid taking an oath such as one must take in jury service or when being inducted into the armed forces. What he did reject is on-again-off-again truth telling. He was simply saying that we must tell the truth under all circumstances.

B. *The problem of dishonesty is solved by Christian character (v. 37)*. A person's word should be his or her bond. Christians should never need to take an oath to substantiate what they are saying. Their guarantee should be their Christian character.

In the business world you may get a person to sign all kinds of contracts and take all kinds of oaths, but none of these will solve the problem of dishonesty. This problem is solved only by Christian character produced by belief in Jesus Christ that changes the way a person behaves.

IV. The problem of retaliation (Matt. 5:38–42).

Retaliation was unlimited in the early years of humankind. The law of the jungle prevailed, and might made right. If a man knocked out another man's tooth, he could expect to have all of his knocked out. Because of this unrestrained retaliation, the law embodied in Exodus 21:23–24 came into being. This law simply states, "Eye for eye, tooth for tooth."

Though it may be hard for us to understand, at that time limited retaliation was a real advancement in the area of personal morality. This law precisely
defines the amount of revenge that was permitted. But Jesus contended
that repaying evil with evil falls short of the Christian concept of believing
and behaving.

A. *The senselessness of retaliation (v. 38).* Actually, what good does retaliation do? Does it restore a lost eye, or does it replace a broken tooth?
Exchanging retorts and caustic criticism gets us nowhere except in
serious trouble. Violence has always bred violence. So Jesus underscored the senselessness of retaliation.

B. *The alternative (vv. 39–42).* The ancient law of unlimited retaliation
and the later law of limited retaliation was now replaced by Jesus with
the law of no retaliation. Here Jesus was speaking about personal
wrong done by a personal enemy. He was not delivering a discourse on
proper response in the case of modern warfare or unprovoked attack.

We should also keep in mind that Jesus was speaking to committed followers. This is difficult for mature Christians and is certainly
beyond the ability of immature children of the kingdom of God.
The overall implication of Jesus' teaching in this passage is that if we
are slapped in the face, we must neither hit back nor run. Instead,
we must stand our ground, take the insult, and demonstrate that,
as Christians, we would rather suffer wrong than do wrong.

V. The problem of hate (Matt. 5:43–48).

Personally, I believe this to be the ultimate test of the Christian who wants
to believe and behave.

A. *The destructiveness of hate (vv. 46–47).* In verse 46 Jesus said that hate
destroys our rewards. In verse 47 he contended that it destroys our
testimony in that we become no different than the lost people around
us. Hate ultimately destroys the person who hates.

Hate has a way of fastening itself on the person who does not deal
with it quickly and effectively. Hate warps our judgment, breaks down
our personal poise and peace of mind, creates nervous disorders and
high blood pressure, and can actually cause illness and death. These
facts are confirmed by leading physicians in clinical studies.

Thus it is quite obvious why Jesus said we must avoid the destructiveness of hate. We owe it to ourselves, we owe it to our Christian
testimony, we owe it to our church, and we owe it to the Christ we serve.

B. *The destruction of hate (vv. 44–45).* Jesus gives us four steps to take in
the destruction of hate.

1. We must love our enemies. This commandment can be obeyed
only by those who are Christians. Apart from the grace of God,
we can never really love a person who does not love us.

2. The second step is to bless our enemies. This means we must speak well of them. Again, obviously those who know nothing of the grace of God can never bring themselves to bless a person who was cursing them.
3. The third step is, "Do good to them." It is not difficult to do good to those who do good to you, but to do good to those who do you harm requires the lordship of Christ in the fullest sense.
4. Jesus offered a fourth and final step. He asked us to pray for our enemies. Someone has said that our natural impulse is to *prey on* our enemies, not *pray for* our enemies. Yet this is love's requirement of those who believe and behave.

Conclusion

In verse 48 Jesus said, "You, therefore, must be perfect, as your heavenly Father is perfect" (RSV). On the surface this is an impossible imperative, since no one can be as perfect as God. Yet the word *perfect* should not be interpreted to mean sinless or flawless. Rather, we should understand it to mean whole—complete and mature. Jesus seemed to be saying, "Stop acting like a child!" He admonishes us to grow up and become mature as our heavenly Father is mature and thus make our love all-inclusive.

> He drew a circle that shut me out—
> Heretic, rebel, a thing to flout.
> But Love and I had the will to win:
> We drew a circle that took him in!
>
> —*Edwin Markham*

When you draw love's circle big enough to include all humankind, you will exclude the problems of anger, adultery, dishonesty, retaliation, and hate. Then you will be numbered among those who "believe and behave."

WEDNESDAY EVENING, MAY 26

Title: How to "Practice" Your Faith

Text: "Be ye doers of the word, and not hearers only, deceiving your own selves" (**James 1:22**).

Scripture Reading: James 1:22–27

Introduction

There is no doubt that James, in addition to writing this epistle under divine inspiration, was also drawing on a rich background of experience. James was a pastor, and he had had opportunity to observe firsthand the different ways in which Christians practiced their faith. He had seen some of the people develop disappointing and even dangerous habits in regard to their "profession" and their "practice." In our text, James made a proposition, provided an illustration, and drew an application about how to practically apply one's faith.

I. James made a proposition (1:22).

In the previous passage, specifically in verse 19, James told us to be "swift to hear, slow to speak, slow to wrath." He was talking about hearing the Word of truth. But now he is calling our attention to a great danger of which we must be aware in this "swift hearing."

A. *We are not to make the hearing of the Word an end in itself.* James was talking about Christians who love to hear the Word but never get around to putting it into practice.

B. *Christians fall into two categories in regard to this issue.*
   1. Some Christians faithfully listen to the Word and even feel a "spiritual high" because of what they hear, but they never apply the truth of God's Word to their lives.
   2. Other Christians—a distressingly small percentage of the whole— receive the Word with joy and allow it to be disseminated into their life and behavior.

C. *The verb tense in James's exhortation is significant.* He said, "Be ye doers of the word, and not hearers only." The tense is present imperative, which suggests continuity. Literally, it means "keep on being doers of the word." No one becomes an accomplished "doer of the word" in one action. A process of development and growth is involved. Many Christians are like posts instead of trees. If we plant a tree, it begins to grow; if we set a post, it begins to decay.

D. *"Doers of the word" naturally take on the characteristics of their Lord.* One day an elderly Christian woman was getting on an elevator in a large department store. The elevator was dimly lighted, and to make conversation, she said to the elevator operator, "You don't get much sunshine in here, do you?" The operator replied, "Only what folks like you bring in, ma'am." Thus "doers of the word" are those who take the truth of God and, in the power of the Holy Spirit, translate it into everyday, practical illustrations of what God can and will do in one's life.

II. James provided an illustration (1:23–25).

A. *The illustration is that of a man looking at himself in a mirror and walking away, immediately forgetting what he looks like.* Christians who merely "hear" the Word of God do something similar to this. They hear the Word but soon forget it, and it has no influence on them. James implied that the Word of God is like a spiritual mirror to a person's soul. When Christians look into the mirror of the Word, they see the correct and complete delineation of their souls. They see the areas that need to be altered or cleansed.

173

B. *The mirror of the Word has a dimension that is not found in an ordinary mirror.* God's Word not only shows us where we are; it shows what we can become (v. 25). There is an interesting play on words here. The word in verse 24 translated "beholdeth" suggests only a passing glance, without any serious intention to profit from what he sees. But the word translated "looketh into" in verse 25 has the sense of looking carefully, closely, seriously. The same word is used in John 20:5 to describe John as he stooped down to look into the empty tomb. The word suggests a searching inspection of something.

C. *Why did James call this "mirror of the Word" the "perfect law of liberty"?* He called it the "law" because it is the standard by which the Christian life is regulated and directed. And by "liberty," James meant that it is a law that gives spiritual freedom to those who bring themselves under its authority.

III. James drew an application (1:26–27).

A. *He gave three examples of the practice of the Word.* First, he mentioned "the bridling of the tongue" (v. 26). James was talking about carelessness in conversation. To bridle is to restrain, to discipline, to curb. The imagery he used indicates that the tongue is like an unruly horse that needs a bit and bridle to check its wild tendencies. In verse 27 James gave two more examples of practicing one's faith: having compassion for the needy and living an unstained life.

B. *He did not give an all-inclusive definition of religion here.* Rather, he was simply saying that the "externals" of worship are unacceptable to God unless they are accompanied by loving service and a holy life.

Conclusion

Jesus said that we are to be in the world but not of the world. The proper place for a ship to be is in the water, but if the water gets into the ship, it sinks. The proper place for Christians to be is in the world, but if the world gets into Christians, they sink to the depths of unhappiness and sin. It is only as believers practice their faith that they are set in contradistinction to the world and its standards.

SUNDAY MORNING, MAY 30

Title: The Christian Family Grows—Part 1

Text: "But grow in grace, and in the knowledge of our Lord and Saviour Jesus Christ. To him be glory both now and for ever. Amen" **(2 Peter 3:18)**.

Scripture Reading: Luke 15:11–32

Hymns: "We're Marching to Zion," Watts

"Living for Jesus," Chisholm
"Here Is My Life," Seabough

Offertory Prayer: Father, blessed be your holy name to our hearts today. You have bestowed upon us many gifts. You have lavished upon us many mysteries of life. You have required of us obedience by faith. You have promised guidance when our own sight may fail us. You have proven yourself to us over and over. May we, in this offering, express our love in a finite way to you. In Jesus' name. Amen.

Introduction

(This sermon is presented in two parts because of its length.)

Life is made up of a series of stages. God has so arranged our lives that each period is supposed to prepare us for the next one. In the natural consequences of life, we go through these varying developments. Potential for major crises is present during each of these stages. Let us take a positive approach in meeting these developments. I have identified these basic stages as cherished childhood, terrific teens, adventurous adulthood, marvelous middles, and sage seniors.

I. The cherished childhood.

Cherished childhood spans the period of life from birth to puberty. It is during this time that the foundation for an individual's entire life is established. We look back with endearment on these early years of our lives.

Children are not born of their own free will. They are the result of the desire and actions of their parents. Thus parents must be responsible for their children. During the formative years, the mother and father have awesome responsibilities. The older the child becomes, the more responsibility the child must assume.

A. *Major crises.* We will take note of three major crises that all children experience: challenge of authority, struggle with insecurities, and conflict with moral values.

1. Authority. The immediate authority in children's lives are their parents. Children's growth will involve a series of trials and errors. They will experiment with almost everything in their environment in order to learn about life. This includes their parents' authority. At an early age, children will challenge the desires and demands of their parents. This is natural.

2. Security. Security is a trust of present surroundings. Insecurity is a distrust of present surroundings. If children are allowed to have their own way unwisely, as contrasted to the parents' guidance, they will get the feeling they cannot trust their parents. Children will soon begin to think that their parents are not serious when they say what to do or what not to do. This feeling of distrust brings on insecurity in the lives of children.

3. Morality. Many of us have experienced our children coming home from school with nasty words in their vocabulary. Some parents experience the shock of finding out that their child has been copying another child's paper in class. A major crisis arises when a child is introduced to a morality below biblical standards.
B. *Answer.* The rearing of children does not have to be a frightful experience. Here are some natural concepts for Christians to follow in guiding their children safely through early childhood.
   1. Love. Love your children at all times. Tell them that you love them. Do not be afraid to encourage them with kindness. When your child is the most disobedient, this is when he or she needs love the most.
   2. Example. A child longs for an example to follow. The best pattern for the life of a child is the parent. Show your children by your own actions how to act.
   3. Salvation. The greatest experience parents can have is to lead their children to a salvation experience. Parents should so live their lives that they are a continual witness of the new birth to their children. Eternity is a long time to be without Jesus Christ.

II. Terrific teens.

The teenage years encompass the time from the beginning of puberty until an individual becomes independent from his or her parents. The transitional period between childhood and adolescence is difficult, but the teen years are terrific! This is the time when an individual meets some of life's most exciting formative challenges.

A. *Major crises.* Teenagers are responsible for their own deeds even while they are under the authority of their parents. This fact, coupled with an awkward period of development, brings on several specific crises.
   1. Rebellion against authority. Life is a developmental process. Responsibility and authority flow continually from the parents to the child. The parents have all the authority and responsibility over the child when he or she is quite young. The older the child becomes, the more personal responsibility and authority the child must assume. The parents must in turn relinquish responsibility and authority as the child develops. The greatest exchange of this responsibility is during the teenage years when the child is becoming an adult. Sometimes the child may be impatient, while the parents may be too hesitant. This conflict causes rebellion on the part of the teenager.
   2. Lack of purpose. Most teenagers do not have a clear understanding of the purpose for their lives. They try different things, sometimes with success and sometimes with failure and frustration.
   3. Immorality. These crises sometimes push teenagers into experimenting with a new power that has been realized within their

bodies—the power of sex. When individuals reach puberty, they gain a totally new perspective regarding their bodies. New worlds of conflict and temptation open to them.

B. *Answer.* Praise God that there is a source of help for teenagers and their problems. These are years of great sensitivity, potential, and learning. These are the very years during which our God wants to capture the minds, souls, and bodies of his creatures. If individuals become "turned on to Jesus" during their terrific teens, their accomplishments for God are almost without limit.

God gave me the answer to the crises of the teenage years when I was about sixteen years old. Jesus Christ came into my heart, and God immediately placed Matthew 6:33 at the front door of my heart: "But seek ye first the kingdom of God, and his righteousness; and all these things shall be added unto you." Every aspect of life will be placed in its proper perspective if individuals will seek out God's will for their lives.

Conclusion

God's will instills, in both the parents and the teenager, wisdom that enables both to accept and to yield responsibility and authority in unison.

God's will instills a specific sense of purpose and destiny in the life of the teenager. God's will instills a morality and a righteousness in the adolescent during these critical years. God is our Creator and therefore knew from the beginning all of the problems we would face as we matured. Do not think for one minute that he has no plan for you where you are! God has the answer. Praise God he allows us to have access to it.

SUNDAY EVENING, MAY 30

Title: When Your Halo Is Too Tight

Text: "Moreover when ye fast, be not, as the hypocrites, of a sad countenance: for they disfigure their faces, that they may appear unto men to fast. Verily I say unto you, They have their reward" (**Matt. 6:16**).

Scripture Reading: Matthew 6:1–18

Introduction

When we suspect that certain individuals have their religion on parade, we say they are wearing their halos too tight. When your halo is too tight, all kinds of complications set in. When your hat is too tight, you get a headache. But when your halo is too tight, you give other people a headache. You turn them off and make Christianity distasteful and Christ unattractive.

An old slogan of the advertising industry is "Running a business without advertising is like winking at a girl in the dark. You know what you're doing, but she doesn't." The slogan is true. It pays to advertise. Advertisements empty attics and garages of dust collectors and line our pockets with dollars. They stimulate sales and increase profits!

There are some things, however, that advertising kills. One is humility. Advertise it, and it becomes pride. Another is altruism. Advertise it, and it becomes egotism. Advertise spirituality, and it becomes hypocrisy.

Jesus spoke out against wearing our halos too tight. He warned of three areas where we must avoid any ostentatious demonstration of superior piety. To advertise our spirituality is to destroy it!

I. Your halo is too tight when you do good deeds to attract attention (Matt. 6:1–4).

Jesus assumed that we would work and thus did not warn us against idleness. He took our good deeds for granted and in no way was advocating secret discipleship. He was warning us against wrong motives, against doing our good deeds to attract attention to ourselves. T. S. Eliot, in his book *Murder in the Cathedral*, said, "The last temptation is the greatest treason: to do the right deed for the wrong reason."

On the surface it might appear that this teaching conflicts with Jesus' teaching in Matthew 5:16 that we should do our work and live in such a way as to let our light shine before others. In reality the conflict is only surface. When Jesus admonished us to let our light shine, it was for the purpose that we would glorify God and lead others to become his followers. But now he dealt with the practice of individuals putting their piety on parade. The end result of such religion is to glorify oneself and not God. In Matthew 6:2 when Jesus said they will "have their reward," he used a word from the business world. This word signifies the settlement of an account. Thus he was saying that when we do our deeds before others and receive their applause, our transaction has resulted in our good deeds being paid for by the attention from others. For instance, the generous giver is called generous, and thus his or her account is paid in full and closed. Those who do good deeds for the praise of others have received their reward by being acclaimed "truly spiritual people." They have received what they really wanted and all that they will ever get.

When we do good deeds not to call attention to ourselves but as an expression of our love for God, we are following the precepts of Christ. To do good deeds for any other reason is to destroy the blessing and joy of having done them. This happens only when your halo is too tight.

II. Your halo is too tight when you pray to impress others (Matt. 6:5–15).

Something dies within us and within our prayer life whenever we advertise it. To aid us in keeping our prayer life alive and vibrant, Jesus issued a plea, offered a pattern, and made a promise.

    A. *A plea (vv. 5–8).* Quite pointedly Jesus' plea was that we should not pray like the hypocrites do. Our prayers are to be a sincere matter between ourselves and our God. We are not to get lost in needless verbiage. Definite times of the day were set aside for prayer by committed Jews. Beyond attending their worship service at set times, they were expected to pray at 9:00 a.m., 12:00 noon, and 3:00 p.m. every day. From this practice, since the days of Ezra, the prayer life of Israel had become increasingly mechanical and routine. Jesus contended that our halo is too tight when we pray to impress others.

The specified hour of prayer might overtake a person anywhere. Hypocrites were quite pleased if it caught them in a public place. In fact, they often took great care to arrange such a situation. Jesus said in verse 5 that they loved to stand in synagogues and on street corners to be seen by others when they prayed.

Jesus was not condemning public prayer. On many occasions he attended the synagogue and engaged in public prayer. His disciples followed the same practice. Rather, Jesus was asking us to direct our prayer to God instead of to the galleries. If our public prayer is so directed, it will be as private a prayer as we might offer in the quietness of our home.

Jesus asked that we not think of prayer as the repetition of many, many words. Our heavenly Father knows what we need even before we ask. We may liken God to a large reservoir filled with water. Our prayers do not place water in the reservoir; they only open the gates and allow the water to flow. Prayer is never overcoming God's reluctance, but rather is laying hold on his willingness.

B. *A pattern (vv. 8–13).* The best-known prayer in history can be repeated in twenty seconds. It is composed of sixty-six words, fifty of which are one-syllable words. This prayer is simple enough to be understood by a child and yet profound enough to express the heart's desires of the most mature. On one hand, the prayer is personal enough to be prayed in private and, on the other hand, public enough to be prayed by entire congregations in worship services.

Jesus certainly had no intention of stifling spontaneous prayers when he said, "After this manner therefore pray ye" (v. 9). This prayer pattern is not designed as a straitjacket but as a stimulant to meaningful prayer.

Jesus used his favorite term for God when he admonished us to call God "our Father." This expression speaks of the direct access we have to our Father. Heaven had come to denote the majesty of God. Therefore Jesus, in his prayer, spoke of our Father as one who abides in heaven. Such an invocation opens the way for the requests that follow. It is significant that the first petition of the prayer is an expression of adoration: "Hallowed be thy name." To hallow God's name is to hold God's name in respect and reverence.

The reign of God is expressed in the words "Thy kingdom come." In a very real sense, God's reign has already begun, but his consummation awaits the future. As disciples we are to wait and pray. The kingdom of God is both a future promise and a present possession. It is open for business in the here and now, and people can enter it today. But it is our responsibility to work with God in bringing about the realization of his kingdom. Therefore we are to pray, "Thy will be done in earth, as it is in heaven."

Jesus directed his attention from the future to the present in the second half of this prayer. He said that we should pray, "Give us this day our daily bread." It is true that a person does not live by bread alone, but it is equally true that without bread he or she does not live at all. Jesus is clearly saying that God is vitally interested in our physical needs. When we go hungry, God cares.

Our present need is also characterized by the requirement for daily forgiveness. Thus we are to request that our heavenly Father will "forgive us our debts, as we forgive our debtors." Both sin and hunger are daily occurrences. Surely the latter part of that request underscores the fact that an unforgiving spirit in us closes the door to God's forgiveness.

Temptation is an ever-present problem in the Christian's life. Our request is that God will "lead us not into temptation, but deliver us from evil." The very natural human aversion to difficult encounters is expressed in this prayer, as well as a cry for help when such encounters come our way. We are to pray that God will spare us trials that will severely test our faith. When such trials come, we pray that he will give us the ability to live through them victoriously.

C. *A promise (vv. 6, 14–15).* Just how God will reward our secret prayers, we do not know. But that he will do it, we can be most assured, for this is his promise.

After Jesus completed the pattern prayer, he felt it necessary to go back and extract one of the petitions and give it special attention: "as we forgive our debtors." Refusing to forgive others is detrimental to the person who refuses to grant such forgiveness. Unforgiveness can wreck personal health, destroy our sense of well-being, spoil our relation to other people, and build a barrier between us and God.

The person who does not forgive thinks more of grudges than grace and more of halos than holiness. Your halo is too tight when in your prayers to impress others there is no room for forgiving those who have offended you.

III. Your halo is too tight when you fast to appear spiritual (Matt. 6:16–18).

Just like advertising the prayers we offer and the good deeds we do, advertising our fasting destroys whatever blessings it might bring. It appears that the fasting prevalent in Jesus' day had three main purposes. First, it was designed to draw attention from God to the individual who fasted. Second, it was an obvious attempt to prove that repentance was genuine. And third, fasting was often vicarious. That is, it was not designed for one's own personal benefit, but rather to move God to save a nation from its problems.

We are admonished by Jesus not to look dismal like the hypocrites when we fast. Jesus is saying that we are never to put our piety on parade.

Contemporary "fasting" may operate in a different manner. For instance, individuals may arrive at church late so that their attendance will be noticed by everyone. Or they may contribute to good causes with the main intention of being recognized for their generosity. Beware of those seeking public office who go out of their way to announce that they are an "ordained elder" or a deacon, steward, or minister.

The question is, "What is legitimate fasting?" Not long ago I was visiting with a small child who was critically ill. Her mother was at her bedside. Assuming that the mother had not eaten recently, I asked, "Have you had any dinner this evening?" Her reply was simply, "No."

Then I asked if she had eaten any lunch, and then if she had eaten any breakfast. The answer was still no. She looked up at me and said, "Pastor, I've been so concerned about my child that I've really not wanted anything to eat." It is possible to center one's mind so much on God that one does not care for physical food. In such a case, fasting comes from the heart and soul.

In verses 16–18, Jesus explained the great paradox of the Christian's reward. Those who look for rewards and who assume they are deserving never really receive them. On the other hand, those who diligently work for the kingdom of God and who never think they deserve a reward do in fact receive that reward.

Conclusion

Halos are a figment of the imagination created by medieval artists. And in spiritual matters they are doubly a figment of the imagination. Your relation to Christ and to others will become far more meaningful when you not only stop wearing your halo so tight but stop wearing it at all!

JUNE

■ Sunday Mornings

Continue the series "Strengthening Christian Marriage and Family Living" through Father's Day. On the last Sunday of the month, begin a nine-sermon series titled "The Spiritual Struggle for the Renewal of the Church," which will take you through August 22. We need to cooperate with the Father God, who would prune out those branches—attitudes, ambitions, actions—that are counterproductive, so that the church might bear much fruit.

■ Sunday Evenings

Complete the series "Listening to Heaven's Infallible Teacher" from the Sermon on the Mount.

■ Wednesday Evenings

Continue the series from the book of James with the theme "The Practical Expression of Our Faith in Daily Living."

WEDNESDAY EVENING, JUNE 2

Title: Those Who Please God

Text: "If ye fulfil the royal law according to the scripture, Thou shalt love thy neighbour as thyself, ye do well: but if ye have respect to persons, ye commit sin, and are convinced of the law as transgressors" (**James 2:8–9**).

Scripture Reading: James 2:1–1

Introduction

As we noted earlier in this series of studies, the epistle of James is doubtlessly the most practical treatise in all of Holy Scripture. James made no attempt to teach theology; he left that to others. Being a pastor, dealing with individuals day after day, he was far more concerned with the application and expression of the Christian faith. In many respects, this second chapter may be considered the heart of James's message, for in it he gave a description of the character of faith. He showed that the expression of this kind of faith is that which pleases God in our lives.

I. First, let's examine the precept that James set forth (2:1).

A. *Probably the most common sin among believers is the sin James spelled out in this passage—showing favoritism.* In fact, it is such a common practice that we often allow it to exist without our consciences even bothering us about it. But James was saying, in effect, "Do not hold to the Christian faith—which sees every believer saved by grace through faith, not of works—and at the same time practice discrimination between different classes of people in the fellowship. For this is a shameful demonstration of hypocrisy!" Because we cannot know everything there is to know about a person, we cannot possibly judge a person correctly. This truth was driven home vividly to Peter at Cornelius's house. He had resented the mission God had given to him—to go and preach to Gentiles—yet when he saw what God had wrought among them, he declared, "Of a truth I perceive that God is no respecter of persons" (Acts 10:34).

B. *James spoke of having "the faith of our Lord Jesus Christ," and he drew a comparison between that and our having "respect of persons."* What was he saying? In essence, "Let there be agreement between what you profess has taken place on the inside and what you express on the outside." James was simply reiterating the general theme of his epistle: "Be ye doers of the word, and not hearers only" (1:22).

C. *Note that James called Jesus "the Lord of glory."* Jesus Christ should be the glory of every believer at all times. As we observe our fellow believers and are tempted to criticize and discriminate between them, let us remember that within every believer is the glory of God in Jesus Christ. It is the same glory, and before God there is no partiality shown.

II. Second, let's consider an illustration of this precept (2:2–4).

A. *James painted the picture of two men coming into the church.* One was a rich man, finely and elaborately dressed, and the other was a poor man, dressed in keeping with his meager means. Then James showed, hypothetically, how we might treat these two worshipers in the church assembly. From the descriptions of the men given, it is unlikely that either was a believer. Yet when they arrived, the richly dressed man was shown great respect, not because of his true worth but because of his outward appearance of wealth and position. In contrast, the poor man was treated harshly, with no warmth or compassion.

B. *James then made an application.* "Have you not made distinctions among yourselves, and become judges with evil thoughts?" (v. 4 RSV). He was saying that it is wrong to honor the rich at the expense of the poor. Both stand on the same level before God and should be treated accordingly. James said two things about those who practice partiality.

   1. They have made distinctions among themselves. In other words, they are at odds with themselves. There is a wide difference between profession and practice.

   2. They are "judges with evil thoughts." James brought a serious charge against any professing believer who shows partiality or respect of persons.

III. Third, let's see why having respect of persons is sinful (2:5–11).

A. *The principle James stated is simply, "Hath not God chosen the poor of this world rich in faith, and heirs of the kingdom which he hath promised to them that love him?" (v. 5).* Here he set forth three blessings that God has bestowed on the poor.

   1. They are chosen of God. God chose them through his Spirit, convicted them of sin, and drew them with love toward himself.

   2. God has made the poor "rich in faith." Their wealth does not consist in gold rings or fine apparel but in faith.

   3. He said that they are "heirs of the kingdom." They possess, and have become a part of, the kingdom of God.

B. *Then James became practical.* "Do not rich men oppress you, and draw you before the judgment seats?" (v. 6). And not only so, but the rich were those who most often blasphemed the name of Jesus. Of course, this was not a blanket condemnation of all rich people. Some wealthy people in the early church were generous and faithful servants of God, just as they are today. But on the whole, this was not the case.

C. *The principle involved is that partiality is a violation of the royal law of God (v. 8).* What is the "royal law"? It is the law of love expressed in the command "Thou shalt love thy neighbor as thyself." Why "royal"? Perhaps because Christ, the true King, is its disseminator.

Conclusion

Verse 12 is James's conclusion of this passage: "So speak ye, and so do, as they that shall be judged by the law of liberty." James gives both an appeal and a warning here. The appeal is that obedience to the royal law be expressed both in speech and action. The warning is that those who show no mercy will find none at God's judgment (v. 13). So how do we please God? By showing mercy and love to all people regardless of their station in life.

SUNDAY MORNING, JUNE 6

Title: The Christian Family Grows—Part 2

Text: "According to my earnest expectation and my hope, that in nothing I shall be ashamed, but that with all boldness, as always, so now also Christ shall be magnified in my body, whether it be by life, or by death. For to me to live is Christ, and to die is gain" **(Phil. 1:20–21)**.

Scripture Reading: Philippians 1:15–2:4

Hymns: "One Day," Chapman
"I Am Resolved," Hartsough
"Blest Be the Tie," Fawcett

Offertory Prayer: God of mercy, how we adore you. When our hearts reflect on your greatness and our smallness, we are amazed that you even notice us. But you do! We praise you for this. As this offering is extended from our hearts to yours, may it be an expression of our love to you. In Jesus' name we pray. Amen.

Introduction

Five basic stages make up life's maturing process. These five periods are identified as cherished childhood, terrific teens, adventurous adulthood, marvelous middles, and sage seniors. Last week we covered the first two of these, the cherished childhood and the terrific teens. Today I want us to note how our heavenly Father guides us through the crises and challenges of the stages of adventurous adulthood, marvelous middles, and sage seniors.

I. Adventurous adulthood.

Teenagers have some special concerns as they reach adulthood. They are bombarded with questions like "How will I make my living? Whom will I marry? Who pays the bills now? Where will I live? Do I need insurance?" Nature forces them to face the reality of each of these issues.

Adulthood is the stage in life when individuals leave the shelter and protection of their parents and establish a home of their own. They choose a vocation, secure the proper education, and develop the necessary skills. They usually marry and rear a family during these years. Adventurous adulthood generally ends when the individual has completed formal education, attained basic financial security, brought children through their formative years, and approached the "fortyish" period of life.

A. *Major crises.* As with every other period, the adult years bring certain challenges to the individual. The areas of concern involve the selection of and preparation for a vocation, establishment and development of a family, and the individual's basic attitudes toward life. There are three specific crises many adults experience in these areas.
   1. Vocation. People cannot perceive all of the problems and shortcomings that may be involved in the particular vocation they select. When the new wears off and problems and limitations appear, many decide they are in the wrong vocation. This is a crisis, especially if their family requires continuing support.
   2. Marriage. Most people do not take marriage as seriously as they should when they approach it. But once the wedding and honeymoon are over, marriage becomes a very serious matter.
      Crisis comes when an individual feels that an improper marriage has taken place. What do you do? Do you give up and try again with someone else? Do you just walk away from it all? How do you escape a marriage that should not have been? Is there room for immorality within a bad marriage?

3. Materialism. The secular world forces the Christian to give consideration to finances. One of the greatest temptations of the success-minded adult is to become oriented to a materialistic lifestyle. He or she is tempted to lose sight of important values.

B. *Answer.* In Romans 12:1–2 God provides an answer for adults with problems and burdens. He calls for people to dedicate their entire beings to the way of righteousness.

The problems and perplexities of a bad marriage can be worked out. Divorce can be avoided. Immorality can be shunned. Victory in the home is available to persons completely yielded to God.

If you conform your will to the eternal will of God, even your vocation will be directed by him. Materialistic ideals will give way to Christian ideals. God has the answer to our every need: it is through surrender to his way.

II. Marvelous middles.

Middle age may easily be the most marvelous of all periods of life. It is during this span of life that God sends a second generation into the home. Grandchildren are great joys to the heart. During your marvelous middles you come to a new appreciation of your spouse. You should have more creativity and more time to express it. The body tends to slow down, but the mind speeds up.

A. *Major crises.* No attempt is made to identify the exact age limit to this period called middle age, but the realistic individual will recognize it. Certain crises are awaiting those advancing to this stage in life.

1. Nonacceptance. Many people have difficulty accepting the fact that they have reached middle age. Many people have a fear of growing older. This fear is due to ignorance of the joys of this time of life.

2. Vocation. It is during the marvelous middles that individuals may realize that they will never be the president of their company. There is a letdown when reality hits and dreams are vanquished. If these individuals have had the wrong goals all along, this letdown can be absolutely devastating.

3. Marriage. Middle age sometimes brings on a marital crisis. The man or woman may seem to have lost some youthful sexual power. Satan tells these people they have to prove themselves. Foolish escapades may disrupt the golden opportunities of middle age. Many spouses neglect one another for the sake of their children. Then when their children leave home, they suddenly find themselves staring across the table at a spouse they have never really known.

4. Stress. Both mental and physical stress are common during this period. The body is not as active or as strong as it once was, yet people still have basic goals and desires to fulfill.

B. *Answer.* The individual who has reached middle age needs dynamic guidelines. Paul, a middle-aged man or older, wrote these words of wisdom to us: "Not that I speak in respect of want: for I have learned, in whatsoever state I am, therewith to be content. . . . I can do all things through Christ which strengtheneth me. . . . But my God shall supply all your need according to his riches in glory by Christ Jesus" (Phil. 4:11, 13, 19).

This message of our Lord to our souls will meet every single need we have. It will keep us pure before our Lord and respectable before our spouse. It will keep us happy in our endeavors.

III. Sage seniors.

We refer to the older ones in our Christian community as the sage seniors. Those who have been exposed to God's grace for so many years are wise in spirit and kind in heart. Yet this is the most difficult period of life. This is the time for which all other ages are meant to prepare us.

A. *Major crises.* The crises facing these giants in the faith would crumble teenagers and young adults. Only those who have faced years of experience can stand under these challenges.

1. Death. This is the usual time when a spouse of many years is lost and close friends pass away. The time until one's death is now limited to years instead of decades.
2. Vocation. Retirement has come and with it a fixed income. Inflation becomes a hungry giant that constantly eats away at the retirement check.
3. Health. The body grows weak and health begins to fade away. Dependency on others for some very common matters tends to be depressing.
4. Dreams. All dreams have passed for this life. Even many hopes and expectations for one's children are obviously going unfulfilled.

B. *Answer.* All is not lost. Rather, the years of the sage seniors may be the very best of all. God wants us to enjoy life until our very last day. He has given us the words to help us do just that in Philippians 4:6–7: "Do not be anxious about anything, but in every situation, by prayer and petition, with thanksgiving, present your requests to God. And the peace of God, which transcends all understanding, will guard your hearts and your minds in Christ Jesus" (NIV). God's "keeping power" is ours through Christ Jesus. That is the answer to any problem faced by our sage seniors.

Conclusion

Every person at every age has his or her own crises and challenges. God is gracious to give to each a sufficient answer. His answers are yours for the acceptance.

SUNDAY EVENING, JUNE 6

Title: The Good Life

Text: "But seek ye first the kingdom of God, and his righteousness; and all these things shall be added unto you" **(Matt. 6:33)**.

Scripture Reading: Matthew 6:19–34

Introduction

Many years ago, in an effort to boost circulation, the St. Petersburg, Florida, *Times* ran clues to a treasure of two hundred dollars that had been buried somewhere in the greater St. Petersburg area. Two thousand people gathered in front of the newspaper building on the day the final clue was printed. During the next thirty minutes, several unusual things happened. A half dozen people were injured in automobile wrecks. A number of women passed out in the crowd gathered in front of the *Times* office building. Four people had to be rescued from waist-deep mud. And the stakes on a building site were torn up by a crowd in its mad search for the hidden treasure. In retrospect the newspaper stunt was a big success; circulation had increased 5 percent.

In a very real sense, the lure of gold can become a mania. A popular American pastime is the effort to get something for nothing. The search for the good life is often an all-controlling interest. Frequently it leads to all sorts of unusual behavior, some of which is pathetic, humorous, or tragic.

Since Jesus knew this to be so, he dedicated much of his time to the human search for the good life. Christ saw men and women losing their souls in their effort to discover things that would make them happy. In the Sermon on the Mount, he dealt with this subject in a direct manner. He said that the good life is a life of wise investments, unwavering loyalty, and simple trust.

I. The good life is a life of wise investments (Matt. 6:19–23).

Why is the good life a life of wise investments? Because the things we live for determine the direction of our lives. The great philosopher Spinoza said that the three things people want most are honor, riches, and satisfaction of lust.

A. *Treasure on earth.* The truth is that most of us are not piling up treasures on earth. We hardly have enough to pay our bills and taxes and fulfill our financial obligations to family and community. In this passage, however, Jesus was not so much concerned with the amount of money we have as he was with the direction of our lives and the quality of our daily existence. Jesus realized that our attitude toward things, regardless of the amount we might have, determines the direction of our souls and the destiny of our lives.

Rugs and garments and tapestries were some of the goods persons hoarded and relied on for financial security in Jesus' day. All of these things could easily deteriorate or be stolen. Jesus contended that accumulation of these things is no protection against the invasion of warped judgment and barrenness of soul.

An eighty-four-year-old rag picker who had died in abject poverty was buried in a pauper's grave in New York. Several days after his burial, the city authorities discovered a fortune of more than $500,000 belonging to the old man in a Brooklyn warehouse vault. His name was Henry Chapin Smith. He was a graduate of Harvard and had been a classmate of Robert Frost and a friend of the philosopher Henry James. His life stands as a mute reminder of the futility of placing our trust in things.

The principle Jesus sets forth is that whenever we depend on money alone for security, life has a way of folding up no matter what the level of security may be. Jesus contends that these are unwise investments.

B. *Treasures in heaven.* But how can we lay up treasures in heaven? How can we make wise investments? We make wise investments when we invest in acts of forgiveness, understanding, and love. We increase in our richness toward God when we turn away from deeds that are shoddy and cheap and wrong. Deposits are made in the bank of heaven in our name when we live with courage, love, faith, and hope. Whenever we live this kind of life, we accumulate wealth that will last forever.

Jesus made a statement in verse 21 that most of us fail to understand: "Where your treasure is, there will your heart be also." It is important that we realize that he did not say where your heart is, there will your treasure be. He was simply saying that where we make our greatest investment is where we begin to have our greatest interest. Your heart and interest may not be in a particular project or program, but when you invest heavily in it, you become vitally concerned with its outcome. A good life is a life of wise investments.

II. The good life is a life of unwavering loyalty (Matt. 6:24).

There is nothing intrinsically wrong with wealth. What is wrong is putting wealth before God or, more than that, making wealth our god. In this passage Jesus is not advocating poverty but priority. Immediately verse 33 comes to mind, where Jesus said, "Seek ye first the kingdom of God, and his righteousness; and all these things shall be added unto you." This is no prohibition against wealth, but it is an admonition to get our priorities in order.

Divided loyalties make for disturbed minds and confused goals. Divided loyalties cause all kinds of physical and mental illnesses. The investigations of modern medicine and psychiatry underscore in a striking way the truth of these words of Jesus that "no man can serve two masters." When we attempt to do so, we are caught in the middle every time.

But how can we develop a life of unwavering loyalty? How can we be careful not to attempt to serve two masters? The answer is surely in Paul's statement in Philippians 3:13: "This one thing I do." When we focus our attention and power on a single object, we discover strength that we never knew we had. But when we cannot decide on our goals and priorities, our life becomes weak and we can become paralyzed in any effort to move forward.

Jesus said in Luke 17:32, "Remember Lot's wife." She was a good example of divided loyalty. She had known God from her childhood, but she had fallen too much in love with the things of Sodom. She sincerely wanted God, but she also wanted Sodom. Finally, the day of decision came. She made a feeble start toward God, but then she looked back toward Sodom. She was reaching for God with one hand, but with the other she was reaching back for the things of Sodom. Her divided loyalty brought misery and ultimately destruction.

We must settle once and for all who is master of our lives and where our loyalties will remain. Once that decision has been made, we can experience the good life that comes through a life of unwavering loyalty.

III. The good life is a life of simple trust (Matt. 6:25–34).

The antithesis of trust is fear and worry. We may worry about what we will eat or what we will drink or what we will wear or what will happen tomorrow. Jesus was well acquainted with the universal plague of fear. His solution was simple trust in God.

a) *Simple trust observes God's care in nature (vv. 25–31).* Jesus drew on God's care for creation to substantiate his claims. He reminded his listeners that the birds of the air are cared for, the flowers of the field are clothed, and even the grass is not forgotten. Jesus then made his point. Since God cares for these, he surely cares for those who are made in his image.

A little poem sums up beautifully this lesson of Christ:

> Said the sparrow to the robin,
> "I should really like to know
> Why these anxious human beings
> Rush around and worry so."
>
> Said the robin to the sparrow,
> "Friend, I think that it must be
> That they have no heavenly Father
> Such as cares for you and me."
>
> —*Elizabeth Cheney*

b) *Simple trust is reassured by God's knowledge of our needs (vv. 32–33).* Jesus was not arguing in this passage against planning, saving, or working.

He does not want us to neglect our responsibilities, and he was not advocating idleness. Rather than showing trust, these reveal a spirit of presumption. The real thrust of this passage is captured in the New International Version translation of the phrase "Take no thought." It more accurately translates this as "Do not worry." This idea is repeated five times in verses 25–34.

Certainly we must consider what we will eat or what we will wear or our state of health or our future. But we must never allow these things to become an obsession. If we do, they will become a burden to our soul, and we will find ourselves continually anxious and fearful. But how can this be avoided? The answer is simple yet profound. We can be assured that God both knows our needs and will supply them, for simple trust is reassured by the knowledge that God is aware of all our needs.

c) *Simple trust lives one day at a time (v. 34). The Living Bible* translates this verse, "So don't be anxious about tomorrow. God will take care of your tomorrow too. Live one day at a time."

This is not an admonition to avoid facing life seriously. Rather, we are being told that troubles can best be met by dealing with them one at a time. We are assured that God will grant the strength required for the troubles of tomorrow when they come just as he provides that strength for today.

Much of our anxiety about tomorrow will subside when we realize that many of today's difficulties are not permanent. An elderly minister was once asked to quote his favorite Scripture verse. His reply came without hesitation, "And it came to pass." Then this grand old man of God explained that through his many years he had come to realize that difficulties and wars and debts and burdens to humankind "come to pass."

Too often we feel that the adversity of today or the problems that we fear tomorrow will be with us unto death. History calms this fear. In our effort to live one day at a time, we must never borrow trouble from tomorrow. Are not most of our worries about the future? We worry about surgery we may never have, a child who goes wrong but in time turns out well, or enemies who eventually become our friends. Insurance companies have gotten wealthy by insuring people against fear of future disasters that never happen.

Conclusion

Cecil B. DeMille told how, many years earlier in his life, he was commissioned to write a play that later became *The Return of Peter Grimm*. The story concerned the continuation of life after death.

DeMille went on to share how he drew inspiration for that story from a water beetle on a lake where he was canoeing. He was reading and resting and searching for an idea. As DeMille looked down at the water, he saw a small water beetle that crawled up on the little boat, stuck its talons into the woodwork, and died. DeMille said he simply left it alone and returned to his reading. The sun was hot, and about three hours later he looked up from what he was doing to see the little beetle parched, with its back cracking open. He watched, and out of the back of the dead beetle he saw a new form with wings emerging. DeMille said it was a most beautiful dragonfly, reflecting the many colors of the rainbow. Then the dragonfly began to move its wings and lift itself from the boat. It flew farther in one second than the water beetle had crawled in hours. For a moment it hovered over the lake just a few inches from the water with the beetles below. They were totally unaware of its presence.

DeMille flipped the shriveled remains of the old water beetle's husk from the canoe into the lake. It quickly sank into the mud-covered bottom. Other beetles crawled awkwardly to see what it was. Then they backed away from it. DeMille asked, "If God does that for a water beetle, don't you believe he will do it for you and me?"

And when God does this for us, we will be thankful that, through our wise investments, unwavering loyalty, and simple trust, the good life we have known here gives way to a better life hereafter.

WEDNESDAY EVENING, JUNE 9

Title: When Faith Is Alive

Text: "What does it profit, my brethren, if a man says he has faith but has not works? Can his faith save him? . . . Faith by itself, if it has no works, is dead" **(James 2:14, 17 RSV).**

Scripture Reading: James 2:14–26

Introduction

Someone has said that faith is like calories: you can't see them, but you can see their results. Tonight we study a section of James's letter that is probably the most misunderstood passage in the entire letter. Some see this passage as a contradiction of Paul's teaching concerning the way of salvation. But when the teachings of both Paul and James are understood properly, there is no conflict. Three things must be kept in mind as we study these verses.

A. *The situations presented by James were entirely different from those presented by Paul.* Paul had in mind those who denied the doctrine of salvation by grace through faith and insisted on ceremonial works, whereas James was saying that true faith expresses itself in deeds. Paul was talking about the *way* of salvation, and James was talking about the *life* of a person after he or she has been saved.

B. *While Paul and James used many of the same words, they put different meanings into them.* By "works" Paul meant works of the Jewish law—ceremonies and rituals. For James, "works" were works of love, proof that faith was alive and real.

C. *James's intention was not to contrast two opposing methods of salvation.* His intention was to show two kinds of faith—one genuine and the other false, one alive and the other dead.

I. James said that true faith produces (2:14–17).

A. *He tried to show that things such as mental agreement, or saying we accept Christ, do not mean much unless they are proved by the fruits of faith at work.* Almost with an air of disgust, James said, in essence, "What good is faith without works? Does it help anyone?"

B. *Note that James did not write, "If a man* has *faith," but "If a man* says *he* has faith."John Bunyan, the author of *Pilgrim's Progress,* had a character named Talkative, and of that character he said, "Religion has no place in his heart, or house or conduct; all he has lies in his tongue, and his religion is just something to make a noise with." This is the kind of person James was describing.

C. *Note the statement, "Can faith save him?" (v. 14).* An adjective is implied that does not appear in the wording here. It is better read, "Can *that* faith save him?" The reference is to that false, fruitless faith James had just described.

II. James's theme is that true faith is alive (2:18–20).

A. *This is another difficult area of the epistle.* James seems to have been dramatizing here, as he often did in this epistle. He felt so certain of what he was saying about faith and works that he saw an imaginary man rising in support of what he had been saying. This man turned to the one in the assembly who made a profession of faith but did not prove it by works. This may well have been the man James described in the preceding illustration, who had said to the cold and hungry, "Be ye warmed and filled" (2:16). With righteous indignation, the first man burst out, "You hypocrite! Of what use are your long prayers, of what use is your profession of faith, since you just had the opportunity to practice it and failed to do so?"

B. *What is the principle here?* Faith is something that dwells in the deepest recesses of the heart, and only God can see it. Others can only see the outward appearance. But if there is faith deep in the heart, it cannot but manifest itself in outward expression. Ralph Erskine, a great Scottish preacher of the seventeenth century, used to say, "Faith and works are the two feet with which a man walks in Christ." One without the other produces a spiritual cripple.

C. *James showed a bit of "sanctified wit" (v. 19)*. In spite of the fact that demons are afraid of God, they do not obey him. Fear can never inspire obedience that pleases God. Much so-called religion today is prompted by a slavish fear. If we try to obey and serve God out of this kind of fear, our obedience and service will never be accepted.

III. James said that true faith produces obedience (2:21–26).

A. *James was not teaching that Abraham's justification or "acquittal" before God depended on his works to the exclusion of faith.* He was not even saying that his justification depended on works in addition to faith. He was saying that one's justification before God is simply by faith, but it is the kind of faith that moves the heart and regulates the life; it is a faith that does not lie dormant but manifests itself in active obedience.

B. *For his second illustration, James chose Rahab, who was as far removed from Abraham as night is from day.* James insisted that her experience with God teaches the same lesson as that taught by Abraham's experience. Just as the body without the life-giving spirit is dead, so faith, which is a mere shell of profession if it is void of fruit, is dead also (v. 26).

Conclusion

This kind of fruitless faith brings no glory to God and yields no benefit to the person who has it. What James was saying is that the union between faith and works is as close as the union between body and soul.

SUNDAY MORNING, JUNE 13

Title: Gifts That Fathers Can Give

Text: "If ye then, being evil, know how to give good gifts unto your children . . ." **(Matt. 7:11)**.

Scripture Reading: Matthew 7:7–11

Hymns: "Brethren, We Have Met to Worship," Atkins
"Break Thou the Bread of Life," Lathbury
"Wonderful Words of Life," Bliss

Offertory Prayer: Loving God, we thank you for being our heavenly Father. Thank you for being merciful and generous. Thank you for this good day in which we have the privilege of rejoicing and worshiping with our brothers and sisters in Christ. As we come bringing our tithes and offerings to indicate our love and our desire to share the good news of your love with those around the world, may these gifts be blessed. May we truly believe that it is more blessed to give than to receive. In Jesus' name. Amen.

Introduction

Our text compares giving by earthly fathers to their children with the good gifts the Father God bestows on his children. This illustration concludes that if human fathers are inclined toward gift giving, the divine Father is even more so inclined. If earthly fathers seek to be wise in the giving of gifts, we can rest assured that the heavenly Father gives with even greater wisdom.

Some gifts fathers find impossible to give because of their economic circumstances. Other gifts are more important than any gadget or toy fathers can give to their children. Let us examine some of these important gifts in the form of an acrostic using the letters in the word "Father."

I. F—Faith (I Tim. 5:8 RSV).

When Paul said, "If any one does not provide for his relatives, and especially for his own family, he has disowned the faith and is worse than an unbeliever," surely he is including the provision of faith itself.

A. *Faith in God is a gift fathers should give.* If a father will put confidence in God and lovingly seek to obey him, in the overwhelming majority of cases, his children will be able to receive this gift. They will face life with a confidence in God that will bring stability to them. A father who does not have a faith to give sends his children out into the world impoverished.

B. *Faith in God's Word is a gift fathers should give.* God's Word speaks to our deepest needs. Each father should love God's Word. He should read and study God's Word, reverencing it and making it such a part of his life that his children will also want to love this precious gift from God.

C. *Faith in oneself is a gift fathers should give.* It is extremely important for children to have confidence in themselves. A father should encourage his children to develop a good self-image. Children can have high self-esteem if they see love and assurance in the eyes of their parents.

D. *Faith in the future is a gift fathers should give.* Many times fathers are pessimistic and critical of the circumstances in which they find themselves. It is easy for fathers to impart a negative attitude to their children. Instead, fathers should seek to instill optimism and hope in the minds of their children.

II. A—Acceptance.

A man with two children once came to his pastor with feelings of insecurity that bordered on deep depression. In their discussion, the pastor discovered that this man had experienced rejection by his father at an early age. This man's father wished that his son had not been born as early as he was after their marriage. Consequently, the father gave his son the impression that he was not accepted and not appreciated.

Every child deserves the right to be accepted and appreciated by his or her parents. If children are to accept their own uniqueness and face life with a good self-image, they need full acceptance by their parents.

III. T—Time.

There are many different ways to spell the word *love*. Probably the best way for a father to spell love toward his children is with the letters t-i-m-e.

Often a grandfather gives more attention and more time to his grandchildren than does the father. As a result, children have great affection for their grandparents. Could it be that when children come along, the father is so busy trying to make a fortune, or simply trying to meet his financial obligations, that he fails to spend time with his children? By the time grandchildren come along, the man has either made his fortune or given up trying and concentrates on the thing that is of greater worth. He has time to give to his grandchildren. Let fathers take a lesson at this point.

    A. *It takes time to teach our children the things they should know.*
    B. *It takes time for a father to train his children.*

IV. H—Help.

The psalmist declared, "My help comes from the LORD, who made heaven and earth" (Ps. 121:2 RSV). Our Lord is the greatest helper anyone can have. However, much of his help comes through our earthly fathers.

    A. *Each father can be a helper by encouraging his children to admire the right kind of heroes.*
    B. *Each father can be a helper by sharing his knowledge.* One of the great tragedies of life is the inability of fathers to pass on to their children the benefits of their experience. Perhaps some fathers are poor communicators. Perhaps some children are poor listeners or learners. A father's intellect and experience should always be available to his children when they desire it.
    C. *Each father can be a helper by having his children always in his heart with love and affection.* Certainly a father should concentrate on not being a hindrance to his children.

V. E—Encouragement.

Everybody needs encouragement. Particularly the members of our household need encouragement.

    A. *Each father needs to be a constant source of encouragement to his wife.* A father needs to give his wife affection and support and work by her side to maintain the family.
    B. *Each father needs to encourage his children.* He needs to be a cheerleader to each of them, encouraging them to set high goals for their lives and

rejoicing in every step of achievement toward these goals. A father needs to avoid being a faultfinding critic who, seeing only the failures, makes comments that undermine the child's sense of worth.

VI. R—Rock, resource, reverent example.

A father should be a source of strength to his family.

A. *A father can serve as a rock of defense in times of struggle and difficulty for his children.* This requires faith, commitment, and effort.
B. *A father can be a resource in many different ways for his children.* He should not think of himself only as a financial resource. He should be available to assist his children as he has opportunity.
C. *A father can be an example of reverence.* Fathers should teach their children to revere God, womanhood, motherhood, life, and morality.

Conclusion

The greatest gifts that parents can give to their children are not those that can be purchased at a department store and wrapped up in beautiful paper. Give your children the gifts of faith, acceptance, time, help, encouragement, and reverence.

SUNDAY EVENING, JUNE 13

Title: The Sin of Censoriousness
Text: "Judge not, that ye be not judged" (**Matt. 7:1**).
Scripture Reading: Matthew 7:1–5

Introduction

Christ's statement, "Judge not, that ye be not judged" points its accusing finger directly at each of us and implies that we have been found guilty. This is one of the most disturbing passages in all Christ's teachings. Jesus centers his attention on the prevalent sin of censoriousness, the sin of nit-picking, faultfinding, and cutting other people down to our size.

In Greek mythology there is a story about a robber chieftain named Proclustes. Anyone who invaded his territory was taken to Proclustes's cave, where he had an iron bedstead. Each captive was carefully measured on the bed. If the captive was too short, he was stretched. If he was too long, his ankles and legs were cut off until he was short enough. The myth records that Theseus invaded the territory of Proclustes and killed him, but he did not destroy his iron bed. In fact, his bed is still around.

Proclustes's bed may be found in our homes, in our offices—anywhere in our lives. We look around for people to measure. Then we stretch those who are too short and cut off those who are too long. They must exactly fit our bed.

Jesus, being aware of human nature, realized the propensity of individuals to measure everyone else by themselves. He had observed people trying to force others to fit exactly into their own concepts. Thus Jesus gives us clear and stern instructions: "Judge not, that ye be not judged"! This is not a subtle suggestion or a gentle nudge. "Judge not" is an imperative!

I. A prohibition.

A present imperative with a negative is used in verse 1, where Jesus said, "Don't pick on people, jump on their failures, criticize their faults—unless, of course, you want the same treatment" (MSG).

A. *What Jesus was not prohibiting.*

1. Jesus was not prohibiting the due process of law. Often this statement of Christ has been misunderstood and misapplied. The Russian writer Tolstoy is best known for his book *War and Peace.* He became a most conscientious Christian during the latter part of his life. He took literally each word of the Sermon on the Mount. He believed that this message was intended as a divine blueprint for a new social order that Christ had come to establish. For example, when Jesus said, "Judge not, that ye be not judged," Tolstoy concluded that every courthouse should be destroyed and the judicial system should be set aside. Yet our Lord never meant for his words to serve as a replacement for the law. The due process of law and the grace of God are not antithetical. They simply operate in different realms. The spirit of the entire teachings of Christ would never advocate anarchy. Jesus knows human nature well enough to know that government and a judicial system are necessary.

2. Jesus was not prohibiting the practice of moral judgments. Jesus himself passed moral judgment on others. For instance, he called the Pharisees a generation of vipers and whitened sepulchres. He announced that if they did not repent, they would surely perish.

   Because of our hesitancy to make moral decisions, we tend to drift into an indiscriminate moral neutrality. Consequently, we quote this passage, "Judge not, that ye be not judged," and in so doing abdicate our responsibility to make moral judgments. Actually, the correct position is that we should judge morally and thus be prepared to be judged morally.

B. *What Jesus was prohibiting.* He was attacking the sin of censoriousness. He was addressing the hypercritical, faultfinding attitude that encourages us to stretch people out or chop them off so they will conform to our bed.

   Here Jesus placed himself in diametrical opposition to those who would inflict slow death on others by relentless criticism. Employers sometimes do this to employees. Parents do it to their own children. Teachers, by this means, destroy pupils, and ministers wear down their church members. "Judge not, that ye be not judged."

II. A promise.

In verse 2 Jesus said, "For in the same way you judge others, you will be judged, and with the measure you use, it will be measured to you" (NIV). This promise reflects the law of reciprocity, a law that states that we always get back what we give out. This may not be the highest motive for appealing to others—that they should be Christlike—but it is a motive based on fact. Dishonesty begets dishonesty, stealing begets stealing, and censoriousness begets censoriousness. Yet the bright side of this law is that the opposite is also true: truth begets truth, faithfulness begets faithfulness, and love begets love.

The fact remains that our censoriousness not only causes others to be censorious toward us, but we are also hurt from two other sources—ourselves and God. "With what measure ye mete, it shall be measured to you again." This is simply a restatement of such passages as "Whatsoever a man soweth, that shall he also reap" (Gal. 6:7), and "They that take the sword shall perish with the sword" (Matt. 26:52). Modern psychology bears witness that the attitudes of censoriousness, grudge-bearing, hatred, and related attitudes are destructive to a person's body and mind.

Charles Allen pointed out that our censoriousness reveals five things about us: our sins, our jealousies, our ignorance, our inability to deal with our own problems, and our lovelessness. So each time we judge another, we are saying to all who have ears to hear, "This is the kind of unloving person I am." Paul addressed himself to this same problem in Romans 2:1–3. He said, "You, therefore, have no excuse, you who pass judgment on someone else, for at whatever point you judge another, you are condemning yourself, because you who pass judgment do the same things. Now we know that God's judgment against those who do such things is based on truth. So when you, a mere human being, pass judgment on them and yet do the same things, do you think you will escape God's judgment?" (NIV).

There are four reasons why we receive God's judgment when we are censorious toward others. First, censoriousness hinders God's work; second, it assumes God's office as judge; third, it destroys what God has given—character and influence; fourth, it is contemptuous toward the grace of God, which is extended to those whom we would destroy by censoriousness.

III. A perplexity.

In Matthew 7:3–4, Jesus said that the sin of censoriousness creates a real perplexity. In his typical humor, Jesus painted a picture of a man with a log in his eye trying to pick a splinter out of another man's eye! A perplexing situation indeed! Not one of us is without sin; not one of us is free of glaring defects in our own life. Jesus was saying, "Look at the ridiculous role you are playing. With a glaring flaw in your own life that everyone else can see, you nitpick at the small problems in the lives of others." If there is anything that Jesus does not want his followers to be, it is hypocrites.

Jesus set the example in this matter. When he saw Zacchaeus, he wanted to help him. This man had been cheating and defrauding the public. Jesus could have said, "I know who you are, Zacchaeus; you're one of those terrible tax collectors. You've earned the bad reputation that is yours. Come down out of that tree, fall on your knees before me, and confess your sins publicly. If you get your life straightened out, you might be good enough to come and join my followers." Instead of standing in judgment on this fallen man, Jesus established a relationship of love. By the tone of his voice and the actions that followed, Jesus said to Zacchaeus, "I love you very much." In the light of God's love, Zacchaeus became keenly aware of the fault in his life.

IV. A proposal.

In verse 5 Jesus made a proposal. We have our hands full in correcting the problems in our own lives without being censorious in our judgment toward others. We could spend our time quite constructively if we concentrated on our own faults, leaving the faults of others to the goodness and grace of God. Jesus' proposal is quite difficult to carry out. We naturally find ourselves asking how we can execute this proposal and what we can do about the temptation to be censorious toward others.

First of all, we should recognize censoriousness as sin. It *is* a sin, just as stealing or lying or immorality is a sin. In God's eyes, being critical and hurtful toward others is serious sin. Second, we should confess our tendency to judge as a sin. Only through confession will we ever rid our lives of the deadly sin of censoriousness. Third, we must quit doing it. It is not enough to own up to the sin and ask God to forgive us. We must claim the grace of God that will enable us to quit being censorious.

Three good filters through which we should pass every word that comes from our mouth are: Is it true? Is it necessary? Is it kind?

Conclusion

One day while walking in Florence, Italy, Michelangelo came across a piece of discarded marble. He had it brought to his studio. Someone else had started to work on the marble but had cast it aside as useless. Michelangelo said, "There is an angel imprisoned in this piece of marble, and it is my task to bring out that angel." This is exactly what our business is. We are to see the good in people and by the grace of God bring it to the surface. Too many people are willing to throw others aside as human rejects. May God grant that we will become people who release the angels imprisoned in the twisted forms of humanity. May God save us from joining the ranks of those who stand idly by and point out the flaws and faults in others.

WEDNESDAY EVENING, JUNE 16

Title: The Tongue Is a Terror

Text: "And the tongue is a fire, a world of iniquity: so is the tongue among our members, that it defileth the whole body, and setteth on fire the course of nature; and it is set on fire of hell" **(James 3:6)**.

Scripture Reading: James 3:1–12

Introduction

James had a great deal to say about the tongue. In fact, he devoted an entire section of his letter to it. Even so, he was not introducing a new thought. He spoke about the tongue earlier when he warned that we must be "swift to hear, slow to speak" (1:19). In that same context, he exhorted us to "bridle" our tongues (1:26), suggesting that they often have the tendency to run ahead of our thoughts. Even though there are many references to the tongue throughout the Bible (see Prov. 13:3; 18:21; 21:23; Pss. 34:13; 39:1), James spoke more strongly about its dangers than any other Bible writer.

I. James spoke of the power of the tongue, both from the standpoint of evil and of good (3:2–5).

He used three illustrations to prove the power of the tongue.

A. *In the first illustration, James drew a parallel between the horse and the human body (v. 3).* A horse, unrestrained, seeks to satisfy its physical needs. It is an illogical being. If it is to accomplish anything useful, anything not merely for the satisfaction of its own desires, it must be directed by a logical being, a thinking person. So it is with the human body. Humans cannot direct themselves, for if they do, they will seek the satisfaction of self instead of seeking the glory of God, which is the specific purpose for which they were created. What do we do to harness a horse? We make use of a bit and bridle. By controlling its tongue, we can control the whole body. The horse does not bridle itself—it must be bridled by someone else. Likewise, people cannot control themselves. They must defer to a greater power.

B. *The second illustration James used has to do with great ships (v. 4).* James did not know anything about the great ocean-going vessels of our day, but even in his day there were ships that could be described as "great." How were the movements of these great vessels controlled, even under the most adverse conditions? "By a very small rudder wherever the will of the pilot directs" (RSV). The point of these first two illustrations is made in verse 5: "Even so the tongue is a little member, and boasteth great things." That is, in relation to the other members of the body, the tongue is little. But it can achieve great

201

results. This is not an empty boast. The tongue can sway people to violence or move them to the highest and noblest action.

C. *The third illustration is found in the fire (v. 5).* "How great a forest is set ablaze by a small fire!" (RSV). James contrasted the smallness of a spark with the greatness of the fire that can result.

II. James spoke of the vicious nature of the tongue (3:6–8).

A. *First, James said that "the tongue is a fire."* We know that fire under control can be a great blessing. With controlled fire, people can overcome the cold, cook their food, and drive the engines of industry. But fire out of control leaves desolation and tragedy in its wake. So the tongue, like fire out of control, scorches and consumes!

B. *James then said that the tongue is "a world of iniquity."* The word translated "world" here (*cosmos*) also means "ornament," or "decoration." The good and sanctified tongue will condemn unrighteousness, but the evil tongue will complement and "decorate" it, making it appear as if it were righteous. James concluded this metaphor by saying that the tongue that does this "is set on fire of hell." That is, the uncontrolled fire of the tongue is fed by the never-dying flames of hell.

C. *James said that the tongue is wild and untamable (vv. 7–8).* A person may control the tongue, but it must be ever kept under careful guard; the leash can never be removed from it.

III. James spoke of the inconsistency of the tongue (3:9–12).

A. *The tongue is notoriously inconsistent, James said.* With it we bless God and curse others who are made in God's image. He was saying that it is abnormal and inappropriate to bless God in prayer and praise yet speak evil of members of God's family.

B. *James illustrated this inconsistency with two figures drawn from nature (vv. 11–12).*
   1. The first is the figure of a fountain of water. Is it possible for a "salt spring [to] produce fresh water"? (NIV).
   2. The second figure concerns fruit. "Can a fig tree . . . yield olives, or a grapevine figs?" (RSV). That like produces like is a law of nature.

Conclusion

An unbeliever hired a professing Christian to paint his house. He knew that this Christian could pray beautiful prayers and could quote a great deal of Scripture. But when it came to painting, he didn't fill the nail holes with putty like he was supposed to, and he didn't paint the tops of the doors, where no one could see them. The non-Christian later said, "Now I know that his prayers and his piety don't mean much. I prefer Christians who will fill up the nail holes and paint the tops of the doors!" What we say must be backed up with actions.

SUNDAY MORNING, JUNE 20

Title: The Influence of Fathers

Text: "If a son shall ask bread of any of you that is a father, will he give him a stone? or if he ask a fish, will he for a fish give him a serpent? Or if he shall ask an egg, will he offer him a scorpion? If ye then, being evil, know how to give good gifts unto your children: how much more shall your heavenly Father give the Holy Spirit to them that ask him?" **(Luke 11:11–13)**.

Scripture Reading: Matthew 10:37; Luke 11:11–13; 2 Corinthians 12:14

Hymns: "Faith of Our Fathers," Faber
"How Firm a Foundation," Rippon
"Faith Is the Victory," Yates

Offertory Prayer: Our heavenly Father, we are continually overwhelmed by your matchless grace and glory. We see your grace when we look at ourselves. We see your glory when we look at you. With this offering we express our thanksgiving for your grace to us. We express our praise for your glory before us. Use this offering to further your kingdom. In Jesus' name we pray. Amen.

Introduction

A mother is extremely dear and close to the heart of her offspring. For the first two years of a child's life, a good mother lovingly nourishes and tends to her child. The life of an infant is dependent on the mother's care and concern. Though the mother continues to love and to watch over the child, an environment larger than that of the mother begins to influence the child. Soon the outside world has an awesome influence on the child's formative years. Circumstances brought on by the father help determine this larger environment. In many homes the father's work determines the place of residence, the standard of living, and the social environment.

It is imperative that the role of the father is understood. Let us look at two major factors—the influences that are operative on the father, and the influences of the father on the world around him.

I. Influences on the father.

By the very nature of his role, the father is exposed to many of life's pressures. He usually functions with more efficiency when he has responsibilities and/or pressures. Let us note the varied influences in the life of the father.

   A. *Family.*

      1. Past. The father is a product of his parents and each relationship he had with his brothers and sisters. A woman should never marry a man with the idea that she will make him over, for he is a product of the past.

      2. Present. A father's present life is intricately involved with his wife. Much care must be taken when an individual seeks to select a mate for life.

      3. Future. Children are a major part of their father's future. They are great responsibilities to the father.

B. *Personal abilities.*

      1. Natural inclinations. Each man has certain personal inclinations, such as talents, health circumstances, and so on, that greatly determine his direction in life.

      2. Education. The amount of education (formal or otherwise) that the father receives will either help or hinder him in his responsibilities.

      3. Vocation. Most men are free to choose the employment they desire. Different vocations bring about different social and economic factors. A man should take into consideration the long-range effects his vocation will have on his family.

      4. Recreation. Every man selects the way he spends his leisure time. His manner of recreation will directly influence a major segment of his life.

C. *Finances.* It comes as no shock to anyone that a father, as well as everyone else, is greatly influenced by finances.

      1. Earning pressure. The father is under pressure to earn enough money to support his family in accordance with the lifestyle he has set for them.

      2. Spending pressure. As the family's needs increase and inflation bites away at the income, a father is pressured to try to curb his family's expenditures.

      3. Saving pressure. A long-range plan for the family requires a system of savings. This is a big responsibility for the father.

      4. Emergency pressure. It is inevitable that unexpected sicknesses and expenses will arise. A father must make provision for these matters through insurance, savings, and so on.

D. *Spiritual.* The foremost responsibility and/or pressure experienced by the father is in the realm of the spiritual.

      1. Personal conversion. The head of the family, the father, needs to be born again.

      2. Personal growth. The family should be able to see spiritual growth in the life of their leader.

      3. Involvement of family. The father is responsible for getting the entire family involved in valid worship of God.

      4. Environment. The father needs to place his family in an environment that will aid them in spiritual growth.

II. Influences of the father.

A father should never underestimate the power of his influence on his family and on the world in which he moves.

A. *On his vocation.*
1. Diligence. It is a biblical honor for a man to be diligent on his job and to influence others to be the same way.
2. Integrity. Honesty and respectability are contagious traits. Blessed is the father who infects others with them.
3. Creativity. Progress is made through the influence of a creative man. Father, be that creative man!

B. *On his society.*
1. Witness. A lost world needs the example of a believing father to guide its inhabitants to salvation.
2. Economics. If a father can be victorious in his own financial affairs, he may be very influential to those around him.
3. Morality. How majestic it is to see a family man stand tall in face of the immoralities surrounding him.

C. *On his family.*
1. Wife. The greatest influence of the father will first be felt by his wife. She is the closest person on earth to him.
2. Children. Children usually live the life that is exemplified before them.
3. Parents. Seeing their son grow up to be a respectable father makes parents proud.
4. In-laws. Many family problems are solved before they arise when the father shows his in-laws that he loves their daughter and their precious grandchildren.

D. *On his church.*
1. Presence. The local church needs a family man who will attend worship and see that his family does the same.
2. Talents. When a father commits his talents to God to be used through the local church, he wields an awesome influence over his family.
3. Financial. As a father supports the local church financially, he reveals his priorities to his family.
4. Service. The best way to teach children they need to serve God is for the father to show them how it is done.

Conclusion

The role of the father must not be underestimated. His influence cannot be overstated. Father, are you a plus or minus in the lives of those around you?

SUNDAY EVENING, JUNE 20

Title: Handle the Holy with Care

Text: "Give not that which is holy unto the dogs, neither cast ye your pearls before swine, lest they trample them under their feet, and turn again and rend you" **(Matt. 7:6)**.

Introduction

Possibly the hardest saying of Jesus ever recorded is found in Matthew 7:6. Jesus Christ, who came in love to give his life as a ransom for many, is quoted as calling some of these people "dogs" and "swine." If you or I used such words in addressing others, people would be shocked by our attitude, and those addressed would feel insulted and offended.

Jesus went on to say that such people are unworthy of God's holy truths and that we are wasting our time trying to persuade them. In fact, he said that if we persist in our efforts in trying to win such people, we are running the risk of being assaulted and torn to shreds by the very ones we are trying to help.

Matthew 7:6 on the surface seems to be in direct conflict with other statements attributed to Jesus, such as, "Unto him that smiteth thee on the one cheek offer also the other" (Luke 6:29), and "Bless them that curse you, do good to them that hate you, and pray for them which despitefully use you, and persecute you" (Matt. 5:44).

Is there any way we can reconcile Jesus' statement in Matthew 7:6 with these and many other of his teachings? What is the purpose of such a shocking statement being interjected in the middle of Jesus' Sermon on the Mount? What was Jesus saying? This verse divides itself into four segments—a restriction, a reason, a response, and a repercussion.

I. A restriction.

"Give not that which is holy unto the dogs, neither cast ye your pearls before swine" is obviously a restriction. On the surface this command seems to call for an exclusiveness that is foreign to the spirit of our Lord. We must remember, however, that the church was an island surrounded by a sea of immorality and paganism. Ever present was the danger that it would be infected with the diseases of the world. It is not that the early church failed to be evangelistic, for indeed the church was consumed with a burning desire to win everyone to faith in Jesus Christ. On the other hand, the church was keenly aware of the necessity of keeping their morals pure and doctrines unpolluted. Otherwise the Christian faith would eventually be swallowed up by the surrounding sea of immorality and pagan worship. The key to understanding this statement is found in the word *holy*. When Jesus spoke of that which is holy, he was surely referring to truth.

A. *The truth of the gospel.* Paul spoke of "the truth of the gospel" in Galatians 2:14. In John 8:32 Jesus said that "the truth shall make you free." Since the gospel can do such wonderful things, why then does Jesus place a restriction on offering such truth to "dogs" and "swine"?

We generally assume that Jesus spent most of his time preaching to the unsaved in evangelistic endeavors. He did minister to the lost and the "unchurched," but he spent most of his time speaking to people who were religious yet lost. He spent even more time with those who had embraced him as Lord and Savior. The vast majority of his parables and teachings were directed toward those who had become his followers. And through such teaching he attempted to equip them to carry the gospel to the rest of the world.

Jesus never declined an opportunity to share the good news with publicans and sinners. Yet in this particular statement, Jesus had in mind religious people who reveal no real interest in him and who, in fact, are openly hostile toward him and do everything to oppose him. As you read again the many incidents found in the gospel accounts where the Pharisees antagonized him, you will fail to find a single incident where Jesus turned and preached the simplicity of the gospel to them. He refused to cast his pearls before swine.

There will always be those to whom the preaching of the cross of Christ is foolishness. These people respond to an offer of God's grace with hate and hostility. It is to this group that Jesus restricts our sharing of the beautiful truth of the gospel. In fact, the implication is that to disobey his restriction is to do more harm than good.

B. *The truth in general.* Jesus spoke of truth in general in John 3:19–21, where he talked about the light coming into the world. He said that people love the darkness of sin rather than light because they desire to do evil. The truth we offer in behalf of Christ is not to be thrown out indiscriminately. Our enthusiasm to reach others for Christ must be tempered with knowledge. If we violate Jesus' restriction and attempt to force the truth of Christ on others, we should not be surprised when we are met with hatred and insults.

In Matthew 5:14, Jesus said of the Pharisees, "Leave them alone." There will always be those who say in words and attitude, "Don't confuse me with the facts; my mind is made up!" After you have done your best to share with others the truth of the gospel and that truth is neither welcome nor accepted, then, in essence, Jesus said, "Handle the holy with care. You have done all any person can do, and God's divine restriction prohibits you from any further efforts to convince that rejecting soul of this truth."

II. A reason.

The Living Bible translates this verse in part to read, "Don't give holy things to depraved men." And what is the reason for such a restriction? Jesus answered this by describing those who refuse to accept the truth and revere the gospel. Certainly we are not to be censorious or judgmental toward others. In his parable of the sower, Jesus clearly communicated that we are not to prejudge people as being rocky ground, the wayside, or thorns.

The question naturally comes, who are the "dogs" and "swine"? Let us allow Scripture to interpret itself for a moment. Simon Peter must have heard this statement and later in one of his writings said, "It is happened unto them according to the true proverb, The dog is turned to his own vomit again; and the sow that was washed to her wallowing in the mire" (2 Peter 2:22). Yet people are not born with the nature of a dog or pig. A person must choose of his or her own volition to assume this depraved nature. The apostle Paul said that un-Christlike attitudes can disrupt the fellowship of the church. "But if ye bite and devour one another, take heed that ye be not consumed one of another" (Gal. 5:15).

Christ used the analogy of a pig to illustrate the nature that has lost all sense of values. To offer "the pearl of great price" to such a person is to have that pearl trampled underfoot.

We must remember that ours is not to judge others. Our responsibility is to avoid needlessly exposing the truth of Christ to those who are completely lacking in appreciation and are sure to reject it.

III. A response.

In this verse Jesus warned us lest the response of such degenerate people be that "they trample them under their feet." Solomon captured this same truth in Proverbs 23:9 when he said, "Speak not in the ears of a fool: for he will despise the wisdom of thy words." There have always been those people who are repelled by the gospel and even stirred into hostile antagonism. Jesus himself did not speak as he stood before Herod, even though the ruler asked many questions. This does not mean that such people are hopeless, but as heavy rain runs off hard-packed ground, so the Word of God rolls off hard hearts. Just as hardened earth must first be softened by a gentle rain, it often takes much time and a great deal of patience to penetrate the hearts of hardened people.

What Jesus was really saying is not so harsh as it may appear at first. He was simply teaching us that there are those who lack background, training, or the ability to comprehend the gospel of Christ. Before they can grasp the truth of the gospel and allow it to take root, the Holy Spirit must have time to work with them. To attempt to argue with such people is to do more harm than good. To try to force the gospel on them and twist a profession of faith from them is perhaps to close the door forever. To run ahead of God and attempt to do this is to violate God's restriction, to ignore the reasons offered, and to be met with an unfavorable response.

IV. A repercussion.

Jesus said that if we choose to violate his command, we run the risk that those who reject him will "turn and tear [us] to pieces" (NIV). Christian history verifies this truth. Acts 7:51–60 recounts the story of Stephen, who steadfastly and honestly proclaimed the truths of Christ. He laid the guilt of people at their feet where it belonged. But the end result was that he lost his life.

John the Baptist, in Mark 6, confronted Herod with his sin. He was speaking the truth to a man who desperately needed to hear it, but the end result was that John the Baptist lost his head and won no convert.

Jesus Christ at his trial (Matt. 26:59–68) held his peace for quite some time. Then, when asked if he was the Son of God, he replied, "Yes, it is as you say" (v. 64 NIV). The result was that the high priest tore his clothes, accused Jesus of blaspheming, and pronounced him worthy of death. Those in the crowd joined in with this spirit of hostility by spitting in Jesus' face and hitting him.

Conclusion

What then is the remedy? How are we to relate to these Christ rejecters? Are we to walk off and leave them as hopeless spiritual derelicts? Is the message of Christ simply for those who seem willing to embrace it?

What our words cannot do, our lives can do. Certain individuals may be calloused toward any Christian truths we may speak. But they are open to a flesh-and-blood demonstration of what the gospel of Christ can do in the life of someone else.

The challenge that is ours in light of Christ's warning to handle the holy with care is found in some other words spoken by Christ. "Let your light so shine before men, that they may see your good works, and glorify your Father, which is in heaven" (Matt. 5:16).

WEDNESDAY EVENING, JUNE 23

Title: Who Is Wise?

Text: "Who is a wise man and endued with knowledge among you? let him shew out of a good conversation his works with meekness of wisdom" **(James 3:13)**.

Scripture Reading: James 3:13–18

Introduction

In James 3:13 James seemed to change his subject. The first twelve verses of this chapter are devoted to the tongue. Now he turned to the subject of wisdom. In these six verses, he approached his subject from three perspectives. First, he discussed the proof of wisdom; then he dealt with false wisdom; and finally, he concluded with a declaration of the essence of true wisdom.

I. The proof of wisdom (3:13).

A. *"Who is a wise man and endued with knowledge among you?"* Perhaps two of the most sought-after qualities of human life are wisdom and knowledge. Judging from the verses that follow, James seemed to mean that the wise person is the one who possesses true knowledge of things both human and divine; "endued with knowledge" speaks of one who is able to apply that knowledge to the practical details of life.

B. *Understanding that wisdom is not something acquired, but rather given by God, James put forth a challenge to those who feel they have both wisdom and knowledge.* "Let him shew out of a good conversation his works with meekness of wisdom." James was saying, "Prove your wisdom!" How can we do this? By seeing to it that our life matches our profession of faith.

C. *How are we to do this?* "With meekness of wisdom," or as the NIV translates it, "By deeds done in humility that comes from wisdom." The beautiful thought James put forth here is that meekness, or humility, is to be the natural accompaniment of wisdom. Where there is no meekness or humility, there is no wisdom.

II. False wisdom, which does not have its origin with God (3:14–16).

A. *James said there are telltale signs that let us know when this wrong kind of wisdom is present in our lives (v. 14).* These evidences are "bitter envying and strife." The word translated "envying" is the same Greek word from which the word *zeal* is derived. The word literally means "to boil or bubble up." Zeal can be both good and bad. One's zeal—or fire—will either warm others or burn them! Thus, when others feel the bitterness of our zeal, they will surely come to the conclusion that the wisdom we seem to possess is not heavenly wisdom at all!

B. *James outlined the distinctive traits of false wisdom (v. 15).* First he described it negatively: "This wisdom descendeth not from above, but is earthly, sensual, devilish." Then in verse 16 he described the destructive consequences of this false wisdom.

III. True wisdom, which is "from above" (3:17–18).

A. *James said that it "is first pure."* That is, it is undefiled; it is free from the self-interest that characterizes false wisdom. By "first pure," James meant that true wisdom is *above all else* pure. He continued by saying that heavenly wisdom is "peaceable, gentle, and easy to be intreated." Worldly wisdom produces contention and strife. True wisdom is "peaceable." It delights in promoting and making peace. It is reasonable, forbearing, and courteous, and it does not always insist on its own rights. True wisdom is compliant, conciliatory, willing to yield yet without compromise to evil.

B. *Then James said that heavenly wisdom is "full of mercy and good fruits."* The word "mercy" speaks of compassion and pity shown toward those who are miserable and in need. It is a characteristic of God himself. Finally, James said that true wisdom is "without partiality, and without hypocrisy." It is without prejudice and does not show respect of persons. It makes no distinctions. It is genuine, sincere, and unpretentious.

C. *"Peacemakers who sow in peace raise a harvest of righteousness" (v. 18 NIV).* One of the characteristics of a wise Christian is righteousness. Being righteous involves growth. If we are to bear visible fruits of righteousness before the world, we have to grow from the seed stage.

Conclusion

What kind of wisdom characterizes your life? Is it a false wisdom that is selfish, ego-centered, and inconsiderate toward others? Or is it a wisdom existing in you because Jesus Christ, the essence of true wisdom, lives in you? Seek wisdom that is born of God.

SUNDAY MORNING, JUNE 27

Title: Renew My Church

Text: "I beseech you therefore, brethren . . . be not conformed to this world: but be transformed by the renewing of your mind" **(Rom. 12:1–2)**.

Scripture Reading: Romans 12:1–6

Hymns: "Rejoice, Ye Pure in Heart," Plumptre
"Serve the Lord with Gladness," McKinney
"He Keeps Me Singing," Bridges

Offertory Prayer: Holy heavenly Father, we come to offer our thanks to you for this your church, which is also our church. We thank you for what it means to this community and to your work around the world. We rejoice now in the opportunity to bring our tithes and offerings to you that the ministry of your church in this community might be prosperous. Bless these offerings also to the coming of your kingdom into the hearts of men and women beyond this community. In Jesus' name we pray. Amen.

Introduction

The church is struggling for renewal today. Romans 12 spells out the nature of the struggle: conformity to the world or transformation according to God's will. It is the struggle of the Corinthian church between the carnal and the spiritual. It is the struggle of Laodicea between the cold, the lukewarm, and the hot.

The burning question today is what will we do with the church? Will we attack it, criticize it, neglect it, or quit it? Not even Jesus did that, although he saw the churches in deep trouble.

What is our response? Our prayer should be the prayer of Francis of Assisi when he knelt in the empty and forsaken chapel by San Damiano—"Renew my church!" If that prayer is to be answered, three truths must be used as steps to the survival of the church.

I. Admission that the church is in trouble.

William Russell Maltby said that Jesus promised those who follow him only three things: they would be absurdly happy, entirely fearless, and always in trouble. The trouble I refer to, however, relates to the church's effectiveness. Church leaders list several areas where the church is in trouble.

A. *The problem of divisions.* Only Christ Jesus could bring unity between Jews and Gentiles in the early church. Today the divisions in the church are activists versus pietists, the social gospel versus the personal gospel, and evangelism versus the deeper life. In each of these cases we need balance.

B. *The problem of inconsistency.* There is a gap between what we profess and what we produce. The Christian life is *"the way* of life," yet the way we walk isn't always consistent with the way we talk. Christians ought to be leading the way!

C. *The problem of irrelevancy.* The outside world says the church is concerned with programs, not people, and that even the programs are irrelevant. If the church, possessing salvation and hope, does not witness by life and word, its existence becomes irrelevant.

D. *The problem of inability.* We are the salt of the earth and the light of the world. We have the power to preserve society and dispel moral darkness, but we fail to use it.

E. *The problem of isolation.* Elton Trueblood said the church is isolated geographically to a particular place, a building. It is isolated temporally to a particular time, Sunday morning. It is isolated in personnel, limiting responsibility to professional clergy, to the staff. We have lost contact with people.

F. *The problem of irreverence.* The church lacks reverence for the Lord of the church, for his Word, and for his plans for the church.

In the light of its problems, our prayer is "Renew our church!"

II. Affirmation that there is hope for the church.

God is not finished with the church yet! Some powerful Scripture passages proclaim the victory of the church.

A. *Matthew 16:18.* "And the gates of hell shall not prevail against it." This is a promise for the life and victory of the church. This is the church on the offensive, battering down the strongholds of Satan. Let the church take heart!

B. *Matthew 18:20.* "Where two or three are gathered together in my name, there am I in the midst of them." The Lord Jesus Christ is our hope so that we need not despair.

C. *Revelation 2 and 3 contain these words.* "He that hath an ear, let him hear what the Spirit saith unto the churches." As long as these words exist, there will be salvation and survival for the church.

D. *Revelation 3:20.* "Behold, I stand at the door, and knock: if any man hear my voice, and open the door, I will come in to him, and will sup with him, and he with me." Let Jesus into his church! Let him give us renewal and resurgence!

E. *John 12:24.* "Unless a grain of wheat falls into the earth and dies. . . ." Death is the key to the life of the Christian and the life of the church—death to our will, our goals, our plans, our self-existence. Christ then gives life!

Hunger for new life in the church is growing. People believe the church is worth saving, and God's Word says it can be saved.

There is one other thing we must have.

III. Awareness that the time is short.

Time is short because the church is losing spiritual sensitivity. Time is short because Jesus is coming again. Time is short because people die without the gospel in their hearts.

Conclusion

I have hope for the church because our hope is in the Lord Jesus Christ. As he is, so are we in the world. The time is now that we are to present ourselves to him for his usefulness. If we build the altar, he will send the fire!

Sunday Evening, June 27

Title: Prayer Is for Real

Text: "Ask, and it shall be given you; seek, and ye shall find; knock, and it shall be opened unto you" (**Matt. 7:7**).

Scripture Reading: Matthew 7:7–11

Introduction

Prayer is for real! It cannot be explained away psychologically as an expression of wishful thinking. Nor can it be ignored as the residual of some ancient social custom. Prayer is neither child's play, nor is it a religious exercise. It is as much a part of life as breath itself.

But the question still comes, though often unspoken, "Can we, in a scientific age, continue to believe in prayer?" This question is not peculiar to our generation. People have always questioned the value and effectiveness of prayer, even in the time of Christ. Some have honest doubts, some are skeptics, and still others question the value of prayer because they have observed professing Christians misusing prayer.

In this portion of the Sermon on the Mount, Christ unequivocally said, "Prayer is for real! Ask, and it *shall* be given you; seek, and ye *shall* find; knock, and it *shall* be opened unto you."

In Jesus' assertion that prayer is for real, he offered a pattern, a promise, and a proof.

I. A pattern.

Jesus offered a pattern for prayer in Matthew 7:7. It is a pattern of asking, seeking, and knocking. The followers of Christ recognized that he, more than any other person, could teach them how to pray. They were fascinated with his preaching, yet they never asked him to teach them how to preach. They would sit for hours and listen to him teach, yet they never asked him to instruct them in how to teach. But when they heard him pray, they came to him and said, "Lord, teach us to pray" (Luke 11:1).

Jesus continues to stand as the supreme authority on prayer, for his whole life was bathed in the spirit of prayer. He knows what it can accomplish, and he knows the power it can exercise. In his Sermon on the Mount, Jesus outlined the pattern to be followed.

A. *"Ask."* To ask means that we acknowledge our need and admit our own helplessness. We all experience times when we can only come before Christ asking. We are very much like a blind man on a corner who asks for someone to take him safely across the street. He asks and at the same time offers nothing in return.

True prayer is always offered in this spirit. Such prayer can never be ours if, like the self-righteous Pharisee, we compliment ourselves and criticize others. Prayer has nothing to do with personal merit or promise of doing better in the future. Real prayer is couched in the words of the publican who said, "God be merciful to me a sinner" (Luke 18:13). Therefore, asking means that we acknowledge our need.

Asking means that we address ourselves to a person. We cannot ask some inanimate object for a response. Thus, when we pray, we address ourselves not to a thing, but to a personal God who hears and cares. Certainly Jesus was saying that God is always approachable. He is present with his ears open and his hands extended.

Asking also means that we can pray specifically. Paul said, "Let your requests be made known unto God" (Phil. 4:6). Ours is not to filter out our requests before offering them to God, but like a little child, we are to open our hearts to God. He is a good and loving Father who will answer those requests that he knows are best for us. And he will answer them in such a way as to fulfill his will.

To pray is to seek God's will. Many times we do not know what God's will is, so we simply let our request be made known and ask God to grant it only according to his will. In such a spirit we can pray with confidence, knowing that if we pray according to God's will, he will hear us.

B. *"Seek."* Seeking conveys the concept of effort. In the model prayer, in which Christ told us to pray for our daily bread, he was not instructing us to sit down and passively do nothing. Rather, he was indicating that we should ask God to give us the opportunity to earn our daily bread. When a farmer prays this prayer, it means that he is asking for the opportunity to prepare the ground, plant seed, cultivate the crops, and tend the plants. And when we pray, "Thy kingdom come," we are praying that we will become so committed in the matter of personal soul winning and building up one another that God's kingdom will be hastened.

C. *"Knock."* The third step in Christ's pattern of prayer is to knock. Knocking carries with it the concept of effort plus persistence. Jesus illustrated this with the story of a man who continued to knock late at night on his neighbor's door until the man got up and answered his request. In Luke 18:1 Jesus taught that we are "always to pray and not lose heart" (RSV). We may allow lack of understanding or disappointment or bitterness to cause us to give up. How long must we keep on praying? Until the answer comes.

II. A promise.

In Matthew 7:8 Jesus offered us the promise that if we ask, we will receive; and if we really seek, we will find; and if we continue to knock, the door will be opened to us. The verbs *ask*, *seek*, and *knock* are present imperatives. Thus Jesus is telling us to keep on asking, seeking, and knocking. We are never to be discouraged in prayer.

God promises that he will always answer our prayers. He may not answer them in our way, but he will always answer them in his way, which is the best way. He alone has perfect love, perfect understanding, and perfect wisdom.

The question comes, "To whom is this promise made?" It is certainly not a blank check written out to humankind in general. It is a promise made to followers of Christ who are sincere enough to keep on asking, seeking, and knocking. Prayer is real when the pattern is followed and the promise is accepted.

III. Proof.

In verses 9, 10, and 11, proof is offered. Here Jesus used the analogy of a father kindly responding to the request of his son. Then he drove home the point that if we as frail, sinful human beings desire to answer our children's requests, our heavenly Father surely desires to answer the requests we bring to him. Proof that prayer is for real is found in the God to whom we pray. It is found in his nature, his resources, his wisdom, and his love.

Conclusion

Prayer can become real in your life if you follow these simple steps: First, decide what your need is and get it clearly focused in your mind. Second, in light of what Scripture teaches, determine if your desire is right. Third, put your request in writing. This will help clarify your thinking.

As you talk to God, get in such a place or such a state of mind that other things will not distract you. Remember that you are talking to God and not to a human being. Share with God what you will do as his instrument to help bring about the answer to your own prayer. Answered prayer is more often a cooperative effort between a person and God than simply unilateral action on the part of God.

When your prayer is finished, never forget to be grateful to God and express that gratitude through thanksgiving. Be willing to accept God's answer, whatever it may be, remembering that God's will is always best.

When you have taken these steps, you will discover through the pattern, the promise, and the proof Christ offers that prayer *is* for real!

WEDNESDAY EVENING, JUNE 30

Title: When the Humble Person Is Exalted

Text: "Do you suppose it is in vain that the scripture says, 'He yearns jealously over the spirit which he has made to dwell in us'? But he gives more grace; therefore it says, 'God opposes the proud, but gives grace to the humble'" (**James 4:5–6 RSV**).

Scripture Reading: James 4:1–10

Introduction

As we study the epistle of James, we need to remember that James was writing to Christian Jews of the dispersion—Christians living among non-Christians all over the world.

Christians today continue to live among those who are strangers to God's grace. The world has succeeded in penetrating the hearts and lives of many believers today. Therefore James's words are just as relevant to us as they were to the Jewish Christians. In these first ten verses of chapter 4, James wrote about worldliness, or self-gratification, in the Christian's life.

I. James said the obsession to gratify self is the cause of wars and fighting among God's people (4:1–2 RSV).

Christians have said that the chief end of man is to glorify God and to enjoy him forever. But another philosophy of life originates in the sinful human heart that says that happiness and pleasure constitute the chief goals of life; in other words, the chief goal of humanity is the gratification of self rather than the glorification of God. James asked two questions.

A. *The first question is, "What causes wars, and what causes fightings among you?"* James was not referring to international wars but to feuds and conflicts that develop among the people of God. The two words "wars" and "fightings" are significant. The Greek word for "wars" describes a continual or chronic state of feuding or hostility, whereas the word for "fightings" suggests flare-ups or outbreaks resulting from this tension.

B. *With his second question, James answered his first: "Is it not your passions that are at war in your members?"* Very plainly James was saying that quarrels and conflicts arise among God's people because having their own way is their chief aim. James further specified that this warring is "in your members." He was not talking about the members of a congregation but about the members of our bodies. In other words, he was saying that these external wars start within us!

C. *James became more specific as he developed the relationship between passions and wars (v. 2).* He was simply telling us what can and does happen when people choose the gratification of self rather than God as a way of life.

II. This passion to satisfy self undermines the effectiveness of prayer (4:3 RSV).

A. *If we have our sights set on things below, it is only natural that we seek those things.* Jesus said, "Where your treasure is, there will your heart be also" (Matt. 6:21). Even after we become Christians, it is possible for us to place the wrong value on material things in relation to God's purpose for our lives (see Matt. 6:33).

B. *What did James mean when he said, "You ask wrongly"?* He may have been referring to asking for the wrong things (which can be done as the result of ignorance), but most likely he meant asking with evil intent, with wrong motives. He clarified with the next phrase: "To spend it on your passions." God will neither hear nor answer that kind of prayer.

III. Our tendency to gratify ourselves is abhorrent to God (4:4–6 RSV).

A. *James spoke of "unfaithful creatures" (v. 4).* He was talking about unfaithfulness to God. "Do you not know that friendship with the world is enmity with God?" To be a friend of the world is to be an enemy of God.

B. *James enforced what he said with a quote from Proverbs 3:34.* "God opposes the proud, but shows favor to the humble" (v. 6 NIV). "The proud" are those who arrogantly defy God and refuse to admit his sovereignty over the world and over their lives.

IV. This tendency of unregenerate humankind demands repentance (4:7–9).

A. *This paragraph consists of a series of brief exhortations uttered with the quick staccato of military commands.* Each command calls for the self-seeking and worldly-minded Christian to return to God. James sounds very much like an Old Testament prophet in these statements.

B. *The essence of repentance is revealed in James's appeal to "be wretched and mourn and weep" (v. 9 RSV).* This is the picture of the person who realizes what his or her sinfulness has done to a righteous and loving God.

Conclusion

The result of our doing all that James has said is reflected in verse 10: "Humble yourselves in the sight of the Lord, and he shall lift you up." We must acknowledge God's right to rule in our lives. We must also recognize that we are nothing—and only as we become nothing can God be everything in our lives.

SUGGESTED PREACHING PROGRAM FOR THE MONTH OF

JULY

■ **Sunday Mornings**

Continue with the theme "The Spiritual Struggle for the Renewal of the Church."

■ **Sunday Evenings**

Begin a thirteen-message series called "The Doctrine of God."

■ **Wednesday Evenings**

Continue with the lessons from James, "The Practical Expression of Our Faith in Daily Living."

SUNDAY MORNING, JULY 4

Title: Renew My Church to Ministry

Text: "Be ye transformed by the renewing of your mind" **(Rom. 12:2).**

"But unto every one of us is given grace according to the measure of the gift of Christ. . . . For the perfecting of the saints, for the work of the ministry, for the edifying of the body of Christ" **(Eph. 4:7, 12).**

Scripture Reading: Romans 12:1–6; Ephesians 4:7–12

Hymns: "All Hail the Power," Perronet
"O for a Thousand Tongues," Wesley
"Praise to God, Immortal Praise," Barbauld

Offertory Prayer: Heavenly Father, we thank you for life with all its privileges and joys. We thank you for giving us the power to work and earn a living. We come today bringing tithes and offerings as an indication of our desire to dedicate ourselves completely to you. Help us that we might dedicate our bodies as living sacrifices of devotion to you, that others may see the beauty of holiness and come to hunger for a knowledge of Jesus Christ. Bless these tithes and offerings so that others will come to know Jesus as Savior and Friend. In Jesus' name we pray. Amen.

Introduction

God's plan for the church is for each person to present himself or herself as a living sacrifice, not conformed to this world, but transformed by the renewing of the mind, fully demonstrating God's will. Further, it is God's plan that all members of the body function according to the measure of faith God has imparted to them and minister as the grace of God directs them. So the prayer goes on. "Renew our church! Make it a church where every member of the body answers the call to the ministry of believers." What does this mean? Look at it from two viewpoints.

I. Scriptural understanding of a universal ministry.

    A. *Romans 12:3–6 contains several insights that describe ministry.*

        1. Paul spoke of the grace given to him (v. 3).

        2. God has given all believers a measure of faith to express but not all to the same degree (v. 3).

        3. All believers are members of the body of Christ, but not all have the same function. However, all believers do have a ministry.

        4. All believers have gifts given to them by grace, but not all have the same gift (v. 6).

        This Scripture passage calls us to be renewed in our minds toward the church because God has given every member of the body a call to ministry. We are not to think more highly of ourselves; rather, we are to think more soberly (v. 3).

    B. *Ephesians 4:7–12 adds to this concept.*

        1. Every believer is given grace according to the measure of the gift of Christ (Eph. 4:7). Every believer! This compares with Romans 12:3.

        2. God gives some gifts to believers so they can prepare other believers for ministry. Paul said that God gave different believers different roles to fulfill "equip [God's] people for works of service, so that the body of Christ may be built up" (Eph. 4:12 NIV). God gives gifts not to be hidden or neglected, but to fulfill his purpose. Are you building the body or hindering it?

        Furthermore, Ephesians 4:7–12 agrees with the passage that says all believers have been created in Christ Jesus for good works (Eph. 2:10) and with the truth that all believers are priests (Rom. 1:6; 1 Peter 2:5–10). Although our gifts and ministries may differ, no believer is exempt from serving God to build up the body of Christ.

        Therefore, as Christians, let us know our gifts, our ministries; let us value our gifts as precious from the Lord; let us accept them with spiritual satisfaction; and let us use them to fulfill Christ's gracious calling!

II. Practical application of a universal ministry.

    Since Christians form a universal ministry, several practical applications can be made.

    A. *Christ is the head of the church, ministering through his body.* Just as he ministered on earth, he now ministers through us.

B. *If we confine ministry to the pastor or the church staff, we miss God's plan for the church.* This confines too few people to a work that is too big to be done.

C. *Everybody is a servant, not a spectator.* We must leave the stands and get on the playing field. We must leave the balcony and get on the stage. All are players; God is the coach! All are actors; God is the director!

D. *There will be a price to pay.* We must die to self and live in obedience to God's perfect plan. This is why Romans 12:1 precedes 12:3. Commitment calls for a living sacrifice!

E. *If we are to go into battle, we need to be trained and equipped.* Troops need to be trained. All believers are to be part of the crew; God has no passenger list—that is, no one should be merely along for the ride.

Conclusion

A pastor in Dallas, Dr. Ernest Estelle, was dying of cancer some years ago. At a luncheon he said, "A long time ago I realized that there was nothing so significant about Ernest Estelle standing alone, so I decided to identify myself with something that is greater and would last longer than Ernest Estelle. I gave myself to the Lord Jesus Christ and his church. As I look back, I made no mistake about that. All that is worthwhile to me now that I face death is wrapped up in that decision." May this be true for each of us!

SUNDAY EVENING, JULY 4

Title: The Image of God

Text: "God created man in his own image, in the image of God created he him; male and female created he them" (**Gen. 1:27**).

"Howbeit every nation made gods of their own" (**2 Kings 17:29**).

Scripture Reading: Genesis 1:24–28; 2 Kings 17:27–29

Introduction

These two Bible texts present a contrast and a choice: God created people in his own image, and people created gods in their image.

After the fall of the northern kingdom of Israel, the king of Assyria made a new policy. He decided that the people he had transplanted to the captive province of Samaria ought to embrace the religion of that land. Accordingly, he arranged to send one of the captured priests to the ancient shrine of Bethel to teach these people "how they should fear the LORD" (2 Kings 17:28). It didn't work! Governmental plans for religion seldom do. "Every nation made gods of their own" (v. 29).

Which will it be for us: Will we live as those made in the image of God, or will we make gods in our image? This is our problem: Who is created in whose image? Is the god we worship merely a projection of ourselves, or is he, as the hymn writer said, "Our Maker, Defender, Redeemer, and Friend"?

Like a coin, our message today has two sides.

I. On one side of the coin, people today have created a god in their own image.

"Howbeit every nation made gods of their own." In their mythologies, the Greeks and the Romans created gods in their own image. Their gods were not contrasted as being totally different from other people. They conceived of their gods as being like themselves, with the only difference being not in kind but in power. This was not revelation but projection. Unfortunately, like the ancients, people still make gods of their own. What is this god like that humankind has created in its own image?

A. *This god that humankind has created is merely "Superman."* These days God is referred to as "the man upstairs," or "the big guy," or "someone up there who likes me," and so on. It is only a step from such familiarity to idolatry. Many moderns think of God as an easygoing, good-natured, grandfatherly being. This is not "the God and Father of our Lord Jesus Christ" but a god in our own image that we have fashioned ourselves.

B. *This god that humankind has created grows and changes.* This startles us. Those who propose this idea are called "process theologians." In simplest terms, they teach that God has not yet grown up but is still growing and maturing. These theologians do not mean that our ideas of God are developing. That is, or ought to be, true. They do not mean that we are maturing theologically. They mean exactly what they say: that God has not yet grown up.

C. *This god that humankind has created is subject to death.* He is mortal. Some theologians proclaim boldly, even gladly, "God is dead." One well-known theologian has said, "God is dead, and the church is his tombstone. Hallelujah!" In theological circles, nothing could be "deader" than the "God is dead" theology. Perhaps this was a symptom, not a disease.

D. *This god that humankind has created is a power to be manipulated.* This is a "positive thinking" cult that construes religion as a surefire means of getting what one wants, presenting God as a vast reservoir of obedient power that we can manipulate for our own purposes. This is nothing more than primitive magic, which is the attempt to master techniques that will harness the superhuman forces of life for personal ambitions.

E. *This god that humankind has created is advanced science.* Is science the answer to all our questions? Can one who is in need of technical information, or one who is ill, or one who is troubled by some psychological problem merely go to scientists to obtain an answer? Has science taken over a social function that was originally satisfied by religion, the function of offering ultimate security? Has belief in science replaced, in large measure, belief in God? Must our doxology be, "Praise science from whom all blessings flow"? This is not to berate or underestimate the advances and contributions made by science. But the hope of salvation by the advances of science is a false hope. This is a god that people today have created in their own image. And what a god!

II. On the other side of the coin, God created people in his own image.

"God created man in his own image, in the image of God created he him; male and female created he them" (Gen. 1:27). This sounds almost like Hebrew parallelism after the best form of Hebrew poetry. As told in Genesis, creation's story is a great religious poem of six beautiful stanzas. Here we are concerned only with its climactic phrase, the creation of people. "God created man in his own image." What do these words mean? At least two things.

A. *God is a person.* He has created humans as persons akin to himself. A human being is the only creature formed after the pattern of the divine. This is the first great truth with which the Bible comes to grips. It is basic, fundamental, and lies at the foundation of everything else.

The God of the Bible is personal. Little that people do, except sinning, is omitted from the catalog of God's activities as he is pictured for us in Scripture. All our relationships with him are clearly personal. God is a person, and he has created every human being as a person.

B. *As a person, God has intellectual, moral, and spiritual qualities.* He has created people with these same qualities. However hard to define, people have a uniqueness that gives us a subtle superiority over the rest of creation. This opens up for us problems, discoveries, joys, powers, and temptations that make us special creatures.

1. "In his own image" means, for one thing, that like God, people are rational beings. We have a mind. We have the ability to think. "In the image of God" implies that, at least, people are like God in having a mind and a capacity for living by plan and purpose.

2. "In his own image" also means that, like God, people are moral beings, free to make moral choices. Planted deep in the heart of humankind is the earnest desire to be free. Once we begin to believe that we are created in God's image, it becomes difficult for us to be enslaved. God has limited his own freedom by giving people their freedom. This is natural and necessary, since God created people in his own image. A significant part of that image is the right of self-determination. God has given us this right, and he continues to respect it. He will not cancel his gift.

3. Further, "in his own image" means that, like God, people are spiritual beings capable of spiritual relationships. The Bible ushers us into the presence of the living God.

Conclusion

It is by faith in God as he revealed himself in Christ Jesus that people respond to the great truth of their being created in the image and likeness of God. We were made to walk and talk with God. We can have fellowship with our Creator.

Respond by faith and faithfulness to God, who comes to you in human flesh through Jesus Christ. He wants to dwell within you as the living Spirit.

WEDNESDAY EVENING, JULY 7

Title: Who Is a Sinner?

Text: "Therefore to him that knoweth to do good, and doeth it not, to him it is sin" **(James 4:17).**

Scripture Reading: James 4:11–17

Introduction

There are two kinds of sinners in the world. First, there are those who reject Jesus Christ and consequently dwell in spiritual darkness. Among these, there is extreme divergence. Some are openly defiant and hostile toward God, while others are passive and even apparently kind toward Christianity. Second, there are those who are "saved by grace." They are clothed in the righteousness of Jesus Christ, and when God looks on them, he sees them secure under the blood of his Son. Yet these believers in the Lord Jesus still live in unredeemed bodies and therefore fight a continual, lifelong battle with temptation and sin. These are the kind of sinners James was talking about in our text. He was describing Christians who fall victim to sin.

I. James depicted the Christian who criticizes other Christians (4:11–12).

A. *In addressing the need for Christians to permit God to humble them, James mentioned how those who have won some victory may become proud and arrogant in their attitude toward other Christians.* They allow Satan to worm his way in, and they find themselves "evaluating" the lesser victories of their brothers and sisters. The position of victory is often more dangerous than the position of defeat.

B. *James was not talking about the fools who irresponsibly criticize everybody but themselves.* He was speaking of those who are so wise in their own conceit that when it comes to others, they are not able to exercise good judgment at all. Some Christians have come to think so highly of themselves that when they speak of others, criticism and devaluation become automatic.

C. *James enforced his command by reminding us of two facts.*

    1. Those who are guilty of slandering others "speaketh evil of the law, and judgeth the law" (v. 11)—they set themselves above the law of God and count it unworthy of their obedience.

    2. "There is one lawgiver, who is able to save and to destroy" (v. 12). In other words, God is the one who holds the final judgment.

II. James depicted those who arrogantly disregard God (4:13).

A. *Actually, there are three areas of human disregard.*

    1. Verses 1–10 show the human disregard for God in preference for the world and the pleasures of the world.

    2. Verses 11–12 show the human disregard for God in judging one's fellow Christian.

    3. Verses 13–17 show the human disregard for the providence of God. Humans, in their pride, do not want to acknowledge that they cannot determine their own fate and make their own plans.

B. *Notice James's illustration.* He said that those who make plans without God say, "Today or tomorrow we will go to this or that city, spend a year there, carry on business and make money" (v. 13 NIV). Certainly profit-making is essential in any business, but when it becomes a passion and the motivation behind all our activities, we are on dangerous ground.

C. *Why is it wrong to let the profit-making motive become a consuming passion in our lives?* James told us in verse 14, "Why, you do not even know what will happen tomorrow" (NIV). Humankind stands between the past and the future, and when we refuse to trust God with our tomorrows, we are torn between the memory of the past and the ignorance of the future.

D. *What are the lessons to be learned from these facts?*

    1. We should take full advantage of today and its opportunities.

    2. Our ignorance of what tomorrow holds does not mean that we should not think about tomorrow and make provision for it. Most of the duties for which God holds us responsible call us to work for tomorrow.

III. James depicted the mystery of life (4:14–15).

A. *Here is one of the greatest questions ever asked.* "What is your life?" James's answer is profound: "It is even a vapour, that appeareth for a little time, and then vanisheth away" (v. 14). He was illustrating the swiftness and transitory nature of life.

B. *The great tragedy is that most people confuse life with the circumstances of life.* Life is largely independent of its circumstances. A person may be rich yet unhappy or poor yet happy. A person may be in prison yet sing, as did Paul and Silas, while another may be free yet be sad and depressed.

C. *James's meaning is that when we are fully aware of our duty yet fail to perform it, we sin (v. 17).* It is not enough to know to do right; we must do what we know we ought to do. James was talking about sins of omission.

Conclusion

When emperors were crowned at Constantinople in the ancient past, the royal mason would set before the emperor a certain number of marble slabs. The new emperor was to choose one of these for his tombstone. The point of this custom was for the new emperor to realize that he would do well at his coronation to remember his funeral. Life is time, and the purpose of time is to prepare for eternity. There is no more profound question in all of Scripture than this one that James placed before us: Who is a sinner? May God help us to consider that question with great soberness.

SUNDAY MORNING, JULY 11

Title: What You Believe Matters

Text: "One Lord, one faith. . . . Till we all come in the unity of the faith" **(Eph. 4:5, 13).**

Scripture Reading: Ephesians 4:4–6, 11–16

Hymns: "O God, Our Help in Ages Past," Watts
"'Tis So Sweet to Trust in Jesus," Stead
"God Will Take Care of You," Martin

Offertory Prayer: Our loving Father, we thank you for adopting us as your children. With eyes wide open to your mercies, we come to dedicate ourselves to you afresh. Help us to use our talents and testimony that others may know Christ. As we bring our tithes and offerings, we pray your blessings upon them. Help us meet the expenses of the ministry of this church and engage in ministries to the ends of the earth. In Jesus' name we pray. Amen.

Introduction

What we believe is basic to the renewal of the church. If we are to be equipped for ministry today, we must not only know what we stand for and what we stand against, but also what we stand on! What we believe will ultimately determine what we do.

The Bible speaks of a general faith, something that everybody has—even Satan. It also speaks of a saving faith, as in Ephesians 2:8: "For by grace are ye saved through faith; and that not of yourselves: it is the gift of God." And it also speaks of "the faith," that is, the truths that have been revealed through Jesus Christ and God's Word, which we have accepted. These are not just intellectually grasped; they are personally and spiritually received. Jude 3 says that we are to "contend for the faith which was once delivered unto the saints." Therefore what you believe matters! Four questions about what you believe must be answered.

I. Is your faith really "your" faith?

Is your faith yours or your parents'? Is it yours or your friends'? Is it your faith or just a doctrine of the church? Has "the faith" really become yours, or is it like a sign in a bookstore window that reads Secondhand Theology for Sale? We don't need a secondhand theology; we need a first edition! This faith must become ours by personal experience. It is not enough to say, "I know the truth." We must say, "The truth is mine!"

If we are growing in Christ, the truths of God's Word become real and illumined in our minds by the Holy Spirit. One such occurrence for me was while I was a seminary student and pastor. I believed the resurrection of Jesus, but I truly came to know it personally in my heart by means of the work of the Holy Spirit in my life.

II. Is your faith working?

What is your faith accomplishing? Does it have power in your life?

A. *A real faith will meet your personal needs.* Faith determines how we live, where we stand, and what we do. It provides a foundation that can withstand the storms of life (Matt. 7:24–27).

B. *A real faith will give you something to share.* When we truly believe, we witness to him whom we believe (2 Tim. 1:12).

 People everywhere need help. People are lost to God, to their families, to the church, and to themselves. Do you have a word for them? Do you know how to tell someone to be saved? Do you have in your mind your own testimony of salvation? Do you know Scripture verses for sharing this truth? What you believe matters!

III. Is your faith basic?

The distinction between an opinion and a conviction is that an opinion is something you hold while a conviction is something that holds you. How many convictions do you have? A basic faith is composed of convictions.

A. *A basic faith consists of beliefs that really matter.* What you believe about Jesus Christ and how he relates to salvation, victory, and destiny matters. What you believe about the Bible matters. Do you truly believe that it is God's Word? What you believe about the Holy Spirit matters. What you believe about salvation and the church and all of the basic doctrines of the Bible matters.

B. *A basic faith is personal.* What do you believe? What do you believe about God, the Trinity, Jesus Christ, the Holy Spirit, witnessing, stewardship, and the many basic truths of the Scriptures? Write out your own personal theology and be strengthened in what you believe.

C. *A basic faith is one worth dying for.* Would you die for what you believe? Many have, such as Stephen, Paul, and Polycarp in ages past; Bill Wallace and Jim Elliot in the last century; as well as Christian martyrs who die in far-off places every day. What do you believe that you would hold at any cost?

IV. Is your faith Christ-centered?

The foundation of our faith is Jesus Christ. The disciples stood firm on Jesus' testimony of who he was. They had the Old Testament, but their walk of faith began with an encounter with Jesus Christ. They met him and followed him, and he changed their lives!

The earliest known confession is "Jesus is Lord" (Rom. 10:9 RSV). He is the center of our faith.

Conclusion

The acid test of genuine saving faith is spiritual maturity, Christlikeness, the stature of the fullness of Christ. It is not enough just to be orthodox; we are to be Christlike! This is being renewed in our faith.

SUNDAY EVENING, JULY 11

Title: The Justice of God

Text: "Will not the Judge of all the earth do right?" (**Gen. 18:25 NIV**).

Scripture Reading: Genesis 18:22–33

Introduction

When in 1938 Richard Whitney, president of the New York Stock Exchange, was sentenced to only five years in Sing Sing prison upon conviction of a $225,000 embezzlement count, with a parole possible in three and one-half years, there was general resentment all over the United States. This was pointedly illustrated by a St. Louis judge when a young man was convicted in court of stealing two dollars from a gas station. "Richard Whitney got five years for stealing $225,000," said the judge. "That would be $45,000 a year, $120 a day, $5 an hour. You stole $2. That would be twenty-four minutes. That is your sentence." In this story, *justice* is the key word.

The basic meaning of the word *just* is "straight" or "right." Those who have lived their lives straight in line with the moral law of God are just, or righteous. The foundation on which the whole world stands is God's justice.

After God revealed to Abraham his intention of destroying Sodom, the great patriarch prayed that God would spare the whole city for the sake of the righteous in it. "Will you sweep away the righteous with the wicked? . . . Far be it from you to do such a thing—to kill the righteous with the wicked alike. Far be it from you! Will not the Judge of all the earth do right?" (Gen. 18:23–25 NIV).

Our main concern is the theological question Abraham asked of God: "Will not the Judge of all the earth do right?" Abraham's prayer is based on his faith in the justice of God. His was a fair question, and a just God welcomed it, just as he welcomes honest inquiry from his people today.

God is just. This is where we begin. This is our initial premise. But what significance does this tremendous fact have for our lives? The justice of God does at least four things for us.

I. The justice of God assures.

A. *The justice of God assures us that prayer makes sense.* Abraham's prayer was based on his faith that God is a righteous God. In the great moral perplexities of life, it makes sense to fall back on those qualities in God that are his very nature. This is our assurance in prayer. This appeal to God's justice rather than to his mercy touches the foundation of things. Thus those true believers who are face-to-face with problems that are too much for them take them to God in prayer.

B. *The justice of God assures us that our world rests solidly on a moral foundation.* God supports what is right and opposes what is wrong. The universe is not a moral chaos where any kind of conduct is indiscriminately accepted. The God who governs the world examines, weighs, and judges the motives and actions of humankind with an impartiality unswayed by the wealth, prestige, or position of the one under examination.

C. *The justice of God assures us that the final consummation will be right and good.* In the end the right will prevail, for God is on the side of the right. Sometimes there is seeming confusion between good and evil in the world; we don't understand God's ways and grow impatient with him. Still our hearts find refuge in the sure belief that God will do what will be seen in the end as right.

II. The justice of God implies.

1. *The justice of God implies his judgment on the wicked, the sinful, and the rebellious.* The moral constitution of the world is such that every sin carries within itself the seeds of the sinner's destruction, its own judgment. This is true because a God of justice rules at all times and under all circumstances.

2. *The justice of God implies his vindication of the innocent and the oppressed.* Unless God opposes the evil that destroys us, he cannot be for us. The Greeks defined justice as giving every person his or her due. Their idea of balancing two sides against one another is expressed

in that familiar symbol of justice, the scales. In sharp contrast to the Greek idea is the prophetic image from Amos, who said, "But let justice roll down like waters, and righteousness like an everflowing stream" (Amos 5:24 RSV). Amos is telling us that God does what is right actively, not passively. Justice exists in relation to a person. Justice is something that is done by a person. An act of injustice is condemned, not because a law has been broken, but because a person has been hurt, a person whose anguish may reach the very heart of God.

3. *The justice of God implies his correction of earthly injustice in the life to come.* The faith that one day all accounts will be balanced, all discrepancies made right is one of the most powerful reasons for belief in life after death. It could never be right that Elijah and Jezebel, Herod Antipas and John the Baptist, Paul and Nero, should in the end fare the same. It will not be. God is just.

III. The justice of God requires.

A. *The justice of God requires a cross in the heart of God.* Jesus died for our sins on Calvary's tree. But long before, yes, from the foundation of the world, a cross was raised in the heart of God. Paul wrote to the Corinthians, "All things are of God, who hath reconciled us to himself by Jesus Christ."

B. *God was in Christ, reconciling the world unto himself (2 Cor. 5:18–19).* The justice of God requires that "the soul that sinneth, it shall die" (Ezek. 18:4). God requires that "whatsoever a man soweth, that shall he also reap" (Gal. 6:7). Then how could any of us, with our corrupt, sinful nature, ever hope to cross the gulf that separates us from a holy God? How could God's justice ever be satisfied so that his mercy could be made possible? There was only one way; and that was to provide a substitute to die in his place.

C. *The justice of God requires justification by faith as the gift of God.* "God presented Christ as a sacrifice of atonement, through the shedding of his blood—to be received by faith. He did this to demonstrate his righteousness, because in his forbearance he had left the sins committed beforehand unpunished—he did it to demonstrate his righteousness at the present time, so as to be just and the one who justifies whose who have faith in Jesus" (Rom. 3:25–26 NIV). How can sinners ever be declared righteous? How can they be pronounced, "Not guilty"? How can they ever be justified? The New Testament answers, "By faith." Faith is the condition of God's free gift. In that same third chapter of Romans, Paul also said, "There is no difference between Jew and Gentile, for all have sinned and fall short of the glory of God, and are *justified freely* by his grace through the redemption that came by Christ Jesus" (vv. 22–24 NIV, emphasis added).

D. *The justice of God requires righteousness on the part of his children.* Since God is righteous, he expects righteousness from his children. Because God is both all-knowing and all-just, those who do not strive to be just and righteous cannot please him. The Bible, especially the Old Testament, emphasizes that sacrifices, rituals, and prayer have no value if they are not accompanied by righteousness of life (see Amos 5:15).

IV. The justice of God warns.

A. *The justice of God warns that we are not to doubt God's character.* Even though in our hearts we are committed to God's justice, our experiences and observations often cause us to ask questions. God welcomes honest inquiry, but we are not to doubt him. Under tremendous pressure, the prophet Jeremiah said, "Righteous art thou, O LORD, when I complain to thee: yet I would plead my case before thee" (Jer. 12:1 RSV). Jeremiah was saying, "You are a just God, but all the same I want to ask a question." And here is his question: "Why does the way of the wicked prosper? Why do all who are treacherous thrive?" (12:1 RSV). In every age this question has caused great saints of God to harbor dim, gray doubts about the justice of God in their hearts. But we must not do this.

B. *The justice of God warns us not to pit love and justice against each other.* With God they are one and the same thing. Justice is love expressed toward people in human relations. Too often we have viewed love as soft and naive sentiment, and justice as a hard-nosed demand for punishment. This contradicts the spirit of the New Testament. Jesus was never more just than when he forgave the adulterous woman, never more loving than when he drove the money changers from the temple. Love and justice are one.

C. *The justice of God warns us not to ask for justice but for mercy.* A man once told Billy Graham, "When I get to heaven, all that I will ask is justice." Billy Graham replied, "My friend, if all you get is justice, then you will go to hell. You won't need justice. You will need mercy." And so will we all!

Conclusion

A final word: Any study of the justice of God is bound to throw us back on the grace of God. God is a God of justice, but he is also a God of mercy and grace.

WEDNESDAY EVENING, JULY 14

Title: A Warning to the Rich

Text: "Go to now, ye rich men, weep and howl for your miseries that shall come upon you. Your riches are corrupted, and your garments are moth-eaten" (**James 5:1–2**).

Scripture Reading: James 5:1–6

Introduction

In our study of the final chapter of James, we find that this wise pastor has some direct words about relationships between Christians within the body of Christ. It seems that James began this teaching in 4:13, which deals particularly with arrogance and self-centeredness in the Christian's life. Although poverty was far more widespread than wealth in the early church, some people had been blessed materially. Some wealthy landowners who belonged to the church were misusing their wealth and taking advantage of those who worked for them. Whether they were genuine Christians we do not know. They may have accommodated themselves by using the church for selfish advantage. In any event, James spoke plainly and sharply to them, and his words are good advice for all of us.

I. These rich men had taken for granted the material blessings God allowed them to receive (5:1–3).

A. *There may have been a secondary purpose in James's mind as he penned these harsh words to the rich.* Some people in the church, though not wealthy, may have been seeking after riches. They may have begun to be a little prosperous, and the taste of prosperity was sweet in their mouths. So these words might also have been "preventative medicine" for some of the Christians. James spoke plainly first about the doom of the rich who placed their confidence in material things. He had mentioned the rich in two earlier passages. In 1:10 James reminded wealthy Christians that their wealth would soon pass away. Then in the opening verses of chapter 2 he referred to the unbelieving rich.

In the passage we are studying tonight, James appears to be delivering a broadside to the rich, speaking in the manner of an Amos or a Micah, declaring that the judgment of God will inevitably fall on them and on their wealth.

B. *James began his warning by telling the self-centered rich to "weep and howl" because of God's judgments, which were soon to come upon them.* Someone has said that there are four classes of people when it comes to the matter of possessions: (1) those who are rich in this world and poor toward God; (2) those who are poor in this world and rich toward God; (3) those who are poor both in this world and in the next; and (4) those who are rich in this world's goods, but because they hold them with a loose hand, are rich in the next world also. Sad to say, this last class is not a very large one.

What was James calling these deceitful rich people to do? He told them, "Weep and howl for your miseries that shall come upon you" (v. 1). This is not the weeping of true repentance, though. For they will have realized too late that their wealth is not a passport to heaven and into the presence of God. They will "weep and howl," but it will avail them nothing.

C. *In the ancient world wealth was of three types—food, costly garments, and precious metals.* James did not name all three of these specifically, but what he had to say in verses 2 and 3 suggests that he had them in mind. He said, "Your riches have rotted" (literal translation). This could refer to food that the rich had hoarded and that had become unfit for human consumption. (Compare the manner in which the Israelites attempted to hoard manna in Ex. 16.) The garments James mentioned were expensive clothes that had become moth-eaten and consequently without value. Also, the wealthy people's gold and silver were covered in rust. Though gold does not actually rust, this was probably James's way of saying that their money had lost its value. Then he added, "Ye have heaped treasure together for the last days" (v. 3).

II. James listed the sins of the rich (5:4–6).

A. *The first sin was injustice.* These rich men in their greed had withheld wages from those who worked for them. James dramatically pictured the wages of these defrauded laborers crying out (the Greek word means "to shriek") to God for vengeance (v. 4).

B. *The second sin was extravagance.* "Ye have lived in pleasure on the earth, and been wanton; ye have nourished your hearts, as in a day of slaughter" (v. 5). This is a picture of people wallowing in luxury and immorality. Like cattle fattened for slaughter, they have grown fat in body, mind, and spirit.

C. *The third sin was violence against the righteous.* "Ye have condemned and killed the just" (v. 6). James was probably referring to legal or judicial actions taken against the poor.

Conclusion

James pulled no punches, as in fiery, righteous indignation he condemned those who have misused the blessings of wealth God had allowed them to receive. Instead of using their prosperity to bless others and to glorify God, they had used it to curse and destroy. Even though many godly men and women through the ages have used their wealth to bless others and advance God's kingdom on earth, the temptations that accompany material affluence are legion.

SUNDAY MORNING, JULY 18

Title: Renew My Walk

Text: "Be ye transformed by the renewing of your mind" (**Rom. 12:2**).

"He that saith he abideth in him ought himself also so to walk, even as he walked" (**1 John 2:6**).

Scripture Reading: Romans 12:1–2; 1 John 2:1–6

Hymns: "There's a Wideness in God's Mercy," Faber
"O Master, Let Me Walk with Thee," Gladden
"Make Me a Blessing," Wilson

Offertory Prayer: Holy Father, you have been so very generous to us. Help us to recognize that every good and perfect gift comes from you. Help us to give ourselves to you as you have so freely given your riches to us. Today we come bringing our tithes and offerings that we may provide financial support for your work in this congregation and throughout the world. We pray your blessings on Christian professors in colleges and universities. We pray your blessings on Christian doctors and nurses. We pray your blessings on evangelists as they carry the good news to the ends of the earth. Bless these gifts to your honor and glory and to the salvation of the world. In Jesus' name we pray. Amen.

Introduction

The day of the church is not over! The church belongs to Christ. He is the Head; the church is his body. The life of Christ is the life of the church, and that life can be renewed by him who is our life.

The church must choose its direction—the world's plan or God's plan, the mold of the world or the mind of God. This is what renewal is, because when the church yields to God's plan, it is renewed spiritually.

The prayer "Renew my church," is a prayer to "Renew my walk." It is God's plan that the church be renewed in mind, ministry, faith, and walk to a life that is disciplined by Jesus Christ.

A renewed walk involves a disciplined life. Notice two aspects of that walk.

I. The roots of a disciplined life.

A. *A disciplined life is a living sacrifice.* The words "living sacrifice" describe the Christian life as a disciplined life in the daily walk. In the background is the sacrificial system in the temple. The word "present" is a technical term for presenting the Levitical offering. Such offerings required a priest, an altar, and a sacrificial animal.

Today we are not required to offer an animal; we are to present ourselves. We are priests to God; we have our altar, Jesus Christ; and our lives are the sacrifice. We present ourselves in death; that is, we die to ourselves, our goals, and our conformity to the world.

Luke 9:23 speaks of taking up our cross daily. That means death to our sinful way of life. Have you built an altar in your life? Have you put yourself on it? Have you put all that you have on it? The disciplined life does just that!

B. *A disciplined life thinks soberly.* Romans 12:3 says that we are "to think soberly." The word "sober" is translated "self-controlled," or "disciplined." A disciplined mind so governs all passions and desires that the believer becomes conformed to the mind of Christ.

We are to think disciplined thoughts about ourselves and not think more highly of ourselves than we ought. We are not to be proud or self-absorbed but sober and disciplined. We are to evidence a humble, surrendered attitude.

This is the kind of life God gives to the believer (2 Tim. 1:7).

C. *A disciplined life is a yoked life.* Matthew 11:29 says, "Take my yoke upon you, and learn of me." Disciples are those who learn from another; they adhere to the person and teachings of their teacher. Thus disciples of Jesus are those who learn from Jesus. They adhere to his person and his teachings. They are yoked to Jesus.

A yoke is a symbol of submission; therefore a disciplined life is one submissive to the authority of Jesus Christ. Three words are involved in this kind of submission.

1. Control. The disciplined life is under Christ's control. The disciplined person has a meek spirit. The word "meek" is pictured as the taming of a wild horse. When a horse is tamed, it is "broken" by its rider, brought under the rider's control. A disciplined life is "broken" by Christ's control.

   Jesus' life was perfectly disciplined. He was always under his Father's control. And as Jesus was to his Father, so are we to him! We are to be under his control constantly, our will trained to his will. We must strive to be consistent, disciplined, trained.

   Our family had an Old English sheepdog that was trained and obedient, but occasionally he would demonstrate his animal nature by snapping at someone. He acted disobedient and undisciplined. Many times we are like that dog. Self snaps back at God and at others; we are disobedient to Christ's control; and our attitudes and activities are undisciplined. The yoked life is one of Christ's control over us.

2. Consent. We become disciplined when we consent to be disciplined. We present ourselves as a living sacrifice (Rom. 12:1) by coming to Jesus as Matthew 11:28 invites us. We take his yoke and learn more about him. No one forces us to do these things. If we are to walk as he walked, we must yield ourselves to him.

3. Completeness. This word involves all of life under Christ's control. It is the total discipline he demands. How disciplined are we to be? The following Scripture passages answer this question: 2 Corinthians 10:4–5 talks about "bringing into captivity every thought to the obedience of Christ." Matthew 4:4 says that we must give account of "every idle word." Luke 9:23 says that we must "take up [our] cross daily." And 1 Thessalonians 5:18 commands, "Give thanks in all circumstances" (NIV).

   So all of life is to be under Christ's control. He is to be the center of all our goals, our single focus (Luke 11:34; Phil. 3:13).

II. The fruits of a disciplined life.

The roots of a disciplined life will be evidenced in the fruits of such a life. Ask yourself these questions.

A. *How disciplined is your attitude toward yourself, God, and others?* Do you have love for the Lord and for your neighbor?

B. *How disciplined are your words?* "Let the words of my mouth, and the meditation of my heart, be acceptable in thy sight" (Ps. 19:14). "Death and life are in the power of the tongue" (Prov. 18:21).

C. *How disciplined are your morals?* We are to seek the most thorough moral purity.

D. *How disciplined is your worship?* "Enter into his gates with thanksgiving" (Ps. 100:4). "Not forsaking the assembling of yourselves together" (Heb. 10:25).

E. *How disciplined are you in the grace of giving?* Is giving a grace that you experience or a task that you endure? Jesus said, "Give, and it shall be given unto you" (Luke 6:38).

F. *How disciplined are you in your devotional life?* There is no mastery in the Christian life apart from a disciplined devotional life of Bible reading and prayer. Jesus taught prayer as both private and public, silent and spoken, seeking and waiting. Disciplined prayer is personal, honest, specific, and consistent. We are to read the Bible expectantly, submissively, and regularly.

G. *How disciplined are you in your ministry?* God has given a ministry to every believer. This is both a privilege and a responsibility.

Conclusion

To renew my walk may mean a change of masters and a change of direction. It will result in fulfillment instead of frustration. It will mean a life of rest in my soul. This is the prayer the church needs to pray: "Renew my church, Lord, and renew my walk!"

SUNDAY EVENING, JULY 18

Title: The Call of God

Text: "And the LORD came, and stood, and called as at other times, Samuel, Samuel. Then Samuel answered, Speak; for thy servant heareth" (**1 Sam. 3:10**).

Scripture Reading: 1 Samuel 3:1–14

Introduction

Awakened from sleep, the boy Samuel heard someone calling his name. Thinking that the aged priest Eli had called, Samuel ran quickly to his bedside, but Eli had not called. After the third time this happened, Eli realized that the voice must be the voice of God. He told the boy to listen well and, if the voice came again, to say, "Speak, LORD; for thy servant heareth" (1 Sam. 3:9). When the voice came the fourth time, Samuel did as he had been instructed. The message he received from God was not a pleasant one. Eli's blasphemous sons were about to be punished, and so was Eli because he had not restrained them.

This ancient story reflects a simpler view of life than ours. God still speaks to people. God calls us even now. Consider several pointed questions.

I. When does God call?

A. *God calls when our hearts are impressionable and tender.* This is true in the time of childhood, especially so when a child has been nurtured in the things of God. This was true of the boy Samuel, who had never known anything else. This is true in a time of sickness, which teaches us our weaknesses and our dependence on God. This is true in a time of sorrow, for sorrow is one of God's great ministers. This is true in a time of disappointment and defeat.

B. *God calls when we have reached the end of our rope and know we have.* It has been truly said, "Our extremity is God's opportunity."

C. *God calls when we seek his face.* The first tenet of biblical religion is that God—not us—took the initiative to bring about our salvation. Yet everywhere the Bible encourages us to approach God, to call on his name, to seek his face. Those who seek God's face will hear God's call in their souls (Dan. 10:12).

II. Why does God call?

A. *God calls to offer salvation from our sins.* Christians are referred to in the New Testament as "the called" (Rom. 8:28). We find such phrases as "the called of Jesus Christ" (Rom. 1:6), "the called according to his purpose" (Rom. 8:28), and "called to be saints" (1 Cor. 1:2). The meaning of all this is that God took the initiative in our salvation (1 John 4:10). We are to call on the name of the Lord because he first called us (Rom. 10:13).

B. *God calls to judge us.* God's call often comes as his response to human wickedness, to announce his judgment. When God called Samuel in the night, he gave him a message of judgment on Eli and all his house (1 Sam. 3:12–13).

Do we think God will be soft and sentimental about our sins, like some doting, earthly parent, and fail to judge us because of our sins? Not so! His judgments are sure.

C. *God calls to humble us, to remind us of his sovereignty.* The moral foundations of this universe rest on this inflexible fact. A silent power, rigorous and austere, works certain retribution or reward, as the case may be. Let us not think the sovereignty of God will be set aside just because we may not believe in it. The nature of this universe does not change to suit our whims. God is in charge whether we realize it or not. Things are not slipping out of his hands.

D. *God calls to enlist us in service and to assign to us tasks.* God commissioned certain people to act as his prophets. But God's call to enlistment does not come only on the high level of the prophets. He also calls ordinary people like you and me into his service to do ordinary tasks—and sometimes extraordinary tasks. If God has called you to serve him, if God has assigned you some task, that job may get done without you. But your failure to enlist will spoil his plan for you, for nobody else can do what God had intended for you to do.

III. Who does God call?

A. *God calls nations and leaders of nations.* There is no more striking illustration of the fact of God's sovereign rule in history than in the references to Cyrus, king of Persia. In Isaiah 44–45, Israel is in captivity, but their captors, the Babylonians, have fallen before Cyrus and the rising tide of the Persian Empire. It is God's purpose, we learn here, to use Cyrus as an instrument to restore the Jews to their own land. He even referred to Cyrus as "my anointed."

B. *God calls churches to do his will.* Acts 13:2 says, "As they ministered to the Lord, and fasted, the Holy Ghost said, Separate me Barnabas and Saul for the work whereunto I have called them." This call came to a church.

C. *God calls individuals to do his will.* In his call, God's point of contact is the individual. There is no other door, no other way. Nations, parliaments, institutions, and churches are all made up of individuals. If God knocks at their doors, he must knock at the door of individual hearts. When he has something he wants done, he calls on an individual.

IV. Where does God call?

A. *God calls us where we are.* God called Paul on the road to Damascus as he neared the city. He called Isaiah in the temple as he pondered the nation's sad predicament precipitated by King Uzziah's death.

B. *God calls us in the course of our daily work.* He called Amos from following the flock. He called Elisha from following the plow. He called missionary William Carey from the shoe cobbler's bench.

C. *God calls us even when we are trying to run away.* Elijah lost heart and left his post of duty, but God found him in a cave on Mount Horeb and asked, "What are you doing here, Elijah?" (1 Kings 19:9 RSV). God called Jonah, who fled from his call, but God's voice found him and brought him back to his task. We may try to hide from God, but we cannot escape him.

V. What responses does God receive when he calls?

Every person must answer for himself or herself.

A. *We may ignore his call.* Through conscience, God's call is constantly breaking in, calling us to follow him, to serve him, to honor him, to worship him; and so often we ignore him.

B. *We may reject his call.* Some do so deliberately, stubbornly. Others do so painfully, sorrowfully, but the result is the same. The rich young ruler who came to Jesus considered Jesus' terms of discipleship and rejected them. So we read, "He went away sorrowful" (Mark 10:22 RSV); nevertheless, he went away.

C. *We may accept God's call.* We may say yes to him. The towering mountain peaks in the history of revelation have been those who have heard God's voice saying, "Whom shall I send, and who will go for us?" and have answered, "Here am I; send me" (Isa. 6:8).

Conclusion

Let me make this matter very personal. Let me leave it at your very doorstep.

Christian friend, God is calling you as an individual. What will you do about it? What will your response be?

Unsaved friend, God is calling you. He is calling now. Don't turn him away. Instead, hear his voice and respond to him. Will you?

WEDNESDAY EVENING, JULY 21

Title: Being Patient in Affliction

Text: "Take, my brethren, the prophets, who have spoken in the name of the Lord, for an example of suffering affliction, and of patience. Behold, we count them happy which endure" **(James 5:10–11)**.

Scripture Reading: James 5:7–11

Introduction

Beginning with verse 7 of the final chapter of James's epistle, James's entire tone changed. Note that he reverted to the word "brethren" as his word of address. His theme in these verses is a call for steadfastness in times of great affliction and trial. He made an appeal for several things.

I. James exhorted Christians to be patient under trial (5:7–8).

A. *James began his letter with an exhortation to "let patience have her perfect work, that ye may be perfect and entire, wanting nothing" (1:4).* Then he began its conclusion with a similar appeal: "Be patient therefore, brethren, unto the coming of the Lord" (5:7). The word "therefore" doubtlessly points to the sufferings that poor Christians were undergoing at the hands of the merciless rich, which is the theme in the first six verses of this chapter. The inference is that all the oppression they were undergoing would be brought to justice, and they were to exercise godly patience under trial.

B. *The word James used for "patience" is significant; it means to be long-tempered, not short-tempered.* It suggests a self-restraint that enables one to bear insult and suffer injury without resorting to a hasty act of retaliation.

C. *James told us why we are to be patient.* When James said that we are to be patient under affliction unto the coming of the Lord, he was talking not only about duration—the length of time we are to bear insult and trial—but also the reason for our willingness to be long-suffering. The idea is that suffering Christians are not to take matters into their own hands; rather, they are to know that God is able to avenge them, and they are to wait for *him* to act.

II. James showed Christians how to be patient under trial (5:7, 10–11).

He used three illustrations to support his point.

A. *First, James illustrated the experience of the farmer (v. 7).* The farmer patiently waits for his land to produce a crop. He prepares the soil, sows the seed, and keeps the fields free of grass and weeds. Then he waits expectantly. James made an application: "Be ye also patient; stablish your hearts" (v. 8).

B. *Next, James illustrated the experience of the prophets (v. 10).* "Take, my brethren, the prophets, who have spoken in the name of the Lord, for an example of suffering affliction, and of patience." There are two ways in which the prophets were an example to us—in their sufferings and in their patience.

C. *Finally, James illustrated the experience of Job (v. 11).* We know from reading the book of Job that Job sometimes gave vent to outbursts of frustration and even anger. But in spite of his trials, he maintained a persistent trust in God. This is what James meant when he referred to "the patience of Job." He used a different word entirely from the word meaning "long-suffering," which he had been using all along. For Job did not show a great deal of long-suffering, though he clearly showed steadfastness, which is the meaning of this kind of "patience."

Conclusion

The very fact that James spoke of God as "full of compassion and mercy" (v. 11 NIV) suggests that our Lord feels with us when we are undergoing these hard times. The writer of Hebrews underscored this thought when he said of the Lord Jesus, "We do not have a high priest who is unable to empathize with our weaknesses" (4:15 NIV). Therefore we must remember that our Lord is hurting with us when we are enduring the hard times of life. From it all will come the strength to grow and develop as mature sons and daughters in his family.

SUNDAY MORNING, JULY 25

Title: The Spirit for Renewal

Text: "Be ye transformed by the renewing of your mind" **(Rom. 12:2).**

"Not by works of righteousness which we have done, but according to his mercy he saved us, by the washing of regeneration, and renewing of the Holy Ghost" **(Titus 3:5).**

Scripture Reading: Romans 12:1–2; Titus 3:1–5

Hymns: "Love Divine, All Loves Excelling," Wesley
"The King of Love My Shepherd Is," Baker
"Breathe on Me," McKinney

Offertory Prayer: Holy heavenly Father, we thank you for the gift of life. We especially thank you for the gift of eternal life through faith in your Son, Jesus Christ. We thank you for the gifts you have given us that our lives might be fruitful and productive in your service and in ministries of helpfulness to others. Today we come for worship that we might give ourselves to you afresh. Accept our tithes and offerings and bless them in helping us to give ourselves more completely to you. In Jesus' name we pray. Amen.

Introduction

The key to renewal is not our plans, our programs, or our techniques; rather, it is the person of the Holy Spirit. Titus 3:5 says that the Holy Spirit both regenerates and renews the believer.

If we are not careful, we may find ourselves in a situation like that in the story of some "bush missionaries." They camped for several days near a monkey colony. When they returned to the camp one day, they saw the monkeys scurrying about, appearing to imitate the missionaries. In the center of the camp the monkeys had gathered firewood into a pile and were sitting around it as though warming themselves. Their only problem? They lacked the fire!

The church can be like that: we can have firewood but no fire! The fire is the Holy Spirit, and the Holy Spirit is the Spirit of renewal.

I. The hope of renewal.

Someone has said that the Holy Spirit is the displaced member of the Godhead. There is an apparent absence of the Holy Spirit in the life of the church and an apparent ignorance of his ministry. What do you know about the Holy Spirit and his ministry in your life? There are two basic terms used in the New Testament to describe the ministry of the Spirit to believers.

  A. *The indwelling of the Holy Spirit.* The Holy Spirit enters the life of a
     person when he or she is born again. The death, burial, and resur-
     rection of the Lord Jesus Christ provide the means of salvation; the
     Holy Spirit effects it.

1. He convicts us of our need for salvation (John 16:8).
2. He regenerates us in salvation (John 3:6–7).
3. He takes up residence within us at conversion (see John 14:16–17; Rom. 8:9).
4. He seals us to the day of redemption. He is our assurance of salvation (Eph. 1:13–14).

B. *The infilling of the Holy Spirit.* This is a term that refers to the control of the Spirit. Ephesians 5:18 says, "Be not drunk with wine, wherein is excess; but be filled with the Spirit." It is not a picture of an empty vessel being filled; rather, it describes the situation that occurs when one is filled with wine. It means that every part of a person's body is affected—how he or she walks, talks, thinks, and sees. It is the idea of control. When the Holy Spirit is in control, something happens in our lives.

1. He delivers us from the defeat of self (Rom. 7:8–25).
2. He cultivates Christlike qualities (Gal. 5:22–23).
3. He teaches us (1 Cor. 2:9–10).
4. He leads us (Rom. 8:14).
5. He assures us (Rom. 8:16).
6. He strengthens us (Eph. 3:16).
7. He empowers us for witnessing (Acts 1:8).

II. The how of renewal.

There are five things to remember as to how our lives are brought under the Holy Spirit's control.

A. *Decision.* We must decide to live a Spirit-filled life. It is an act of our will. A positive response means that we have the Holy Spirit living inside of us; even more importantly, we allow the Holy Spirit to have us!

B. *Daily.* Being filled is not a onetime event. It is not a spiritual vaccination. Instead, it is a continual experience. Ephesians 5:18 contains a present tense verb, "be filled." Being filled with the Spirit is a daily experience.

C. *Devotional.* The Spirit-filled life is nurtured by our devotional life. They go hand in hand. We need time with God's Word and time for prayer if we want to be the spiritual people Christ would have us to be.

D. *Doubtless.* The Spirit-filled life is a life of faith. We are saved by faith, we live by faith, we walk by faith, and we are filled with the Holy Spirit by faith—not by feelings, but by faith. Let us be done with doubting! Let us trust God's Word for this relationship.

E. *Discovery.* The Spirit-filled life is one of the daily discoveries of God's riches. Romans 6:13 is the pattern for discovery. "Yield yourselves unto God . . . and your members as instruments of righteousness unto God." This means self—every part of our being. When we continually submit ourselves to God's will, the discovery of the Holy Spirit's ministry is real!

Conclusion

Lawrence of Arabia went to London following his exciting military life and took with him a number of Arab chieftains. It was their first trip outside the desert, and they were awed with the city. They were most impressed with the water faucets in the hotel rooms—they came from a barren desert land to a place where simply by turning a handle at any time water would rush freely.

After they left, the hotel management made an unusual discovery. The water faucets had been removed! The Arabs had taken them. They thought they could take the faucets back, turn the handle, and water would pour out. How impossible! The faucets were not connected to the water supply!

And it is just as impossible for us as Christians to produce power and Christlike qualities apart from being controlled by the Holy Spirit.

SUNDAY EVENING, JULY 25

Title: The Gentleness of God

Text: "And thy gentleness hath made me great" **(Ps. 18:35).**

Scripture Reading: Psalm 18:32–45

Introduction

At no other place in the Bible is this exact word used to describe God. *The Interpreter's Bible* says that the word "gentleness" here is a mistranslation but then goes on to say, "But we cannot afford to lose the older reading. . . . The phrase is so apt a description of God in Christ and the graciousness of his redemption that we must keep it as a part of our permanent mental furnishing" (J. R. P. Schlater, "Psalms 1–41," *The Interpreter's Bible*, ed. George A. Buttrick [Nashville: Abingdon, 1955], 4:99–100). All things considered, the old translation is good. An absolutely literal translation misses the spirit of the original language and conveys a meaning the sacred writer did not intend. Gentleness is an apt word to apply to the infinite God. It was not the brazen bow or the shield of brass that made the psalmist victorious, but the helpful strength of a gentle God.

Four questions about this matter are in order.

I. How should we see God's gentleness?

Three points of view will help us.

A. *We should see God's gentleness against the background of his power.* Only the strong can be truly gentle. What may be mistaken for gentleness in others may not be restraint at all but merely weakness. The truly

243

strong can be truly gentle, and the greater the power, the more arresting does the gentleness become.

B. *We should see God's gentleness against the background of his righteousness and purity.* Let us never imagine that the gentleness of God is only an easy tolerance. Whatever else it may be, it is not that! It leans against a background of a righteousness that burns like fire.

Also, this gentleness is strangely moving when we remember that it is joined with purity. There is a type of gentleness that springs from an easy, tolerant good nature. To be gentle with sin is an easy matter if that sin is a light thing in our eyes. But when we are tempted to think of God like that, it is time to "survey the cross." When we measure such things by Calvary, we are awed by God's gentleness.

C. *We should see God's gentleness in Jesus Christ.* Isaiah prophesied, "He shall feed his flock like a shepherd: he shall gather the lambs with his arm, and carry them in his bosom, and shall gently lead those that are with young" (Isa. 40:11). To a pastoral people, that was the most apt description of gentleness they knew. All power was his, but he was gentle. Paul saw this and entreated the Corinthians by "the meekness and gentleness of Christ" (2 Cor. 10:1).

II. Where can we find God's gentleness?

There are traces of it everywhere, but note four specific suggestions.

A. *We find the gentleness of God in nature.* For the most part, those mighty forces sleep. There is power sleeping in the winds that would drown all our navies, in earthquakes that would overthrow all our cities, in blight and insect ravages that would destroy all our harvests.

Yet how gently this great machine of nature works. How gently the sunbeam touches the baby's face. How gently the mighty force of gravity holds the foot of the little child on the earth and poses the tiny gnat in the air. The Creator moves in infinite delicacy through countless ages revealing his gentleness.

B. *We find the gentleness of God in the Bible.* The way it was written demonstrates this. The Bible is different from anything the wisest person could have imagined. Men of genius, had they been consulted, would have agreed that it must be a book for the select few, not for the multitudes. The notion of teaching unlearned people, slaves, and little children the deep things of God would have seemed as folly to them. But "the foolishness of God is wiser than men" (1 Cor. 1:25). The Bible is a book for the cottage, the schoolroom, the hospital, as well as for the palace, the university, and the cathedral.

C. *We find the gentleness of God in other people.* Long ago, a farm family moved to the city so that a son could continue in high school. He dreaded the transition to a large school. The first day of school was a long and traumatic day for him. His naïveté, his mistakes, and his appearance made him a laughingstock from the first period to the last. But the kindness of a teacher to an embarrassed, timid boy that day did more to help than she ever realized. The boy found God's gentleness in this teacher's kindness. The gentleness of God in people is a powerful, curative force. In all the world there is nothing else like it.

D. *We find the gentleness of God in his own personal dealings with us.*
   1. He saves us from our sins. Like nature, the Bible has its severe side, a severity aimed solely at our deadliest enemy, sin. The terrible judgments the Bible records stand as sure warnings to us, for God does not desire that anyone should perish but that all should come to repentance (2 Peter 3:9). But the crowning revelation of God to us is "the meekness and gentleness of Christ" (2 Cor. 10:1), who saves us from our sins.
   2. Not only does God save us from our sins, but he keeps us safe in the hollow of his hand. Think of the temptations that would have overcome us had not the gentleness of God taken them away.

III. What does God's gentleness tell us about God?

Note three things.

A. *God's gentleness reveals his perfect understanding of his children.* In his sight we are all ailing children. Have you ever noticed how, when a child is seriously ill, everyone in the house grows strangely gentle? Jesus said, "They that are whole need not a physician; but they that are sick" (Luke 5:31).

B. *God's gentleness reveals our abiding value in his sight.* Included in Jesus' instructions to the Twelve as he sent them out two by two are some astounding words. These are to be taken literally, but I sometimes think we do not consider them seriously: "Are not two sparrows sold for a farthing? and one of them shall not fall on the ground without your Father. But the very hairs of your head are all numbered. Fear ye not therefore, ye are of more value than many sparrows" (Matt. 10:29–31). Indeed, God did so love the world (John 3:16). We are all important to him. That is why he is so gentle with us.

C. *God's gentleness reveals his infinite patience with even the worst of us.* Every mother knows how hard it is to be gentle with a provoking child, and some are provoking most of the time. But no child was ever so provoking to the tender heart of his or her mother as you and I must be to God. When we sin, when we fail to trust him, when we grow bitter, when we become despondent, how ceaselessly provoking this must be to his infinitely loving heart. But "love is patient and kind" (1 Cor. 13:4 RSV).

IV. What does God's gentleness accomplish in our lives?

A. *God's gentleness encourages us to pray.* Of course our omniscient Father already knows the things we need. But God does not squelch us. He does not deprive us of our main comfort in life, our anchor in trouble, our closest, highest fellowship. Rather, Jesus said, "Ask, and it shall be given you; seek, and ye shall find; knock, and it shall be opened unto you" (Matt. 7:7). In other words, "Pray, and I will hear you."

B. *Little by little, God's gentleness makes us into what he wants us to be.* David was great politically, intellectually, and artistically, but the greatness of which he spoke must be understood as spiritual. The psalmist humbly but exultantly recognized that the gentleness of God has ennobled his nature and crowned him with glory and honor.

Conclusion

Can Christians not say, "His gentleness purges and purifies our lives"? By means of testing and trials we are disciplined. The dross is purged away (1 Peter 1:7). Sometimes when gold is in the fire, it may seem that God is not very gentle. But remember, when gold is in the fire, the goldsmith is not far away.

Unsaved friend, would you despise the gentleness of God? If you will not be driven to heaven, then will you be drawn? His gentleness will assure to you "great salvation" (Heb. 2:3).

WEDNESDAY EVENING, JULY 28

Title: A Ministry to the Whole Person

Text: "Brethren, if any of you do err from the truth, and one convert him; let him know, that he which converteth the sinner from the error of his way shall save a soul from death, and shall hide a multitude of sins" **(James 5:19–20)**.

Scripture Reading: James 5:12–20

Introduction

With this passage we come to the end of one of the most practical letters in all the Bible. There were no holds barred as James dealt with many areas of the Christian life. He addressed the wrong use of the tongue, showing what great harm and destruction can be wrought by this little member. He addressed those who have been blessed of God materially but who have misused their wealth, even to the hurt of others.

Then, about halfway through his letter, James changed his approach. As he began to deal with the "whole man," his words became unusually kind and compassionate. If James had been following the modern-day style of letter writing, he probably would have placed his "complimentary close" at the end of verse 11 and added a "postscript" beginning with verse 12. For from the twelfth verse through the end of the chapter, he dealt with matters that he did not bring out in the body of the letter.

I. James's first message in the "postscript" is watching one's speech (5:12).

Here he dealt with the common practice of swearing in his day.

A. *We know that swearing has always been a common practice.* But James said, "Above all things, my brethren, swear not." Why "above all things"? He had just talked about trials and afflictions. When a person is under great stress, he or she may be tempted to say, "Why? Why has all this come upon me? What have I done to deserve this?" The use of God's name in the trials of life can become an expression of anger rather than an expression of praise. In times of affliction, we must guard our speech, for what we say in those difficult hours is very important. A Christian's conduct under pressure always affects others.

B. *We may have trouble trying to determine all that James meant in verse 12.* Some interpret his words to constitute an absolute prohibition of oath-taking. But if we carefully examine both the Old and New Testaments, we will find many instances where God himself, his prophets, and his apostles make use of oaths, or what we would call vows. What James was actually exhorting us to do here is support what we say by what we are and what we do. Many times our works are more persuasive than our words.

II. James's second message in the "postscript" is praying under all conditions (5:13–18).

James made an earnest appeal for Christians to let prayer and praise be part of every aspect of their lives.

A. *First, he mentioned suffering (v. 13).* "Is any among you afflicted?" Here James was talking about any kind of trouble, physical or mental troubles, personal or family troubles, or whatever. What is the proper attitude of Christians under such circumstances? "Let him pray." Prayer can either move God to take away the affliction or give us grace to bear it (see 2 Cor. 12:9).

B. *Second, he asked, "Is any merry?" (v. 13).* James's advice is appropriate: "Let him sing psalms." Let us not forget to praise God in times of joy just as we remember to pray to God in times of trouble.

C. *Third, he dealt with the sick (v. 14).* When James spoke of affliction in verse 13, he was talking about suffering in a broad and general way. His reference to sickness is more specific. The Greek word suggests that it is a sickness that incapacitates a person. Those who are sick are to "call for the elders of the church," whose presence will encourage and hearten them, and make them more conscious of the effectiveness of prayer. The elders are to pray for the sick person, "anointing him with oil in the name of the Lord." Oil in the Scriptures is a gracious symbol of the Holy Spirit. In Bible times it was also a medicine. But here anointing with oil may have been intended as an aid to the sick person's faith.

   D. *Fourth, James summarized the matter of prayer (v. 16).* He drew two conclusions.

      1. There is a need for confession of sins. He was not saying that we are to confess all our faults to all of our fellow Christians. But we are to confess to those whom we may have offended.

      2. James encouraged intercessory prayer. "And pray one for another" (v. 16). All of the people are to pray, not just the elders. James then said that there is great power in the prayer of a person who is right with God.

Conclusion

James concluded his epistle by urging Christians to reclaim those who have fallen away (vv. 19–20). Here the "pastor heart" of James surfaced. He was talking about those who are spiritually sick. To "convert" those who have wandered astray means to bring them back to the way of truth, to turn them around. It is God's plan and purpose to use his people as instruments in the saving of souls from death and in the covering of a multitude of sins.

AUGUST

■ Sunday Mornings

Complete the series "The Spiritual Struggle for the Renewal of the Church." On the last Sunday of the month, begin a new series titled "The Nature and Ministry of the Church." These messages focus on the home, the school, the church, and the state—the four great institutions that give meaning and stability to Western civilization.

■ Sunday Evenings

Continue the series "The Doctrine of God."

■ Wednesday Evenings

"Great Imperatives from the Apostle Paul" is the theme of messages based on Paul's first letter to the Thessalonian believers.

SUNDAY MORNING, AUGUST 1

Title: Renew My Witness

Text: "Be ye transformed by the renewing of your mind" (**Rom. 12:2**).

"That which we have seen and heard declare we unto you, that ye also may have fellowship with us: and truly our fellowship is with the Father, and with his Son Jesus Christ" (**1 John 1:3**).

Scripture Reading: Romans 12:1–2; 1 John 1:1–4

Hymns: "O Worship the King," Grant
"Rock of Ages," Toplady
"We've a Story to Tell," Nichol

Offertory Prayer: Holy Father, we thank you for the good feeling it gives us to know that you need us and desire us to cooperate with you in sharing the news of your love with a needy race. Accept the love of our hearts. Accept the praise of our lips. Accept these tithes and offerings from our hands and hearts as we bring them for holy use in extending your kingdom to the ends of the earth. Bless both the gifts and the givers in the name of him who taught us that it is more blessed to give than to receive. Amen.

Introduction

What were the first and last words of instruction Jesus gave to his disciples? See Matthew 4:19 and Acts 1:8. Jesus said, "Follow me, and I will make you fishers of men," and "Ye shall be witnesses unto me." His first and last words were related to witnessing. Since there is no question that we are called to a life of witnessing, may our prayer be, "Lord, renew my witness!"

Jesus used many figures of speech to describe the nature of his mission. He called his followers "the salt of the earth" and "the light of the world." He gave them "the keys of the kingdom." He looked on himself and his work as "bread" and "water." His kingdom was like "leaven," and he came to cast "fire" on the earth.

What common idea do all of these represent? Each represents some kind of penetration. Salt penetrates meat to preserve it. Light penetrates darkness to dispel it. Keys penetrate a lock to provide an opening. Bread penetrates the body for nourishment and life. Water penetrates the earth for moisture. Leaven penetrates the dough to make it rise. Fire has penetrating power and continues only as it is given new fuel. Fire is extinguished when it is contained.

This is what we are to be—Christ's penetrating power in the world! The church exists for this purpose. Apart from it we have no reason to exist. "Renew my witness" is a prayer we can pray that God will surely answer. If we are to renew our witness, we must do two things.

I. We must refine our definition of witnessing.

Witnessing is not just ringing doorbells in the community or handing out pieces of literature. Neither is it just asking an individual if he or she is born again or quoting the customary soul-winning passages. Witnessing is what 1 John 1:3 talks about: "That which we have seen and heard declare we unto you." Witnessing is telling something that comes from our own experience, something we know. Witnessing is sharing what Christ has done in our lives. It is pointing to the one who has performed the miracle of new life in us. Witnessing is knowing Jesus Christ personally and telling the lost about him in his power.

Witnessing has two basic elements.

A. *A way of life.* We demonstrate that there is a change within us, that we have a new way of life. One man testified, "I used to go every Sunday to the priest's house and learn how to be a good Christian. When we did well, we got sweets and tea to take home. Once I got a prize for learning the four gospels by heart and reciting them nonstop in the church." Who spoke these words? Nikita Khrushchev! Life with Christ provides both inner and outer evidence of his life in us. This illustrates that it is not enough just to do good works; the primary thing is that we be a new person in Christ.

B. *A word of mouth.* Witnessing must go beyond one's life to a verbal explanation if we are to truly witness. The Word must become flesh! We are to verbalize our witness, supported by the Word of God.

II. We must recover the New Testament way.

Someone has suggested that there has been a shift in methods from the first century to the twenty-first.

A. *A shift from personal to impersonal evangelism.* Most of our evangelism today is the mass type that is to a large extent impersonal. We are certainly not to discard mass evangelism; rather, we are to make sure that we do not substitute it for the basic New Testament way, personal evangelism.

B. *A shift from people-centered to church-centered evangelism.* The church has been charged by its own leaders of changing the Great Commission from "going to tell" to "coming to hear." Jesus told us to make disciples as we go; to go into all the world and preach the gospel; to search until we find lost sheep. When we fail to do this, we miss the masses of people because the masses will not come to church.

Someone has said, "The problem is not that the churches are filled with empty pews but that the pews are filled with empty people."

Conclusion

A well-known host of a television cooking show told about receiving Christ. First his wife believed in Christ; soon after, he began to read the "red words" in the Bible. He was eventually saved and used thirty minutes of his air time asking people to forgive him for all the filth he had spoken on his program in the past. That is a living witness! "Lord, renew my witness!"

SUNDAY EVENING, AUGUST 1

Title: The City of God

Text: "Glorious things are spoken of thee, O city of God" (**Ps. 87:3**).

Scripture Reading: Psalm 87:1–7

Introduction

Woven into the very fabric of the Bible is the dream of a city to come, the city of God. To the Jews, Jerusalem was a figure, a type, a symbol of this city of God about which they dimly dreamed. When the psalmist said, "Glorious things are spoken of thee, O city of God," he was referring to Jerusalem. The psalm as a whole makes this clear. But behind the curtain of the years, shadows may be seen moving about in the eternal city as the light shines through.

Three things about the city of God claim our attention.

I. The vision of the city.

a) *Ancient seers saw that vision.*

    i. The psalmist of old saw the vision of that city. Psalm 48 was written to commemorate God's deliverance of Jerusalem in the days of King Hezekiah. The angel of death passed in the night through the sleeping hosts of the Assyrians and left 185,000 dead bodies around the city. The psalmist said, "As we have heard, so have we seen in the city of the LORD of hosts, in the city of our God: God will establish it for ever" (v. 8).

ii. Earlier Abraham had seen the vision of the city of God. Called out of his own city, with only God's promise to lean on, Abraham wandered from place to place following God's will for his life. In Hebrews 11 the writer's benediction on Abraham is this: "By faith he sojourned in the land of promise, as in a strange country, dwelling in tabernacles . . . for he looked for a city which hath foundations, whose builder and maker is God" (vv. 9–10). This was most meaningful to Jewish readers, who had a history of slavery, exile, and now dispersion with the city of Jerusalem laid waste. The eyes of those who belonged to the Lord turned to the future. With Abraham they looked for a city "whose builder and maker is God."

iii. The prophet Isaiah also saw the vision of that city. "In that day shall this song be sung in the land of Judah; We have a strong city; salvation will God appoint for walls and bulwarks" (Isa. 26:1). In that famous sixtieth chapter, Isaiah described the glories of the restored city. The chapter begins, "Arise, shine; for thy light is come, and the glory of the LORD is risen upon thee" (v. 1). It escalates to a climax as the prophet said, "They shall call thee, The city of the LORD, The Zion of the Holy One of Israel" (v. 14).

Where is this city of the prophet's vision, and when is its glory to be revealed? Beyond any doubt, Isaiah 60 originally celebrated the return from captivity. Later generations took this chapter as foretelling their liberation from their oppressors. In any case, the Jews would answer, "The place is Jerusalem, and the time is the near future."

But surely the prophet's vision meant more than that! Suppose the prophet had seen the promise of this chapter literally fulfilled, with Jerusalem the capital of a world empire receiving tribute from afar. Suppose he had seen gold and silver as plentiful in the city as brass and iron. Would these tokens of prosperity have satisfied him? No. Isaiah would have said, "This is not what God showed me in the vision. It is only what I said I had seen because it could not be described more accurately. Now the supernatural light has all gone out of the picture; the religious value of the vision has vanished."

b) *Others besides the Jews have had their vision of the city of God.* The Greek philosophers had their heavenly city of which all good men were already subjects. But had we asked these Greek philosophers, "Where is your heavenly city, and when is its glory to be revealed?" they would have answered, "The place is everywhere and nowhere; the time is now, always, and never. It is not in time nor in place. It is where God is, for it is in His mind" (Ralph William Inge, *The Things That Remain* [New York: Harper Bros., 1958], 13).

c) *The vision is too great for the framework in which we try to interpret it.* If we should ask the average Christian today, "Where is the city of God, and when is its glory to be revealed?" he or she would no doubt reply, "The time is in the unknown future and the place is beyond the stars." The vision is a real revelation of God, but we do not see it clearly, and we do not understand it completely. We try to find a time and a place for it in our own world, within our own thoughts, to which it does not really belong.

In his poem "The Seekers," the English poet John Masefield stated this thought winsomely. His poem begins and ends:

> Friends and loves we have none, nor wealth nor blest abode,
> But the hope of the City of God at the other end of the road.

II. The features of the city as seen in the vision.

How can that city be identified? What is heaven like?

A. *We seek a city that is like a family with God as Father, Jesus Christ as Elder Brother, and the Holy Spirit as Comforter.*

B. *We seek a city where brotherhood prevails.* It is a city without walls (Isa. 26:1) because no enemies are there and the redeemed dwell together in brotherly love. This city is the full realization of the community of humankind. Paul said, "Eye hath not seen, nor ear heard, neither have entered into the heart of man, the things which God hath prepared for them that love him" (1 Cor. 2:9).

C. *We seek a city that is a moral bastion, a fortress of ultimate integrity.* The Bible's climactic chapter describes it: "And there shall in no wise enter into it any thing that defileth, neither whatsoever worketh abomination, or maketh a lie" (Rev. 21:27).

D. *We seek a city that is a workshop.* The notion that in heaven we will be stretched out eternally on flowery beds of ease has unquestioned appeal to some, but it is mistaken. Heaven isn't that kind of place. People who have never worked and won't work wouldn't fit there. They wouldn't like it. That city will be a place of creative and satisfying work for God where "his servants shall serve him" (Rev. 22:3).

E. *We seek a city where our real citizenship is.* Paul told the Philippians, "Our citizenship is in heaven. And we eagerly await a Savior from there, the Lord Jesus Christ" (3:20 NIV). The Christian view of the city of God is realistic. The city of God already penetrates this present life but has not yet come to fruition. Meanwhile, we must conduct ourselves as citizens of Christ. The vision of that city to come colors and influences the life we now live.

253

III. Note the values of this vision for our lives.

A. *The vision of that city has strengthened and sustained God's great saints of all ages.* Of those heroes of faith in Hebrews 11, the writer said, "These all died in faith, not having received what was promised, but having seen it and greeted it from afar" (v. 13 RSV). But then he went on to say, "But as it is, they desire a better country, that is, a heavenly one. Therefore God is not ashamed to be called their God, for he has prepared for them a city" (v. 16 RSV). That was the faith that undergirded their lives.

B. *The vision of that city sustained the early Christians.* Was Hebrews written after the destruction of Jerusalem in AD 70? If so, it must have been written in part to comfort those Hebrew Christians. One statement seems to suggest this: "For here we have no lasting city, but we seek the city which is to come" (13:14 RSV). But if Hebrews was written before Jerusalem was destroyed, the shape of things to come would have been clearly apparent, and these words would have prepared them for that awful catastrophe.

C. *The vision of that city gave Christians through the centuries the power to rise out of the ashes to rebuild the earthly city.* In the fifth century, the Goths sacked Rome and destroyed it. In the midst of this tragedy, Augustine wrote his famous work *The City of God*, in which he portrayed a new and glorious city rising out of the ruins. His book reminds the reader that Christ's church will survive all catastrophes, all civilizations, all cultures.

D. *The vision of that city will sustain us today.* Nuclear war could destroy four-fifths of the human race in a few days. That is a stern reality, and we ought to face it. Should this come to pass, the remnant of the race must rise phoenix-like from the ashes and rebuild.

　　The power that raised up a new civilization out of the ashes of the Graeco-Roman world was their faith that knew all along that "here we have no lasting city" (Heb. 13:14 RSV). In their faith in that heavenly city they rebuilt the earthly city.

E. *Above all, the vision of that city will not only sustain us, it will give us the power to go on.* Once we have seen the vision, once we have had even a glimpse of the city of God, we can go on and on and not falter, for "we seek the city which is to come" (Heb. 13:14 RSV).

Conclusion

　　This is the vision, its features, its values. Let us go on in the faith that the lights are on in the Father's house in the city of God.

WEDNESDAY EVENING, AUGUST 4

Title: The Ministry of a Comforter

Text: "Therefore comfort one another with these words" (**1 Thess. 4:18 RSV**).

Scripture Reading: 1 Thessalonians 4:13–18

Introduction

The words of our text are directed to believers in Jesus Christ. Each of us is commanded to participate in a ministry of bringing comfort to others. We are to render this ministry with the precious promises and provisions of God described by the apostle in the preceding verses (1 Thess. 4:13–17).

I. The need for comfort.

Sooner than we can imagine, we will either be in need of comfort or be associated with someone who needs comfort. Very seldom does a month pass in which death does not touch the life of someone who is near and dear to us. We are not to remain unconcerned in the presence of grief.

A. *"But we would not have you ignorant, brethren, concerning those who are asleep" (v. 13 RSV).* While there is much speculation concerning death and the afterlife, there is great ignorance concerning what the New Testament teaches regarding God's provisions for those who die with faith in Jesus Christ. Each believer should study the New Testament to fully appreciate the resurrection of Jesus Christ. We need to delve into great passages of Scripture like 1 Corinthians 15.

B. *"That you may not grieve as others do who have no hope" (v. 13 RSV).* Believers grieve over the death of someone near and dear just as unbelievers grieve. When a person dies, all of those who knew him or her feel loss, and this brings pain. While believers experience grief, Paul tells us that we must not grieve as do unbelievers, for their sorrow is the sorrow of those who have no hope. A nonbelieving husband was heard to say in connection with the death of his Christian wife, "If I were only a Christian, it would not be so bad." He knew that apart from Jesus Christ he had no hope of ever experiencing his wife's presence again.

A perceptive observer on the mission field noticed the radical difference between the grief of believers in contrast to that of unbelievers in the presence of death. He expressed the judgment that if this were the only benefit that came as a result of being a Christian, it would be worth all the effort and expense put forth by the missionaries. As followers of Christ, we are encouraged to refrain from grieving as though we have no hope.

II. The basis for the Christian's comfort.

The apostle Paul said we are to "comfort one another with these words" (v. 18). What are the words to which he was referring?

A. *"We believe that Jesus died and rose again" (v. 14 RSV).* Our only hope of victory over death and the grave is based on the fact that Jesus Christ,

God's Son, died for our sins. He conquered the power of death and the grave on our behalf. The resurrection of Christ provides us with a revelation of what God has planned for those who trust Christ as Lord.

The occasion for these words of instruction and comfort grew out of the pain that these early believers were experiencing when friends and loved ones entered into death prior to the expected return of Jesus Christ. Paul affirmed that when Christ returns to claim his own, believers who have experienced death prior to that event will be with him.

B. *Those who are alive at the second coming of Christ will not have precedent over those who have died prior to that event (v. 15).* Some people interpret these verses of Scripture in terms of a detailed explanation of our Lord's return. We will get closer to the truth if we interpret them in terms of instruction and comfort to distressed believers a short two or three decades after the ascension of our Lord. Paul was affirming that both living and dead believers will share equally in the wonderful victory of the triumphant return of Jesus Christ. He was affirming that "we who are alive, who are left, shall be caught up together with them in the clouds to meet the Lord in the air; and so we shall always be with the Lord" (v. 17 RSV). He was dealing here with the pain that is experienced when death separates the living from the dead. He was affirming that the day will come when we will be together in and through Jesus Christ.

III. Being a comforter.

Each of us will need the comfort that comes from the God of all comfort and the Father of mercy (2 Cor. 1:3–4). Each of us is encouraged, even commanded, to be a source of comfort to one another. To comfort means to encourage, to impart assurance of victory, to help others know that death will have no final victory over us or our loved ones who know Jesus Christ as Lord and Savior.

A. *We need to study the Scriptures.* If we would be obedient to this imperative, and if we would be a source of help to others, we need to know what the Scriptures teach about the Lord's provisions for those who trust him.

B. *We need to claim the promises of God.* The New Testament contains many promises to those who trust Jesus Christ. Only as we claim these promises on a personal basis can we experience God's great comfort.

C. *We can be the channel through which God's help comes to others.* Our presence and our words of assurance and sympathy will bless others in their times of grief.

Conclusion

Determine that with God's assistance you will be a source of help to others in their times of sorrow and grief.

SUNDAY MORNING, AUGUST 8

Title: Renew My Vision

Text: "Be ye transformed by the renewing of your mind" **(Rom. 12:2)**.

"But when he saw the multitudes, he was moved with compassion" **(Matt. 9:36)**.

Scripture Reading: Matthew 9:36–38; Luke 7:13; 10:33; 15:20; Romans 12:1–2

Hymns: "Guide Me, O Thou Great Jehovah," Williams
            "Open My Eyes That I May See," Scott
            "He Leadeth Me!" Gilmore

Offertory Prayer: Loving Father, help us see the beauty of your love for us and for your world. Help us see this world's need for the message of your grace through Jesus Christ. Help us see where we fit into your plan for communicating the way of salvation to those around us and to those in other parts of the world. Thank you for giving us that which we can use to proclaim the good news to the ends of the earth. Accept these tithes and offerings as expressions of our desire to worship you in spirit and in truth. In Jesus' name. Amen.

Introduction

There was something special about Jesus' power to see. The Greek word for "see" has something special about it. It means not just seeing something as an object, but seeing with understanding. It means to see through something, to see something in its true condition. So when Jesus saw people, he saw them as they really were.

If the church is to be renewed, we must see the people around us with the eyes of Jesus. A prayer for renewal is, "Lord, renew my vision!"

Renewing our vision means to do the following:

I. Open our eyes to see people in their need.

If anyone knew the true condition of people, it was Jesus. He could see into the heart and discern whether a person had faith (Mark 2:5). John 2:24 says, "He knew all men." Matthew 9:36–38 pictures how Jesus saw the multitudes. "They fainted" (v. 36). They were tired and weary with life. They needed spiritual rest. They "were scattered abroad" (v. 36). This expression is from a verb meaning "to throw, cast, or hurl." People are thrown around by life's circumstances, and they are without the leadership and protection of a shepherd. Multitudes have no God, no faith, no love, no home. They are without roots, and they have no hope.

Jesus also saw people like a ripe harvest (v. 37). There is always someone ready for the gospel of hope in Christ. When we open our eyes to others' needs, we see people spiritually lost and critically hurting with all types of needs. To adequately fulfill God's purpose, we also must see life in its true condition.

257

II. Open our hearts to care.

Seeing means much more than just being aware of spiritual needs; it means responding to those needs. It means loving and receiving people.

Compassion is a deeply moving attitude. Jesus "was moved with compassion" (Matt. 9:36). Compassion represents love for someone so deep that we involve ourselves until the hurt is healed. The good Samaritan is a poignant illustration of compassion (Luke 10:25–37).

In a vacation Bible school "decision" service in California, a Mexican-American boy didn't respond to the invitation, although he later indicated that he had considered it. When asked why he didn't respond, he said, "I didn't think you'd want me." How many people feel this way?

III. Open our souls to prayer.

There is no true vision without prayer. Jesus said, "Ask the Lord of the harvest, therefore, to send out workers into his harvest field" (Matt. 9:38 NIV).

Laborers for the harvest always come in answer to prayer. The Holy Spirit, in the atmosphere of prayer, calls people to special ministries (see Acts 13:2–3). We need to pray for laborers who minister to needs as well as for the people with those needs (John 17:9, 11, 15, 20).

IV. Open our lives to go.

A true vision means that we make ourselves available to become involved in the needs of people. How do we do this? We acknowledge our place in the body of Christ to be his servant to minister to others. We open our lives to touch people with our love, words, and genuine help. Also, we open our lives to tell people the good news of salvation. We teach them the Word of God. We minister to their total needs. One man, after sharing Christ with others, said to his pastor, "I didn't know there were needs like this. It opened my eyes to why we need to go."

How can you respond specifically?

A. *Respond to the opportunities you have personally, wherever they are.* Opportunities to help others may arise in your family, in your neighborhood, at your workplace or school, in the church, or among strangers.

B. *Respond to opportunities your church offers you.*

C. *Don't wait for a giant step.* Just take the first step, however insignificant and unseen it may be.

Conclusion

A church received a telephone call from a desperate person. The caller said, "My father has cancer and is dying. Would you send someone to see him?" Someone from the church went and discovered that the dying patient was not a Christian. As a result of the visit, he was saved! And before the visit was over, five other members of the family received Christ into their lives. How wonderful!

Without waiting for someone else to respond, let us pray, "Lord, renew my vision!"

SUNDAY EVENING, AUGUST 8

Title: The Humility of God

Text: "Who is like unto the LORD our God, who dwelleth on high, who humbleth himself to behold the things that are in heaven, and in the earth!" **(Ps. 113:5–6)**.

Scripture Reading: Psalm 113:1–9

Introduction

A Carthusian monk was explaining the strong points of his little-known order. "As for learning, we are not to be compared to the Jesuits," he said. "When it comes to good works, we don't match the Franciscans. As to preaching, we are not in a class with the Dominicans. But," he concluded, "when it comes to humility, we're tops!" Nothing is more nauseating than phony humility. Humility is such a delicate thing that those who dare to think that they have it prove by that single thought that they don't.

The humility of God is the thought at the center of Psalm 113. This is the first of the six psalms that are known as the "Hallel" because the dominant note in all six is praise. The Hallel was sung as a part of the Passover observance. When Mark tells us, "When they had sung a hymn, they went out to the Mount of Olives" (14:26 RSV), we may assume that a part of the Hallel is what they sang. Imagine the King of Kings and Lord of Lords singing with his disciples, "Who is like unto the LORD our God, who dwelleth on high, who humbleth himself to behold the things that are in heaven, and in the earth!" (Ps. 113:5–6).

Two contrasting thoughts about God support and complement one another in this psalm. The psalmist praises the name of God on two counts. He is high, yet he is lowly—above the nations and above the heavens yet humbling himself to behold the heavens and the earth. The thing that exalts humankind, the contemplation of creation and its glories, humbles God, so far above his creation is he in awful majesty and might. He humbles himself.

These two thoughts about God must always be held together if we are to avoid extremes. As we think about his humility, we raise three questions.

I. In broad terms, what is humility?

Consider six affirmations.

A. *Humility is the realization that we do not know it all.* When a little girl came home from her first day at school, her father teasingly asked, "Did you learn everything today?" "No," she answered with obvious disappointment, "I have to go back tomorrow." It is good to realize that we have not learned everything, that we "have to go back tomorrow."

259

B. *Humility is the prerequisite to honesty.* This is the kind of honesty that can keep pride from blinding us to our own vices as well as to the virtues of others. True humility can free us from the blindness of prejudice, envy, and hatred. It can enable us to rejoice in the gifts and achievements of others.

C. *Humility is the willingness to listen.* Jesus said, "If any man have ears to hear, let him hear" and "Take heed what ye hear" (Mark 4:23–24). Jesus also said, "Take heed therefore how ye hear" (Luke 8:18). Will Rogers once said, "I never met a man from whom I could not learn something." He was a truly humble man because he was willing to listen.

D. *Humility is the disposition to serve.* Those who think they are too big to serve others are really confessing that they are too little. Jesus performed the lowliest service that one person could render another, and his dignity suffered not one whit because of it. He said, "I am meek and lowly in heart" (Matt. 11:29). Those who prefer to be servants in the house of God rather than dwell in the tents of the wicked are truly humble people.

E. *Humility is God's way to, and condition for, power.* Only the humble does he deem worthy to trust with power. What person ever had greater power with God than Moses? Yet Moses is described as "very meek, above all the men which were upon the face of the earth" (Num. 12:3).

  Many years ago an American college student, visiting in the home of Beethoven in Bonn, asked permission to play Beethoven's piano. The caretaker reluctantly permitted her to do so. After playing a few bars of the "Moonlight Sonata," she remarked, "I suppose all of the great pianists have played this instrument during visits here." "No, miss," the guard said. "Paderewski was here two years ago, but he said that he was not worthy to touch it."

F. *Humility is one of the greatest things in Christian character.* Greatness begins with humility. Jesus said, "Whosoever will be great among you, let him be your minister; and whosoever will be chief among you, let him be your servant" (Matt. 20:26–27). The word translated "minister" here means an ordinary hired servant; the word translated "servant" means a bond slave, owned body and soul by his master. This is humility.

II. What is the significance of God's humility?

What insights into his nature does his humility give us?

A. *The psalmist said that God's humility attests to his greatness.* Read Psalm 113:2–5 again. The greatness of God is a theme of which the psalmists never tire and which they never exhaust.

  1. God's greatness is above all duration of time. "Blessed be the name of the LORD from this time forth and for evermore" (v. 2). This is time sublime. Moses prayed, "Before the mountains were

brought forth, or ever thou hadst formed the earth and the world, even from everlasting to everlasting, thou art God" (Ps. 90:2).

2. God's greatness is above all the expanse of space. "From the rising of the sun unto the going down of the same the LORD's name is to be praised" (Ps. 113:3). The mightiest mountain is but a speck; the earth itself is but a speck in the system to which it belongs; and our solar system is but a speck in the numerous systems in this vast universe. Draw the line where you will, the immeasurable lies beyond; but above that immeasurable sits God enthroned.

3. His greatness is above all nations: "The LORD is high above all nations, and his glory above the heavens" (v. 4). This verse affirms that Israel's God is King of the earth.

4. His greatness is beyond all comparison, for the psalmist said, "Who is like unto the LORD our God, who dwelleth on high!" (v. 5). At the dedication of the temple, Solomon prayed, "Behold, heaven and the heaven of heavens cannot contain thee" (2 Chron. 6:18). But though God's seat is on high, he humbles himself in regard to us.

B. *God's humility explains his works and his ways.* Read Psalm 113:6–9 again. His majesty alone would overwhelm us by its awful grandeur. His condescension alone would lead us to presumption. We must avoid both extremes. He raises the poor out of the dust and the needy from the trash heaps where they struggle to survive. He exalts the ordinary man to be a prince among the people. Remember David, who was elevated from shepherd boy to be king of Israel. Wonderful are God's works "and his ways past finding out" (Rom. 11:33).

C. *God's humility demonstrates his matchless love.* "What is man, that thou art mindful of him?" (Ps. 8:4). What is man, indeed? Man is one who is loved by the God of might who "humbleth himself." Love that goes upward from a person's heart to God is adoration. Love that goes outward from a person's heart to another is affection. Love that stoops is grace. God stoops to us.

God has demonstrated his love. When we were dead in trespasses and sin, he came, taking onto himself the form of a servant in the likeness of men. And that was not all. "Being found in fashion as a man, he humbled himself, and became obedient unto death, even the death of the cross" (Phil. 2:8). Now we know that God is love.

III. What should result in our lives from even a glimpse of God's humility?

To realize that, for our sakes, God humbles himself—that he stoops all the way down to where we are—should change our lives.

A. *This truth, truly accepted, will help us on toward spiritual maturity.* Humility is a crucial factor in Christian growth. If we are humble, we will make life a long experience of learning wonderful things out of God's Word, out of God's world, and from God's people. Those who cease to "hunger and thirst after righteousness" (Matt. 5:6) are not humble. They are filled with pride.

B. *This truth should urge us to see ourselves in the perspective of God's universe.* Humility is the way we feel when we see ourselves as part of God's world. Humility is the only honest reaction when we see ourselves as part of God's world and feel his claim on us.

C. *This truth should make us willing to let God be God in our lives.* We should let God put us in our proper place. We should be glad for that place, whatever it is. Humility leads us to make the right estimate of ourselves; it also helps us accept God's estimate of us and God's place for us.

D. *This truth should inspire us to imitate our Lord.* Paul told the Philippians, "Let this mind be in you, which was also in Christ Jesus" (2:5). What did he mean? He meant for us to imitate Christ in his humility. In Philippians 2:6–8 he expanded this thought fully. Jesus calls his followers to do the same work he did. Benjamin Franklin once said, "To be humble to superiors is duty; to equals, courtesy; to inferiors, nobleness." How noble is our God!

Conclusion

Such a faith would make a great difference in our lives. God is high and lifted up, transcending all human thought, imagination, and reason. Yet he is with us as we set out on the day's adventure and as we commit ourselves to sleep. He is with us when troubles and temptations come and when success spreads its subtler danger in our path. So near is he that when we cry out he hears our faintest whisper and answers our feeblest prayer.

WEDNESDAY EVENING, AUGUST 11

Title: The Habit of Prayer

Text: "Pray constantly" (1 Thess. 5:17 RSV).

Introduction

The King James Version translates our text, "Pray without ceasing," and *The Living Bible* paraphrases it, "Always keep on praying."

Paul is informing the dear disciples of Thessalonica that they should develop the habit of prayer and then never break that good habit.

Jesus told his disciples a parable to the effect that they "ought always to pray and not lose heart" (Luke 18:1 RSV). It is the will of our heavenly Father that we form a consistent habit of prayer and then not break that habit.

For the good of our own spiritual lives and for the advancement of God's kingdom, we should give ourselves constantly to prayer. This is not to imply that we should assume some pious pose or that we should enter some type of convent or monastery to give ourselves to uninterrupted prayer.

Prayer has both a human and a divine side: we talk with the Father, and the Father communicates with us. True prayer is always a dialogue in which we bring our confessions, our thanksgivings, our petitions, and our intercessions to the Father. The most valuable part of the prayer experience is the listening side, in which we let the Father speak to our needs.

I. We should have the habit of prayer because the Father God listens.

A. *The Father is eager to bestow his gifts upon us.*
B. *The Father gives only gifts that are good for us (Matt. 7:11).*
C. *The Father gives gifts that are in harmony with his purpose.*
 1. We can discover God's character by studying the Bible.
 2. We can understand God's gifts as we follow the Holy Spirit's leadership.
 3. We can know what to expect from God when we pray (John 15:7).

II. We should have the habit of prayer because of our great need.

We find that the great prophet Daniel had the habit of praying three times each day (Dan. 6:10–11).

A. *We should always pray a prayer of confession when we have any consciousness of sin in our lives (1 John 1:9).*
B. *We should pray when we stand in need of wisdom (James 1:5).* Wisdom is God-given insight that enables us to see the end from the beginning of a particular course of action.
C. *We should pray when we are tempted by Satan to do evil (James 4:7–8).*
D. *We should pray when we or our loved ones experience the pain and suffering of illness (James 5:13–18).*
E. *We should pray when we are in any kind of need for God's grace and help (Heb. 4:16).*

Conclusion

We should develop the habit of prayer and not break it, because God yearns for fellowship with those who are near and dear to him and because God has placed a hunger in our hearts for fellowship with him.

SUNDAY MORNING, AUGUST 15

Title: The Secret to Renewal

Text: "Be ye transformed by the renewing of your mind" **(Rom. 12:2)**.

"Yield yourselves unto God, as those that are alive from the dead, and your members as instruments of righteousness unto God" **(Rom. 6:13)**.

Scripture Reading: Romans 6:6–13; 12:1–2

Hymns: "Break Thou the Bread of Life," Lathbury
"I Hear Thy Welcome Voice," Hartsough
"Our Best," Kirk

Offertory Prayer: Blessed Father, thank you for being the giver of every good and perfect gift. Thank you for the gift of your Son. Thank you for the gift of your precious Holy Spirit as a permanent presence in our hearts. Thank you for giving us the privilege of cooperating with you to the end that your kingdom might come upon earth, even as your will is done by the angels in heaven. Accept these gifts as tokens of our desire to be totally involved in your service. In Jesus' name we pray. Amen.

Introduction

Spiritual renewal is the answer for the church today. It is God's will for the church to be renewed and transformed; it is not God's will for the church to be shaped by the mold of the world. It is God's will that the church be renewed to ministry, renewed in faith and a disciplined life. It is also his will that the church be renewed to witnessing, and this happens only as it experiences the renewing of the Holy Spirit.

There is a secret to renewal, and it involves two steps.

I. Yield yourselves to God.

The key word to spiritual renewal in the Christian life is "yield." It is the same word translated "present" in Romans 12:1. It is also the word that is used to describe the presenting of an offering in the sacrificial system in the temple. The worshiper presented or yielded his sacrifice to the priest to be offered. It is an act of worship whereby we personally acknowledge that we belong to God. This act is the secret of renewal of life. Notice three things about this act.

A. *It is a realistic act.* In the Christian life it is just as real as the decision to accept Jesus Christ as Lord and Savior.
   1. It is a definite act. In Romans 6:13 the second use of the word "yield" is in the aorist tense of the Greek language. The verse may read, "Do not go on yielding your members at sin's disposal, but once for all decisively yield yourselves to God." There must be a time in your life when you present yourself to God and from then on consider your whole life to belong to him.
   2. It is a transfer of your life to God. Your life is no longer your own, but his!
   3. It is an act of the will as well as an act of obedience.
B. *It is a reasonable act.* This is what Romans 12:1 indicates: "Present your bodies a living sacrifice . . . which is your reasonable service." It is reasonable if we want to have victory.

The believer in Christ has a dual nature, while the lost person has only one nature, "the old man." Something happens when a person is born again. New life comes in, divine life, Christ's life, in the person of the Holy Spirit. The new believer now has a new nature. The old nature, the self-life, is dealt with by Christ's death, but it not evicted from our lives. As believers we now have a dual nature—a higher nature and a lower nature, an old life and a new life, the flesh and the Spirit, the self-life and the Christ-life. These are enemies, and they struggle for full control of one's life. Believers have the choice as to which to yield themselves. How we choose is the secret to victory.

C. *It is a resisted act.* The flesh resists the Holy Spirit (Gal. 5:16–26). The resistance masses itself at some point in your life so that surrender becomes the key to victory. What is it that stands between you and renewal? Must some cherished idol in your life be yielded to God if victory is to come? Nothing will substitute for the act of yielding yourself to God. This is the secret to spiritual power in our lives. Jesus must be Lord of our lives!

II. Yield your members to God.

The word "members" refers to the parts of one's body, thus the areas of our lives. These members are "weapons" either for righteousness or sin, for God or Satan. We are to yield ourselves and our members to God. This makes Romans 12:1 clearer when it says, "Present your bodies." Your body is important. Present it to God!

A. *Yield your eyes to God.* Your eyes control what you see and what you read. Make a covenant regarding your eyes.

B. *Yield your ears to God.* Your ears control what you hear. Be discerning about what you hear.

C. *Yield your mouth to God.* What you say and how you say it are important. Colossians 4:6 says, "Let your conversation be always full of grace, seasoned with salt" (NIV).

D. *Yield your mind to God.* Let your thoughts and attitudes be formed by God's Word.

E. *Yield your hands to God.* Let him govern what you do and how you work—your actions and your service to others.

F. *Yield your feet to God.* Go to the places God would have you to go, but walk away from places that would be detrimental to your spiritual or physical life.

G. *Yield your knees to God.* Kneel in prayer before God regularly.

H. *Yield your lungs to God.* Yielding your lungs means abstaining from the foul habit of smoking.

I. *Yield your stomach to God.* Gluttony is displeasing to God.

J. *Yield your face to God.* Your countenance should reflect the light of Christ who lives within you. You can look at a person's face and determine his or her character qualities. Do you smile or frown?

Are you serving others, or are you expecting others to serve you?

Conclusion

This is the secret then. Yield yourself and your members to God. Build an altar and place yourself and the areas of your life before God. He promises you victory and renewal as you do!

SUNDAY EVENING, AUGUST 15

Title: The Faithfulness of God

Text: "Thy faithfulness is unto all generations" **(Ps. 119:90).**

Scripture Reading: Psalm 119:89–96

Introduction

God's laws never fail. In the physical realm, the sun, moon, stars, and seasons are dependable because God is faithful. Likewise, in the spiritual realm God's laws never change. Ezekiel wrote in the Old Testament, "The soul that sinneth, it shall die" (18:4). And Paul wrote in the New Testament, "Be not deceived; God is not mocked: for whatsoever a man soweth, that shall he also reap" (6:7). God's laws are steadfast because God is faithful.

God's faithfulness is a rock under our feet, a strong arm around our shoulders, a sure light upon our way, and an apt word in our discouragement.

This passage from Psalm 119 emphasizes God's character, including his sovereignty, his integrity, and his dependability. Verse 90 states an important biblical theme: "Thy faithfulness is unto all generations." Let's look at five places where this theme surfaces in the New Testament.

I. The faithfulness of God is his protection in our temptations.

"No temptation has overtaken you that is not common to man. God is faithful, and he will not let you be tempted beyond your strength, but with the temptation will also provide the way of escape, that you may be able to endure it" (1 Cor. 10:13 RSV). How could this be true? Because God is faithful.

For the Christian there is foe, there is fight, there is a victory. With the first two affirmations we have no problem, but we sometimes doubt the third. Napoleon Bonaparte once said, "God is on the side of the biggest battalions." He was right, but not in the sense he meant it. God is on the side of the biggest battalions, for his battalions are the biggest. "Fear not: for they that be with us are more than they that be with them" (2 Kings 6:16).

"If this is true," you ask, "why do temptation and sin so often lay me low?" God is our supreme commander. We must fight the battle the way he directs. If we go wandering off like stray sheep, if we fight in our own strength, if we use the weapons of the flesh and not of the Spirit, the enemy will pick us off one by one (2 Cor. 10:3–5).

Unless we do go wandering off on our own, we are secure within God's fold, within the citadel of his peace and strength. Paul told the Philippians,

266

"The peace of God, which passeth all understanding, shall keep your hearts and minds through Christ Jesus" (4:7). God will guard those who are his own and keep them safe.

II. The faithfulness of God is his explanation of the orderliness of our physical universe.

In his first epistle, Peter said, "Let them that suffer according to the will of God commit the keeping of their souls to him in well doing, as unto a faithful Creator" (4:19). Mark well the phrase "unto a faithful Creator." The more we ponder these words, the more wonderful they appear! God is faithful in the return of the seasons and the orbit of the stars, and he is faithful to provide sustenance for every living creature he has made.

> Summer and winter, and springtime and harvest,
> Sun, moon, and stars in their courses above
> Join with all nature in manifold witness
> To Thy great faithfulness, mercy, and love.
> —*Thomas Chisholm, "Great Is Thy Faithfulness"*

God is the faithful Creator. It is logical, therefore, that his faithfulness should be the theme of the Bible. But why does Peter, when ministering to these suffering saints, lay emphasis on God's faithfulness as Creator? Isn't this the reason? We are apt to concentrate our thoughts entirely on the birth, the cross, the burial, the resurrection, and the intercession of our Lord and to forget that behind all these, deep in the nature of God, the almighty Creator, there are ever-flowing fountains of faithfulness and love.

God is faithful. His physical creation, therefore, is orderly and dependable. "What then," we ask, "is wrong with this world in which we live? Why the weeds, briars, and thorns that infest the ground; and why floods, hurricanes, cyclones, and other calamities of nature?" Humans, by their sin, have upset God's perfect environment, his balance of nature. This is a part of God's judgment, a part of humankind's penalty (Gen. 3:17–19). What is wrong with our physical environment? Nothing, except people themselves, and their thoughtlessness and sin in upsetting the balance of nature. But for all that, God is faithful. He is the bulwark of scientists in their research, the ally of physicians in the healing arts, the assurance of astronomers in their study of the universe, the protection of every living thing.

III. The faithfulness of God is his pledge of the efficacy of our faith.

Because God is faithful, we can trust him. Paul told Timothy, "It is a faithful saying: For if we be dead with him, we shall also live with him: if we suffer, we shall also reign with him: if we deny him, he also will deny us: if we believe not, yet he abideth faithful: he cannot deny himself" (2 Tim. 2:11–13). The value of any faith is in its object. We are faithless again and again. We disappoint God. We betray others. But "if we believe not, yet he abideth faithful: he cannot deny himself" (v. 13). We can put our weight on God because he is faithful.

The missionary John G. Paton translated John 3:16 into the crude language of the South Sea Islanders like this: "God so loved the world that he gave his only begotten Son that whosoever leans his whole weight on him should not perish but have everlasting life." To "lean one's whole weight on" was their word for faith. We can lean our full weight on God because he is faithful. An unknown poet has said,

> Nothing before, nothing behind,
>   The steps of faith
> Fall on the seeming void, and find
>   The solid rock beneath.

IV. The faithfulness of God is his assurance of our security.

A. *Because God is faithful, we know that he will never desert us.* Why will God strengthen and guard his own? Because he is faithful. Paul said, "The Lord is faithful, and he will strengthen and protect you from the evil one" (2 Thess. 3:3 NIV). Because God is faithful, the security of his own is absolutely assured.

B. *Our salvation through Christ has three features.*

1. It is personal, the rescue and redemption of a person by a person—and that person is Jesus Christ.
2. It is planned. God's plan of salvation was no afterthought. It is the plan of the ages.
3. It is permanent. A Christian life begins; it continues on and on; and one day it will consummate in glory. Peter said that those despised and persecuted saints "are kept by the power of God through faith unto salvation ready to be revealed in the last time" (1 Peter 1:5). Our Lord is faithful; therefore his own are secure.

V. The faithfulness of God is his guarantee of forgiveness.

"If we confess our sins, he is faithful and just to forgive us our sins, and to cleanse us from all unrighteousness" (1 John 1:9). Confession of sins is God's condition of forgiveness; his faithfulness is his guarantee. By confessing our sins to God, we admit their reality, their enormity. Silence conceals the sin it refuses to acknowledge. Confession to God drags the sin into the light and shows it to ourselves in all its foulness.

John promised, "If we confess our sins, he is faithful and just to forgive us our sins." This anticipates by nearly two thousand years the modern psychiatric principle whereby patients who unburden themselves of their guilty memories experience purging and cleansing.

But will it work? Thousands of people through all the centuries could testify that it will. The attributes of God that lead to the punishment of those who will not repent lead to the forgiveness and cleansing of those who do. He meets free confession with free forgiveness.

Conclusion

The faithfulness of God—how wonderful is this truth! Let us thank God for it! Let us exult in it! Indeed, his "faithfulness is unto all generations."

WEDNESDAY EVENING, AUGUST 18

Title: The Value of an Attitude of Gratitude

Text: "Give thanks in all circumstances; for this is the will of God in Christ Jesus for you" (**1 Thess. 5:18 RSV**).

Introduction

A positive mental attitude is essential for living a victorious life. Thus it is imperative that we develop the habit of being thankful at all times and in all circumstances. William Law said, "For it is certain that whatever seeming calamity happens to you, if you thank and praise God for it, you turn it into a blessing." If we develop the habit of being thankful at all times, we will open the door so God can provide divine assistance during life's disappointments and tragedies.

I. The habit of being thankful must be learned.

    A. *The natural reaction to disappointment is to complain and be depressed.* Instead of responding in this manner, we need to take inventory of the things for which we can be thankful.

    B. *We must acquire the habit of giving thanks at all times.* Luke's record of Jesus healing ten lepers (17:11–19) reveals that only one had developed the habit of being thankful. Most of us are like the nine who neglected to give thanks even in a time when something very wonderful had happened to them.

    C. *As followers of Christ, we need to give attention to our habits.*

        1. Bad habits are destructive.

        2. We need to earnestly work at developing good habits, especially the habit of being thankful at all times. As British poet John Dryden said, "We first make our habits, and then our habits make us."

II. The wisdom of developing the habit of being thankful.

The psalmist said, "It is good to give thanks to the LORD" (Ps. 92:1). Not only is it a good thing to give thanks to the Lord, but it is a good thing to give thanks to others. Many benefits come to those who have developed the habit of counting their blessings and being thankful.

A. *The habit of giving thanks will produce joy.*
   1. Our thankfulness brings joy to the heart of our Father God.
   2. Our thankfulness brings joy to the hearts of those around us.
   3. Our habit of giving thanks brings joy to ourselves as we recognize the things for which we can rejoice.
B. *The habit of giving thanks will strengthen our faith in God's goodness.* Paul encouraged the Philippian Christians as they brought their petitions before God's throne of grace to be sure to express their thanks for God's past and present blessings (Phil. 4:6–7). One of the best ways to overcome despondency is to count our blessings and thank God for his goodness in the past.
C. *The habit of giving thanks will increase our capacity to love.* We are commanded to love others as we love ourselves. This is the great commandment for harmonious human relationships.
   1. If we have the habit of being thankful, our love for our family members will increase.
   2. If we have the habit of being thankful, our love for our friends and associates will increase.
   3. If we have the habit of being thankful, our love for our Father God will increase as we recognize how much he has done for us.
D. *The habit of giving thanks will help us have an optimistic attitude toward life.*
   1. It is easy to be pessimistic and spend our life in despondency.
   2. By being thankful for what we are and what we have, we can move in the direction of being an optimist.
E. *The habit of giving thanks will add beauty and joy to the privilege of living.* Instead of moaning and groaning about the negative things along the road of life, we can and should become grateful.

III. Developing the habit of being thankful.

How do we respond to this imperative for living the genuine Christian life?

A. *Let us recognize that the ungrateful life is a self-destructive way of life. It brings hurt to us personally and also to those around us.*
B. *Let us confess this sin of ungratefulness and ask God for forgiveness.*
C. *Let us earnestly desire to make a change in our outlook on life.* Let us regard anew the various events that we encounter along the road of life.
D. *Let us respond positively to the truth that God will work for good in all events of life.* To do this we must look to him in faith and love and hope (Rom. 8:28). We can begin to express thanks to those around us for the little things they do for us.

Conclusion

It is God's will for us that we develop the habit of being thankful at all times. God will help us. Let us pray for open eyes to see his goodness. Let us ask him to help us be more thankful, particularly toward those who are helpful to us. Developing the habit of being thankful is not an option if we want to live a victorious Christian life.

SUNDAY MORNING, AUGUST 22

Title: Renewing the Church's Most Important Quality

Text: "But I have this against you, that you have abandoned the love you had at first" **(Rev. 2:4 RSV)**.

"We love him, because he first loved us" **(1 John 4:19)**.

Scripture Reading: 1 John 4:7–19; Revelation 2:1–7

Hymns: "I Love Thy Kingdom, Lord," Dwight
"Come, Holy Spirit, Love Divine," Judson
"Jesus, I My Cross Have Taken," Lyte

Offertory Prayer: Holy Father, help us this day to receive the gifts that you have for us. Help us to know that only what we put into eternal things will remain with us for eternity. Help us to lay up many treasures in heaven by investing our time, talents, and energy in the hearts and souls of people. Help us, Father, to so give ourselves to you that we will be pleasing in your sight. In Jesus' name we pray. Amen.

Introduction

Renewal in the Christian's life must not overlook the renewal of its most important quality—love. Love is essential in the life of a Christian and of the church. Ephesians 4:15–16 calls attention to our "speaking the truth in love" and "the edifying of [the church] in love." Without love there is no true growth.

The church at Ephesus left its first love. The Lord Jesus Christ reveals how important "first love" truly is. According to 1 Corinthians 13, a church may have many things, but without love it is nothing!

If Jesus desires and demands that first love be returned to the Christian's life, how can it be renewed? The answer is by observing the order of love. First John 4:19 says, "We love him, because he first loved us." First love is his love for us. First love is so full of his love for us that love is our response to him and to others.

How is our first love lost? By forgetting his love for us. We begin to think only of our love for him and for ourselves. This is not enough. We get the love relationship reversed.

How is our love renewed? By concentrating on God's love for us. By thinking, reviewing, and meditating on his first love. As we do this, we become so full of his love for us that we have a new love inside us. Our love begins to be renewed and restored. Notice two basic thoughts about love.

271

I. God's unconditional love for us.

Anything that is unconditional is not subject to conditions or limitations. It is not dependent on certain responses being produced. How does God love us unconditionally?

A. *God does not love us sentimentally.* His love corrects us and disciplines us. In love he chastens us. Revelation 3:19 says, "Those whom I love, I reprove and chasten" (RSV).
B. *God loves us whether we respond or not.*
C. *God's unconditional love has no limits.* He loves all people everywhere. His love is not limited to friends; it also includes enemies. It is also not limited as to how long it loves.
D. *God's unconditional love is not based on our performance.* He loves us in spite of our disobedience, rebellion, selfishness, and weakness.
E. *God's unconditional love cares for each of us as someone special.*

II. Our unconditional love for others.

If God loves us unconditionally, we ought to love ourselves and others without strings attached. When we love unconditionally, we do the following:

A. We love others whatever their response.
B. We love others without setting limits for our love. We love everyone. We refuse no one. We love constantly, even as Jesus loved his disciples. He loved them to the end.
C. We love others based not on what they do but on who they are. We all make many mistakes. Our love is not based on another person's performance.
D. We love others without expectations. When we love with expectations and those expectations are not fulfilled, we tend to become inwardly hurt. So we love according to their needs and not our expectations. If we yield our expectations of the other person to God, not only are we free to love, but the other person is free to respond.

   What if we expressed true unconditional love in our families, in our communities, and in our churches? This is the way we are supposed to love, but how is it possible?

   1. Let us admit that we cannot love this way. We must admit our inability yet realize that it is God's command.
   2. The only way we can love as God loves is to have his love in us. We are to yield ourselves to the Lord to let his love flow through us and onto others. This is how his love is perfected in us (1 John 4:17). His ability is released by our availability.

Conclusion

When we are full of God's love for us, our love is renewed with all its capabilities. Why not determine right now to let God's love in you love someone else? Write down the name that comes to mind and let God's love in you tell you how to love that person. You will be amazed at what begins to happen!

SUNDAY EVENING, AUGUST 22

Title: The Love of God

Text: "I have loved thee with an everlasting love" **(Jer. 31:3)**.

Scripture Reading: Jeremiah 31:1–6

Introduction

The better acquainted we are with God's love, the more our hearts will be drawn out in love to him. Jeremiah wrote, "The LORD hath appeared of old unto me, saying, Yea, I have loved thee with an everlasting love: therefore with lovingkindness have I drawn thee" (31:3). How little real love there is for God! One reason for this is that our hearts are so seldom occupied with the wondrous love of God for his people. However wonderful human love may be, it is but a poor reflection of the divine. Consider three questions about God's love.

I. What are the characteristics of God's love?

As Christ taught us, God's love for us is utterly beyond enlightened self-interest, the Golden Rule, or good Samaritanism. Christ manifested the only absolutely selfless love.

   A. *The love of God is unmerited.* There is nothing in the objects of God's love to call it forth, nothing in his creatures to prompt it. The love one human being has for another is because of something in them, but the love of God is free, uncaused, unmerited. In effect, Moses told Israel, "God loved you only because he wanted to, not because you deserved to be loved" (see Deut. 7:7–8). "We love [God], because he first loved us" (1 John 4:19). God loved us before we had in us a particle of love for him. What is there in me, what is there in you, to attract the love of God? Nothing! To the contrary, there is much to repel. Yet he loves us.

   B. *The love of God is eternal.* Such a concept transcends the grasp of our minds, but it is nonetheless true. God himself is eternal, and "God is love" (1 John 4:8). Since God had no beginning, his love had no beginning. Love is more than a feeling. It is an act. God's love is not only eternal, it is also historical. How clear is our text on this point: "I have loved thee with an everlasting love."

   C. *The love of God is universal.* He loves all people. "God so loved the world" (John 3:16)—the good and the bad, the healthy and the sick, the rich and the poor, the saint and the sinner, every creature in this world. God loves all people as they are—the deranged, the dirty, the diseased, and the sinful—and he sent his Son to save them all (1 Tim. 2:4).

D. *The love of God is infinite.* Everything about God is infinite. His essence fills heaven and earth. His wisdom is infinite; he knows all things. His power is unbounded. So his love is without limit. "Because of his great love for us, God, who is rich in mercy, made us alive with Christ even when we were dead in transgressions—it is by grace you have been saved" (Eph. 2:4–5 NIV). The love of God cannot be estimated.

E. *The love of God is immutable.* As with God himself, there "is no variableness, neither shadow of turning" (James 1:17), so his love knows neither change nor diminution. During Jesus' last night on earth, one disciple would betray him; another would ask, "Lord, shew us the Father" (John 14:8); and another would deny him three times. And in the critical hour, all would forsake him. Nevertheless, John tells us, "Having loved his own which were in the world, he loved them unto the end" (John 13:1). Nothing can separate us from God's love (Rom. 8:35–39).

F. *The love of God is holy.* It is not regulated by caprice, passion, or sentiment but by principle. God's love is no mere weakness or softness. God will not wink at sin, even in his own people.

II. What are the results of God's love?

What does God do because of his love for us?

A. *Because God loves us, he saves us.* He prepared his matchless plan of salvation. In fact, it was conceived in his loving heart before the foundation of the world. God alone is the author of our salvation. God alone wrought the change seen in believers (Eph. 2:4–5). This change in sinners is grounded in God's boundless mercy and love. God's love is that divine disposition that sees something infinitely precious in people in spite of their sin.

B. *Because God loves us, he sent Christ to die on the cross.* "God so loved the world, that he gave his only begotten Son" (John 3:16). He loved us. Love has been defined, once and for all, by the act of Christ giving his life for us. Paul wrote to the Galatians about Jesus as "the Son of God, who loved me, and gave himself for me" (2:20). To the Romans, Paul wrote, "While we were yet sinners, Christ died for us" (5:8). Love substituted itself, that the one loved might be freed. The cross is the uncovering of the realism of love.

C. *Because God loves us, he sent the Holy Spirit.* "Behold, I stand at the door, and knock: if any man hear my voice, and open the door, I will come in to him, and will sup with him, and he with me" (Rev. 3:20). He stands not only at the door of a lukewarm church, but also at the door of an unsaved individual. If you are not a Christian, he is standing at your door offering you the gift of love.

D. *Because God loves us, his children, he helps us.* Because he lives within us by his Holy Spirit, his power is available to us.

At times Jesus' philosophy of life may seem to be negative, but it always leads to the positive and the joyful. Jesus said, "If any man will come after me, let him deny himself, and take up his cross, and follow me" (Matt. 16:24). To some, this may sound like taking the joy out of life. Quite to the contrary, it is love seeking the highest and best for his own.

III. What should be our response to God's love?

How should we respond to a love so great?

A. *We should respond with conviction of sin.* Realizing that a pure and holy God loved us enough to die in our place should break our hearts, striking conviction, deep and strong, into our souls.

B. *We should respond with conversion from sin to Christ.* Conviction is not enough; we must totally commit our lives to Christ for all time to come. These days some scoff at the idea of instantaneous conversion. Though we must grow and develop in the things of Christ, there is no other kind of conversion.

C. *We should respond with commitment to Christ's way, the way of love (1 Cor. 12:31).* Christian commitment is to be for the things Christ is for and against the things he is against. Love hates war, racial discrimination, injustice, inhumanity, and dishonesty. Love will not cease its efforts until it does all it can to change conditions. If we love God, everything else will fall into place.

D. *We should respond with community in Christ.* Christians are saved to live in a community of believers. Of course one must be saved even to be eligible to be baptized into the fellowship of a church, but a converted person outside the fellowship of a church is a hopeless contradiction.

Conclusion

Love is not a luxury in our world. It is the profoundest practical need of humankind. Psychologist Karl Menninger once said, "Half the diseases are due to hate, and half the accidents are due to hate." He continued, "Love is the remedy." Then he universalized it: "Love is the medicine for the sickness of the world." Yes, it is—God's love, that is. We should love God because he first loved us.

WEDNESDAY EVENING, AUGUST 25

Title: Don't Quench the Holy Spirit

Text: "Do not quench the Spirit" (**1 Thess. 5:19 RSV**).

Introduction

The negative imperative in our text, "Do not quench the Spirit," reveals that it is highly possible that each of us can be guilty of doing so. And doing so is to grieve the heart of our Father God, to deprive ourselves of his benevolent ministry, and to withhold from others that which they could receive through us if the Spirit were permitted to do his good work.

Have you choked the life out of the Spirit within you? Have you poured water on the creative fire of the Holy Spirit? To face these and other questions concerning our response to the Holy Spirit will cause each of us to plead guilty. How do we avoid the possibility of making a negative response to the Holy Spirit?

I. Let us recognize the presence of the Holy Spirit within us (I Cor. 3:16; 6:19–20).

It is possible that we have quenched the Spirit by our very failure to recognize that he was and is God's gift to us at the time of our conversion experience (Acts 2:38; Gal. 3:2). Some people have the mistaken idea that they must wait for a kind of spiritual extravaganza before they experience the Holy Spirit's presence. He came quietly but significantly in the moment you received Jesus Christ as Lord and Savior (Rom. 8:9). Let us stand in awe before the significance of this truth that the eternal Spirit has come to dwell within us.

II. Let us cultivate the fruit of the Spirit with cooperation (Gal. 5:22–23).

Our heavenly Father's purpose for us is to bring us into conformity to the image of his dear Son (Rom. 8:28–29). The Father God is in the process of helping us in that direction day by day. He has bestowed the gift of the Holy Spirit within us to make that possibility real. Paul told the Colossians that Christ in them was the hope of glory (Col. 1:27). Becoming genuinely Christian is not a matter of our lifting ourselves up by our own spiritual bootstraps. Instead, it comes about as we respond positively and continuously to the work of the Holy Spirit. He seeks to reproduce within us the very nature and personality of Jesus Christ.

In the nine graces of the Spirit, we find a verbal portrait of Jesus Christ. We also see a vision of what we can be as we are led by the Holy Spirit (Gal. 5:16–18).

III. Let us listen to the Spirit with joyful obedience (Heb. 3:7–11).

There is no way God can lead us into our personal promised land in the here and now if we neglect to hear the voice of the Spirit and refrain from obeying his Word. No one can do your listening and obeying for you. God is at work for good in each of us. To experience the fulfillment of his promise, we must listen and obey.

Conclusion

It is no accident that each of the seven epistles to the seven churches of Asia Minor concludes with the exhortation, "He who has an ear, let him hear what the Spirit says to the churches" (Rev. 2:7 RSV). The Holy Spirit is present in your heart if you are a believer, but you must listen to and obey him to reap the benefits of his presence. Let us discover his presence afresh by responding positively to his gracious work within us. Let us rejoice in what God wants to do in us by his Spirit.

Don't pour water on the fire of the Spirit!

SUNDAY MORNING, AUGUST 29

Title: The Church and Its Beginning

Text: "And I say also unto thee, That thou art Peter, and upon this rock I will build my church; and the gates of hell shall not prevail against it" **(Matt. 16:18)**.

Scripture Reading: Matthew 16:13–19

Hymns: "Built on the Rock the Church Doth Stand," Lindeman
"I Love Thy Kingdom, Lord," Williams
"Onward, Christian Soldiers," Sullivan

Offertory Prayer: Our Father, for the beauty of the earth and for the magnificence of its bounty, we give you thanks. We ask your forgiveness for our sins of ingratitude and presumption. Increase our sensitivity to your blessings around us, and open our hearts and hands to respond by sharing that with which we have been blessed. Receive these gifts we bring and use them for your glory. In Jesus' name we pray. Amen.

Introduction

What do you think about when you first hear the word *church*? Some think of a building, a physical structure. It might be a modern steel building in the suburbs with an open ceiling, acoustical panels on the walls, interlocking chairs, a large stage, and a Plexiglas pulpit. Others envision a majestic and imposing edifice with stained-glass windows, cushioned pews, and beautiful furnishings. Still others, when the word *church* is mentioned, think of a service—a ceremony or ritual—that takes place on Sunday morning, in which hymns are sung, prayers are offered, and a sermon is delivered.

These are all connotations of the word *church*, and they all are right if we have firmly planted in our minds the denotation, the original and basic meaning of the word. The purpose of this morning's message is to establish in our minds the basic meaning of church that Jesus has given to us. This was not Peter's idea of the church or Paul's concept or Matthew's or John's. It came directly from Christ who "loved the church, and gave himself for it" (Eph. 5:25).

277

The verses of our text are divided into three parts. First is the *prologue.* A prologue is like a preface or introduction in which the author sets the stage or prepares the reader for what he is about to say. Second is the *presentation.* Here it is a single verse in which Jesus revealed the foundation, mission, and security of the church. Finally, there is an *epilogue,* or concluding section or statement in which the author attempts to round out or sum up the design and purpose of what he has said.

I. The prologue.

A. *What happened in the area of Caesarea Philippi has been called the "watershed" of the gospel.* All that went before and all that comes afterward flow from this event. At this point Jesus was only six months away from his death on the cross. Did these men, his disciples, truly understand him and his mission on earth? They had been fascinated by his teaching, thrilled by his miracles, and awed by his divine personality. But did they truly understand him and what he came to do? Certainly Jesus knew their hearts, but they had never articulated their thoughts about him; they had never verbalized their faith. Paul said in Romans, "With the mouth, confession is made unto salvation" (10:10). There is something about speaking one's faith that validates it.

B. *In our imagination let's join the disciples and Jesus.* The setting is a relaxed one, because Jesus has taken the disciples apart from the milling crowds. On every hand in this historical section of Palestine are monuments of ancient kings and conquerors; there are also relics of the ancient Canaanite religions as well as the current pantheistic cult.

   In the midst of all this, Jesus asks a question he has never asked his disciples before: "Whom do men say that I the Son of man am?" (Matt. 16:13). No doubt this is a jolt to the disciples. It is a probing question. One by one they begin to answer. Of course Jesus isn't asking the question to receive information from his disciples, for he knows what others are saying about him. He is simply preparing the disciples for the question of all questions: "Whom do you say that I am?" It does not matter what the others are saying. I am not interested in your reciting a creed to me. Rather, tell me who you believe I am!

C. *Perhaps the disciples begin to glance at one another as Jesus' words fall like heavy stones on their hearts.* They may begin to smile. Doubtless there is a throbbing excitement in Peter's voice as he speaks for all of them: "Thou art the Christ, the Son of the living God!" Peter speaks what his heart has already accepted as truth. Immediately Jesus recognizes the reality of Peter's confession (v. 17). The stage is set. This is Jesus' "prologue."

II. The presentation.

A. *After Peter's confession, Jesus reveals to his disciples the most fantastic concept the world has ever known (v. 18).* He begins by saying, "Thou art

278

Peter. . . ." The name Peter (*petros*) means "a little stone or rock." When Jesus first met this man, he said to him, "Thou art Simon the son of Jona: thou shalt be called Cephas" (John 1:42). Cephas, the Aramaic form of the Greek name Peter, is by interpretation "a stone." Now Jesus is saying, "Peter, you have become a stone!" And what is the evidence? His confession of Christ. Peter is still unstable, but at long last the "rock" is beginning to harden. Through the sorrow of the crucifixion, the victory of the resurrection, and the glory of Pentecost, Peter will keep on becoming the rock that Jesus has predicted he will become.

B. *But Jesus is not through (v. 18).* After he commends Peter, Jesus changes his emphasis completely. "And upon this rock I will build my church." The word Jesus uses for "rock" is *petra*, in the neuter gender. It means a great ledge of rock, such as would be the foundation for a huge building or large city. Peter was "a little rock" broken off the great ledge, the *petra*. Undoubtedly the *petra* refers to Christ himself, and when individuals make a confession of faith in Jesus Christ, they partake of his nature. And upon the Rock, Christ Jesus, he would build his church. The church belongs to Christ, who "loved the church, and gave himself for it" (Eph. 5:25).

III. The epilogue.

A. *Now Jesus is about to summarize this electrifying revelation he has given his disciples (v. 19).* "And I will give unto thee the keys of the kingdom of heaven: and whatsoever thou shalt bind on earth shall be bound in heaven: and whatsoever thou shalt loose on earth shall be loosed in heaven." What does Jesus mean by "the keys of the kingdom"? No, he is not telling Peter that he will be the first pope of the church and, as such, have the authority to retain or forgive sin. Instead, in Jesus' day, the keys to a house were entrusted to the slave who was the "steward" of the owner. Keys are used to lock and unlock doors. Each time Christians take the Word of God and proclaim it, they are unlocking the very portals of heaven for a lost person. But if they fail to share it, teach it, and preach it, they are keeping those doors locked to someone who needs entrance! Jesus is saying that the preaching of the cross, as Paul would later attest, may sound like foolishness to the world, but it is Jesus' way to introduce lost souls to eternal salvation.

B. *It is a glorious privilege to have "the keys of the kingdom" committed to us.* But it is also an awesome responsibility. We hold in our hands that which contains the power to transform the world! And if people go away from us because of our silence, it will not be the fault of the gospel or of the Christ whom it preaches, but of his church, his people who have played truant to the task that God has placed before us.

Conclusion

Jesus' words here are a monumental part of the New Testament. All the way through this passage there is a ringing note of victory, of conquest. Yet at the same time this is the most serious challenge God's people have ever received. As believers we are members of his church, his body, and we are founded on the Rock, Jesus Christ. We are charged with the keys that will unlock the doors of heaven—and that is the gospel of redemption. What are we doing about it?

SUNDAY EVENING, AUGUST 29

Title: The Constancy of God

Text: "For I the LORD do not change; therefore you, O sons of Jacob, are not consumed" **(Mal. 3:6 RSV)**.

Scripture Reading: Malachi 3:1–6

Introduction

Everything earthly changes. A retired man visited his birthplace and reported, "I visited the town of my boyhood days and found almost everything changed. The community school and the little church are both gone. The mom-and-pop stores and restaurant are gone, and franchise businesses have taken their places. An interstate highway cuts my uncle's farm into two equal parts. But the God about whom my parents, my grandparents, and my uncle taught me has not changed. His goodness and mercy have followed me and blessed me all the days of my life."

So said the prophet, "For I the LORD do not change; therefore you, O sons of Jacob, are not consumed." This prophet of old grasped the truth of the constancy of God. He sought to show his people its implications. Let us explore some of these implications from two points of view.

I. What does the constancy of God mean from God's point of view?

A. *Even though humans have changed their attitude about sin, God has not and will not.* The humanist says, "Sin? There is no such thing, really. A bit of the beast survives in us, traces of selfishness, but not sin! Sin is a Jewish taboo, a Victorian convention." A psychologist has said, "Sin is a psychopathic aspect of adolescent mentality."

Some who do not agree with the humanist and the psychologist apply the wrong test to their deeds. They justify their deeds by the test of popularity. They feel that if everyone is doing a certain thing, it must be all right. Others justify immoral acts by the test of legality. But just because something is legal does not make it moral. For others the eleventh commandment is, "Thou shalt not get caught." But sin has not changed; sin is still rebellion against God. And the person who rebels is God's enemy.

280

This is the marvel of the cross. "While we were enemies," Paul tells us, "we were reconciled to God by the death of his Son" (Rom. 5:10 RSV). It is because God does not change his attitude toward sin that Christ went to the cross.

B. *God does not change in his love toward all people.* We are valuable in his sight. God loves every man, woman, boy, and girl in this world.

C. *God does not change in his evaluation of human souls.* David asked, "What is man, that thou are mindful of him?" (Ps. 8:4). Jesus said, "How much then is a man better than a sheep?" (Matt. 12:12). Both texts, though thousands of years apart, suggest the supreme worth of human personality. God's evaluation of human worth does not change.

D. *God does not change in his plans and purposes.* His methods may change. His approach may vary. He may even discard one group because of disobedience and choose another to be used in carrying out his plans, but his program does not change. Dr. E. Y. Mullins once said, "The apparent changes in God are simply his unresting desire to bless men."

God's goals remain the same.

   1. God's first goal is the salvation of all who will believe. Paul said in 1 Timothy that it is God's will for all people to be saved (2:4).

   2. God's second goal is the indoctrination of the saved. Paul continued in 1 Timothy by saying that God desires all people to come to the knowledge of the truth. Part of Jesus' great commission is "Teaching them to observe all things whatsoever I have commanded you" (Matt. 28:20).

   3. God's third goal is the consummation of the kingdom. Paul said, "Then the end will come, when [Christ] hands over the kingdom to God the Father after he has destroyed all dominion, authority and power" (1 Cor. 15:24 NIV).

E. *God does not change in his judgments and mercy.* Our passage illustrates this. "Then I will draw near to you for judgment; I will be a swift witness against the sorcerers, against the adulterers" (Mal. 3:5 RSV). God's changeless nature guarantees this. With God, judgment is written into the very nature of things. Thus God's judgment is clearly seen in history. Consider, for example, the Genesis accounts of the flood and of the destruction of the Tower of Babel.

But history also illustrates God's mercy. At the crisis in the history of his nation, Samuel said to his people, "If ye do return unto the LORD with all your hearts, then put away the strange gods and Ashtaroth from among you, and prepare your hearts unto the LORD, and serve him only" (1 Sam. 7:3). What was the result? "Then the children of Israel did put away Baalim and Ashtaroth, and served the LORD only" (v. 4). When the people repented, God's mercy broke through. God's mercy never fails, for God changes not. "The mercy of the LORD is from everlasting to everlasting upon them that fear him" (Ps. 103:17).

II. What does the constancy of God mean from the human point of view?

What implications does it carry?

A. *The constancy of God warns us of the certainty of God's judgment.* His judgment is on the unrepentant, upon those who rebel against him. Sin has not changed, nor has its penalty. "The soul that sinneth, it shall die" (Ezek. 18:4). The wages of sin is still death (Rom. 6:23), and nothing can unwrite that law.

B. *The constancy of God assures us of the dependability of his promises.* He has promised to receive us, answer our prayers, sustain us, and protect us. He has promised relief from our burdens and strength for our trials. He has promised abiding fellowship (Matt. 18:20), power (Luke 24:49; Acts 1:8), and eternal life (John 10:28). His promises are not empty words. His changeless nature is their guarantee.

C. The constancy of God guarantees the security of believers. God's changeless nature is bound up with his sovereignty. Sovereignty means security. The security of believers is predicated on the sovereignty of the God who does not change (John 10:27–29). This is the rock on which our faith rests. The value of faith is in its object, and the object of our faith is Christ. If one who has trusted himself or herself to God's care were to be lost, it would be necessary for God to change, and he changes not.

D. *The constancy of God provides the incentive for living.* Because God changes not, life has meaning, purpose, and direction. If we are going in the same direction hand in hand with God, life has incentive. Otherwise life is meaningless and empty.

E. *In her poem "Lament," Edna St. Vincent Millay describes the brave efforts of a widow to help her small children adjust to the death of their father.* She makes them clothes out of his old clothes. She gives them their father's trinkets to play with. The poem ends on this plaintive note: "Life must go on, I forget just why." Many people are saying the same thing.

Conclusion

Two questions plague the minds of modern men and women. What does life mean? And what in this world can be trusted to stay the same? Both questions are answered in a changeless Christ. Outside of Christ individuals are free to choose what kind and how great a sinner they will be. They are alienated from the ground of their being. But life takes on new meaning when a person enters a relationship with a changeless God through Jesus Christ.

SUGGESTED PREACHING PROGRAM FOR THE MONTH OF
SEPTEMBER

- ## Sunday Mornings

    Complete the series "The Nature and Ministry of the Church."

- ## Sunday Evenings

    Complete the series "The Doctrine of God."

- ## Wednesday Evenings

    The Wednesday evening messages this month deal with the topic "The Problem of Pain and Suffering." The messages come from the heart of one who has experienced suffering in those dear to him.

WEDNESDAY EVENING, SEPTEMBER 1

Title: Thorn in the Flesh

Text: "And he said unto me, My grace is sufficient for thee: for my strength is made perfect in weakness. Most gladly therefore will I rather glory in my infirmities, that the power of Christ may rest upon me" **(2 Cor. 12:9).**

Scripture Reading: 2 Corinthians 12:1–9

Introduction

Some people seem to enjoy talking about their afflictions. This was not the case with the apostle Paul. He does, however, tells us in today's Scripture passage about his affliction—his "thorn in the flesh." We are grateful that he shared such an experience with us. We often ask about our trouble, "Why did God send this upon me?" Maybe God did not send it at all. Paul said the thorn was "a messenger of Satan" sent to torment him (2 Cor. 12:7). Much of our suffering is due to our own folly. Satan deceives us.

I. What was Paul's thorn in the flesh?

A. *We are not really sure.* It may have been figurative, or it may have been literal. If figurative, it could have been a bad temper, remorse for having persecuted the church, some personal adversary, or carnal temptation. If literal, it might have been malaria, an eye disease, epilepsy, arthritis, or maybe an unhealed wound from some beating.

   What is your thorn? It may be anything exceedingly trying or difficult. It may be a weak body, a great sorrow, or some gnawing burden. It may be a bad heart, disappointment, failure, or weakness.

283

It may be someone who is always getting under your skin. A person may be born with a thorn or discover it late in life.

B. *We do not know what tormented Paul.* I'm glad we don't. If we did, it would help us only when we had that particular affliction. As it is, his thorn represents every affliction. There is one thing we can say: his thorn in the flesh repudiates the philosophy that if you live right, you will be healthy and things will go smoothly for you.

Think of how God's people have suffered. Job had something like skin cancer. Moses had a stammering tongue. Jeremiah was overwhelmed with a sense of his own deficiencies. Peter had a bad temper. Francis of Assisi had tuberculosis. Fannie Crosby was blind. Ignatius of Loyola was physically disabled. Joni Eareckson Tada is a quadriplegic. If you have a thorn, you stand in the company of some of the great people of history.

II. How can we deal with our thorns?

A. *You can refuse to admit it.* You can try to escape it through drink or pleasure. You can harden yourself to it.

B. *How did Paul deal with his thorn?*

1. Paul prayed about it. He admitted his problem and pleaded with the Lord to take it away (2 Cor. 12:8). Moses faced the bitter complaints of his people through prayer. Elijah, upon feeling helpless and powerless on Mount Carmel, cried out to God. David, when his heart was broken by his own failure and sin, prayed. You can learn the secret of a power beyond your own through prayer.

2. Paul relied on the grace of God. Each time Paul prayed that God would remove the thorn, the answer came back, "No." But God said, "My grace is sufficient for thee." Paul came to know the sufficiency of God's sustaining grace. God's grace is sufficient in our weakness, in our suffering, and in our sin.

3. Paul gloried in his thorn. He came to thank God for it. The final note to be sounded in any spiritual victory is that of thanksgiving. In Ephesians he spoke of "giving thanks always for all things" (5:20). Weakness, suffering, and trials can bring great spiritual blessings. Perhaps that is the reason Paul said, "Most gladly therefore will I rather glory in my infirmities, that the power of Christ may rest upon me" (2 Cor. 12:9). The word "power" in the Greek is expressively beautiful. In the Old Testament when the presence of God was exceedingly great, that presence was the shekinah glory. It went before the children of Israel on their wilderness journeys. It was also above the tabernacle. It signified the personal presence of God, so Paul said in essence, "My very weakness has made it possible for the shekinah glory of the Lord to dwell over me."

Paul's physical handicap brought spiritual blessings. In the parish church of St. Cuthbert during the last century, George Matheson prayed that his thorn might be removed. What was his thorn? On the eve of his sister's marriage, something happened that broke his heart. He said, "I prefer not to tell it." We do not know what it was. It might have been the message from the doctor that he would soon be blind. It might have been that his sweetheart, whom he loved dearly, refused to marry him when she heard of his blindness. Whatever it was that broke George Matheson's heart, he called it his "thorn in the flesh." Through that experience of his broken heart and the thorn in his flesh, he wrote the hymn "O Love That Will Not Let Me Go." Years later he said, "I have lived to thank God for my thorn."

Conclusion

God gives us grace to bear our pain and bring us to the place where we can glory in our suffering. Thank God for your thorn!

SUNDAY MORNING, SEPTEMBER 5

Title: The Church and Its Growth

Text: "Then they that gladly received his word were baptized: and the same day there were added unto them about three thousand souls. And they continued stedfastly in the apostles' doctrine and fellowship, and in breaking of bread, and in prayers" (**Acts 2:41–42**).

Scripture Reading: Acts 2:41–47; 4:31–32

Hymns: "O Breath of Life," Head
"Pentecostal Power," Homer
"Breathe on Me," McKinney

Offertory Prayer: Our Father, we bow humbly before you, aware that we are undeserving of all your many blessings. Yet we do thank you for all that you have given us. We bring to you today a portion of what we have received. We ask for your blessing upon it. Also, Father, purify the motives behind our giving so that we in turn might be blessed. In the name of Jesus we pray. Amen.

Introduction

A pastor was talking one day with a man who was a member of his church. For no apparent reason, the man never attended church services. When the pastor urged the man to come, he replied rather smugly that he could be just as good a Christian staying home as he could attending church. The two men happened to be seated before a fireplace in which a coal fire was

285

burning. The pastor took the tongs from beside the fireplace and picked out one of the live coals. He placed it on the hearth by itself. That single coal, which had been fiery red when it was in the bed of burning coals, turned gray and began to cool off. Soon it lost all its glow and warmth. Then, without saying a word, the pastor picked up the cold piece of coal and placed it back in the midst of the live coals. Soon it was aglow and began to give off heat once more. The silent little drama drove the message home. The delinquent church member dropped his head in shame and said, "Pastor, I will be in church Sunday morning."

Nothing in the world is as personal and intimate as one's encounter with Jesus Christ, yet each experience is unique within itself. Only two principals are involved: God and the individual. Yet it is not God's will that a Christian continue alone or that he or she live the Christian life in isolation. It was God's plan from the beginning that believers in the Lord Jesus Christ be joined together in spiritual fellowship, in a special kind of oneness. This was the basic characteristic of the church that was conceived in the heart of God before the foundation of the world.

On the eve of the day of Pentecost, we read that the disciples "were all with one accord in one place" (Acts 2:1). Just as warmth and fellowship exist in the togetherness of the church, so does growth happen in that environment. Our theme this morning is the church and its growth. In our Scripture passages we will discover three directions in which the church grew in the first century. It is God's will that it continue to grow in these same directions.

I. The growth within.

"Then they that gladly received his word were baptized: and the same day there were added unto them about three thousand souls. And they continued stedfastly in the apostles' doctrine and fellowship, and in breaking of bread, and in prayers" (Acts 2:41–42). In these brief words we have the four fundamentals of Christian growth.

A. *They were baptized.* Because they had already "received his word" with gladness and open acceptance, they publicly identified with Christ through baptism. It was their way of saying to the whole world that they had begun a lifelong experience of death to self in order that they might come alive daily in Christ.

B. *They were taught.* "They continued stedfastly in the apostles' doctrine." This was spiritual nourishment, food for the souls of these young believers, and they absorbed it. They were consistent ("continued stedfastly") in receiving the Word of God. It was their sustenance, their strength. The result was that they grew both numerically and spiritually. This is a vital phase in the Christian's life that is often overlooked. Sometimes the church, in its commendable efforts to win the lost to Christ, fail to teach them consistently and properly in the way. As a result, many remain spiritual babies, causing the church to give a weak and often ineffective witness before the world.

C. *They experienced fellowship.* Fellowship, *koinonia*, is one of the most beautiful words in the New Testament. It means more than a social get-together. It describes a communion, a sharing between those who have something special in common. Because of the Spirit of Christ within them, the early believers began to love one another, share their burdens, and pray together. They had a delightful sense of community, of belonging to one another.

D. *They prayed together.* The early Christians continued steadfastly not only in the apostles' teaching and in fellowship, but also in prayer. Their communication with God was not neglected. This was their lifeline, their contact with the very throne of grace. They practiced what Paul later expressed to the Thessalonians—praying without ceasing (1 Thess. 5:17). They knew what it meant to remain in a spirit of prayer and openness before God.

II. The growth without.

In Acts 2:43–47 we have an indication of the growth of the church "without," that is, the radiating effect of the church on the unbelieving world.

A. *Note that "fear came upon every soul" (v. 43).* A reverence and respect for these Christians and their faith struck at the hearts of the unbelievers. This fear could also be interpreted as conviction, a tool of the Holy Spirit in dealing with unbelievers. But sadly, not all who feared in their heart because of the testimony of these believers responded in repentance. It is so today. Some unbelievers are struck by the sincerity of Christians but fail to follow through. They stop short of repentance.

B. *Furthermore, these Christians were "praising God, and having favour with all the people" (v. 47).* These first-century Christians were continually held in high regard by unbelievers. Perhaps this is a serious indictment against many modern Christians. Often professing Christians live in a spiritually substandard way. Those who are unsaved, always yearning to find justification for their life lived apart from God, find delight in pointing out Christians who are not consistent in their profession.

C. *"And the Lord added to the church daily such as should be saved" (v. 47).* God was at work in the midst of his people. They were glorifying and praising him. The result was a continual response on the part of the people around them—not seasonal or spasmodic growth but genuine and consistent growth. Too often after great revival campaigns, during which scores of people come to know Christ as Savior, we go back to business as usual. That was not the case with the first-century Christians. Growth without took place because they "continued stedfastly" in teaching and fellowship.

III. The growth beyond.

"And when they had prayed, the place was shaken where they were assembled together; and they were all filled with the Holy Ghost, and they spake the word of God with boldness. And the multitude of them that believed were of one heart and of one soul" (Acts 4:31–32).

A. *Marvelous things happened in Jerusalem.* But they certainly could not keep the gospel there. It was too big to be contained in one city! So God began to prepare them for growth beyond. His preparation came in a strange way: it started with persecution. When the early believers began to experience hostility and pressure from the unbelieving world, what did they do? They prayed!

B. *After the church prayed, something happened.* "The place was shaken where they were assembled together." They experienced a physical sense of God's overpowering presence among them. Perhaps he was saying to them in a symbolic way that he would shake Jerusalem and the world beyond with the message they were proclaiming.

C. *Then they spoke God's Word boldly.* The message of Jesus Christ and his resurrection brings new life flowing from a living Christ into dying and dead people and institutions, awakening and empowering them.

Conclusion

God has made provision that Christians of every age can speak his Word with boldness and in so doing shake the structures of the society in which they live. God did not intend for the church to stop growing after the first century. The same principles of growth that he instituted in the early church are those that must be operative in the church today. We must not be ashamed to confess him before others. His Word must be faithfully and consistently taught, or else no inner growth can take place. A *koinonia* fellowship, a communion and oneness, must exist among the people of God. Believers must pray continually for a holy boldness to proclaim the good news of salvation to the ends of the earth.

SUNDAY EVENING, SEPTEMBER 5

Title: The Urgency of God

Text: "I must work the works of him that sent me, while it is day: the night cometh, when no man can work" (**John 9:4**).

Scripture Reading: John 9:1–12

Introduction

How does God regard time? Although God is eternal, he has a program of redemption for mortal beings, who are "of few days, and full of trouble"

(Job 14:1). God's commands and commissions are throbbing with urgency. His business requires haste. Jesus is our example: so compelling was his task, so urgent was he in spirit that he crowded into three and one-half years labor that could have graced a century.

Concerning this urgency, let's consider two facts and then, based on these two facts, consider two questions.

I. Consider two facts.

A. *First, we are slow to do God's work.* In almost every realm an impelling sense of urgency grips us. "Hurry! Hurry!" is the watchword of the day. We must eat faster, learn faster, travel faster, and sell faster. This sense of urgency has touched about everything in modern life except the program of the church. How leisurely is our pace. No sense of urgency weighs on our minds concerning God's work. In the work-a-day world, our theme is rush, rush, rush. "Got to make a living, you know." But when it comes to serving God, we say, "We'll get to that one of these days. There's no hurry; we have plenty of time."

B. *Second, God is urgent.* This fact is thrown in bold relief against the dark shadow of the first. Most people think of God as having no concern with the passage of time. When they read Peter's statement, "One day is with the Lord as a thousand years, and a thousand years as one day" (2 Peter 3:8), they emphasize the thousand years in God's sight equaling one day. Seldom do people focus attention on the statement the other way around. Anyone who has watched through a long night at the bedside of a dying loved one will understand how a few hours can seem like an eternity. So it must be with God as he watches the dying multitudes, whom he loves and for whom Christ died, going into eternal damnation. Our delay in sharing the gospel must weigh heavily on his heart. God's love demands haste.

The New Testament is an urgent book. It is filled with such phrases as, "Go quickly, and tell his disciples" (Matt. 28:7), "Arise up quickly" (Acts 12:7), and "I come quickly" (Rev. 22:20). The only reason Jesus ever asked his disciples to tarry was that they might be filled with the power of the Holy Spirit (Luke 24:49).

II. Consider two questions that arise from these two facts.

A. *First, why are we so slow?* There are several reasons.

1. We are so slow because we do not realize how important God's work is. We think primarily of our own earthly wealth and material obligations. We let God's business get along the best it can. People often want God to hurry, especially when his presence would banish their sorrow and suffering. The rest of the time they assume that God will be content to wait until they have

289

made their fortune, until every earthly obligation has been met, or until a more convenient day arrives.

2. We are so slow because we cannot discern the unerring and unseen operation of spiritual laws and forces. God works silently and unseen, but he works! Let every Christian remember that for those who are not Christians, time is running out. Witnessing to them is urgent.

A group of men in the Swiss Alps made their living in an unusual and precarious way. Equipped only with a sharp, pointed steel bar, a long rope, and a leather satchel, they roamed about the mountains searching for the eggs of rare species of birds. They would bring these home, hatch them by artificial means, and sell the little birds thus obtained to zoos for fabulous prices.

One day one of these men saw on a ledge below him a nest containing three eggs of a species of bird for which he had searched for years. He secured his steel bar in the rock, fastened his rope to it, and climbed down the face of the cliff to the ledge below. But in his excitement, he did a thing that all of his training and experience had taught him not to do: he let go of the rope. Instantly the realization overwhelmed him that when his rope ceased to swing, it would be far beyond his reach, and he would perish there with those precious eggs. His only chance was to leap out into the void and grasp the rope as it swung toward him. At the first swing of the rope, he was not ready. The second swing was shorter, but still he could not bring himself to jump. When the rope started toward him the third time, he knew it was now or never. He leaped out into space, seized the rope, and climbed to safety.

In this illustration, the man could see the rope and would know when it would be too late to save himself. Like the rope, the pendulum of God's clock is swinging. The difference is that no one knows how short the swing or how brief the time.

We are so slow because we do not understand the urgency of God. As a little boy, I loved to go to the circus, but the sideshow barkers frightened me with their cry, "Hurry, hurry, hurry!" It is no cheap sideshow, but the main issue of life, with which God is concerned. The heartbeat of God sets the tempo. "Hurry! Hurry!" he would say. "For those I love die so fast." How urgent is our God!

B. *Second, what results from our lack of urgency concerning God's work?* Several answers may be suggested.

1. By our lack of urgency, we bring pain to the heart of God. God has furnished all things needed for our salvation. Jesus bore this out when on the cross he cried, "It is finished" (John 19:30). God's plan of salvation is complete. Atonement has been made. How it must grieve his heart when we are so slow to show others his way.

290

2. By our lack of urgency, we let irreclaimable opportunities to reap God's harvest fall to the ground. Our text tells us when we are to work for him: "While it is day: the night cometh, when no man can work." The opportunity passes. One of God's angels in Revelation cried, "Thrust in thy sickle, and reap: for the time is come for thee to reap; for the harvest of the earth is ripe" (14:15).

3. By our lack of urgency, we do so little to win a lost world to Christ. Although much is being done in all types of missions, the surface has hardly been scratched.

Conclusion

There are two prayers we all should pray. First: "God, give us a vision of yourself, of a God who is in a hurry. Give us a vision of your work, its importance, its urgency. And give us a vision of ourselves, how slow and lackadaisical we are."

Second: "God, help us realize that the King's business requires haste. Show us how great your program is, how urgent your cause. Urge us on, Lord, that we may be in a hurry to do your work. Amen."

WEDNESDAY EVENING, SEPTEMBER 8

Title: Why Do Good People Suffer?

Text: "But it is good for me to draw near to God: I have put my trust in the LORD God" **(Ps. 73:28)**.

Scripture Reading: Psalm 73:3–17, 28

Introduction

Following the funeral service for his father, a man and his young son walked out of the church to their car to drive to the cemetery. The son looked up through his tears and asked, "Why did it have to be Granddaddy?"

We find the question "Why?" in the hearts of young and old alike. Many things happen for which we can find no answer. Have you ever asked this question? If so, you stand in good company. The psalmist tried to live a good life. He endured pain, suffering, and tragedy yet saw the wicked prosper on every hand. He saw their pride. He heard them speak against God. He heard them laugh at goodness. They did not seem to suffer like good people. The bewildered psalmist cried out, "Why do the wicked prosper and the righteous suffer?"

Why do good people suffer?

I. People suffer because of sin.

We disobey the laws of God and suffer for our rebellion. David suffered because he sinned against God. People sow wild oats; then one day they reap an awful crop. Adam and Eve were driven from the garden of Eden because

291

they sinned. Today people are driven from the gardens of happiness and blessing into the deserts of misery and trouble because of their rebellion against God. The springs of life dry up. The flowers wilt and fade away. The birds cease their singing because sin has entered the heart.

II. People suffer because of the frailty of human life.

Jesus said to his disciples, "In the world ye shall have tribulation" (John 16:33). Jesus promised his people in the beginning that because they lived in the world, they would suffer. We suffer because of our own mistakes, foolishness, and sin, and also because of the mistakes, foolishness, and sin of others. Some people break the speed limit and run stoplights. They make foolish choices. They walk in the counsel of the ungodly. They seem to court disaster.

Can you measure the amount of suffering that is due to floods, fire, tornadoes, earthquakes, hurricanes, and storms at sea? Such disasters are simply a part of our existence in a world of natural law.

Can you measure the amount of suffering that is due to disease, weakness, and frailty of body? And how much suffering is due to accidents of all kinds? We suffer simply because we live in a fallen world.

III. People suffer because it builds character.

Paul said, "We glory in tribulations also: knowing that tribulation worketh patience" (Rom. 5:3). God allows suffering in his world because it produces character. It educates. It disciplines. It brings out the best in people. Milton wrote more lastingly because of his blindness. Tennyson wrote more beautifully because of his suffering. Through suffering we learn that it is sweet to walk with the Lord and keep company with his people.

IV. People suffer because it deepens spiritual growth.

The psalmist said, "Before I was afflicted I went astray: but now have I kept thy word" (Ps. 119:67). James put it like this: "Count it all joy, my brethren, when you meet various trials, for you know that the testing of your faith produces steadfastness" (James 1:2–3 RSV). Suffering is often redemptive. We learn through our pain to depend more fully on God. It is said that one should darken a bird's cage when teaching it to sing. If the hand of the Lord had not darkened the windows, many of us never would have learned to sing or be strong at all. Lay hold on God in times of suffering and pain even if your attempt is no stronger than a prayer, and you will find that he has laid hold on you.

V. People suffer because it teaches how to trust God.

We learn through suffering to trust God even when we don't understand. In John 13:7 we read, "Jesus answered and said unto him, What I do thou knowest not now; but thou shalt know hereafter." There are some things we will never understand on this earth. Mystery is woven into the fabric of life.

Sometimes I wonder if the questions that bother us are really as big in God's eyes as they are in ours. Have you ever watched a child cry or throw a temper tantrum because he or she didn't understand why one block wouldn't stay on top of another, or why a doll's arm wouldn't stay where it was placed? That is big to a child, but to a parent it is such a trivial thing. If we could only see life from God's perspective, what a difference it would be! Maude Royden wrote, "Christ does not give us reasons, at least not at the first instance. He gives us strength without telling us why the pain has come and gives us reasons only beyond the victory."

It has been said that the worst sentence ever passed on Christians in the early days of persecution was to be sentenced to the mines of Numidia. Their chains were shortened so they could never be able to stand upright again. Often one eye was knocked out. They were then given a lamp and a pick and sent into the mines to dig until they died. Being watched by merciless overseers, these Christians knew they would never come out of the mines alive. Still God placed songs on their lips. Their radiant witness and their grateful prayers are recorded on the walls of the mines. One word of courage there occurs over and over again. It is the word "life." Their persecutors could shut them away from the world, but no enemy could shut God in Christ away from them. In their darkness they saw the Light of the World. They drew close to God and found the secret of life.

Conclusion

May you draw near to God in time of suffering and find that he draws near to you and makes you a stronger, happier, and better person.

SUNDAY MORNING, SEPTEMBER 12

Title: The Church and Its Undershepherds

Text: "He gave some, apostles; and some, prophets; and some, evangelists; and some, pastors and teachers; for the perfecting of the saints, for the work of the ministry, for the edifying of the body of Christ" **(Eph. 4:11–12)**.

Scripture Reading: Ephesians 4:11–16

Hymns: "Stir Thy Church, O God, Our Father," Butler
"To Worship, Work, and Witness," Webb
"A Charge to Keep I Have," Wesley

Offertory Prayer: Our Father, we come thanking you for opening the windows of heaven and pouring out blessings upon us in such abundance that we cannot contain them. We offer you these gifts of ours, meager within themselves, but capable, with your blessings, of meeting the needs of your kingdom's work. Father, may our giving always be spontaneous and with love. In Jesus' name we pray. Amen.

293

Introduction

Words often change in meaning over the years. Take, for example, the noun *ministry* and the verb *to minister.* In the New Testament and within the early church, these were precious and meaningful words applicable to all believers. In our generation, however, they have become "professional" words. A minister is generally conceived of as a person who fills a role apart from the body of believers in the church. Ministers are usually trained for their place of leadership. Also, the verb form, *to minister,* is usually thought of as an activity of the minister or other staff members of the church to whom we also refer as ministers. In no way was this the meaning and use of the word in the New Testament and in the early church. Thus, as a challenge to the undershepherds of the church and to all the people of God, let us examine what Paul is saying to us in this passage.

I. The Holy Spirit gives the assignment.

"And he gave some, apostles; and some, prophets; and some, evangelists; and some, pastors and teachers; for the perfecting of the saints, for the work of the ministry, for the edifying of the body of Christ" (Eph. 4:11–12).

A. *Paul began by naming the primary office-bearers of the church.* I believe the offices of apostle and prophet have passed away. With the completed revelation of God's Word, there is no longer any need for these offices. That leaves, then, two offices mentioned here: the evangelist and the pastor-teacher. These officers function, on the basis of the Scripture passages that follow, as "undershepherds" of the flock—not as imperial overlords or dictators.

B. *What are these undershepherds to do?* Their major task is to be aimed at "the perfecting of the saints, for the work of the ministry, for the edifying of the body of Christ." The word translated "perfecting" is rich in meaning. It means to fit the saints, as a tailor or seamstress would fit clothing on a person. It means to complete the equipment or dress of the saints; here we could refer to the list of pieces of armor Paul enumerated in Ephesians 6. The word "perfecting" also means to repair—and there it is used in a disciplinary sense. Some children of God had become careless in their spiritual lives, and their equipment or spiritual dress had become ineffective. Perhaps they had become undisciplined. Their values and priorities were all mixed up. The undershepherds were to help these people repair their priorities. And what was all of this for? "For the work of the ministry."

C. *Interestingly, the Greek word from which we derive our word* deacon *is* diakonia, *which means "ministry."* It is not a word reserved for the professional staff members of the church, but a word describing the function of every member of the body of Christ. In Matthew 20:26 Jesus said, "Whosoever will be great among you, let him be your minister"—and the word is *diakonia,* the word we translate "deacon"! If only we could destroy this concept that ministry is a word reserved for the professionals—or even for the deacons. Ministry is for all of God's children.

D. *When each of us functions as a spiritual minister, the body of Christ will be edified.* The work of the evangelist, the pastor-teacher, the deacon, and the undershepherds of the flock is always to build up and never to tear down. According to Scripture, God has called his undershepherds to the business of construction.

II. Paul outlined the aim.

A. *"Till we all come in the unity of the faith" (Eph. 4:13).* We are to create unity. It would be wonderful if every member of the body of Christ made himself or herself to be a creator of unity within the fellowship and never a source of discord. There is no greater blessing to a church fellowship than the presence of those men and women who love unity and harmony and who actively seek to create it among the believers. They know what to say and how to say it; they know what to do and when to do it! And conversely, they know when not to speak and when not to act. How does this come about? It comes as every member of the body of Christ agrees to be controlled by the Holy Spirit.

B. *And what else? "That we henceforth be no more children, tossed to and fro, and carried about with every wind of doctrine."* Now the church has always had within its family those who have remained babies in the faith— those who have refused to grow spiritually. They are like children, and they are most often dominated by a desire for that which is novel or spectacular. They are ever at the mercy of the latest fad or gimmick that some other church is using. They are always under the influence of the last person with whom they have talked or the last preacher they heard preach.

Paul said, "Start growing up! Stop being infants, weak and at the mercy of everything and everybody that comes along!" A part of the task of every true minister in the body of Christ is to help the spiritual babies start to grow. It may be to the discredit of the undershepherds if the flock over which God has given them charge is filled with spiritual infants.

C. *How do we help them grow?* By "speaking the truth in love." Every word in that sentence is vital and quivering with life. "Speaking"— communicating by word and example and conduct. "The truth"—the gospel, the Word of God, which will not return to the Lord void, but will accomplish its purpose. "In love"—the secret of motivation. Even the Word of God can be spoken without the constraint of love. When this happens, God's Word will repel rather than soften and inspire.

Conclusion

"From him the whole body, joined and held together by every supporting ligament, grows and builds itself up in love, as each part does its work" (Eph. 4:16 NIV). This is the mission of the people of God, his ministers. This is both the aim and the assignment of every member of the family of God. When the undershepherds lead the people to become dependent on God and not on them, the members of the body, sometimes fragmented, sometimes spiritually infirm and out of fellowship, will start fitting together, firmly adhering to one another, complementing one another.

Then the love of God, like the ligaments of the body, will bind us together, supplying power to each of us as we have need. When this happens, we will be built up in a spirit of love; our Lord will be glorified; and because of the radiating love of the body, sinners will be converted and his name glorified.

SUNDAY EVENING, SEPTEMBER 12

Title: The Winds of God

Text: "And suddenly there came a sound from heaven as of a rushing mighty wind, and it filled all the house where they were sitting" **(Acts 2:2)**.

Scripture Reading: Acts 2:1–13

Introduction

There is something mysterious about the wind. If you don't believe that, try to explain the wind to a child, or try to understand an explanation of the wind in scientific terms. Because the wind is so mysterious, it is fitting that it is used as a symbol of God's powerful Holy Spirit.

What preceded the passing of the children of Israel through the Red Sea? All through the night the trembling host of Israel cringed in fear between the chariots of Egypt and the sea while the terrible winds of God cut a path through the heart of the waters (Ex. 14:21).

We are told that when Elijah begged to see the face of God, "a great and powerful wind tore the mountains apart and shattered the rocks before the LORD" (1 Kings 19:11 NIV).

Of the reaction of the onlookers on the day of Pentecost we read, "At this sound the multitude came together, and they were bewildered, because each one heard them speaking in his own language. And they were amazed and wondered, saying, 'Are not all these who are speaking Galileans?'" (Acts 2:6–7 RSV). We also read, "And all were amazed and perplexed, saying to one another, 'What does this mean?'" (v. 12 RSV).

How we need the winds of God to blow upon us! When they do, it makes all the difference in the world. The Christian movement experiences a new birth of power, and people marvel at God's wondrous works. The unsaved ask in awe, "What does this mean? By what power have you done this?" And scores cry out, "Brethren, what shall we do?" (Acts 2:37).

Let us gather this thought into one simple affirmation. Wonderful things happen when the winds of God begin to blow.

I. Ordinary people do extraordinary things when the winds of God begin to blow.

Simon Peter was an ordinary man. Unstable, wishy-washy, and impulsive when Jesus first met him, Peter nonetheless became the heart of early Christianity just as Paul became the brain. Someone said of Peter, "He never worried about what he had said because he never thought about what he was going to say before he said it." Yet at Pentecost when the winds of God began to blow, those who heard him "were pricked in their heart" (Acts 2:37), and three thousand people were converted.

Augustine was a willful man, breaking the heart of his mother, who never ceased to pray for him. Then, in Milan, he met Ambrose, whose influence eventually led him to Christ. When the winds of God began to blow, Augustine's dream of "the City of God" was all that survived the ashes of the Roman Empire.

Francis of Assisi was an ordinary man until one day when he saw a loathsome leper by the wayside and the Spirit of God struck his heart in a mighty conversion experience. Retracing his steps, Francis ran to kiss the leper, whom ten seconds before he had despised as an unclean thing. When the winds of God began to blow, Francis of Assisi ran to God as easily as he ran to sea as a boy.

Until the winds of God began to blow, Martin Luther was just another ordinary, brown-clad monk seeking peace in his heart, but by God's power he was used to change the history of the world. Wesley, Spurgeon, Palmer, Booth, Crosby, Moody, Truett, and a host of others—although they were ordinary men and women, God used them mightily to do extraordinary things when the winds of God began to blow.

You and I may be ordinary people, but if we would wait on God in prayer and in faith until the winds of God shook us to the depths, he could use us to do some extraordinary things.

II. Ordinary churches do extraordinary things when the winds of God begin to blow.

What are our churches doing that amazes and confounds an unsaved world? The great sin of our churches is that of being ordinary, that of doing the same old things in the same old way over and over again. What chances have we taken for God? What risks? When have we laid it on the line, trusting the power of God to see us through?

In our churches the time is here when we must no longer be ordinary. We dare not! Every ordinary church must begin by the power of God to do extraordinary things if it is to make an impression on this world in which we live.

After their failure at Kadesh-Barnea, the children of Israel wandered in the wilderness in the region of the "Mount of God" for forty years as judgment on their disobedience. In Deuteronomy, however, we read, "Then we turned, and took our journey into the wilderness by the way of the Red Sea, as the LORD spake unto me: and we compassed mount Seir many days. And the LORD spake unto me, saying, Ye have compassed this mountain long enough: turn you northward" (2:1–3). Where he leads, we must follow!

Conclusion

This new era must be the era of the Holy Spirit. We need only for the winds of God to begin blowing, that in every worship place there would be heard from heaven a sound like the rushing of a mighty wind.

WEDNESDAY EVENING, SEPTEMBER 15

Title: Ministry of Christ to Mental Health

Text: "I can do all things through Christ which strengtheneth me" (**Phil. 4:13**).

Scripture Reading: Philippians 4:6–13

Introduction

Many people are breaking under the stress of today's problems. Rising numbers of people are being diagnosed with mental disorders, and more than ever are being treated with drugs and spending time in mental hospitals. Because of a sense of shame or embarrassment and because insurance companies often won't pay treatment costs, many people are not receiving the help they need. Christ, the Great Physician who came to help the sick, ministers to our mental as well as our physical health.

I. Overcome anxiety through faith.

If anyone had grounds for anxiety, the apostle Paul did. He faced limitations of physical health, suffered night and day from a thorn in his flesh, and was brutally mistreated. He was imprisoned, shipwrecked, beaten, stoned, and dragged out of the city for dead. Yet he told of the secret of God's peace. "Have no anxiety about anything, but in everything by prayer and supplication with thanksgiving let your requests be made known to God" (Phil. 4:6 RSV). Paul lived a life of faith.

II. Overcome inadequacy through divine strength.

Many people suffer from such an appalling sense of inadequacy that they cover their feelings with a crust of pride. Others turn to daydreaming and live in a world of make-believe. The Bible says, "But as many as received him, to them gave he power to become the sons of God" (John 1:12). God gives us strength to face our weaknesses and overcome them. Roy Rogers

298

once confessed that he had been plagued by a terrible inferiority complex. He was haunted by inadequacy, lived in fear, and could not speak in public. His life changed when he surrendered to Christ.

III. Overcome resentment through love.

People get stung by the circumstances of life and turn to bitterness. They become bitter because they have not received as much ability as others, or have not been loved by their families, or have faced too many hardships. There is a practical reason why the Bible tells us to love: the basic cause of resentment is our failure to love. It is for want of love that the personality disintegrates. Bitterness imprisons; love releases life. Bitterness paralyzes; love empowers. Bitterness sickens; love heals. Bitterness blinds us to life; love opens our eyes to the needs of those around us.

IV. Overcome aimlessness and depression through the guidance of Christ.

Paul said, "For God hath not give us the spirit of fear; but of power, and of love, and of a sound mind" (2 Tim. 1:7). Christ gives his people mastery over evil impulses and destructive moods. He saves us from an aimless life by giving us something to live for. Being a Christian does not solve all our problems, but Christ always provides inner strength so we can triumph over them.

V. Overcome guilt through the forgiveness of Christ.

Psychologists tell us that behind many nervous breakdowns, emotional maladjustment, and mental disorders lies a sense of guilt. We cannot push guilt out of our hearts. We cannot argue it away. We cannot simply thrust it out of our minds and forget it. There is only one healthy way to rid ourselves of guilt—through confession, repentance, forgiveness, and a new start with Christ. The psalmist said, "Blessed is he whose transgression is forgiven" (Ps. 32:1).

Conclusion

Christ brings happiness and health to those who follow him. David counseled his soul:

> Praise the LORD, my soul;
>> all my inmost being, praise his holy name.
> Praise the LORD, my soul,
>> and forget not all his benefits—
> who forgives all your sins
>> and heals all your diseases,
> who redeems your life from the pit
>> and crowns you with love and compassion,
> who satisfies your desires with good things
>> so that your youth is renewed like the eagle's. (Ps. 103:1–5 NIV)

We would do well to follow David's advice and praise the Lord for his provision for our health and our forgiveness.

SUNDAY MORNING, SEPTEMBER 19

Title: The Church and Its Mission

Text: "Provided that you continue in the faith, stable and steadfast, not shifting from the hope of the gospel which you heard, which has been preached to every creature under heaven, and of which I, Paul, became a minister. Now I rejoice in my sufferings for your sake, and in my flesh I complete what is lacking in Christ's afflictions for the sake of his body, that is, the church" **(Col. 1:23–24 RSV)**.

Scripture Reading: Colossians 1:19–29

Hymns: "The Church's One Foundation," Stone
"Wonderful Words of Life," Bliss
"We Are Called to Be God's People," Jackson

Offertory Prayer: Our Father, grant us the free spirit of giving as you have demonstrated it to us in the incomparable gift of your Son. Help us realize that no gift to you is complete until we give ourselves along with our substance. As best we know how, we offer you ourselves, weak and sinful creatures that we are. Accept us, Father, along with our gifts, and make us conform to your holy will for our lives. In Jesus' name we pray. Amen.

Introduction

A church does not choose its mission any more than an aide chooses what task he will perform for the general or a herald chooses what message he will deliver in the name of the king. A mission suggests orders, and whenever people are sent on a mission or assigned a task to perform, they have received directions from a higher authority. Furthermore, those who are dispatched to fulfill a mission are not at liberty to change the orders or rearrange the assignment at will. God has chosen to carry out his plan and purpose on earth through the agency of the church. No other plan is set forth, or even mentioned, in the Bible.

In our study of the church so far, we have examined the nature of the church, the growth of the church, and the undershepherds of the church. This morning we will consider the mission of the church. The words of our text, Colossians 1:25–29, comprise Paul's commission from God in his own words. The essence of God's commission to Paul is identical with the mission assigned to the church. Therefore we will discover that the mission of the church is, first, to fulfill the Word of God; second, to proclaim the mystery of the indwelling Christ; and third, to preach a universal gospel.

300

I. To fulfill the Word of God.

"To make the word of God fully known" (Col. 1:25 RSV). How can the church do this? The first chapter of Colossians shows us three ways.

A. *The church must exalt Christ.* "He is before all things, and in him all things hold together. He is the head of the body, the church; he is the beginning, the first-born from the dead, that in everything he might be pre-eminent. For in him all the fulness of God was pleased to dwell" (Col. 1:17–19 RSV). This is one of the most magnificent statements in the Bible concerning the position of our Lord Jesus Christ in regard to his preincarnate glory, and it also establishes him as the head of the church. Paul said that Jesus Christ was one with the Father before anything was made. And not only so, after everything was created, he became the one in whom everything holds together. So this is our springboard. This is the way in which the church "make[s] the word of God fully known"—by exalting the incomparable Jesus Christ as Lord of Lords and King of Kings.

B. *The church must recognize its role as a colaborer with God in the ministry of reconciliation.* "And through him to reconcile to himself all things, whether on earth or in heaven, making peace by the blood of his cross. And you, who once were estranged and hostile in mind, doing evil deeds, he has now reconciled in his body of flesh by his death, in order to present you holy and blameless and irreproachable before him" (Col. 1:20–22 RSV). What happened when people sinned? The most tragic fragmentation the world has ever known came about! When Adam and Eve succumbed to Satan in the garden of Eden, there was a moral explosion. Immediately, God, who had rested from his creative work on the seventh day, began a new work—the work of redemption, the end result of which was reconciliation, or the bringing back to himself of that which had been separated from him.

Then, to further compound the mystery of God's sovereign grace, God made another decision in regard to this business of reconciliation: he decided to use the church. Paul said, "And all things are of God, who hath reconciled us to himself by Jesus Christ, and hath given to us the ministry of reconciliation" (2 Cor. 5:18). God was saying to the church, "This is a vital part of your mission on earth. You are to be colaborers with me in this ministry of bringing sinners face-to-face with their sins and with my saving grace!"

C. *The church must consistently encourage growth and stability among its own.* "Provided that you continue in the faith, stable and steadfast, not shifting from the hope of the gospel which you heard, which has been preached to every creature under heaven, and of which I, Paul, became a minister" (Col. 1:23 RSV). What was Paul saying? When a person is born into the family of God, the church's task is to teach and establish the new Christian in the faith. Sometimes young Christians get off on doctrinal tangents because the church is derelict in providing the proper spiritual diet. Thus the church that makes the Word of God fully known through its teaching and pastoral ministry sees its people grow in the grace of our Lord. It sees them become established in the faith.

II. To proclaim the mystery of the indwelling Christ.

Paul said of Christ's indwelling believers that it was "the mystery hidden for ages and generations but now made manifest to his saints. To them God chose to make known how great among the Gentiles are the riches of the glory of this mystery, which is Christ in you, the hope of glory" (Col. 1:26–27 RSV).

A. *The mystery of Christ indwelling the believer was clouded in ages past.* Through the prophets and through Old Testament symbols and sacrifices and types, God prepared his people for this grand and magnificent truth—that he would one day come to live within his people in the person of his Son.

B. *Furthermore, this truth about "Christ in you, the hope of glory" has been made manifest.* Phillips says that it means "as clear as daylight." Not many experiences are quite as thrilling as that of watching the sunrise. It is a miracle! When the earth is shrouded by the darkness of night, the whole psychology of life is changed. All kinds of evil and crime find compatibility in the darkness. But after the night has ended, the eastern horizon begins to change. There seems to be a struggle as the long fingers of light heralding the rising sun begin to stab through the darkness.

When you see it, you know what is happening. There is no mistake! The sun is about to rise, and struggle though it may, the darkness is already defeated; it has no recourse but to slowly dissipate, fade away, and give place to the light. The same thing happened in the spiritual realm. The first finger of divine sunlight pierced the darkness of Ur of the Chaldees and lighted and warmed the heart of a man named Abraham. And the light kept coming, little by little, until Jesus came and the sun rose in its fullness and in its brightness.

C. *What was the result?* "Christ in you, the hope of glory." We can say with all joy and assurance that the mystery is now an open revelation to those who will receive it. The sun has risen. "The Word became flesh and dwelt among us, full of grace and truth; we have beheld his glory, glory as of the only Son from the Father" (John 1:14 RSV).

III. To preach a universal gospel.

A. *It is a universal gospel.* Paul said, "Him we proclaim, warning every man and teaching every man in all wisdom, that we may present every man mature in Christ" (Col. 1:28 RSV). This gospel is not to be proclaimed to only a select few or to an elite group. In his powerful sermon on Mars Hill in Athens, Paul declared, "The times of ignorance God overlooked, but now he commands all men everywhere to repent" (Acts 17:30 RSV). In other words, the first note of the gospel is a clarion call to repentance. That is the doorway. For unless we repent of our sin, we cannot enter the kingdom of heaven. This call to repentance is issued to all people. It is universal in its scope.

B. *It is also a warning.* The word Paul used, translated "warning," means to put in mind, to admonish. This warning is about the impending danger of losing one's soul. Therefore the mission of the church is to be faithful in the warning aspect of its message.

C. *"Teaching every man in all wisdom."* This correlates beautifully with our Lord's great commission. After we have warned unbelievers of the danger of continuing in their sin, we are to teach them how to find deliverance from sin and guilt and find peace with God.

Conclusion

So there we have it. The mission of the church is to make the Word of God fully known by exalting the Lord Jesus Christ, fulfilling our role as colaborers with God in the ministry of reconciliation and encouraging growth and stability among the saints. We are to proclaim the mystery of the indwelling Christ and preach a universal gospel—warning and teaching all people that God, in his grace and mercy and inconceivable compassion, can save from sin and give assurance of eternal salvation.

SUNDAY EVENING, SEPTEMBER 19

Title: The Fatherhood of God

Text: "For you did not receive the spirit of slavery to fall back into fear, but you have received the spirit of sonship. When we cry, 'Abba! Father!' it is the Spirit himself bearing witness with our spirit that we are children of God, and if children, then heirs, heirs of God and fellow heirs with Christ, provided we suffer with him in order that we may also be glorified with him" **(Rom. 8:15–17 RSV).**

Scripture Reading: Romans 8:12–17

Introduction

Old Testament saints conceived of God's fatherhood almost solely in the national sphere (Ex. 4:22; Isa. 1:2). But even in the Old Testament you can see people's thoughts, as in the Psalms, moving to something more personal (Pss. 68:5; 103:13).

Jesus gave the word *Father* new depth and content. He did this not so much by what he said as by the way he lived. He alone lived the kind of life God's fatherhood should inspire and imply. He said, "I come from the Father," meaning his father, whose nature he perfectly reflects. Note three things about the fatherhood of God.

I. Implications of God's fatherhood.

A. *God's fatherhood implies that God is accessible to us.* The way to God is open. This does not mean that we can be irreverent in our approach to God or that we can take liberties with him. But it does mean that the barriers between us and God are down. The veil before the Holy of Holies is torn in two from top to bottom (Matt. 27:51), and the way to God lies open.

B. *God's fatherhood implies that God's authority over us is like that of a father over his children.* Many conflicting claims are made on us, but we must hold to our faith in God, the almighty Father. In all things we are responsible to him.

   In the home in which Jesus lived, the father was a symbol of authority. By "Father" Jesus did not mean the kind of indulgent father often found in American families. The Jewish father loved his children intensely, but he expected unquestioned obedience and honor that continued all through his life. In Jesus' mind the word *Father* carried connotations of obedience rather than mere indulgence.

C. *God's fatherhood implies that the blackness of sin is revealed.* If the power behind the universe were sheer impersonal law, our sins would be sins against law. But if, as Jesus revealed, the power behind the universe is a loving Father, our sins are sins against love. To call God "Father" is ultimately to make sin intolerable. It was not law we crucified on Calvary's cross, but God's holy love, the love of a Father God.

D. *God's fatherhood implies that the wonder of forgiveness is clear.* Before Jesus came, people asked, "Can God forgive?" Call God "Father" and know that he is, and the question becomes, "How could God not forgive a truly penitent heart?" In one parable Jesus pictured God running out to meet the returning prodigal, to gather him, just as he was, into his arms. If, because God is Father, sin stands in a new light, so does love's victory over sin, which is forgiveness.

II. Results of God's fatherhood.

A. *Since God is our Father, he concerns himself with our concerns.* Jesus taught us that our food, clothing, and shelter are God's concerns. "For your heavenly Father knoweth that ye have need of all these things" (Matt. 6:32). He continued, "If ye then, being evil, know how to give good gifts unto your children, how much more shall your Father which is in heaven give good things to them that ask him?" (7:11).

B. *Since God is our Father, he knows and loves us as individuals.* An earthly father does not love his family in general; he loves each child in particular. What we do poorly, God does perfectly. He knows us. He loves us one by one as individuals. "God so loved the world" (John 3:16) is one side of the coin. The other side is "There is joy in the presence of the angels of God over one sinner that repenteth" (Luke 15:10). Augustine said, "He loves us every one as though there were but one of us to love."

C. *Since God is our Father, he disciplines us as his children.* God is a Father, not an uncle. One man speaks fondly of his uncle. He says, "He would let me do almost anything. Sometimes I would be punished when I got home because of the things he let me do." An uncle will indulge a boy's desires because he does not have to accept full responsibility. To love means to desire the best for another and to exercise discipline to encourage it. God will not always hold back his anger against those who trifle with his love. "For whom the Lord loveth he chasteneth" (Heb. 12:6).

D. *Since God is our Father, he saves us from our sins as individuals.* As Father, he acts personally to call persons to respond to his love in repentance and faith. He is Father, and we are potentially his children. As long as we know who he is and who we are, and act accordingly, we may have a personal relationship with him. Through Jesus Christ he is our Father and we are his children (John 1:12).

E. *Since God is our Father, he blesses us through his Holy Spirit.* Three words in the text describe the privileges that come to the Christian through the Holy Spirit.
   1. "Children." How wonderful to be a child of God!
   2. "Heirs." We inherit what is his.
   3. "Joint-heirs with Christ." As God's children we are heirs of all he is and all he has.

III. Assurances of God's fatherhood.

A. *God's fatherhood assures us concerning suffering and pain.* People were once prone to think that pain and suffering were signs of God's condemnation and judgment. Sometimes people may bring their suffering on themselves, but not invariably so.

   Not only has Christ cleared that awful thought away, but he has shown us that some kinds of suffering, far from being God's condemnation, are actually God's election to a singular honor. This was true of Jesus. God "spared not his own Son" (Rom. 8:32) because he had a purpose for him, a great and glorious world-redeeming purpose. So does God often deal with his children.

B. *God's fatherhood assures us concerning prayer.* In prayer we do not send our voices out into an empty void. The God whom we seek in prayer we are to call "Father." That is the very center of our Christian faith.

A teacher asked a class of third-grade girls to answer the question "What is a father?" One girl wrote, "A father is a person you can tell anything and he will listen to you." Our heavenly Father is a person we can tell anything and be assured that he will listen to us.

C. *God's fatherhood assures us concerning the future.* Relief and encouragement come when we rest our minds in the thought that God knows what lies ahead and that he is in control.

As God's children we have to learn, but sometimes the tuition is needlessly high. Our heavenly Father would save us from a lot of mistakes if only we would ask him first and then listen and do what he tells us. He knows what the future holds.

D. *God's fatherhood assures us concerning our salvation.* Salvation is the work of the Holy Spirit on the merits of the redeeming work of Christ, whereby we become children of a loving Father God. Saved for how long? The security of the believer is predicated on the fatherhood of God. Even to raise the question "How long?" is to cast a slur on the God whose name is "Father." God never disowns his children. We may disown him, but he never disowns us. If we are Christians, we are his children.

Conclusion

Years ago a newspaper reporter went to interview the great concert artist Roland Hayes. The reporter found him at lunch, not in the hotel dining room, but in a dingy little room next to the kitchen—and this simply because he had dark skin. The reporter was indignant, but Hayes stopped him, saying, "This doesn't bother me. Before I went away to school to struggle hard for the training I have, my mother had a talk with me. She didn't say much, but she impressed one thing indelibly upon my mind. 'Roland,' she repeated over and over, 'remember who you are. Remember who you are.' She kept drumming that in until finally I asked, 'Who am I, Mama?' She replied, 'Roland, you are a child of God. He is your Father. Never forget that. You are a child of God.'"

So is every Christian.

WEDNESDAY EVENING, SEPTEMBER 22

Title: Learning from the Illness of a Loved One

Text: "These things I have spoken unto you, that in me ye might have peace. In the world ye shall have tribulation: but be of good cheer; I have overcome the world" **(John 16:33)**.

Scripture Reading: James 1:1–2

Introduction

"Why do good people suffer?" This question has baffled people for centuries. In fact, the problem of a loving God and human illness was raised long ago in the book of Job. Recently I met a man who struggled with this question when his wife was suffering greatly with arthritis. At times the husband resented the limitations caused by his wife's illness and confinement. There were moments when he even questioned God's ways. Sometimes friends and family members were not only unsympathetic but openly critical. All of this speaks of the mystery that surrounds suffering. We can, however, learn some lessons from suffering.

I. We learn that trouble, sickness, and grief come to all.

We think subconsciously that if we do God's will, tithe our income, and serve others that nothing tragic will happen to us. But Jesus said, "In the world ye shall have tribulation" (John 16:33). There are some things all of us have to bear, for both good and bad experiences come to us all. They usually balance out in the long run; but if not, one day God will reveal the reason and reward the faithful.

II. We learn the meaning of patience.

The Bible says, "Glory in tribulations . . . knowing that tribulation worketh patience" (Rom. 5:3). Patience is the power to hold out, to refuse to quit, to keep on keeping on. It is the ability to go on when you feel like giving up.

III. We learn to be more compassionate toward the sick.

Many people think of sickness as weakness. It is hard to be sympathetic with people who are ill. People with diseases that leave them bedridden and in constant pain often feel guilty, for sickness was a part of the curse on humankind in the fall. Paul called his thorn a "messenger of Satan" (2 Cor. 12:7). Healing and good health are God's will for his people. Trials can minister to our spiritual growth, however (James 1:2–4). Christ went about healing the sick and showing compassion. Caring is Christlike.

IV. We learn the reality of God's love.

Love has the power to heal, but it may involve a long process. Fear, guilt, frustration, and depression do not come all at once. Neither does healing from grief come all at once. We may wonder, "If God loves me, why did this happen?"

If you have struggled—really struggled in the depths of your soul—with this question "Why?" you are in good company, for both Job (Job 3:11) and David (Ps. 73:3–14) asked this question. Even Jesus, when hanging on the cross, asked, "My God, why . . . ?" (Mark 15:34).

Early in the 1900s a minister and his son had laid their wife and mother to rest in a distant place. They made the long ride back home in the funeral coach.

They were tired and went to their separate berths to retire. After a little while, the son came to his father crying and asked if he could sleep with him. He tried to go to sleep but was still suffering an awful sense of loneliness. In the darkness he asked, "Daddy, is your face turned toward me?" In the days ahead there were times when the minister said there was not a star in the sky of his life, and he too would ask, "Father, it is so dark, I cannot see you. Is your face turned toward me?"

Conclusion

In the midst of the baffling mystery of disease, pain, and grief, we can be sure of God's unchanging love.

SUNDAY MORNING, SEPTEMBER 26

Title: The Church and Its Worship

Text: "I exhort therefore, that, first of all, supplications, prayers, intercessions, and giving of thanks, be made for all men; for kings, and for all that are in authority; that we may lead a quiet and peaceable life in all godliness and honesty. For this is good and acceptable in the sight of God our Saviour" (**1 Tim. 2:1–3**).

Scripture Reading: 1 Timothy 2:1–15

Hymns: "Living for Jesus," Chisholm
"I Am Thine, O Lord," Crosby
"Speak to My Heart," McKinney

Offertory Prayer: Our Father, we praise your name because you have lifted us from the miry clay, put our feet on the rock, and established our lives. You have forgiven our sin and made us new creatures through your Son. We thank you also for giving us countless material blessings. Every possession is a reminder of your grace. We worship you this morning with our hearts, hands, and gifts. Please receive what we have to offer as an expression of our love and devotion. Use our tithes and offerings to help others know your wonderful blessings we so freely enjoy, through Jesus Christ our Lord. Amen.

Introduction

Worship is the dynamic of the church. It is an act of meeting God in which believers are empowered, encouraged, and enlightened. In today's Scripture reading, Paul discussed one facet of the church's worship—prayer.

I. The place of prayer in worship (I Tim. 2:1–8).

A. *The importance of prayer.*
  1. This we gather by implication and command. Approximately one-sixth of this letter is devoted to instructions concerning prayer. Obviously Paul considered prayer to be important.

2. Paul practiced prayer. On the Damascus road, having met Christ face-to-face, Paul prayed. In the midnight hour, with his back bleeding and his hands and feet in chains, the apostle prayed. When he considered the lost condition of humanity, he prayed.

3. Actually, people have always prayed. They pray for rain in times of drought. They pray for food in times of famine. They pray for victory in times of battle. They pray for strength in times of weakness. They pray for health in times of sickness. They pray when they can do nothing else.

4. Now Paul exhorted the church to make their requests known to God in prayer. "I exhort therefore, that . . . prayers . . . be made" (v. 1).

B. *The characteristics of prayer (v. 1).* Many people have a limited view of prayer. Prayer *is* asking, but it is more. In our text the apostle mentions four types of prayer that are to be used in public worship (and in private also).

1. "Supplications" is the first word used. This is prayer that expresses the idea of personal insufficiency. It is prayer for divine help and grace. All prayer must begin at this point.

2. "Prayer" is the second word. It is an appeal to God based on past mercies. It includes acts of adoration and confession.

3. "Intercessions" is the third word. It embraces the idea of going into a king's presence to submit a petition. It implies going to someone on behalf of a third party. The prayer of Abraham for Sodom, the prayer of Moses for Israel, and the prayer of Paul for his worldly brothers all illustrate this concept. It is what Christians must do for other Christians and for the unsaved people of this world. Certainly we limit the King of the universe by failure in this area.

4. "Thanksgiving" is the final word. It is gratitude to God for all his benefits, such as we see so prevalent in the psalms.

C. *The circumference of prayer (v. 2).*

1. Prayer must encompass the world. Paul said we are to pray "for all men." God's love is for all, "for God so loved the world." Christ died for all. In fact, unless we pray for all, we certainly will not witness to all. The scope of our sincere prayers indicates more than anything else the measure of our concern.

2. Specifically Paul said we are to pray "for kings, and for all that are in authority." At this time the church was the subject of great persecution. Those "in authority" were the ones instigating this bitter persecution, yet Paul told Timothy to pray for them.

   Jesus said in the Sermon on the Mount, "Love your enemies, bless them that curse you, do good to them that hate you, and pray for them which despitefully use you, and persecute you"

(Matt. 5:44). On the cross he practiced this, saying, "Father, for-give them; for they know not what they do" (Luke 23:34).

3. Only with this kind of prayer can we expect society to be what it ought to be. This alone can make it possible for us to "lead a quiet and peaceable life in all godliness and honesty." "Quiet" indicates the idea of tranquility from without. "Peaceable" indi-cates the idea of peace from within. We are called to be Christian citizens showing our concern and highest desire for our country.

4. Paul believed that prayer could change things. Even the king and those in authority could be changed. Most of us place limitations on the omnipotent God by thinking that some people cannot be changed by prayer. We mark certain ones off our list because we think they are beyond prayer, but Christ did not—not even his enemies who were crucifying him.

D. *The charter of prayer (vv. 3–8).* Paul now gave reasons why we ought to pray.

1. "This is good and acceptable in the sight of God our Saviour" (v. 3). Such prayer as we have been discussing is "good and acceptable" because it is obeying the command of God. It is in keeping with the Spirit of Christ.

2. God's desire is for all people to be saved (v. 4). Therefore our prayer should encompass all people.

3. There is one mediator between God and humanity (v. 5). Christ is our High Priest who intercedes with the Father for us. We can "come boldly unto the throne of grace" (Heb. 4:16) because Jesus "gave himself a ransom for all" (v. 6).

4. This charter for prayer stresses the universality of the gospel of our Lord and Savior Jesus Christ. It is for all people, and anything less than this is a mockery of Christianity. He has made possible the redemption of the entire world—young and old, rich and poor, black and white.

5. Such prayer is in accordance with God's will (v. 4). Sometimes we may be uncertain if our prayers are according to his will, but there can never be any doubt about prayer for the salvation of people for whom Christ died.

E. *The conditions of prayer (v. 8).*

1. In worship we are to pray "lifting up holy hands." This refers to the position of prayer. It does not exclude other positions (kneeling, etc.); it simply stresses this one. It is the picture of a person standing before God with arms lifted and hands open toward God.

2. Paul mentioned three conditions for effective prayer. People have always felt that a wrong life or a wrong motive was a barrier to access to God. Isaiah 1:15 says, "When ye spread forth your hands,

I will hide mine eyes from you: yea, when ye make many prayers, I will not hear: your hands are full of blood." To be effective in prayer, we must have:

    a. No sin—we must have "holy hands." David said, "If I regard iniquity in my heart, the Lord will not hear me" (Ps. 66:18). Isaiah 59:1–2 indicates this truth: "Behold, the LORD's hand is not shortened, that it cannot save; neither his ear heavy, that it cannot hear: but your iniquities have separated between you and your God, and your sins have hid his face from you, that he will not hear."

Do you remember as a child coming to the dinner table and hearing your mother say, "Let me see your hands"? If they were dirty, you could not eat until you had washed them. In like manner, God says that you cannot sit at his table of abundance until you have cleansed your hands and your heart.

    b. No anger—we must be "without wrath." Jesus said that those who came to worship but remembered that a fellow Christian had something against them, must first be reconciled to that person before offering their gift (Matt. 5:23–24). If we are not right with others, our Father will not listen to us. Jesus taught us to pray, "Forgive us our debts, as we forgive our debtors" (Matt. 6:12). Anger, wrath, and hatred will destroy our prayer life.

    c. No doubting—we must have faith. "Without faith it is impossible to please [God]; for he that cometh to God must believe that he is, and that he is a rewarder of them that diligently seek him" (Heb. 11:6). James said, "But let him ask in faith, nothing wavering. For he that wavereth is like a wave of the sea driven with the wind and tossed. For let not that man think that he shall receive any thing of the Lord" (James 1:6–7).

II. The place of women in worship (I Tim. 2:9–15).

Paul next turned his attention to women and their place in public worship. "In like manner" refers to the men whom he mentioned previously.

    A. *The background of this passage is the paganism in which the early church found itself.* The immorality and indecency of some women in the pagan worship of idols caused Christian women to carefully guard against every appearance of evil.

    B. *The beauty of women was to be found in their inward character and not in their outward appearance.*

    C. *Women were not to be leaders in public worship.* They were not to exercise authority over men in teaching.

D. *The service of women was to be in the home.* Paul said, "Adam was not deceived, but the woman being deceived was in the transgression. Notwithstanding she shall be saved in childbearing" (vv. 14–15). This does not refer to salvation from sin, but to salvation from uselessness. Since women were not allowed to teach in public, they were provided with an even greater field of service. In the home, by means of rearing and instructing and winning their children, women truly became "the hand that rocks the world."

Conclusion

In light of all that Paul said, let us pray and serve as God would have us and in the place he would have us.

SUNDAY EVENING, SEPTEMBER 26

Title: The Grace of God

Text: "By the grace of God I am what I am" (**1 Cor. 15:10**).

Scripture Reading: 1 Corinthians 15:1–12

Introduction

Perhaps John Newton felt as deeply the wonder of God's grace as did anyone. He once explained that the crowds who attended his services came not to hear him preach but with the curiosity of people who wished to see lions tamed in a circus. They came to behold a trophy of the grace of God.

Paul was also a trophy of God's grace. God's grace saved his soul, disciplined his mind, enriched his life, empowered his ministry, and sustained him to the end. Thus he could say, "By the grace of God I am what I am." Every Christian can and must say this. What has God's grace done for us? Note five things.

I. We are saved by the grace of God.

Christianity was initiated solely by God's grace. "He first loved us" (1 John 4:19) "and sent his Son to be the propitiation for our sins" (1 John 4:10). "For by grace are ye saved" (Eph. 2:8). We did not deserve to be saved. What we deserved would be quite different. We cannot secure salvation for ourselves.

People were not saved by works in the Old Testament, as some erroneously believe, but by grace in the New. God has always dealt with his people graciously. Amos urged his people to repent and walk in the right way with the hope "that the LORD God of hosts will be gracious" (Amos 5:15). For Amos, salvation was by grace alone.

Paul's testimony was, "By the grace of God I am what I am." When we think of what he was—a blasphemer, persecutor, destroyer of churches—and when we think of what he became—apostle to the Gentiles, missionary, statesman,

312

founder of churches, soul-winner, and Christian martyr—we are bound to ask, "What made the difference?" There can be but one answer, and that is the grace of God.

II. We are disciplined by the grace of God.

The words *discipline* and *disciple* come from the same root. There can be no discipleship without discipline. We cannot be saved by discipline, but our salvation cannot be effective unless disciplined.

There is no conflict between grace and discipline. Paul put the two together like this: "For the grace of God that bringeth salvation hath appeared to all men, teaching us that, denying ungodliness and worldly lusts, we should live soberly, righteously, and godly, in this present world" (Titus 2:11–12). Paul was saying, "God's grace saves us. God's grace teaches us on the one hand to renounce and on the other hand to realize." A truly disciplined Christian emerges by the grace of God.

III. We are enriched by the grace of God.

Paul told the Corinthians, "For ye know the grace of our Lord Jesus Christ, that, though he was rich, yet for your sakes he became poor, that ye through his poverty might be rich" (2 Cor. 8:9). God's grace will enrich our lives. It will make them full and rich and free. Paul raised a question that is devastating to our pride: "For who sees anything different in you? What have you that you did not receive? If then you received it, why do you boast as if it were not a gift?" (1 Cor. 4:7 RSV).

But grace, so conceived, is a two-way street. If we take God's gifts with a willing hand, we belong forever to the giver. God's grace is not cheap. It is a very expensive gift, for if we receive the gift, we belong to the giver. He will bind our hearts with cords of love. Would we want to have it otherwise?

IV. We are empowered by the grace of God.

Paul told the Corinthians, "[God] said unto me, My grace is sufficient for thee: for my strength is made perfect in weakness" (2 Cor. 12:9). Paul had been given "a thorn in the flesh" (2 Cor. 12:7). He called it "the messenger of Satan to buffet me, lest I should be exalted above measure" (v. 7). Three times he prayed for its removal, but God's answer was no. Paul did receive a promise, however: "My grace is sufficient for thee: for my strength is made perfect in weakness." Our forefathers called this "enabling grace."

In one of Robert Louis Stevenson's stories, "The Ebb Tide," one of his characters cries out, "Everything's grace. We walk upon it, we breathe it, we live and die by it, it makes the nails and the axles of this universe."

V. We are sustained by the grace of God.

Not only does God give us strength for each day, but his grace sustains us in every trial and from every pitfall. He keeps us from falling.

Some people have an inadequate concept of salvation. We are saved by the grace of God. They see that! But they have the idea that salvation, received by grace, God's great gift that we could never deserve, can be lost by our own poor works, our failures. They seem to think that God saves us by his grace and then removes his hand and leaves us to hold on if we can. Of course we are no more able to keep ourselves saved than we are able to save ourselves in the first place. It takes God's wonderful grace to save us from our sins. It takes his wonderful grace to keep us out of Satan's clutches.

By God's grace he saves us. By his grace he keeps us from falling. Our Lord said, "My sheep hear my voice, and I know them, and they follow me: and I give unto them eternal life; and they shall never perish, neither shall any man pluck them out of my hand. My Father, which gave them me, is greater than all; and no man is able to pluck them out of my Father's hand" (John 10:27–29). That is the grace of God. His grace sustains us. At all times and under all circumstances, he keeps us. When Martin Niemoeller was a prisoner of Hitler during World War II, he wrote a friend, "In the old days I used to be a bearer of the gospel; now that gospel is bearing me."

Conclusion

We are saved, disciplined, enriched, empowered, and sustained by the grace of God. And this is only one sermon. If we could tell it all, "even the world itself could not contain the books that should be written" (John 21:25).

WEDNESDAY EVENING, SEPTEMBER 29

Title: Affliction

Text: "Look upon mine affliction and my pain; and forgive all my sins" (Ps. 25:18).

Scripture Reading: Psalm 25:16–22

Introduction

Since human departure from God in the garden of Eden, suffering and affliction have been people's common lot in every age. People have had to labor for their bread and women have had to bear children in pain.

Jesus said, "In the world ye shall have tribulation" (John 16:33), and centuries later the poet Longfellow said, "Into each life some rain must fall. Some days must be dark and dreary." Affliction will be ours if we walk long enough along life's highway.

I. Affliction comes because it is the common lot of humanity.

Many people are ignorant and superstitious concerning affliction. Often after loss of possessions, illness, or death, someone will ask, "Why did God do this to me?" Or "What have I done, or failed to do, that God should punish me in this way?" Some people never realize that loss of possessions, heartache, pain, death, and grief are common to all. The good and the bad, the just and the unjust, the believer and the unbeliever are afflicted. We should not blame God or accuse him of these things. Decay, disintegration, and death belong to all living matter, and there is no escape.

Why do God's children suffer? Let's make some observations. Many suffer as the result of storms, floods, fires, disease, poverty, and war. Many afflictions arise out of the near or distant past, for heredity can be merciful or merciless.

II. Affliction comes because of wrong choices.

Much suffering is self-imposed through wrong choices, knowingly or ignorantly made. Many people are afflicted because of their disobedience and rebellion. This is especially true of God's people. Jesus said, "That servant who knew his master's will, but did not make ready or act according to his will, shall receive a severe beating" (Luke 12:47 RSV). And James wrote, "To him that knoweth to do good, and doeth it not, to him it is sin" (James 4:17).

III. Affliction comes as a matter of discipline because of sins.

The Bible teaches that God does impose disciplinary measures on his people because of their sins. It is for our good, and we should seek to know the purpose and design of such correction.

You will recall that God, by the hand of Moses, liberated Israel from bondage. God instructed Moses to lead the people into the promised land. For about forty years they milled around in the wilderness, rebelling against God and against Moses, until God's patience was spent. He decreed that not one of them, except Joshua and Caleb, should ever set foot on the soil of Canaan.

God had led the Israelites with a cloud by day and a pillar of fire by night. He fed them with manna and gave them water to drink. He sought to teach them to depend on him, but they were lacking in gratitude, and God let them die in the wilderness. The people of Israel did not learn their lesson. God's efforts to correct and teach his people to depend on him were futile. There was nothing left for him to do but punish them.

IV. Affliction comes so that God's work can be displayed in our lives.

You will recall that Jesus healed a man who was blind from his birth. The disciples asked, "Master, who did sin, this man, or his parents, that he was born blind? Jesus answered, Neither hath this man sinned, nor his parents: but that the works of God should be made manifest in him" (John 9:2–3).

Jewish theology of that time interpreted all suffering and affliction as a direct penalty for a specific sin. But here was a baffling case. Neither the blind man nor his parents had done anything to cause his handicap.

Affliction should never be a matter of doubt, debate, or controversy. It should be a means of glorifying God. The blind man's affliction became a means of displaying God's work in his life.

Conclusion

The benefits of affliction are many. Listen to God's Word!

Job said, "He knoweth the way that I take: when he hath tried me, I shall come forth as gold" (Job 23:10).

The writer of Hebrews said, "Now no chastening for the present seemeth to be joyous, but grievous: nevertheless afterward it yieldeth the peaceable fruit of righteousness unto them which are exercised thereby" (Heb. 12:11).

Job said, "Behold, happy is the man whom God correcteth: therefore despise not the chastening of the Almighty: for he maketh sore, and bindeth up: he woundeth, and his hands make whole" (Job. 5:17–18).

David wrote, "Before I was afflicted I went astray: but now have I kept thy word" (Ps. 119:67).

Solomon said, "My son, despise not the chastening of the LORD; neither be weary of his correction: for whom the LORD loveth he correcteth; even as a father the son in whom he delighteth" (Prov. 3:11–12).

Our attitude toward the discipline of our heavenly Father should not be rebellious, sour, bitter, or complaining. If we cannot understand our affliction, then let us believe "that all things work together for good to them that love God, to them who are the called according to his purpose" (Rom. 8:28).

William Cowper wrote,

> God moves in a mysterious way
> His wonders to perform;
> He plants His footsteps in the sea
> And rides upon the storm.
>
> Ye fearful saints, fresh courage take,
> The clouds you so much dread
> Are big with mercy and shall break
> With blessings on your head.
>
> Judge not the Lord by feeble sense,
> But trust Him for His grace.
> Behind a frowning providence,
> He hides a smiling face.
>
> His purposes will ripen fast,
> Unfolding every hour.
> The bud may have a bitter taste,
> But sweet will be the flower.

SUGGESTED PREACHING PROGRAM FOR THE MONTH OF
OCTOBER

■ **Sunday Mornings**

In times like these, we are in need of God's guidance more than ever. The suggested theme for the Sunday morning messages is "Finding and Following God's Guidelines."

■ **Sunday Evenings**

Begin a series of expository messages based on the apostle Paul's letter to the Ephesians, using "Making a New World" as the theme.

■ **Wednesday Evenings**

"The Parables of Jesus Continue to Speak" is the suggested theme for a series of studies focusing on some of Jesus' great parables. This series continues through the end of the year.

SUNDAY MORNING, OCTOBER 3

Title: Trusting God's Guidance

Text: "Trust in the LORD with all thine heart; and lean not unto thine own understanding. In all thy ways acknowledge him, and he shall direct thy paths" (**Prov. 3:5–6**).

Scripture Reading: Proverbs 3:1–8

Hymns: "Glorious Is Thy Name," McKinney
"Take My Life, and Let It Be Consecrated," Havergal
"Wherever He Leads, I'll Go," McKinney

Offertory Prayer: Heavenly Father, we begin this new year aware that our daily steps may be the walk of faith or the walk of disobedience. Help us to so commit ourselves to you that we will walk in the confidence of your guidance. Let this time of dedication of our gifts become for us a time of new commitment to follow where you lead and to do what you ask. We ask this in the name of Jesus Christ our Lord. Amen.

Introduction

We cannot see into the future, and without God's wisdom we will not see the present with understanding. At best, we expect to experience, beyond our current limited horizon, some complex and confusing turns in our paths that will test our highest knowledge and deepest commitment. We will have hills to climb and bumpy roads to traverse. How will we fare? Do we have any assurance that we can safely and successfully make it to our destination?

Our text says we can make it—and victoriously if we will trust God's guidance. "Trust in the LORD with all thine heart; and lean not unto thine own understanding. In all thy ways acknowledge him, and he shall direct thy paths."

This is an excellent watchword for the year, a battle cry for the testing times, a comfort and strength for our uncertainty. It is a sufficient substitute for a road map, even though our eyes cannot discern the turns, the stops, the difficulties, or the pleasures ahead. What does this text say to us?

I. God can guide us in our everyday living.

In every decision, every action, in every development of our lives, God will direct our paths.

A. *The analogy of a road builder and maintenance chief are suggested in the word "direct."* These assure that we travel to a desired destination as the road is built and maintained.

The Hebrew language contains several words for road or path, including words that refer to a highway, a way, a narrow path, a broad path, a trodden path, and a customary path or road. The word in Proverbs 3:6 is the customary or usual path or road. God relates to us as road builder and maintenance chief in the customary or day-to-day travels of our lives.

God cuts the road straight and keeps it useful. That is what is meant by the promise "He shall direct thy paths." We can get where we ought to be because God is available to prepare the way. He is active in all our affairs. We may not see the road builder and the maintenance chief during every mile traveled, but we do not move an inch without their help. This analogy does not say enough, however.

B. *God goes with us.* The God who can guide us does, in fact, become personally involved with us on every inch of our journey. He promises, "I will instruct thee and teach thee in the way which thou shalt go: I will guide thee with mine eye" (Ps. 32:8); "For this God is our God for ever and ever: he will be our guide even unto death" (Ps. 48:14); "The LORD shall guide thee continually" (Isa. 58:11); "Howbeit when he, the Spirit of truth, is come, he will guide you into all truth" (John 16:13).

II. God can guide us, but three conditions determine his guidance.

A. *Acknowledge him.* First, "in all thy ways acknowledge him." That is, in all the steps of your journey, see that you acknowledge God as your guide. We have likely had the experience of meeting a person on the street whom we knew well but who was preoccupied in thought or conversation and did not respond to our greeting. We either smilingly passed on by that person, spoke again, or touched the person on the shoulder. No slight was intended; our acknowledgment was simply missed. We also have experienced times when a preoccupied family member did not hear what we said, though we spoke directly to him or her. If this can happen in our relationships with friends and family members, it surely can happen in God's relationship with us. By our preoccupation we may miss his guidance. So if we have God's guidance, we must pay attention to him with the sensitivity of a faith that is alive and expectant, and not just in special moments of devotion and prayer. We are to acknowledge him in all our ways, in the days and the nights, at work and play, in rest or worship, in relationships, and when we are alone.

B. *Trust him.* This brings us to the second condition of God's guidance: "Trust in the LORD with all thine heart." We trust him in the hours of special need when there is no one else to trust. Or we trust him when we are called upon to do some unique assignment with which we feel insecure. But how about our trust level when we are unaware of needs, or when the ordinary experiences of life are in process? Trusting God, like loving him, must be total in degree. We must desire to please him totally in the ordinary experiences of every day.

C. Think of two professing Christians, both of whom affirm their faith in Jesus Christ. One is stable and copes with changes so smoothly that to the casual observer it seems easy. The other Christian is insecure. Any threatened difficulty creates a panic. If the currents of trouble are navigated at all, it is by the barest margin. What's the difference? The one with unwavering faith has sought and found God's guidance. The other "double-minded" person is unstable because he does not acknowledge God in all his ways.

D. *Don't depend on yourself.* These first two conditions may be labeled positive conditions. However, there is a third that can be labeled a negative condition: "Lean not to thine own understanding." The Revised Standard Version says, "Do not rely on your own insight." *The Living Bible* says, "Don't trust yourself." This condition suggests the absolute inadequacy of life without God's guidance. We really can't make it on our journey without him, and some people pay an unnecessarily high price to learn that self-management leads to endless defeat.

A family of faith decided not to trust God one day and leaned on their own understanding. God promised to Abraham and Sarah a child, but no child was born. After years of waiting, Sarah, thinking she was helping God out of his dilemma of not being able to provide a child, utilized the surrogate custom of that time. She gave her servant, Hagar, to Abraham. From that union Ishmael was born. In due time the child of promise, Isaac, was born to Sarah and Abraham. Eventually hostility and jealousy between the two women and the two boys came to such a crisis that Hagar and Ishmael were sent away. This personal hostility escalated into national hatred and religious persecution between Arabs and Jews, Muslims and Christians. We only defeat ourselves and God's purpose when we lean on our own understanding.

Conclusion

God wants to give us his guidance. He knows our need for it; he knows our failure without it. But he likewise knows our capacity to follow his direction. He has a unique plan for each of us, and he waits for us to pay attention to him, to trust him with the whole heart, to reject our own abilities to guide ourselves. He can and will guide us when we trust him.

SUNDAY EVENING, OCTOBER 3

Title: Blessings for Believers

Text: "Blessed be the God and Father of our Lord Jesus Christ, who hath blessed us with all spiritual blessings in heavenly places in Christ" **(Eph. 1:3)**.

Scripture Reading: Ephesians 1:1–14

Introduction

When I was in grade school, after the Christmas holidays my teacher would ask each student to stand and describe the various gifts he or she had received for Christmas. My classmates and I thoroughly enjoyed telling about our various gifts.

When Paul wrote to the Ephesian Christians, he began his letter by describing many of the gifts, or blessings, believers had received from the Lord. The greatest of God's many blessings are in the spiritual realm. Let us look at some of them.

I. God selects believers.

God grants to believers the gracious privilege of being selected for membership in his family. The act of being chosen to be a believer rests with God's initiative rather than a person's pursuit of God. Notice the various words that describe God's gift of selection: "chosen" (Eph. 1:4), "predestined" (1:5), and "his will" (1:5).

A. *God's selection marks the point of beginning for believers.* The blessing of God's selection begins with God. "He hath chosen us in him before the foundation of the world" (Eph. 1:4). This means that our selection is not determined by our virtues or goodness. God begins the salvation process by choosing believers. God's selection does not rule out personal choice, however. Someone has described the process like this: God wants you and Satan wants you. You break the tie.

B. *God's selection underscores his purpose.* Look at God's purpose for selection: "chosen . . . that we should be holy and without blame before him in love" and "predestined" in order to be adopted as his children. The purpose of God's selection is not to demonstrate favoritism but to demonstrate his purpose. Think about this great gift. God has picked you to be in his family. "Blessed be the God and Father of our Lord Jesus Christ" (Eph. 1:3).

II. God redeems believers.

After God selects believers he begins a wonderful process of transformation. Paul described this process with the word *redemption*—"In whom we have redemption" (Eph. 1:7).

A. *God's redemption means a rescue from bondage.* The Greek word for redemption means liberation or emancipation, as of the setting free of a slave by his or her master. The term *redemption* emerged from the Old Testament idea of God's deliverance of Israel from Egyptian bondage. Thus God blesses believers by deliverance. Jesus Christ delivers people from the evil world. He rescues us from the bondage of sin.

B. *God's redemption also means the giving of new life.* When God delivered the Jews from Egyptian bondage, he gave them new territory. Jesus Christ delivers us from a self-centered life to new territory—the selfless life in Christ.

III. God forgives believers.

Closely akin to God's gift of redemption is his gift of forgiveness. God gives "the forgiveness of sins, according to the riches of his grace" (Eph. 1:7).

A. *God's forgiveness means the dismissal of a debt.* The Greek word for forgiveness has the idea of being in debt to a person. Everyone is in great debt to God for graciously sending his Son to release sinners from their debt by his death on the cross.

B. *God's forgiveness also means the restoration of a relationship.* The word translated "forgiveness" refers to a broken and restored relationship with God. Individuals are alienated from God, but he restores the relationship by his grace.

IV. God gives his Holy Spirit.

Perhaps the greatest blessing anyone could give to a person is the gift of self. God has done just that. He has given himself to us in the person of his Holy Spirit.

A. *God proves his presence in believers.* "You . . . were included in Christ when you heard the message of truth, the gospel of your salvation. When you believed, you were marked in him with a seal, the promised

Holy Spirit" (Eph. 1:13 NIV). By the sealing of the Holy Spirit, God assures believers that he is with them.

B. *God promises greater blessings.* "[The Holy Spirit] is a deposit guaranteeing our inheritance until the redemption of those who are God's possession—to the praise of his glory" (Eph. 1:14 NIV). A deposit is a partial payment that guarantees more is to come. God gives his Holy Spirit, and he is the guarantee of many other subsequent blessings.

Conclusion

No one could enumerate all of God's blessings, but let us remember to count ours frequently and to give thanks for them.

WEDNESDAY EVENING, OCTOBER 6

Title: Parable of the Sower

Text: "He that hath ears to hear, let him hear" (**Luke 8:8**).

Scripture Reading: Luke 8:4–15

Introduction

Our understanding of the parable of the sower will be largely determined by our background. Those with an agricultural background have a real advantage. Jesus is describing a man sowing seed in a relatively small field. He plants the seeds a handful at a time by throwing them out over the field. Thus he does not have complete control over every seed, and the seeds fall in various places with differing kinds of soil. Jesus sets forth two major emphases.

I. The first emphasis is placed on the Word of God.

Jesus said, "The seed is the word of God" (Luke 8:11).

A. *We notice throughout the parable that the seeds are all the same kind.* They are all the Word of God. The only difference is the kind of soil on which they fall. To grasp this idea, it is necessary for us to fix in our mind the description of the sower as presented in the introduction.

B. *We also notice throughout the parable that the same person is doing the sowing.* In the Scripture passage, the sower is Jesus. In modern times, the sower is anyone who proclaims the Word.

II. The second emphasis is placed on hearing the Word of God.

A. *The parable places responsibility on the one who hears.* In modern times, far too much emphasis is placed on the one who proclaims and not enough on the one who hears.

B. *Jesus describes four types of people who respond to the Word.*

1. The first group are those who are illustrated by the seeds falling on a trodden path (Luke 8:5, 12). Here the solution is given in a nutshell. Hear! Believe! Be saved! This type of people can hear with the physical ear, but that is the extent of their hearing. Satan immediately takes the Word away so that they may not believe and be saved.

2. The second group are those who are illustrated by the seeds falling on shallow soil (Luke 8:6, 13). The shallow soil is that which has rock a few inches below the top soil. The seeds sprout quickly but have no place to put down strong roots. Jesus used these words to describe those who receive the Word with emotional excitement and superficial enthusiasm but shortly thereafter fall away to outside testing and temptations.

3. The third group are those who are illustrated by the seeds falling among thorns (Luke 8:7, 14). This is a description of people who hear the Word and give the appearance that everything is great but in a short period of time are distracted by life's worries, riches, and pleasures and do not mature.

4. The fourth group are those who are illustrated by the seeds falling on good soil (Luke 8:8, 15). The soil told about here is well prepared. Such people hear the Word, retain it, and by persevering produce a crop. Jesus wants the Word to fall on this kind of soil.

Conclusion

Verse 8 says, "He that hath ears to hear, let him hear." We need to take responsibility for what we do with God's Word. We need to be faithful in seeing that it produces a good crop within us, and we also need to be diligent in sowing the Word so that others may receive it.

SUNDAY MORNING, OCTOBER 10

Title: Seeking God's Guidance

Text: "For this cause we also, since the day we heard it, do not cease to pray for you, and to desire that ye might be filled with the knowledge of his will in all wisdom and spiritual understanding; that ye might walk worthy of the Lord unto all pleasing, being fruitful in every good work, and increasing in the knowledge of God" **(Col. 1:9–10)**.

Scripture Reading: Colossians 1:9–14

Hymns: "Savior, Like a Shepherd Lead Us," Thrupp
          "Great Is Thy Faithfulness," Chisholm
          "Where He Leads I'll Follow," Blandy

Offertory Prayer: Father, your generous provisions for our lives are more than enough to assure us that your work is the most important work on this earth. Help us to be so filled with understanding and appreciation of your work that we will use your gifts to work with you in your kingdom on this earth. May our money serve you as we commit ourselves afresh to the working of your will. In Jesus' name. Amen.

Introduction

God's guidance is available, and we ought to trust it. However, as with other ready resources from God, we need to ask, seek, and knock. To do so clarifies and confirms our openness to do God's will. It sharpens and quickens our desires. Jesus taught us to pray, "Thy will be done on earth as it is in heaven."

There are many good reasons why believers ought to seek God's guidance. However, the one that claimed the apostle Paul's attention as he evaluated the church at Colossae is a sufficient reason to seek God's guidance. Doctrinal compromise and weak Christian conduct would be the result without God's guidance. Pagan philosophy and Jewish legalism were being mixed with Christian beliefs by some religious teachers at Colossae. The result was supposed to be a superior Christianity. Instead, it was inferior.

Our text is Paul's prayer of concern that the church avoid doctrinal compromise by seeking God's guidance and strengthening Christian practices. It features three major requests.

I. That the church "be filled with the knowledge of God's will."

Religious knowledge and the knowledge of God's will are not necessarily synonymous. Much religious knowledge is not only in conflict with God's will but can destroy God's work in the world. We have seen that happen in some of the cults of our day. Paul's prayer request confirms a need for a particular religious knowledge, the knowledge of God's will. Let's remember that such knowledge can be divided into three categories: God's ultimate will, God's intentional will, and God's permissive will.

 A. *God's ultimate will.* Some of God's will is irresistible, unconditional, and inevitable. Regardless of human responses, his plans will unfold. We need the knowledge that God is sovereign over the universe and that his goals will prevail. Those who do his will voluntarily will live with him eternally. Those who disobey will spend eternity separated from him. This portion of our knowledge of God's will may be labeled his "ultimate will."

 B. *God's intentional will.* God's plan for our lives is determined by our choices. He grants us the right to say yes or no in the doing of his will. Not only do we choose whether we receive Christ as Savior and Lord, but we choose the degree of our development. God's desire is that all people be saved and come to the knowledge of the truth (1 Tim. 2:4). Further, he desires for his people to be sanctified (1 Thess. 4:3). He intends that we know his will and do it. This knowledge of his will is marked "intentional will."

C. *God's permissive will.* We can choose to disregard God's will or to follow it. God permits events or circumstances to occur that may serve as discipline. Also, experiences or circumstances not of our own personal making work to test our faith. This is referred to as God's "permissive will."

We must be filled with the knowledge of God's will so that we can avoid doctrinal compromise and strengthen our Christian walk.

II. That the church function in the practice of God's will "in all wisdom and spiritual understanding."

The knowledge of God should always lead to "wisdom" or insight, to the perception of spiritual values and of goals that make the doing of his will primary. That knowledge also leads to "spiritual understanding," or the ability to apply the principles we receive.

The result is that we "walk worthy of the Lord." Our conduct is not only freed from practices of wrongdoing but is filled with the exercise of rightdoing. A three-year-old son was proudly wearing one of his father's World War II ribbons of honor when mealtime came. The dad noticed it and said to his son, "What act of bravery did you perform to get that?" The little boy said, "I didn't get into trouble for thirty minutes." The smiling mother explained that she had offered the ribbon as a reward if the boy would stay out of the kitchen while she worked on a new recipe. So the father hugged his son and said, "Good job!" The boy put on his best grin and replied, "I'm a good boy; I stayed out of trouble." But staying out of trouble is not enough for those who seek and discover the knowledge of God's will. We are to stay in the truth as the way of life.

Many of the practices of God's will do not seem to have a chapter and verse from the Bible as a point of reference. Rather, we stay in the truth by applying biblical principles that express wisdom and spiritual understanding.

As a teenager I was confronted with some issues of right and wrong for which I could find no explicit biblical assistance. I sought from wise leaders some answers that have stayed with me. Those wise leaders suggested that the following questions be raised regarding a particular action.

A. *Will it bring glory to God?* "Whether therefore ye eat, or drink, or whatsoever ye do, do all to the glory of God" (1 Cor. 10:31).

B. *Will it lead into temptation?* "And lead us not into temptation, but deliver us from evil" (Matt. 6:13).

C. *Will it enslave me?* "All things are lawful for me, but I will not be brought under the power of any" (1 Cor. 6:12).

325

D. *Will it defile my body?* "What? know ye not that your body is the temple of the Holy Ghost which is in you, which ye have of God, and ye are not your own?" (1 Cor. 6:19).

E. *Will it damage my influence on others?* "It is good neither to eat flesh, nor to drink wine, nor any thing whereby thy brother stumbleth, or is offended, or is made weak" (Rom. 14:21).

F. *Does it create doubt about doing the will of God in my life?* "For whatsoever is not of faith is sin" (Rom. 14:23). If we seek the highest wisdom and spiritual understanding, we can know God's will and practice it.

III. That the church focus on fully pleasing the Lord by "being fruitful in every good work, and increasing in the knowledge of God."

Pleasing people is important, especially when we love them. Pleasing the Lord is important, but doing so is difficult when there is competition between pleasing people and pleasing God.

We talk about peer pressure on young people. Who can blame them for wanting to be acceptable to their associates? Adults want to be acceptable too. They are strongly tempted to make compromises of Christian principles in the presence of pressure from employers and from friends, as well as from an uncommitted spouse. Seeking God's guidance means striving to please God regardless of the cost to business, friendships, and even family relationships. It is the only way to increase knowledge of God.

The new mission appointee was asked, "Why do you plan to go overseas when you could stay at home and be as useful here in pastoral ministry as you would be there?" He replied, "Because usefulness and place of service are not my highest priorities. God's will for me is the most important issue in my life. I believe he wants me there."

Conclusion

The commitment to seek God's guidance is as important as seeking to be saved. Has this prayer been answered in your life? The missionary apostle prayed it for a church troubled over its understanding of God's will. We, too, need to be filled with the knowledge of God's will, function in the practice of his will, and focus on fully pleasing the Lord in doing his will. Perhaps the most important decision to be made in response to this prayer is to decide to please him above all others. To do so will make you a student wanting to know his will and a servant desiring to obey his will.

SUNDAY EVENING, OCTOBER 10

Title: Improving Your Praying

Text: "Having the eyes of your hearts enlightened, that you may know what is the hope to which he has called you, what are the riches of his glorious inheritance in the saints, and what is the immeasurable greatness of his power in us who believe, according to the working of his great might" **(Eph. 1:18–19)**.

Introduction

If you wanted to learn the game of golf, you would seek out a golf pro. You would not want to teach yourself or seek the instruction of an amateur. Likewise, if you want to learn how to be more effective in your prayer life, you will want to seek the instruction of one who is proficient in the practice of praying. One such person was the apostle Paul. Fortunately, many of Paul's prayers are recorded for us. By studying them we can learn how to pray more effectively.

Let's look at Paul's prayers for the believers in and around Ephesus to see what we can learn.

I. To be effective in prayer you need to know God's personality.

Conversations are enhanced by knowing well the person with whom you converse. If you know something of the other person's temperament and personality, the conversation is more stimulating. The same is true with God. To pray more effectively, you must learn more about the Lord.

A. *You need to know the name of God.* Throughout the Scriptures God has disclosed his nature by the use of numerous names. Paul gave several names of God as he prayed: "Lord Jesus," "God," "Lord Jesus Christ," "Father of glory." Each one of these names described some aspect of God's character. You would not want to talk with someone without knowing his or her name. Getting the name of a person is the first step in conversing with that person.

B. *You also need to know the nature of God.* Closely akin to knowing God's name is knowing God's nature, for his names disclose his divine nature. When you pray, you speak to the unique creator, sustainer, and ruler of history. To pray is to talk with the unique God.

Furthermore, God's names disclose his human nature. God became human at Bethlehem. When you talk to God, you are speaking with someone who knows human nature. "For we have not a high priest who is unable to sympathize with our weaknesses, but one who in every respect has been tempted as we are, yet without sinning" (Heb. 4:15).

II. To be effective in prayer you need to know God's purpose.

Conversation is enhanced when you know something of the other person's purpose and goals in life. When you learn about God's purposes, your prayer life will improve. "That ye may know what is the hope of his calling" (Eph. 1:18).

A. *God's purpose is to reunite the whole creation.* "For he has made known to us in all wisdom and insight the mystery of his will, according to his purpose which he set forth in Christ as a plan for the fulness of time, to unite all things in him, things in heaven and things on earth" (Eph. 1:9–10 RSV). If you talk to God, you must keep God's purpose uppermost in mind.

B. *God's purpose is to use believers to accomplish his purpose.* The church is the body of Christ through whom God brings about his purpose. Whenever you talk to God, you should have a thorough awareness that you will be used to accomplish his purpose.

III. To be effective in prayer you need to know God's provisions.

Paul prayed that believers "may know . . . the riches of [God's] glorious inheritance in the saints" (Eph. 1:18 RSV).

A. *The church is God's special possession called into being by the work of the Holy Spirit.* Paul prayed that believers may appreciate the church as God's special possession purchased with the blood of his Son.

B. *The church is to show God's glory.* Believers have been selected by God to show his glory. They belong to a new kingdom, and their behavior is to match the kingdom principles.

IV. To be effective in prayer you need to know God's power.

Paul prayed that believers may comprehend "what is the immeasurable greatness of his power in us who believe, according to the working of his great might" (Eph. 1:19 RSV). The power of God is expressed in four different words: *dunamis* ("power"); *energeia* ("working"); *kratos* ("strength"); and *ischus* ("might").

A. *Believers need to see what God has done.* How great is the power of God! You have only to look at the resurrection of Christ to know the measure of God's might. God "raised him from the dead, and set him at his own right hand in the heavenly places, far above all principality, and power, and might, and dominion, and every name that is named, not only in this world, but also in that which is to come" (Eph. 1:20–21). God raised Jesus from the dead. That act took a powerful person. Whenever we talk with God, we need to be aware of how powerful he is.

B. *Believers need to appropriate God's power.* When believers pray, they can depend on God's power. We need to seek daily this inexhaustible source of strength.

Conclusion

Paul was a professional when it came to praying. Read his prayer and learn to pray more effectively.

WEDNESDAY EVENING, OCTOBER 13

Title: Parable of the Good Samaritan

Text: "Go, and do thou likewise" (**Luke 10:37**).

Scripture Reading: Luke 10:25–37

Introduction

In this parable Jesus described two types of religion, or two different degrees of religion.

I. Religion based on the law but with no real commitment.

A. *This type of religion has no eternal value.* The lawyer, as presented in Luke 10:25, indicated that he was concerned with the law in the Jewish sense but not in the secular sense. He had a knowledge of the law of Moses and the prophets. This can be illustrated by a person who has a knowledge of the content of the Scriptures but does not show any evidence of the Christian experience of transformation and does not show Christian love.

   The lawyer's question did not spring from a sincere desire to gain insight; instead, the question was intended to trap Jesus. The lawyer had no heart in his religion. He believed he had only to keep the law to be saved.

   Jesus' answer in Luke 10:27 is a summary of the Ten Commandments. The first section refers to a person's relation to God and the last refers to a person's relation to others.

B. *This type of religion has many obvious errors.* It seeks excuses for prejudice (Luke 10:29). It fails to meet the needs of humankind (vv. 31–32). It brings misery to the one who holds such a religion. It does not meet God's approval.

II. Religion based on commitment to God that lends quality to life.

A. *This type of religion is in sharp contrast to the first.* The priest and Levite were professional religionists. The priest was one who offered sacrifices, and the Levite cleansed various things. The Samaritan, however, was a hated person. In Luke 10:37 the lawyer would not so much as say the word *Samaritan.*

B. *This type of religion is demonstrated in compassionate concern.* Religion based on commitment to God overcomes prejudice. Each person, regardless of ethnic background, is precious in God's sight. This kind of religion motivates personal sacrifice for others (10:34). This kind of religion follows through on meeting needs (v. 35). The Samaritan told the innkeeper, "I will repay thee" (v. 35).

Conclusion

The heart of the parable of the good Samaritan is "Go, and do thou likewise." The lawyer asked how to inherit eternal life, and Jesus answered him, "Become like me." Love everyone. Do your best to meet the needs of others.

SUNDAY MORNING, OCTOBER 17

Title: Receiving God's Guidance

Text: "But we have the mind of Christ" (**1 Cor. 2:16**).

Scripture Reading: 1 Corinthians 2:12–16

Hymns: "Love Divine, All Loves Excelling," Wesley
            "Near the Cross," Crosby
            "When I Survey the Wondrous Cross," Watts

Offertory Prayer: Heavenly Father, we receive so much of your good and providential care without thinking to thank you. But let one accustomed blessing be absent from all your gifts and we notice it and complain about it. Forgive us for our selfishness and help us see the absent blessing as your concern that we be more dependent on what you provide and more aware that the missing gift is a means for development of our faith in you. Bless now our response as stewards of all that you have given us, and may we give all to honor your Son. Amen.

Introduction

"But we have the mind of Christ." That claim may seem presumptuous and shocking to those who view the Christian faith as supplemental support for ordinary human experience. But when Jesus is Lord in our lives and each day's highest priority is given to seeking and trusting God's guidance, it is normal to seek and find the mind of Christ.

Like Abraham's servant, who was sent to the old country to find a bride for the son of promise, Isaac, we can say, "The LORD led me" (Gen. 24:27). The reality of this was impressed upon me as a teenager through an experience of a relative who was hosting a foreign missionary in her home. As lunch ended one day, the missionary was asked, "Would you like to go shopping, since your next appointment is not until after the dinner hour?" The missionary replied, "I think I would, but give me a little while to decide for sure." Shortly she excused herself from the table, was gone for fifteen or twenty minutes, and returned to say without any sticky piety in her manner or voice, "Yes, I will go shopping. I checked it out with the Father, and it seems okay."

Is that an intended lifestyle for all believers? It is if we take seriously our text, "But we have the mind of Christ." Receiving God's guidance means that our lives have been possessed by the living God. He has taken up residence within us to enlighten us so that we may walk in the light. He leads us so that it can be said, "For as many as are led by the Spirit of God, they are the sons of God" (Rom. 8:14).

I. If we have the mind of Christ, we have received his knowledge.

We receive the knowledge of Christ from our Guidebook. God reveals himself and what he expects from his people through the Bible. Its words are God's words. There are more than two thousand instances in the Bible where it is said that the words of this Book are identified as the Word of God. Clearly the Bible can help us know how to walk and where to walk. "Thy word is a lamp unto my feet, and a light unto my path" (Ps. 119:105).

Without God's Word as a guide, we walk in darkness. To ignore it or take it lightly is to assure the absence of God's guidance. Jeremiah said, "I know, O LORD, that a man's life is not his own; it is not for man to direct his steps" (Jer. 10:23 NIV).

To receive God's guidance means we must be open to the open Bible, but not because the Bible maps out our daily schedules or gives us detailed prescriptions for every problem. The Bible does, however, present principles, and these principles show us the path. They light up the way. Best of all, the Bible shows us Jesus, the Light of the World. When we have been born anew by the living and abiding Word of God, he is present to instruct us.

When a pastor asked to counsel with a couple about a family problem, he discovered that neither spouse was a Christian. The focus of the discussion moved from the problem itself to Christ, who could give light to their lives. In due time both became disciples. Later the pastor reminded them of his availability to help them think through the problems with which they had first approached him. Their answer was, "With Jesus we've learned how to talk to one another about our problems and to forgive the past. You can be assured we will call you if we need you, but right now we are solving the problems that were irritating us by opening ourselves to his Word and to one another." Indeed, the Bible serves as a helpful Guidebook when we receive Jesus Christ as our Savior. By the knowledge of it, we have the mind of Christ.

II. If we have the mind of Christ, it is because we have received his Spirit.

The reality of the knowledge that we have the mind of Christ because we have received his Spirit causes some who seek a rational explanation for every fact of spiritual experience to blow the fuses of faith. On the other hand, this reality causes others to blow the fuses of practical application. The truth is that both faith and works require the Spirit's guidance to be operational.

We are not merely to set the automatic pilot and keep our hands from the controls of personhood. Rather, we are to be decisively open to impressions that are cultivated by our knowledge of the truth and by our openness to God's guidance. We choose to make our minds a storehouse for the knowledge of God and a distribution center for the doing of God's will. With this highest knowledge and deepest impressions of how to apply truth in our experience, we are walking in the Spirit.

If you have ever been in a foreign land, you know the value of a guide. Persons around you may not speak your language, but a guide does. He helps you understand what you see and what you do. Otherwise, little is appreciated and enjoyed. A friend wrote about his visit to France and Italy. He said that he went to the Louvre in Paris and saw the *Winged Victory, Venus de Milo,* and the *Mona Lisa.* However, he had no guide. In Florence, he said, he had an excellent guide who was an artist and knew the masters and the schools that followed them. The friend wrote, "He led us past dozens of pictures to bring us to the really good ones, and lingered lovingly before them sharing the message and the teachings they had perfected. I learned more in art appreciation in two days in Italy with that guide than in all other museums, including the Louvre." Our Lord does not leave us alone. He comes to us. He dwells within us. He teaches us his truth. Therefore we have his mind.

III. If we have the mind of Christ, it is because we have received his invitation to pray.

Our minds are the battleground in which the forces of righteousness and the forces of evil engage in conflict. The outcome of the battle depends on our submission to God. Through faith we may be in a right position and yet disagree with God's guidance. This is why Jesus said, "Watch and pray so that you will not fall into temptation" (Mark 14:38 NIV). This is why he so frequently turned aside to refresh himself in new submission to the Father's will. His position with God was never in doubt, but he had to renew his submission regularly because of Satan's power.

We are to present our bodies as living sacrifices. That is our position before the Father. We also are to be transformed by the renewing of our minds. This is submission. And how is submission achieved? Through prayer.

Do you remember how Jesus said, "If ye then, being evil, know how to give good gifts unto your children: how much more shall your heavenly Father give the Holy Spirit to them that ask him?" (Luke 11:14). The Holy Spirit is already given to believers as the representative of Jesus. If, however, we respond to Jesus' invitation to pray, to make contact with heaven, to get in tune with the will of the heavenly Father, then the Holy Spirit becomes the power to guide our minds in the conflict. He enables us to choose our actions wisely.

Receiving God's guidance means that we pray intently, frequently, and submissively. In Acts 17:10–11 we note that the new church in Berea "received the word with all readiness of mind, and searched the scriptures daily" (v. 11).

Conclusion

Some amazing experiences take place because we have the mind of Christ. Circumstances that mean nothing to the natural mind take on special meaning. Events that unfold without special religious connotation become a unique means of ministry in the name of Jesus. We cannot always perceive where our circumstances and where these events will finally lead, but we have the mind of Christ, and that is enough.

Remember how the boy Samuel was called from his bed to respond to a voice that spoke to him? Under the wise nurturing of Eli, he learned to answer, "Speak; for thy servant heareth" (1 Sam. 3:10). This is to be our daily prayer as we receive the Holy Spirit's guidance.

SUNDAY EVENING, OCTOBER 17

Title: The Master Designer

Text: "For we are his workmanship, created in Christ Jesus for good works, which God prepared beforehand, that we should walk in them" **(Eph. 2:10 RSV)**.

Scripture Reading: Ephesians 2:1–10

Introduction

Once a man visited another man who worked with wood. With his imaginative mind and skillful hands, the woodworker made attractive products. As the visitor watched the woodworker take a piece of wood and make a beautiful product, he remarked, "God is like that!" God takes a human being and makes a beautiful life. God is the Master Designer. In fact, Paul said, "We are his workmanship." Each believer is God's work of grace. Let us examine the various aspects of God's work with human beings.

I. God has an impossible product with which to work (2:1–3).

Paul painted a pathetic picture of human beings. Such is the world today without God. Sin has caused a terrible plight. It seems as if God has an impossible piece of material with which to work.

A. *The person without Christ is dead.* "You he made alive, when you were dead through the trespasses and sins in which you once walked" (vv. 1–2 RSV). The words "trespasses" and "sins" suggest disobedience to God and a refusal to obey his laws. Such actions and attitudes sever the soul from fellowship with God and destroy spiritual life.

The state of a person without Christ is spiritual death, a resistance to the source of life himself.

B. *A person without Christ is dominated.* "Following the course of this world, following the prince of the power of the air, the spirit that is now at work in the sons of disobedience. Among these we all once lived in the passions of our flesh, following the desires of body and mind, and so we were by nature children of wrath, like the rest of mankind" (vv. 2–3 RSV). The nonbeliever is described by Paul as being directed and dominated by the world, the flesh, and the devil. These words summarize the malevolent influences that control those who attempt to live without God.

Looking at the present state of human beings could cause us to be pessimistic and to conclude that people are helpless. God, however, can take an unholy person and make a beautiful product. He is the Master Designer.

II. God has an incredible power with which to design (2:4–6).

Paul described God's incredible ability to change human beings. God is merciful to humanity, and he desires to help.

A. *The mercy of God prompts the power of God.* The Lord has within his power the capacity to save or to destroy. His compassion motivates him to help human beings. "But God, who is rich in mercy, out of the great love with which he loved us . . ." (v. 4 RSV). The Greek noun translated "mercy" is *eleos* and means "the disposition and readiness to help those in trouble." Out of God's character issues abundant mercy. It is God's disposition to help rebellious human beings.

B. *The power of God changes human beings.* The experience of believers is pictured in terms of the resurrection and exaltation of Christ. He was dead. So we were once dead. We were held under the power of the world, the flesh, and the devil.

Christ was raised from the dead. So Christ grants believers a new kind of life. This spiritual experience is just as real as Christ's death and resurrection. It is demonstrated by changed lives as true as those of the empty tomb and appearances of the risen Lord.

The new life is not a perfect life. We are continually being transformed into the image of Christ.

III. God has an indomitable purpose to accomplish (2:7–10).

After God works on the impossible product with his incredible power, he has a purpose for the finished product.

A. *God wants to show believers as exhibitions of grace.* "That in the coming ages he might show the immeasurable riches of his grace in kindness toward us in Christ Jesus" (v. 7 RSV). All designers want to show their products. God's product can be seen in a changed life. Believers are trophies of God's grace. It is his desire that his children will exhibit his grace forever.

B. *God wants his believers to do good works.* "For by grace you have been saved through faith; and this is not your own doing, it is the gift of God—not because of works, lest any man should boast. For we are his workmanship, created in Christ Jesus for good works, which God prepared beforehand, that we should walk in them" (vv. 8–10 RSV). Good works follow a true relationship with the Lord. When we place our faith in Christ, good works are inevitable results.

Conclusion

If you want to see some of God's great works, look at those around you. You can see what fellow believers have been and what they are now. Only God could do a work like that. He is the Master Designer.

WEDNESDAY EVENING, OCTOBER 20

Title: Parable of the Friend at Midnight

Text: "And I tell you, Ask, and it will be given you; seek, and you will find; knock, and it will be opened to you. For every one who asks receives, and he who seeks finds, and to him who knocks it will be opened" (**Luke 11:9–10 RSV**).

Scripture Reading: Luke 11:1–13

Introduction

The words of today's Scripture reading are not specifically declared to be a parable. However, studies by some New Testament scholars identify it as such. And since a parable is a story used to teach a lesson, I will treat this passage as a parable in today's message.

We find some big little words in these verses—words that are short in the number of letters but big in meaning. One of these words is the two-letter word *if*. Notice how it is used in this passage. First, Jesus said *if* (implied) a mere friend does not want to give because of inconvenience but will give when asked urgently, how much more will God give? Second, Jesus said *if* a mere parent will give and not mock, how much more will the heavenly Father give? Since this is the central message of the passage, let us discuss it by using two phrases.

I. "Because of his importunity" (11:8).

A. *Consider this picture.* It is a picture of sheer desperation. The root meaning of "importunity" is shame. Thus this is the perfect picture of a person lost in sin. In the Scripture passage the man was desperate because he failed to plan ahead. In modern life the reasons are very similar.

B. *Consider this lesson.* The lesson is that a person brings this condition of desperation on him- or herself. It is the result of sinful attitudes and behavior. Humankind is lost because of sin. Some Christians are ineffective because of it.

II. "And I say unto you" (11:9).

A. *These words are intended as words of hope.* Even though a person may be lost in desperation, God is ready, willing, and able to do something about it. He offers hope to those who ask for his help in sincerity. He is able to meet all needs.

335

B. *We need only to ask, seek, and knock.*

    1. These words are continuous action. They do not relate to a singular attitude or activity but to the continuous attitude of a person and his or her relation to God. Christians are to keep on asking, seeking, and knocking.

    2. The passage referred to as the Lord's Prayer reflects this attitude.

        a. One must have an attitude of confidence (v. 2). The term "Father" indicates someone who is close at hand. God is always close by, and believers are to pray with an attitude of faith in him.

        b. One must have an attitude of reverence (v. 2). "Hallowed be thy name." The word "name" denotes all that God is in character. Believers are to treat his name as holy.

        c. One must have an attitude of submission (v. 2). "Thy kingdom come." This refers to the rule and reign of God. Submission begins with an openness to God's will, starting within one's heart and moving out to others.

        d. One must have an attitude of dependence (v. 3). "Give us day by day our daily bread." Bread stands for everything one needs for earthly existence. Believers are to depend on God to supply their "daily bread."

        e. One must have an attitude of penitence (v. 4). "Forgive us our sins." When believers pray for forgiveness, they also confess. Forgiveness means to send away.

        f. One must have an attitude of humility (v. 4). "Lead us not into temptation." This is a prayer for deliverance from temptation. It is also a prayer for strength to resist temptation.

Conclusion

In today's message we have discussed how to have our needs met. Our greatest need is eternal salvation. We need to ask for forgiveness and receive it. Let's do it right now.

SUNDAY MORNING, OCTOBER 24

Title: Testing God's Guidance

Text: "Proving what is acceptable unto the Lord" **(Eph. 5:10)**.

Scripture Reading: Ephesians 5:6–14

Hymns: "Come, Thou Fount of Every Blessing," Robinson
         "All the Way My Saviour Leads Me," Crosby
         "Purer in Heart, Oh God," Fillmore

Offertory Prayer: Heavenly Father, you do not leave us alone to manage your affairs, and we are grateful. Even now your Spirit seeks room within us to be our Helper with each detail. Give us the grace to see our need for his encouragement and the wisdom to follow your guidance in any areas that we have made off-limits to you. Grant that our stewardship may be strengthened as we give our tithes and offerings to you. Amen.

Introduction

God's guidance is available. We can seek it, receive it, and trust it. Information about his guidance is available in his Guidebook. We can check our understanding through the Faithful Guide who is present to instruct us. And we can develop a submissive spirit to his guidance through prayer. But having followed these steps, we may still lack confidence and clarity in doing God's will. Like a do-it-yourself craft kit, some of the instructions are not clear. The process is confusing and frustrating. There is more to it than you originally thought.

Determining God's will can sometimes be confusing, for example, as when people seem to have differing interpretations of the truth. Suppose a new Christian is working as a laborer in an organization whose employees belong to a union. He works diligently, but a foreman of the organization who is also a professing Christian takes aside the hardworking worker and says, "Slow down. If you work too hard it will make the other workmen look bad." But the industrious laborer remembers what the Bible says: "Whatsoever ye do, do it heartily, as to the Lord, and not unto men" (Col. 3:23). What should he do? He's confused.

Confusion in determining God's will may also result from untested principles. A person may feel that the biblical teaching about temperance with food and drink does not mean total abstinence from alcoholic beverages. That person has grown up around people who regularly imbibed. He has experienced none of the family heartaches associated with alcohol abuse. It just doesn't seem wrong to him to drink moderately. As time passes, his teenage son observes his conduct and begins drinking secretly, only not so temperately. The telephone rings one Saturday night and the father learns the price of his influence on his son. "There's been an automobile wreck and. . . ." The father says, "If only I had considered the power of my influence on my son, but now it's too late." The father had heard about the principle of influence, but it hadn't been tested in his life until the tragedy occurred.

How can we overcome confusion and respond to God's guidance with clear obedience to his will?

I. We can walk in the light we already have.

"For once you were darkness, but now you are light in the Lord; walk as children of light" (Eph. 5:8 RSV).

It is important to remember that all of us have been exposed to the darkness of sin and have walked in that darkness. Our previous proximity to the darkness of sin requires that we now live in the light, listening to and

337

following Jesus Christ. We must develop a curious and a quick mind in him. We must recognize that we do not have all the answers but that we are committed to him who does. Otherwise we will be deceived by our adversary Satan.

Walk in the light that you have. Isn't this logical? If you wanted to become a long-distance runner, wouldn't you first begin to run short distances? If your goal is to be able to speak a foreign language fluently, doesn't it follow that you first learn to speak short sentences? Our walking in the light does not mean that we always walk with as much stability as we might. But the child learning how to walk doesn't stop if some of the walking means falling down. In walking poorly we begin to walk with stability.

II. We can test in order to approve what is acceptable to the Lord.

In any school, students are tested. Though it may not always seem so, the purpose of the test is to aid the approving process. Likewise, new machinery is tested on proving grounds so the defects can be eliminated. Our conduct is to be subjected to the testing process for the purpose of being acceptable to the Lord. By this testing we experience clarity in guidance.

Where does this happen? Right out in the world where the darkness is. And out here in the world we are to rely on all the testing devices we can, beginning with the Bible and the Holy Spirit's guidance. How comforting and strengthening to know that "God is at work in you, both to will and to work for his good pleasure" (Phil. 2:13 RSV). In addition to the Word and the Spirit, there are at least four other testing devices.

A. *The conscience of the person being tested.* This inner computer stores information we have received from other resources about right and wrong. As we make decisions, our conscience either affirms or puts down the attitudes or actions we are about to take. Though the conscience that has been exposed to the darkness is not fully trustworthy (see Titus 1:15), when we have been taught the truth, the conscience will bear witness in the Holy Spirit (Rom. 9:1).

B. *The counsel of other Christians.* Believers are instructed to teach and admonish one another (Col. 3:16). No believer is to become our highest authority on truth, yet more experienced believers who show by their lives obedience to the Word should be sought for advice in these confusing issues.

C. *Common sense.* Titus 2:12 tells us that we are to "live soberly"—that is, we are to have a sound, healthy mind. Common sense is never to be accepted as complete sense, for God frequently leads us in ways that do not seem sensible. At the same time, we are to use our minds in the testing ground.

D. *Circumstances.* Let's say that from your relationships with your children and with children in the church you think you should be a school teacher. Yet your education has not equipped you to teach; you cannot obtain a teaching certificate. Your circumstances show you that you either have to go to school again or forget this vocational choice. Yet circumstances alone are never sufficient as a testing device.

These four aids together, however, plus the inspiration of God's Word may verify and clarify God's guidance.

III. We can reprove the unfruitful works of darkness.

To reprove means to rebuke or to silence so as to bring out conviction or confession of guilt. We may do this by our words but more significantly by our conduct. Some may become uncomfortable by what we say and do, but that is the way of God in reaching the hearts of those who are in darkness. The point is that God's guidance is not offered to enable us to live sheltered lives free from contact with people who are motivated by evil. Rather, God's guidance is offered to show us how to live and influence people in an evil world.

A minister's portrait given by John Bunyan has "his back to the world, his face toward heaven, and a Book in his hand." However, it would seem a bit more precise to say in the light of this text, "He has the Book in his mind, his eyes on Jesus, and his body in the world." In this manner we demonstrate the truth and call others to it.

Conclusion

Every person receiving God's guidance does so in the protection of the heavenly habitations. We discover God to be our refuge. Likewise, we discover that the church serves as a shelter from storms. But God's guidance must be tested in the world. This is where the light and the darkness meet. We may be frightened by the conflict, but all that God provides is more than enough as we walk in the light we have, as we test for the purpose of approving what is acceptable to God, and as we reprove the unfruitful works of darkness by our words and deeds.

SUNDAY EVENING, OCTOBER 24

Title: Jesus Makes the Difference

Text: "But now in Christ Jesus you who once were far off have been brought near in the blood of Christ" **(Eph. 2:13 RSV)**.

Scripture Reading: Ephesians 2:11–22

Introduction

Once a man sought to gain membership in a hunting club. The members rejected him because of his reputation for not obeying the rules of sportsmanship. One outstanding community leader, who was a member of the club, interceded on his behalf. He promised the club that he would take full responsibility for the applicant. The man was admitted on the character and strength of another man.

Paul reminded the Gentiles that they had once sought admission into the kingdom of heaven. The sole reason for their admission was the character and work of Jesus Christ. He made the difference.

I. Outside of Jesus Christ people are alienated (2:11–12).

A. *Paul reminded the Gentiles that they were alienated, regarded as outsiders, before they learned of Christ.* The Gentiles were inferior to the Jews in religious privileges. Their state was desperate and godless. Paul described their past state: "You were at that time separated from Christ, alienated from the commonwealth of Israel, and strangers to the covenants of promise, having no hope and without God in the world" (v. 12 RSV). Paul gave five definite indications that the Gentiles were outsiders.

1. "Separated from Christ."
2. "Alienated from the commonwealth of Israel."
3. "Strangers to the covenants of promise."
4. "Having no hope."
5. "Without God in the world."

B. *Outside of Jesus Christ people suffer great consequences.* Paul graphically portrayed the reality of alienation. Those who choose not to live life with God suffer from a life apart from God. This choice makes them strangers to the Lord.

The real outsiders in our age are the nonbelievers. There is no worse tragedy than being alienated from God. This alienation stems from a rebellious heart. Being a stranger does not mean that God arbitrarily cuts certain individuals off from himself. And it certainly does not mean that God is stubborn and will not admit sinners. Being a stranger simply means that simple human rebellion has separated a person from God in this life and in the life to come.

A picture shows a lonely boy looking in at a Christmas celebration. By the look on his face you can tell that he feels forlorn and wants to join in the festivities. If someone would notice him, go to the door, and invite him inside, he would no longer be a stranger. Someone, Jesus Christ, has stepped out and invited us to come inside.

II. Through Jesus Christ people are reconciled (2:13–18).

From the distressing description of what Gentiles had been, Paul turned to describe what had been done for them by Christ. Jesus came to outsiders and made it possible for them to become insiders.

A. *Christ did a marvelous work of reconciliation.* "But now in Christ Jesus you who once were far off have been brought near in the blood of Christ" (v. 13 RSV). At one time the Gentiles were separated from

Christ. Now they live in vital union with God. All of this has been accomplished for them "in the blood of Christ."

B. *Christ's reconciliation brings great benefits.* It brings peace. "For he is our peace, who has made us both one, and has broken down the dividing wall of hostility" (v. 14 RSV). Jesus made possible a harmonious relationship between God and humankind and between fellow human beings.

Christ's reconcilation brings access. "For through him we both have access in one Spirit to the Father" (v. 18 RSV). The new relation is pictured as an access or right of approach. Christians have the privilege of access to God as children do to a loving father.

III. In Jesus Christ people are insiders (2:19–22).

Receivers of Christ's reconciliation become insiders. Metaphorically speaking, strangers become citizens of God's country, children in God's family, and integral parts of a structure.

A. *Jesus gave the Gentiles a sense of belonging.* "So then you are no longer strangers and sojourners, but you are fellow citizens with the saints and members of the household of God, built upon the foundation of the apostles and prophets, Christ Jesus himself being the cornerstone" (vv. 19–20 RSV). Together with Jewish believers, Gentiles form the true Israel of God. They are the seed of Abraham. Jesus Christ is the focal point for both Jewish believers and Gentile believers—"Christ Jesus himself being the cornerstone."

B. *Believers can learn to be insiders.* Once individuals come into the kingdom of heaven, they need to learn the privileges and obligations of kingdom people. Several metaphors teach valuable lessons.

1. A political metaphor teaches that believers are citizens subject to municipal regulation.
2. A physiological metaphor teaches that believers are part of the body and take orders from the head, Jesus Christ.
3. An architectural metaphor teaches that a building is built on the foundation of Jesus Christ.

Conclusion

Do you want to be in the kingdom of God? You have to come through Jesus Christ. Apart from him you are an outsider. Open your life to him and become an insider. Jesus makes the difference.

WEDNESDAY EVENING, OCTOBER 27

Title: Parable of the Rich Fool

Text: "This night thy soul shall be required of thee" **(Luke 12:20).**

Scripture Reading: Luke 12:13–21

Introduction

There are many kinds of barns. There are tobacco barns, dairy barns, and livestock barns. In some cities, the place where they keep the city buses is referred to as the bus barn. The size and shape of a barn says a lot about its use, how much it is used, and the prosperity of the one using it. The condition or maintenance also speaks volumes about pride, investment, and purpose. In this parable barns become symbols of material things. Today we are going to look from three different approaches at barns that are no good.

I. Barns have no inherent eternal value.

    A. *Barns can be symbolic of God's blessings.*

        1. Proverbs 3:9–10 says, "Honour the LORD with thy substance, and with the firstfruits of all thine increase: so shall thy barns be filled with plenty."

        2. This passage refers to the contents of barns. God's blessings are indicated by full barns.

    B. *Barns can be symbolic of worldly security.* It is possible to use barns in a wrong way.

        1. The parable of the rich fool demonstrates this fact. The parable opens with a warning: "Take heed" (Luke 12:15). Worldly security cannot be trusted for long. Seeking pleasure based on materialism leads to destruction.

        2. Barns can become one's worst enemy. This is true when people make materialism their first priority and leave God out. Barns are of no value to people after death.

II. The soul is of more value than material things.

    A. *This is not to say that the whole of a person is not important.* Jesus spent much of his time during his earthly ministry ministering to physical needs. He healed the sick, gave sight to the blind, raised the dead, and so on. His main mission, however, was to save souls.

    B. *This is to say that the soul of a person is most important.*

        1. The soul is most important because it lives throughout eternity after the physical or material is long gone. The soul is the part of a person that lives with God.

        2. The soul is too important to neglect. The lesson of the parable of the rich fool is that if one neglects the soul to the point of physical death, there is no redemption.

III. The word "fool" in this parable refers to emptiness.

    A. *We play the fool if we presume on the time we have to live.* Life is uncertain. Death is certain. None of us knows when we will die, how we will die, or the circumstances surrounding our death.

B. *We play the fool if we leave God out of our life.*
C. *We play the fool if we do not avail ourselves of the best at the earliest possible moment.* The best is the acceptance of Jesus as our personal Savior. The earlier we become a Christian, the better the life we will have. The earlier we become a Christian, the surer our chances are of doing so. The best time anyone has of becoming a Christian is now.

Conclusion

What are you to do in light of this parable? Recognize that you are a sinner. Recognize Jesus as Savior. Ask him to come into your life and save you. Confess him openly and publicly right now.

SUNDAY MORNING, OCTOBER 31

Title: God's Light in Us Offers Guidance to the World

Text: "Ye are the light of the world. A city that is set on an hill cannot be hid. Neither do men light a candle, and put it under a bushel, but on a candlestick; and it giveth light unto all that are in the house. Let your light so shine before men, that they may see your good works, and glorify your Father which is in heaven" **(Matt. 5:14–16)**.

Scripture Reading: Luke 11:29–36

Hymns: "The Light of the World Is Jesus," Bliss
"Lift High the Cross," Kitchin; alt. Newbolt
Wonderful Words of Life," Bliss

Offertory Prayer: Heavenly Father, every good and perfect gift comes from you. We have plenty to eat, warm homes, enjoyable jobs, good health, loving families, and a caring church family. We thank you for every good and perfect gift you send our way. Help us to trust you and to practice being generous. Help us to give sacrificially, to give more than you require—so that we can meet the material and spiritual needs of others and so that you might receive praise and honor. In Jesus' name, amen.

Introduction

The glow of a cigarette on a dark night is visible three-fourths of a mile. The glare of a match can be seen for a mile. Light from a good flashlight is visible for one and one-half miles. Light from a 100-watt lamp can be seen for twelve and one-half miles. The headlights from your automobile are visible for twenty miles on a clear night.

Our Lord taught that Christian influence can light the whole world! Christian influence is described as preservation (salt of the earth) through demonstration (light of the world).

I. The Christian's light can light the world.

A. *When Jesus said, "Ye are the light of the world," he related the mission of the Christian to a familiar Palestinian object.* The houses in Palestine were very dark and had only one small circular window not more than eighteen inches across. Each home had a lamp that was no more than a sauceboat filled with oil with a floating wick. The lamp stood on a lampstand that was no more than a small roughly shaped wooden table. For safety's sake, the lamp was removed from its stand and put under an earthen bushel measure so that it might burn without risk when the family was away from the home.

B. *Light exposes darkness.* The primary duty of the lamp's light was to be seen. Thus our Lord indicates that the Christian is to love in such a way that others might see Christ in his or her life.

C. *As it shone through the small window and as its rays reached the rooms of the house, the lamp served as a guide.* The best guide to the better life is that of a Christian whose influence counts for Christ.

D. *As it shone through the small window, the light warned travelers of dangerous obstacles along the road.* The Christian's influence should serve as a warning sign for all to observe. His or her life should say, "Warning! Walk this way!"

E. *An elderly blind man was seen carrying a lantern on a dark night.* "Since you can't see, why are you carrying a lantern?" asked an interested friend. "I carry a lantern at night," he said, "so that others won't stumble over me."

II. Only the Christian can be the light of the world.

The "Ye" is in the emphatic position. Our Lord is saying, "Ye and ye alone" are the light of the world. No one else can take the place of the Christian in this world, which is dark with sin.

A. *While Jesus was on earth, he was the Light of the World (John 8:12; 9:4–5; 12:35–36).*

B. *Since Christ left the earth, Christians have been given the responsibility of demonstrating him to the world (Phil. 2:15).*

C. *The radiance of the Christian's life depends on how close he is to Jesus Christ (2 Cor. 4:6–7).*

III. The Christian's light cannot be hidden.

A. *Like "a city set on a hill," the Christian's influence cannot be hidden.* A city with shining lights can be seen from all sides on a dark night.

B. *Not all lights have the same wattage.* Some are only 15 watts and others are 500 or even 1,000. God has use for even a dim bulb on a dark night. Regardless of how dimly it shines, the light of a Christian's influence is being observed by someone.

C. *"Bury my influence with me"* was the request of a Christian whose light had not shone very brightly for Christ. When he came to die, he was filled with regret that he had done so little for Christ. But Jesus taught that one's influence cannot be buried with him.

IV. There is a place for every Christian's light.

A. *The Christian is not fired up to fizzle.* Lights are lit for the purpose of shining. The bushel was placed over the lamp only on rare occasions. The lamp was never kindled for the purpose of being covered.

B. *There is a place for every light.* Just as each light in the Palestinian houses sat on its own particular table so that it would shine through the small window and to the rooms of the house, each Christian has a particular place from which he or she is to shine.

C. *Without the elevation of the lamp, the light is wasted.* A lighthouse at Charleston, South Carolina, boasts of twenty million candlepower and is visible for twenty miles. But the secret to its success is the 140-foot structure on which it sets. One must find the will of God for one's life and shine from it to the best of his or her ability.

People walking in darkness need the light of Christians in all sectors of life to guide them to Christ. Thus each believer must bear the responsibility of keeping his or her lamp shining brightly for Christ at all times.

Conclusion

Light makes no noise. Lighthouses sound no drums. They merely shine. The influence of Christians causes others to see Christ in them. But for what purpose? Surely not for their own glory! Christians influence the world toward Christ for the glory of God. With Paul, the Christian asserts, "I am crucified with Christ: nevertheless I live; yet not I, but Christ liveth in me" (Gal. 2:20).

SUNDAY EVENING, OCTOBER 31

Title: A Picture of the Church

Text: "[You are] built upon the foundation of the apostles and prophets, Christ Jesus himself being the cornerstone, in whom the whole structure is joined together and grows into a holy temple in the Lord" (**Eph. 2:20–21 RSV**).

Scripture Reading: Ephesians 2:19–22

Introduction

One minister said, "In nineteen years of pastoral service, I have served six different congregations. For Christmas presents, my wife has started giving me beautifully framed pictures of the buildings that housed these separate congregations. When I look at these pictures, I remember the people and my varied experiences with the congregations."

Paul had a picture of the church. In fact, he used many metaphors to describe the people of God. One of his favorite images of the church was that of "the household of God." The architectural metaphor is an apt metaphor for the people of God. A similar picture can be found in 1 Peter 2:4–8.

Lesslie Newbigin, in his book *The Household of God*, popularized the architectural metaphor of the church. This metaphor suggests many interesting insights about the church.

I. The church rests on a secure foundation.

A. *The foundation is identified.* The cornerstone for the building is identified as Jesus Christ: ". . . built upon the foundation of the apostles and prophets, Christ Jesus himself being the cornerstone" (Eph. 2:20 RSV). The cornerstone is the primary foundation stone at the angle of a structure by which the architect fixes a standard for the bearings of the work. This stone at the base of a building is essential to the integrity of the structure.

   No one can fit into the picture of the church without Jesus Christ. He supports and holds together both the foundation and the walls. It is faith in him that gives every believer a place in the building. It is Christ who gives the structure its unity and strength.

B. *The foundation supports the entire building.* Every part of the building rests on the same foundation. No one can belong to the church without resting on Christ. In their solidarity they share one common theme: "Jesus Christ is Lord."

II. The church demonstrates a harmonious design.

A. *Various parts go into the making of a building.* The construction of a building requires all types of building material, such as concrete, steel, wood, and glass among others. This diversity of material does not call attention to any one of the particular materials. It presents the idea of unity.

B. *Various people go into the making of a church.* The church has a variety of members. Many personality types, cultural backgrounds, educational levels, and other differences comprise the church. The diversity does not create disunity. Instead, unity emerges from the diversity. "For as the body is one, and hath many members, and all the members of that one body, being many, are one body: so also is Christ. For by one Spirit are we all baptized into one body, whether we be Jews or Gentiles, whether we be bond or free; and have been all made to drink into one Spirit" (1 Cor. 12:12–13).

III. The church houses a unique occupant.

A. *Christians ought to be delighted over the Holy Spirit's occupancy.* No building is ever constructed for the sake of being empty. Rather, buildings are constructed to have occupancy. The church has been built to house the Holy Spirit. It has always been God's intention to dwell among his people. God inhabits the lives of believers through his Spirit, and nothing ought to bring them greater delight. Some houses have signs that say, "The Joneses live here." The church should evidence the fact that the Holy Spirit lives here.

B. *Christians ought to be careful about the Holy Spirit's occupancy.* Because the Holy Spirit lives in believers, they need to exercise great care.
1. They should allow the Spirit to control their lifestyle (Eph. 5:18).
2. They should not defile the dwelling place of God (1 Cor. 6:19).
3. They should not do anything to offend the Spirit (1 Thess. 4:19).
   Having God's Holy Spirit within us requires us to take great care in living.

IV. The church blesses the entire world.

A. *Buildings are constructed to help people.* Their purpose may be protection from the weather, a storage place for goods, or a number of other things. God constructs the church to help people. The habitation of God becomes a source of blessing and rejoicing to the world.

B. *The church blesses the world.* No building can compare with people redeemed by the blood of Christ. The church is made of humble people who walk with God, and the world rejoices to see the beauty of their faith and hope.

Conclusion

Look at the church as "the household of God." As you look, make sure you are part of that building. Put your life on the cornerstone, Jesus Christ. He will make you part of the building so you can glorify him.

NOVEMBER

■ **Sunday Mornings**

The biblical teaching of stewardship involves more than the practice of tithing faithfully and bringing generous offerings. "Stewardship Includes Everything" is the suggested theme for the Sunday morning messages.

■ **Sunday Evenings**

Continue the series from Ephesians titled "Making a New World."

■ **Wednesday Evenings**

Continue the series "The Parables of Jesus Continue to Speak."

WEDNESDAY EVENING, NOVEMBER 3

Title: Parable of the Barren Fig Tree

Text: "If it bear fruit, well: and if not, then after that thou shalt cut it down" **(Luke 13:9)**.

Scripture Reading: Luke 13:6–9

Introduction

Lessons abound in this parable. We must not dwell on what we can't understand to the extent that we miss what is so obvious. We need to approach this parable with an honest mind and a prayerful heart. We will look at four lessons this parable teaches us.

I. The necessity of repentance.

   A. *Luke introduces the parable (vv. 1–5).* Twice in the five verses, Jesus tells his listeners that they must repent or perish.
   B. *The parable supports the introduction (vv. 6–9).*
      1. Those who fail to bear fruit must repent.
      2. The need for repentance applies to many areas of life. Those who are lost in sin must repent in order to be saved. Christians who are unfaithful must repent because they are unproductive. The church—Christians collectively—must bear fruit. If the church fails in this area, its members must repent and strive to produce fruit for God's kingdom.

II. Special opportunity (13:6).

   A. *We are judged according to our own opportunity.* No one is held responsible by God for someone else's opportunities. Those who are lost have

348

an opportunity now. If they don't seize it, they may live to regret it. A church may have an opportunity at a given time, but if the opportunity is not seized, it may never be offered again.

B. *Opportunities may not always be available.* For one thing, death will destroy opportunity. Once death overtakes those who are lost, they never have another opportunity to be saved. This is equally true of a Christian and service.

III. Patience (13:8).

A. *The parable of the barren fig tree is a picture of the Lord at work.* He is portrayed as the mediator between God and humankind. He makes intercession for us.

B. *The parable is also a picture of God the Father waiting patiently.* He goes the so-called second mile. He gives another chance. He waits and waits.

IV. The necessity of action (13:9).

A. *The words "Let it alone this year" imply limitation (v. 8).* "This year," to those who are lost, may be the worship service in which they are sitting. It may be a given invitation. "This year," to the fruit-bearing or non-fruit-bearing Christian, may be a week, a year, or another given period of time.

B. *The words "then after that" imply that judgment and destruction come quickly (v. 9).* The listeners are urged not to procrastinate or postpone. The time for them to act is now. The point is to repent.

Conclusion

Second Corinthians 6:12 says, "Behold, now is the accepted time; behold, now is the day of salvation." It is my hope, my prayer, and my plea, that each of you will avail yourself of the opportunity that is presented right now.

SUNDAY MORNING, NOVEMBER 7

Title: God's Commitment Day

Text: "But you are a chosen race, a royal priesthood, a holy nation, God's own people, that you may declare the wonderful deeds of him who called you out of darkness into his marvelous light" (**1 Peter 2:9 RSV**).

Scripture Reading: 1 Peter 2:1–10

Hymns: "Great Is Thy Faithfulness," Chisholm
"Day by Day," Sandell-Berg
"Guide Me, Oh Thou Great Jehovah," Williams

Offertory Prayer: Long ago, Lord, while we were yet in our sin, you came to us offering forgiveness and new life. When your Son, our Savior, Jesus Christ, committed himself to die for us rather than to seek the counterfeit pleasure of a disobedient life, he not only brought salvation to us, but he also set, for all time, the standard for committed obedience to you. Grant that we, too, may be faithful. In Jesus' name we pray. Amen.

Introduction

Many churches have an annual commitment day. The only reason, however, that we can dare ask our people to make a commitment of their lives to God is because God has already made a commitment to us. His commitment day was marked by weeping and sorrow, darkness and angry curses. In the midst of all the pain of a Roman crucifixion, God committed himself to us.

Our text was directed to a people who had been scattered by the persecution of the Roman government. The writer, Peter, gave encouragement and direction to the believers who were living in exile (see 1 Peter 1:1, 6, 17; 2:11; 4:12–19). These early Christians were living in fear for their lives. They needed to know that God had made a commitment to them.

I. God has committed himself to his people.

A. *These were people who belonged to God.* In the midst of the terror and loneliness of exile, it must have been a great encouragement to know they were "God's own people"—they belonged to him. The King James Version translates this phrase "a peculiar people" (1 Peter 2:9). The old Latin word *peculium* referred to property. So the proper translation is not that they were an odd people but that they were people who were God's property.

A small boy was found on a busy city street, dirty and obviously lost. A kind man stopped to see if he could help. When he asked the little boy who he belonged to, the little boy looked up with defiance and angry hurt and replied, "I ain't nobody's nothing!"

Christians may know many kinds of pain, but they never have to experience the pain of believing they are "nobody's nothing." They are God's peculiar people, his property. They belong to him.

B. *Some people do not belong to God.* To say, "You are God's people," is to remind us that though some are God's people, others do not belong to him. That does not mean that they were not created by God or that he does not love them. It simply means that some are not willing to come to him. God's love is not exclusive in regard to race, social status, or nationality—nothing that we cannot change keeps us from Jesus Christ—but some people are not willing to accept his love. People may go to hell unsaved, but they can never go unloved. We can all be God's people. But we must be willing to respond to him.

II. God has committed *himself* to his people.

God did not send a substitute to do what he had to do himself. If he had remained only God, he could not have touched us. If he had been only man, he could not have saved us. No substitute could take his place.

Nor did God send an angel to save his people. These messengers of God move at his will to speak urgent words to his people, but they could not die for the redemption of humankind (cf. 1 Peter 1:12).

A president can send ambassadors to plead the cause of his country. Though they often can be highly effective, if the president himself chooses to go, the whole world stands at attention. Every romantic knows the story of Miles Standish's failure to win the hand of Priscilla. He sent John Alden to plead for the beautiful woman's hand in marriage. It is reported that she said, "Speak for yourself, John." She gave her love to the one who came himself.

Is it any wonder, then, that when the God who gave himself asks for our commitment, he asks not for substitutes for ourselves but for our very selves?

III. God has committed himself to his people so they may declare.

Verse 9 clearly says that God has chosen us that we may declare the strong, virtuous, or wonderful deeds of our Savior God. God's action always has a purpose. He does not save us simply to count us. He calls us to be his people that we may share aloud the glory of his deeds done on our behalf and the radiance of the light that has penetrated our darkness.

A. *We are to declare God's wonderful deeds (v. 9).* The deeds we praise are God's creation of the world and all that is therein; the deliverance of his people from bondage in Egypt; the establishment of the people from whom would come the light to the Gentiles; the coming of Jesus, God's Son, our Savior, born to save his people from their sins; the death and resurrection of Jesus of Nazareth, who is our hope of eternal life; the building of a new people, the church "a chosen race, a royal priesthood, a holy nation, God's own people"; and the anticipation of the final act when Christ will return to call his people to the fulfillment of the kingdom of God.

When the power of those mighty deeds surges through our hearts, we are able to witness to a cynical world with lips and lives that are eager expressions of the joy and victory that have claimed us in Jesus Christ. He has given us bold deeds to declare boldly.

B. *We are to declare the radiance of God's marvelous light (v. 9).* In the creation of the world, the darkness was shattered first by his words "Let there be light." Only later came the light from the sun, the moon, and the stars. The biblical writers have a deep appreciation for the glory of the light that shines in our darkness (Gen. 1:3; Ps. 27:1; Isa. 42:6; 60:3; Matt. 5:14–16; Luke 1:79; 2:32; John 1:4–8; 8:12; Acts 26:18; 2 Cor. 4:6; Eph. 5:8–14; 1 John 1:5–7; Rev. 21:23–25; 22:5).

In the light of God's presence, we are not to be filled with pride or prejudice, but with humility and amazement. No one can declare the glory of God's deeds or the radiance of his light if he or she is filled with the dark prejudice that cuts people off from God's grace. Prejudice is a subtle pride that makes us draw circles around our own religious, racial, or economic groups. We must never yield to its easy call to speak only to those who are like us. God is not willing that any should perish, but that all should come to repentance (2 Peter 3:9). His commitment to us at Calvary is that all should believe. And to all who believe he has given power to become the children of God (John 1:12).

Conclusion

Because God has committed himself fully to you, he can call you to commit your whole life to him—your tithes, abilities, and time. He has held nothing back. He gave himself wholly that you might be his people. He now calls you to commit yourself to declare his wonderful deeds and marvelous light to a world in darkness. He has come that you might go; he has loved you that you might love; he has given that you might give. Our commitment day, therefore, is both our privilege and our responsibility. The one question that remains is: Will we permit God's commitment to shape the nature of our commitment?

SUNDAY EVENING, NOVEMBER 7

Title: A Privileged People

Text: "When you read this you can perceive my insight into the mystery of Christ, which was not made known to the sons of men in other generations as it has now been revealed to his holy apostles and prophets by the Spirit" **(Eph. 3:4–5 RSV).**

Scripture Reading: Ephesians 3:1–13

Introduction

Booker T. Washington founded Tuskegee Institute in Alabama. He came out of a life of slavery and lived to see an abandoned stable and henhouse grow to a million-dollar, world-renowned educational center. Washington traveled extensively, soliciting money needed to build, equip, and staff his college for black teachers. In his autobiography Washington made some interesting observations. He said that people never begrudged his solicitations. They enjoyed giving away their money for such a worthwhile cause. One benefactor said, "Don't thank me, Mr. Washington. I am grateful to you for giving me the opportunity to help a good cause. It is a privilege to have a share in it" (Booker T. Washington, *Up from Slavery* [New York: Doubleday, Bantam, 1956], 128–29).

Though Paul did not use the word *privilege*, this was his prominent thought in Ephesians 3:1–13. He did not describe the church with the words of duty, obligation, responsibility, or other authoritative words. He thought of Christians as extremely privileged people. Believers need to recover a sense of privilege in being Christians.

I. Believers have a great knowledge.

A. *Knowing something that others don't know is a privilege.* The knowledge believers have centers around the significant word *mysterion*, which is translated "mystery." Paul said, "The mystery was made known to me by revelation, as I have written briefly" (Eph. 3:3 RSV). This does not mean something that cannot be known or something difficult to understand. It means something once hidden and now revealed, something graciously communicated by God.

Christians know God's secret plan for his whole creation. Nobody knew the plan until God unveiled a blueprint in the person and ministry of Jesus Christ. Whenever somebody discovers God's plan, it is a marvelous privilege.

B. *Knowing God's great plan is a responsibility.* God revealed this plan to people so that they might share it. To know the plan is not all that God desires. He wants those who know his plan to share it. We can liken this to the responsibility of cancer researchers. Great pressure rests on them to find a cure for cancer, and once they discover the cure, it will be their responsibility to share it.

II. Believers have a unique experience.

A. *The experience with Christ is personal.* Paul often spoke of his encounter with the Lord on the Damascus road. Paul had the unique opportunity of seeing the risen Lord. He knew the gospel both from factual knowledge and from his personal experience. One of the great privileges of believers is to have a personal experience with Jesus Christ.

B. *The experience with Christ is life-changing.* Paul called himself "the very least of all the saints" (Eph. 3:8 RSV). He recalled how he sought to persecute the church. After his encounter with the Lord, he gave his life for the building of the church.

An experience with Jesus Christ is a life-changing event that offers the privilege of turning a person's life around.

III. Believers have a mighty entrustment.

A. *Believers are entrusted with the gospel.* Paul believed that God's revelation and his experiences had been given for his sake and, even more, for the benefit of others. Paul called himself a steward (*oikonomia*), for God had given him the gospel and had told him to share it with the

353

Gentiles. Being entrusted with the gospel is a mighty obligation. We must handle it carefully and diligently.

B. *Believers are entrusted with the spiritual enlightenment of others.* "And to make all men see what is the plan of the mystery hidden for ages in God who created all things" (Eph. 3:9 RSV). Paul was entrusted with the responsibility of letting Gentiles know that the gospel is available to everyone.

Believers must not hoard the gospel; it is for the entire world. The mission to share the gospel is universal in scope.

IV. Believers have a part in Christ's suffering.

A. *Suffering is part of sharing the gospel with the world.* The most priceless enterprises of humankind have been secured by peril, toil, and pain. Paul suffered greatly to get the gospel to Asia Minor, Macedonia, and Rome. The privilege of sharing the gospel with the world will inevitably mean hardship.

B. *Suffering is a glory to believers.* "But now in Christ Jesus you who once were far off have been brought near in the blood of Christ" (Eph. 2:13 RSV). Paul's sufferings were for the benefit of others.

Conclusion

Being a Christian is a privilege. Have you considered your privileges? You can have Christ and be part of a privileged people.

WEDNESDAY EVENING, NOVEMBER 10

Title: Parable of the Leaven

Text: "To what shall I compare the kingdom of God?" (**Luke 13:20 RSV**).

Scripture Reading: Luke 13:20–22

Introduction

The parable of the leaven is a short parable with a single meaning. The Lord gave it to teach a lesson, and as Christians we should learn this lesson. To understand the parable, a discussion of what leaven is and how the parable applies to leaven is necessary.

I. The meaning of leaven.

A. *Leaven is any substance used as a ferment in dough or in a liquid.* Leaven is any material such as yeast or baking powder that lightens dough or batter in baking.

B. *Although leaven may be small in quantity, yet by its influence it thoroughly pervades a thing.* Leaven may be used in a good sense, as in the parable, or in a bad sense, as in the proverb "A little leaven leaveneth the whole lump."

C. *The verb* leaven *means to boil or seethe.* This could result in pernicious fermentation.

II. The uses of leaven in the Bible.

A. *Most often leaven is used in a negative sense.* Here are some scriptural examples.
   1. "Then Jesus said unto them, Take heed and beware of the leaven of the Pharisees and of the Sadducees" (Matt. 16:6).
   2. "Cleanse out the old leaven that you may be a new lump, as you really are unleavened" (1 Cor. 5:7 RSV).
B. *Sometimes leaven is used in a good sense.* This is found in the text of the parable of the leaven.

III. The meaning of the parable (Luke 13:20–22).

A. *The basic teaching is the gradual growth of the kingdom.* Jesus was aware that great things grow from small beginnings. This is contrary to the popular idea of a glorious, mighty empire appearing suddenly full grown. Leaven works little by little.
B. *A basic comparison is found in the parable.* Good is compared with bad in other places in the Bible. Leaven often indicates puffing up or disturbing, souring properties. In this text, however, leaven is thought of as penetrative and energetic warmth.
C. *The major teaching is the prophecy of the diffusion of the gospel.* We are to understand that the leaven is the Word of the kingdom. The highest sense of the Word is the Lord Jesus himself. This is the new power brought into the world from above, not a philosophy, but a revelation. This power works from the inside out. It begins in the inner, spiritual being but eventually brings about a mighty change.

Conclusion

Each of us needs to be aware of the power of the gospel in our world. We need to keep on proclaiming it and trusting it to bring about the divine result.

SUNDAY MORNING, NOVEMBER 14

Title: "We Decided to Quit"

Text: "Give, and it will be given to you; good measure, pressed down, shaken together, running over, will be put into your lap. For the measure you give will be the measure you get back" (**Luke 6:38 RSV**).

Scripture Reading: Matthew 6:19–24

Hymns: "Joyful, Joyful, We Adore Thee," Van Dyke
"I Gave My Life for Thee," Havergal
"Lead on, O King Eternal," Shurtleff

Offertory Prayer: Out of your bounty, O Lord, you have showered us with blessings too numerous to count. We thank you, loving Father, for days in which to live, for family and friends, and for skilled protectors of our lives in medicine, the military, law enforcement, and fire prevention. We thank you also for life beyond the ordinary made possible through our Lord Jesus Christ who came to give us life abundant and eternal. In the life-giving name of Jesus we pray. Amen.

Introduction

The people in the church who have not grown up in it are especially important. The church loses its ability to proclaim and live the gospel in ways that are believable and compelling when the only people in the church are people who have always been there.

Those of you who are new, however, may be confused by our talk about money. You have heard that salvation is free. Then all of a sudden the minister begins talking about tithes—10 percent of your salary, offerings beyond that—and even saying that people who don't tithe are robbing God!

It's interesting to see the astonishment on the faces of people who have never heard of tithing when they learn that some people give 10 percent of their income to the Lord. A man told of a new friend who had never been in church before but who began coming to his church. The friend became an active Christian. After a while the new Christian asked, "What are the dues in our church?"

The longtime church member smiled—he had never heard of tithes and offerings being called "dues." He replied, "There are no 'dues,' but we encourage all our people to give a tithe, or a tenth, of their income to the church."

"Before or after taxes?" the new Christian asked. "Well, I give mine before taxes," the church member answered.

"Man, I just want to give something!" responded the new Christian. "I didn't intend to make the church independently wealthy!"

This, of course, leads to a question.

I. Is the tithe a biblical principle?

Fact 1: The tithe started before the law, as did marriage and prayer (Gen. 28:20–22). Fact 2: The tithe belongs to God (Lev. 27:30; Mal. 3:8–10). Fact 3: Christians are not saved because they tithe, nor are they abandoned by God if they do not tithe. Fact 4: Tithing is not the only responsibility of Christians (Matt. 23:23). Justice, mercy, and faith are more crucial, but tithing is affirmed as being one act that we should not leave undone.

Ann Landers received a letter from a woman expressing what many people must feel when first approached by the subject of money and giving in a Christian context.

Dear Ann,

About a year ago, we joined a church and enjoyed the friendship of the people we met. . . .

Shortly after joining we started to receive the church bulletin. A few weeks ago, smack in the middle of page 1, was a stinging assault on those who do not tithe the full 10 percent. That article was promptly followed by another strong rebuke, same subject.

What if we cannot tithe 10 percent? Where does it say 10 percent in the Bible? And does it mean 10 percent of one's gross or one's net income?

Is it all right to tithe what you can and increase it when you are able? Two weeks ago we decided to quit going to church.

Bugged in Boise
(*Fort Worth Star Telegram*, October 19, 1978, 3D)

Perhaps you identify with that woman's letter. Maybe you're ready to quit because you don't intend to give like that. You don't understand why so much is needed. You don't really believe God could expect that much. You can't imagine how you would pay for your house, cars, utilities, groceries, clothes, and education, and still tithe. Is there a better way than to quit? Our text and Ann Landers's reply point to the answer.

II. The principle of growth.

Ann Landers replied to the woman's letter by saying, "If you cannot tithe 10 percent of your gross or net, give what you can and don't feel guilty. To stop attending church for this reason is a perfect example of throwing out the baby with the bath water" (ibid.).

Our text says that God will bless us as we give. Surely a part of what that means is that as we give, he blesses us so that we grow in our ability to believe that we can give yet more. This is a valid principle for Christians. God starts with us where we are. If we will begin to give of our income on a percentage basis, we can raise the percentage monthly or quarterly or annually until we are giving what we believe we ought to give. The strengths to this approach are threefold. First, we give something rather than postpone giving anything because we cannot give the full amount. Second, we have a plan. Third, we can feel relieved because we have begun to be obedient to God's will.

The weakness to the preceding approach, however, is that God really does ask for a tenth—that is what the word *tithe* means. The widow was praised not because she had given a small gift but because she gave all she had. She gave 100 percent. A minister cannot excuse someone from giving God's required minimum. A minister does not have the right to cheat you of blessings God wants you to have if you would, in faith, begin to do what you know will require God's help if it is to be done. As your income increases—and some people are entrusted with great amounts—you will find that 10 percent is far too little to give. One of the happiest moments of your life will come when you write a check for God's work that simply astounds you because you never thought you could give so much and feel so good about it!

A clear issue before us is how we talk about money in the church. Some people say, "Why not let people know what their fair share is and assess them their dues regularly? Everyone knows the church has to have some money. I'll give my part. Send me a bill, and we can quit talking about money so much." But we can't do it that way. Here's one reason why we can't.

III. The ministry principle is at the heart of a church budget.

Our church shares responsibility for hospitals, children's homes, universities, and seminaries. There are missionaries in our land and around the world who seek to win people to Jesus Christ, help new Christians build churches, minister to the hungry and the sick, and teach the unlearned. They depend on us.

A church budget should never be planned as an instrument to see how little people will be asked to give. Rather, it should be planned prayerfully in answer to the question "What are the needs that God has called us to meet?" We have the opportunity to impact our community and touch individual lives in a saving way. Teenagers, children, and babies need to know that the church loves them in the name of Jesus, and adults need spiritual direction. We must have buildings to provide space for ministering to others. And, of course, the church must be involved in missionary outreach to the whole world.

But there is yet another reason we talk about tithing and giving sacrificial offerings. Here we are at the heart of our text.

IV. The gift principle is the foundation of the church budget.

Jesus said, "Give, and it will be given to you" (Luke 6:38 RSV). Giving allows our souls to be stirred up so that God can replace ideas we have grown accustomed to with fresh blessings that become a new joy to us. Christian growth is directly related to how we learn to handle material possessions. Only a brief look at Matthew 25:14–30 will convince us that how Christians handle their material possessions is a significant measure of what will be entrusted to them in the future.

Matthew 6:21 reminds us that where our treasure is, there our hearts will be also. If we do not invest the tithe in the Lord's work, our hearts will never be invested there either. The first money that comes out of your budget—the basic building block around which you build your budget—ought to be the money God asks of you for supporting the spread of the gospel. Notice that one of the blessings you receive by such giving is that you become more and more a growing, considerate, and sensitive person.

The gift principle is illustrated by a man who had been a generous contributor to Christian causes during a time of plenty in his life. Then he lost everything in a business recession. He was asked if he regretted having given away so much money. His reply was, "No, I cannot regret what I've given, for what I spent I used, what I kept I lost. It was only what I gave that I still have." Every pastor knows men and women with that spirit. And the interesting thing is that although many people who received because of the man's generosity were helped, the person most helped was the man who had learned the meaning of life and the purpose of his possessions. In a time of awful confusion, he knew what was important. In a time of deep distress, he felt no betrayal, for he had done the right thing. In a time of great loss, he was secure, for he knew where his security was really held.

Conclusion

We can decide to quit or we can decide to give and grow. What will it be for you?

SUNDAY EVENING, NOVEMBER 14

Title: The People in Your Church

Text: "That he would grant you, according to the riches of his glory, to be strengthened with might by his Spirit in the inner man; that Christ may dwell in your hearts by faith; that ye, being rooted and grounded in love, may be able to comprehend with all saints what is the breadth, and the length, and depth, and height" **(Eph. 3:16–18).**

Scripture Reading: Ephesians 3:14–21

Introduction

In Ephesians 3:14–19 Paul prayed that the churches would have a distinctive kind of people: indwelt people, broad-minded people, and godly people. Let us consider these qualities and strive to be churches with these traits.

I. The church needs indwelt people.

A. *Christ has a dwelling place in the inner self of people.* "That Christ may dwell in your hearts by faith; that ye, being rooted and grounded in love" (v. 17). This denotes a permanent residency, an abiding presence. Paul prayed that Christ may possess the entire being, purifying the affections, enlightening the understanding, and controlling the will.

   The condition for the indwelling Christ is faith on the part of the believer. Christ is willing and ready to enter in and become the abiding guest.

B. *Christ gives superstrength to believers.* "That he would grant you, according to the riches of his glory, to be strengthened with might by his Spirit in the inner man" (v. 16). Followers of Christ can be more than ordinary people. They can have the powerful resources that are beyond the merely physical element of life. This power comes through the dynamic operation of God's Spirit. He alone can make people strong.

The church desperately needs indwelt people. Only God can give the strength necessary to accomplish the Lord's divine mission.

II. The church needs broad-minded people.

A. *Too often churches are full of narrow-minded people.* Paul prayed for broad-minded congregations. He did not want believers to think of the church in provincial terms. The church has often had a limited vision for the gospel and has restricted God's love and concern to a limited number.

B. *The church needs to comprehend God's world-wide program.* "That ye . . . may be able to comprehend with all saints what is the breadth, and length, and depth, and height; and to know the love of Christ, which passeth knowledge, that ye might be filled with all the fulness of God" (vv. 18–19). Paul wanted the believers to learn that God's love reached to all the peoples of the earth.

God's love is limitless, and an effective church is one filled with people of limitless love.

III. The church needs godly people.

A. *Christ can make a transformation in life.* "That ye might be filled with all the fulness of God" (v. 19). Paul wanted the church to be the tabernacle of God. "The fulness of God" means the sum of God's characteristics. People can be increasingly filled with a godly character. As Christ dwells in hearts by faith, God's character can be seen in the lives of believers.

B. *Christ can make an impression on a secular world.* God living in human beings gives the world a model of the authentic Christian life. The world longs to see God; therefore they will be attracted to people who are filled with "the fulness of God."

Conclusion

Paul's prayer gives insight as to what kind of people believers should be. He desired these kind of people in the church so that God's mission would be accomplished.

WEDNESDAY EVENING, NOVEMBER 17

Title: Parable of the Great Supper

Text: "Come; for all things are now ready" (**Luke 14:17**).

Scripture Reading: Luke 14:15–24

Introduction

What is your favorite food? How do you like it prepared? What kind of surroundings do you prefer as you eat your favorite food, and who do you want with you in order to enjoy it the most? The point of this parable is that God has prepared the very best for each person. The man who prepared the supper is representative of God. The supper is the provision God has made for our salvation. We will discuss this parable under two headings.

I. The invitation.

A. *In describing the invitation, Jesus uses what is sometimes called the journalistic approach.* He answers six pertinent questions.

   1. What? The invitation is from God to all people everywhere. He wants everyone to accept his offer of salvation and deliverance from sin.

   2. Who? The gospel is for everyone. The gospel message is universal. All are invited—the Jew and the Gentile, the rich and the poor, the city dweller and the country dweller, the businessperson and the field laborer.

   3. Why? People need the Lord. They are lost in sin, and they need a Savior. The only way to be saved is to accept Jesus' invitation.

   4. When? The time is now. The words "ready" (v. 17), "quickly" (v. 21), and "compel" (v. 23) each indicate *now*. The master of the house meant business.

   5. Where? Jesus will save you wherever you are and under any circumstances.

   6. How? You must accept the invitation by faith. You must believe that Jesus died to pay for your sins and that he rose on the third day, triumphing over sin and death.

B. *In Jesus' invitation, we can discern some great truths.*

   1. We are not saved by our own efforts. We are saved by simply accepting God's invitation. If we fail to respond in faith, however, we are lost for eternity by our own choosing. God's invitation is extended to everyone.

   2. We are warned of the danger of missing God's blessings. If we do not accept his invitation, we cannot possibly receive his blessings.

II. The excuses.

A. *Notice that these are excuses and not reasons.* There is a clear indication here that the prospective guests did not want to accept the invitation. The parable seems to imply that they had tentatively accepted the master's invitation; they had not previously declined. This shows a lack of consideration for the master's preparations.

B. *Notice that the excuses are ridiculous.* Examine a field at night? Can you imagine someone purchasing something as valuable as a piece of land without inspecting it first? This is an absurd excuse and certainly not a reason. The other excuses are equally ridiculous.

C. *The excuses are transparently false.* Anyone who hears or reads about such alibis can see clearly that the person did not want to attend.

D. *The refusal to go provoked God's wrath (v. 21).* This wrath is righteous damnation. You cannot receive blessings if you do not accept the invitation. The damnation that results from failing to respond to God's invitation is eternal separation from him.

Conclusion

God's invitation is to each of you. If you have not received Jesus Christ as Lord and Savior of your life, I pray that you would accept his invitation right now.

SUNDAY MORNING, NOVEMBER 21

Title: The Secret of Thanksgiving

Text: "O give thanks to the LORD, for he is good; for his steadfast love endures forever!" **(Ps. 107:1 RSV)**.

Scripture Reading: Psalm 107:1–9; Philippians 4:4–13

Hymns: "We Gather Together," anonymous Dutch hymn
"Now Thank We All Our God," Rinkart
"Come, Ye Thankful People, Come," Alford

Offertory Prayer: It is right to give thanks to you, O God. Even those who come today with heavy hearts can rejoice in the knowledge of your love for them and for your presence with them. We lift our voices in happy thanksgiving, for you have blessed us in so many ways. We thank you for giving us an appetite for your Word and a thirst for the living waters of eternal life. We pray in the name of Jesus Christ, who not only spoke his love but showed it as well. Amen.

Introduction

The Psalms have been for faithful Christians the source of song and praise and, along with the Lord's Prayer, the pattern for our most earnest and joyful prayers. Dietrich Bonhoeffer learned much about prayer in his courageous struggle against the Nazis in Germany. He insisted that Christians cannot really learn to pray unless they come to the Psalms. He considered it a dangerous error "to think that the heart can pray by itself. For then we confuse wishes, hopes, sighs, laments, rejoicings—all of which the heart can do by itself—with prayer. And we confuse earth and heaven, man and God. Prayer does not mean simply to pour out one's heart. It means rather to find the way to God and speak with him, whether the heart is full or empty" (Dietrich Bonhoeffer, *Psalms: The Prayer Book of the Bible* [Minneapolis: Augsburg Fortress, 1974], 9).

The Psalms are full of the range of human emotions—all offered to God in prayer. In the psalm before us, the prayer is one of joyous thanksgiving to the Lord. In this text we will discover the secret of thanksgiving.

The first secret of thanksgiving is that we are able to do the following:

I. Celebrate the goodness of God (107:1).

A. *God's goodness is illustrated in different ways throughout the psalm.* He "delivered them from their distress" (v. 6 RSV). He satisfied the thirsty and filled the hungry with good things (v. 9). "He brought them out of darkness and gloom, and broke their bonds asunder" (v. 14 RSV). He healed the sick and delivered his people from destruction (v. 20). When sailors in bitter distress, staggering like drunken men on ships buffeted by mighty storms, cried out to the Lord, "he made the storm be still, and the waves of the sea were hushed" (v. 29 RSV). "He raises up the needy out of affliction" (v. 41 RSV).

B. *The people of God are called to be thankful to a God who is good.* The joy of thanksgiving to a good God is too much for a solo voice. It requires choirs of people. So this psalm is sung as well as prayed by the congregation. The Lord is good. Let his people praise his name.

The second secret to thanksgiving is to do the following:

II. Focus on the main issues of life (107:4, 10, 17, 23–27).

A. *The psalmist painted four pictures of people who have been forced to consider the main issue in life.* First, there are travelers who lost their way in the desert wilderness (v. 4). They circled in a desert where there were no familiar landmarks. Alone, hungry, and thirsty, they were ready to give up when they called to the Lord, and "he led them by a straight way, till they reached a city to dwell in" (v. 7 RSV). The second picture is of captives who suffer in terrible prisons, covered by darkness and bound in irons. The third window through which we view the extremity of life reveals those who are sick and barely able to keep out of the grave. Though all sickness is not a result of sin, sinful ways do bring deadly ills. The fourth description of terror is of sailors who are helpless before a relentless storm (vv. 23–27). The Jews were not known for their prowess at sea. Indeed, the sea was a special terror to the Hebrews. In these illustrations the psalmist reminds us of the primary issues in life.

A person may complain of not having expensive shoes to wear until he sees someone who has no feet. Another person may complain of not being admitted to a prestigious university until she meets a child who is mentally challenged. Thanksgiving wells up in the hearts of men, women, and children who know the difference between necessities and luxuries, and who have learned to be grateful for the basic joys of life itself.

B. *The New Testament gives its own word of grace to those trapped in the despair described in the four pictures of this psalm.* For lost travelers in the desert, Jesus is both the Shepherd and the Way (John 10; 14). For captives in dark prisons, Jesus is the one who gives "deliverance to the captives" (Luke 4:18). For those who are sick, Jesus is the Great Physician who cared for the sick and healed those who came to him. For those at sea who fear for their lives, Jesus is the one who spoke to the storm, "Peace, be still" (Mark 4:39).

Alford "Butch" Summers, thirty years old, was buried under tons of rubble when a Joplin, Missouri, hotel collapsed while he was working there as a welder. He said, "There was no warning. All I could remember was all of a sudden, blam! It just collapsed. No warning. There was no way of warning anybody. Everything was dark. . . .

"Did I panic? Oh, there was a time when I thought I might not make it. But I just kept pounding the pipe and praying a lot and hoping. I mainly laid down and prayed. I did an awful lot of praying. I prayed to Jesus, because he was the only one I knew could get me out of this. I'm not much of a religious man, but if anyone could get me out alive, it had to be Jesus" (*Fort Worth Star Telegram*, November 16, 1978, 3A).

Three and a half days after the collapse of the hotel, Summers was rescued from the two-foot-high cavity where he had been trapped. From his hospital bed, Summers said, "I don't know how long I was there. All of a sudden the world caved in on me." When the world caves in on us, as it did on Butch Summers, or as it did on the people described in the psalm, we cry out to the Lord in our distress, and he does hear us. The secret of thanksgiving is partly discerned when we face trouble and realize that all things are not equally important. When the basics of life are provided, then is the time for great thanksgiving.

The third secret to thanksgiving is this:

III. Remember the source of our help (107:3, 7, 14, 16, 20, 29–30).

Although Summers said he was not much of a religious man, he did know the source of his help. He knew that "if anyone could get me out alive, it had to be Jesus." The people of Israel understood, as this psalm so clearly shows, that God was the source of their strength and deliverance. He had brought them out of bondage; he had led them through the wilderness; he would bring them safely home. If we are to be thankful, we must remember from whom the blessings flow.

A man who had sought to maintain an atheistic viewpoint confessed that he came to a time when he began to believe in God. This came as a result of not knowing who to thank when he delighted in the joy of life, the beauty of a dawn, the glory of the birth of a child, the love in the eyes of his wife.

On reflection he had to admit to himself that the astonishing joy of life was so magnificent that nothing less than God could have made it possible. His desire was to say thank you. Only God was worthy of gratitude.

The fourth secret to thanksgiving is the following:

IV. Take time for gratitude (107:8, 15, 21, 31).

After God's deliverance of the people, noted the psalmist, they took time to be grateful. We have often wondered with some amazement that of the ten lepers whom Jesus healed, only one returned to say thank you (Luke 17:18). We are often guilty of the same carelessness. When we do not give thanksgiving, it is sometimes because we simply are not willing to do so.

On an autumn night in 1860, a steamboat broke up and sank in Lake Michigan one mile from the village of Winnetka, Illinois. Of the 393 passengers aboard the *Lady Elgin*, 279 drowned. Of the 114 survivors, 17 were saved by Edward Spencer, a student at Northwestern University. Spencer was a strong swimmer, but after having made seventeen round trips, he became delirious from the strain. It was reported that he asked again and again, "Did I do my best?" As a result of that night, Spencer became sick and was confined to a wheelchair all through life.

Some years later, on Spencer's birthday, a reporter asked him his most vivid memory of that heroic date in his life. His answer? "I remember that not one of the seventeen returned to thank me" (*Proclaim*, October–December 1978, 30).

Conclusion

Finally, then, the secret of thanksgiving is simple. (1) You must be open to the goodness of God. (2) You must be willing to focus on what really matters. (3) You must remember where your help originates. (4) You must be willing to take time to say thank you. Now you know the secret. Knowing this, you can turn every day into Thanksgiving Day.

SUNDAY EVENING, NOVEMBER 21

Title: Privilege Brings Obligation

Text: "I, therefore, the prisoner of the Lord, beseech you that ye walk worthy of the vocation wherewith ye are called" **(Eph. 4:1).**

Scripture Reading: Ephesians 4:1–16

Introduction

A small boy asked a woman who sat by a municipal swimming pool, "Do you believe in God?" The woman was stunned, but she replied, "Of course I believe in God." On hearing this answer, the boy said, "Good, then you can keep my money and my watch while I go swimming."

The boy felt that belief and behavior belonged together. So did Paul. In his letter to the Ephesians, Paul followed up his instructions with exhortations. He set forth the great doctrines in the opening chapters and applied the doctrines to life in the last three chapters. As Paul entered into his series of practical exhortations, he wrote, "I therefore, the prisoner of the Lord, beseech you that ye walk worthy of the vocation wherewith ye are called" (Eph. 4:1).

Paul had already talked about the numerous privileges of believers. The word "therefore" suggests that he wants to move to the practical application of those privileges. Paul presented the obligations connected with having benefits.

I. Christians are obligated to walk worthily (4:1–2).

A. *Believers should live lives consistent with God's intention.* The word "walk" is used repeatedly throughout the last three chapters of Ephesians (4:17, 17; 5:2, 8, 15). It refers to the course of one's life. To walk worthily means to live a life in harmony with God's will. The word "vocation" speaks of the calling that belongs to every Christian.

B. *Believers have a description of the worthy walk.* Paul described the worthy walk: "With all lowliness and meekness, with longsuffering, forbearing one another in love" (v. 2). Paul listed four spiritual virtues that characterize Christians who walk worthily of their calling. "Lowliness" speaks of their creative dependence on God. "Meekness" describes those who are gentle in their relationships with others. "Forbearance" is a trait of those who bear with the weakness and failures of others. "Love" is the quality of seeking the highest good in others.

II. Christians are obligated to maintain unity (4:3–6).

A. *Believers live under orders to maintain unity.* "Endeavouring to keep the unity of the Spirit in the bond of peace" (v. 3). The word translated "endeavouring" suggests the idea of eagerness and zeal. It could be translated "give diligence."

The disposition of a believer's life is to guard the unity of the body of Christ. The redeemed should make a continuous effort to cooperate with the Holy Spirit.

B. *Believers have a basis for unity.* Fundamental inward experiences bind believers together in spiritual oneness. In Ephesians 4:4–6 the oneness of believers can be seen in three trilogies. The first trilogy speaks of "one body and one Spirit, just as you were called to the one hope that belongs to your call" (v. 4 RSV). Here Paul was teaching about the church as one body of Christ, the Spirit who energizes the church, and the common goal toward which the body is progressing.

The second trilogy is "One Lord, one faith, one baptism" (4:5). The first trilogy focuses on the Holy Spirit. The second trilogy focuses on Jesus. Faith is the experience with Christ, and baptism is the sign of faith in Christ.

The third trilogy is "one God and Father of all, who is above all, and through all, and in you all" (v. 6). This statement teaches that the one sovereign God is the ultimate source of spiritual unity. God is the basis for the believer's unity.

III. Christians are obligated to maintain ministry (4:7–16).

Believers have two supreme obligations: to make disciples of all nations and to disciple the saved. Each member is to do his or her part in these facets of ministry.

A. *God provides the church with gifts in order to maintain the ministry.* God has bestowed various gifts on believers to maintain his work. In Ephesians 4:8–13 Paul dealt at length with the diversity of the gifts bestowed by the Father and explained their purpose—namely, to glorify God, to serve others, and to bring believers joy. To accomplish his purpose, God gives people special abilities. Each person in the kingdom of God has a gift and has a responsibility to maintain the ministry.

B. *God gives gifts to believers for a specific purpose.* "For the perfecting of the saints, for the work of the ministry, for the edifying of the body of Christ: till we all come in the unity of the faith, and of the knowledge of the Son of God, unto a perfect man, unto the measure of the stature of the fulness of Christ" (v. 12). The leaders are to prepare and equip all the members for the service each can render in strengthening the life of the church. Ministers are not appointed to do the work for the members but to prepare the members for their work, that the whole church may be built up as the body of Christ.

Conclusion

If you have believed in Jesus Christ, you have some obligations. Belief is tied to behavior.

WEDNESDAY EVENING, NOVEMBER 24

Title: Parable of the Lost Sheep

Text: "Rejoice with me" (**Luke 15:6**).

Scripture Reading: Luke 15:1–7

Introduction

Good news is in the air: God loves those who are lost and wants to save them. All Christians ought to take delight in being a part of this good news. The parable of the lost sheep tells of the wonderful news of God's love. It is introduced by the grumbling of the Pharisees and scribes because Jesus received sinners. In discussing the parable of the lost sheep, we need to consider two things: the need of the lost and the lost that is found.

I. The need of the lost.

A. *The lost condition is found in the word* lost. The literal meaning of the word *lost* is "to be away from," either in time or space. Those who are lost are separated from God; consequently they are separated from joy and peace and are faced with eternal hell and damnation.

Some people may not realize they are in this condition. They have drifted into separation from God and are unaware of the consequences. The business of God's servants is to open their eyes and stir their souls.

B. *The lost condition is emphasized in the search to find the lost.*

1. The words translated "leave" and "go" (Luke 15:4) show continuous action. This means the shepherd keeps going from one place to another until each lost sheep is found.

2. Jesus' action is even more evident. He left heaven and came to earth, lived and died to pay the debt of sin. He is now alive and at the right hand of God, making continuous intercession. He is at work right now seeking to bring the lost to his fold. He accomplishes this through the drawing of his Holy Spirit when the Word of God is shared.

II. The lost that is found.

A. *Consider the words* joy *and* rejoicing.

1. In verse 5 we find that the shepherd laid the sheep on his shoulders and kept on rejoicing. Isaiah 53:6 says, "And the LORD hath laid on him the iniquity of us all."

2. In Luke 15:6 we read that the shepherd told his friends and neighbors, "Rejoice with me." This, too, is continuous action. He kept calling, and they continued rejoicing.

3. In verse 7 Jesus said that there is more joy over one sinner who repents than over the ninety-nine who have no need to repent.

B. *Consider the joy that comes when one lost person is found.* The Bible says that angels in heaven rejoice. God's children rejoice. The greatest joy of all is found in the heart of the one who repents.

Conclusion

In this message we have discussed a parable that tells of the need for the lost to repent and the joy when one does repent. I want to urge all of you who are lost to come to Jesus right now.

SUNDAY MORNING, NOVEMBER 28

Title: Courage to Say Yes

Text: "When Peter saw [the disciple whom Jesus loved], he said to Jesus, 'Lord, what about this man?' Jesus said to him, 'If it is my will that he remain until I come, what is that to you? Follow me!'" **(John 21:21–22 RSV).**

Scripture Reading: John 21:15–22

Hymns: "Oh, Worship the King," Grant
"God of Grace and God of Glory," Fosdick
"Have Thine Own Way, Lord," Pollard

Offertory Prayer: Gracious Lord, you have given first to us. Though we can never repay you, we do rejoice that we can bring our gifts to you. As you take our offerings and use them to bless your world, we thank you that we can be partners with you and with one another in touching the people of the world. In Jesus' name. Amen.

Introduction

As a young man I discovered that the key to answering many of the questions concerning my life as a Christian was knowing when to say yes and when to say no. Courage to say no is not always easy to come by, but having the courage to say yes when we are called to give our best may be even harder than saying no to the dark temptations of life. Our text confronts us squarely with the challenge to say yes.

I. Peter wanted to say yes, but it was difficult because he had failed before.

A. *Biblical background.*

1. Jesus asked Peter, "Do you love me?" Three times he asked the burning question (John 21:15–17). At first glance it appears that Peter indeed said, "Yes, Lord, I do love you." But a closer look at the Greek text reveals that Peter equivocated. Jesus had asked him, "Peter, do you *agapaō* me?" ("Do you have the highest spiritual devotion to me?") Peter replied, "Lord, you know that I *phileō* you" ("I have a warm brotherly affection for you"). Perhaps Peter remembered his heartfelt but unkept promise, "I will lay down my life for you" (John 13:37 RSV). He had talked more than he could perform. Now he was more reticent in his response. He wanted more than anything to serve his Lord; but how could he say, "Yes, I will *agapaō* you," when he failed so miserably before in the hour of his Lord's crisis?

   So when Jesus asked Peter the third time, "Do you love me?" he used Peter's word, *phileō*. Peter must have been pierced to the heart by Jesus' willingness to accept what Peter could say even if it was not all his Lord had a right to expect from him.

2. Peter's dark failure in the night of his Lord's agony haunted him now. But Jesus would not leave Peter in his defeat. He needed Peter's yes at the level Peter was willing to begin. So with great tenderness our Lord gave his broken servant a new task. "Feed my lambs," Jesus said to him. "Tend my sheep."

B. *Illustration*. A young man grew up in an active Christian home. He married and became the father of a lovely child. But he would not go to church even though he readily admitted his need for it. In probing for the cause of the young man's refusal to become involved at church, his pastor discovered that years before he had in every youth camp rededicated his life to the Lord, only to be discouraged by his failure to live up to his commitment. Finally, he gave up making any promises at all. He was left in failure because he would not hear the call of Jesus to leave his failure behind and follow him.

C. *Application*. Many people have made commitments to serve Jesus Christ as a missionary, as a Sunday school teacher, as a deacon, or as a faithful steward of the possessions God has given. And many have failed to keep their commitments. If you are one who has failed before, what would Jesus say to you? I believe he would ask you, as he asked Peter, "Do you love me? Then do my work: follow me and feed my sheep."

II. The courage to say yes must not depend on another person's response.

A. *"What about this man?"* The disciple John was closely watching the exchange between Peter and Jesus. Peter turned to John and then back to Jesus and asked, "What about this man?" I know that feeling. Weary and doing all I can do, I sometimes grow discouraged because of others around me who seem to do so little. Jesus replied, "What is that to you, Peter? Follow me."

To be sure, it is irritating to be around people who are always willing to "park on someone else's dime." Some of us grow weary in well-doing and are tempted to judge the inadequate or faithless response of others as justification for our reluctance to say, "Yes, Lord. You can count on me."

B. *A man who acted*. A church located near a college campus decided to reach out to college students. Although the church was close to the campus, the people had never had much success in their ministry to college students. That year they made a concerted effort to publicize their services and to warmly invite the students to church. One Sunday morning the church was packed with people. A young man from the college, barefoot and scruffy looking, came in during the first hymn. Unable to find a seat, he walked down the aisle and sat on the carpet in front of the pulpit. He was unaware that his choice of seats would seem out of place to most people in the congregation. Then an old man stood up and walked down the aisle toward the college student. Since the old man had been a leader in the church for a long time, those who saw him were afraid he might say something to correct the young man. You can imagine how they felt when they saw him reach the student and, placing a hand on his shoulder, slowly sit down on the floor beside him. He continued to worship without missing a phrase of the hymn.

III. The courage to say yes is necessary if we are to be victorious.

A. *No victories can be won unless we learn to say, "Yes, I am available to serve."* In our church we are faced with a remarkable challenge. If we were less brave, or if our cause were not so crucial, we might be tempted to run and hide, or maybe to take a leave of absence from our church responsibilities.

B. *God has called us to be his church right here, right now.* We need to say yes to his call to make a difference in this community and throughout the world.

   1. Jesus has the heart of a shepherd. He seeks lost sheep. Frightened or hungry sheep are the object of his special care (see John 10:1–18). So when Jesus asked Peter to take care of his sheep, he was calling him to join in the task of the Great Shepherd.

   2. Great causes do not move forward without great commitment. It is a risk when we set ourselves to do more than we have ever done before. There is always the possibility of embarrassment if we fail. But we can never know the glory of victory if we are unwilling to risk defeat. We as Christians must believe that if God is in the task, it does not matter who is against us. We must nurture the flock to maturity in Christ. We must search for an open place in the hearts of others where we can enter in Christ's name. Single adults who are afraid that life will never make sense must be reached by this church. Families who are holding on by their fingertips must be reached by this church. Young people who are desperate for the assurance that they are loved must be reached by this church.

Conclusion

When Jesus asks, "Do you love me?" commit yourself to caring, sharing, giving, and loving! Although it is not easy to say yes, don't hold back. He will give you the courage to say yes because he believes that you, too, can follow him.

SUNDAY EVENING, NOVEMBER 28

Title: Instructions for New Recruits

Text: "This I say therefore, and testify in the Lord, that ye henceforth walk not as other Gentiles walk, in the vanity of their mind" **(Eph. 4:17)**.

Scripture Reading: Ephesians 4:17–5:2

Introduction

One young man had the responsibility of training Marine Corps recruits. Many of the recruits had not been away from home before, and they needed to learn autonomy. Others were not accustomed to authoritative military life. Still others were not accustomed to the rigidity and toughness of marine training. Every three months the young man worked patiently training a new group of recruits. Part of his joy was to observe them become responsible soldiers.

Many of the people to whom Paul wrote had just accepted Christ. They were new recruits. Paul wanted to give these new believers some instructions. If they heeded his instructions, they would become accustomed to the new life in Christ and would develop into disciplined soldiers for the Lord.

I. Forsake pagan practices (4:17–19).

A. *Everybody has a former life.* Paul addressed believers who were converted from paganism. We often have the tendency to think that all believers were converted from paganism. This is not true. Some have been converted from religious backgrounds with strong morals. Nonetheless, all of us have a former life. This former life is self-centeredness. Any life that seeks to put self at the center dishonors God.

B. *Everybody needs to forsake the former life.* The self-dominated life must be forsaken. Paul described those who lived in sin as "having the understanding darkened, being alienated from the life of God through the ignorance that is in them, because of the blindness of their heart: who being past feeling have given themselves over unto lasciviousness, to work all uncleanness with greediness" (vv. 18–19). Paul enumerated some of the prominent features of the pagan life: vanity, darkness, alienation, ignorance, blindness of heart, callousness, lasciviousness, uncleanness, and greed. It is a grim and revolting picture.

II. Find the Christian conduct (4:20–24).

A. *Christian conduct begins with Jesus Christ.* "But ye have not so learned Christ" (v. 20). The term "learn" describes an experience with the risen Lord. Only by opening their lives to Christ can people start their Christian pilgrimage. When people receive Christ, they are taught that Christian discipleship requires the renunciation of pagan practices and the cultivation of true Christian holiness.

B. *Christian conduct becomes part of believers' lifestyle.* The essence of the Christian lifestyle is defined by three constructions.

1. Christians are to "put off" (v. 22). This is the picture of stripping off an old garment and donning a new one.
2. Christians are to "be renewed" (v. 23). This expression is in the present tense. It denotes continuous progress in the believer's life.
3. Christians are to "put on" (v. 24).This statement is the counterpart of to "put off." The "new man" is the new self, the new life in Christ.

New recruits to Christianity must discover Christ's lifestyle for them. Forsaking old ways is not enough. Taking on Christ's kind of life is essential.

III. Follow Christian conduct (4:25–5:2).

Paul gave six specific commands on how to live the Christian life.

A. *Christians practice truthfulness.* "Wherefore putting away lying, speak every man truth with his neighbour: for we are members one of another" (4:25). Instead of being deceitful and dishonest, Christians should tell the truth.

B. *Christians control anger.* "Be ye angry and sin not: let not the sun go down upon your wrath" (4:26). Anger should not be given a place to take root within the heart.

C. *Christians should not steal.* "Let him that stole steal no more: but rather let him labour, working with his hands the thing which is good, that he may have to give to him that needeth" (4:28). Stealing was an ordinary means of livelihood for pagans.

D. *Christians honor God with their speech.* "Let no corrupt communication proceed out of your mouth, but that which is good to the use of edifying, that it may minister grace unto the hearers" (4:29). Personality may be defined as the power of self-communication. To abuse conversation perverts the personality. People may be blessed or hurt with words.

E. *Christians should not grieve the Holy Spirit.* "And grieve not the holy Spirit of God, whereby ye are sealed unto the day of redemption" (4:30). God is grieved when people rebel against him.

F. *Christians guard their disposition.* "Let all bitterness, and wrath, and anger, and clamour, and evil speaking, be put away from you, with all malice: and be ye kind one to another, tenderhearted, forgiving one another, even as God for Christ's sake hath forgiven you. Be ye therefore followers of God, as dear children; and walk in love, as Christ also hath loved us, and hath given himself for us an offering and a sacrifice to God for a sweetsmelling savour" (4:31–5:2). As children imitate the attitude of their parents, so should God's children imitate their Father.

Conclusion

Come into God's kingdom and receive abundant life. You can't change on your own, but by his Holy Spirit within you, Christ is able to teach you his ways and make you like himself.

DECEMBER

- **Sunday Mornings**

  As we approach the holidays, use "Come, Let Us Adore Him" as your theme.

- **Sunday Evenings**

  Conclude the series from Ephesians, "Making a New World."

- **Wednesday Evenings**

  Complete the series "The Parables of Jesus Continue to Speak."

WEDNESDAY EVENING, DECEMBER 1

Title: Parable of the Lost Coin

Text: "There is joy in the presence of the angels of God over one sinner that repenteth" **(Luke 15:10)**.

Scripture Reading: Luke 15:8–10

Introduction

The word *lost* may be the worst word that can fall from human lips. It is worse than death, as bad as that is. It is worse than pain, and no one likes to be hurt. Because of the emphasis Jesus placed on saving the lost, every person must give serious consideration to the lost condition.

I. That which is lost.

In our Scripture passage, a coin is lost. But the coin is only symbolic.

A. *Think of the value of the coin and relate it to the human soul.*

1. The coin was considered a day's wage. It was essential for the necessities of life. Jesus said the soul is even more valuable. "For what is a man profited, if he shall gain the whole world, and lose his own soul?" (Matt. 16:26).
2. The coin, on some occasions, was somewhat like a wedding band. Ten coins were fastened together and worn around the neck. This necklace had sentimental value. Each human soul is of such value that Christ died so our soul may be saved.

B. *Think of the tragedy of being lost and relate it to the human soul.*

1. A lost coin is useless. It is of no value to anyone or anything. Its purpose is not fulfilled. The same is true of the soul.

2. A lost coin is separated from other coins and from its possessor. It is of no value to the owner. The lost soul is separated from God and Christian fellowship.
3. A lost coin becomes tarnished and dull. A lost soul suffers in hell.
4. A lost coin, as seen in this passage, causes anxiety, suffering, and a loss of time. A lost soul does the same.

C. *Think of the reason for being lost and relate it to the human soul.*
   1. It could have become lost because of carelessness.
   2. It could have become lost because of negligence. It is true that sin is what causes a soul to be lost, but failure to accept Christ makes it stay that way.

II. The seeking.

A. *The act of searching made use of everything available for such a search.* The woman used a candle for light and a broom for sweeping. This is a description of God's search for a human soul.

B. *The act of searching was one of determination and diligence.* The woman exerted much effort. She kept at it. She did not quit. This is an apt description of the Lord's effort to find the lost.

III. The joy over finding the lost coin.

A. *There was joy among the woman's friends and neighbors.* Anytime anyone comes to Jesus, other Christians are made happy.

B. *There was joy in heaven.* God and his heavenly host rejoice when each lost person is saved.

C. *There was joy on the inside.* Although the coin itself could not rejoice, the inner being of the woman was thrilled. A lost person can have inner joy when trusting Christ for salvation.

Conclusion

The reason Jesus told this story was to lead the lost person to accept him as Savior. The reason it has been used in this message is exactly the same reason. We extend an invitation to each person who is lost to accept Christ as Savior and Lord.

SUNDAY MORNING, DECEMBER 5

Title: Reflections of Jesus in Genesis

Text: "And Abraham called the name of that place Jehovah-jireh: as it is said to this day, In the mount of the LORD it shall be seen" **(Gen. 22:14)**.

Scripture Reading: Genesis 22:8–14; 24

Hymns: "As with Gladness, Men of Old," Dix
"Hail, Thou Long-Expected Jesus," Wesley
"Let All Mortal Flesh Keep Silence," Moultrie

Offertory Prayer: O God, as we search for your blessings, let us see you in all areas of our lives. May our eyes be opened to your presence. Forgive us for our spiritual blindness. May we not only seek you here in this time of worship, but let us see Jesus in our homes and in our community. Thank you, Father, for revealing Jesus on all the pages of the Bible. In his name we pray. Amen.

Introduction

Dr. Robert G. Lee used to tell about a famous songwriter who loved the Lord very much. The composer wrote a song with a beautiful romantic tune and a wonderful message about Jesus. He was offered a large sum of money by a secular publishing company if he would change the lyrics. The publishing company asked him to substitute the word "love" for "Jesus." The composer replied, "If you leave out Jesus, you have left out everything."

A professing Christian, after having a powerful experience with God, said to his pastor, "I had been listening to you preach for many years but had not been hearing you. I know you had been preaching the Word of God and Jesus, and I know you had been telling me what I needed to hear, but I had not been hearing it." He continued, "Since I committed my life to Jesus, I now hear what you're saying."

People read the Bible and fail to see Jesus. They go to church and do not come face-to-face with him. Often people are in the environment of Christian experience, but they do not have a relationship with Jesus Christ. They know about him, but they do not know him personally.

In reading Genesis we can see Jesus on almost every page. The problem with the Jews in the first century was that they could not identify the Messiah because they had not really seen him in their Bible. In journeying through Genesis, we see Jesus in many experiences. Genesis does not speak of Jesus' birth, but it does demonstrate his existence.

Two experiences in the life of Isaac illustrate God's plan in Jesus. They show us that God has always had a plan to seek and save the lost.

I. A sacrificing Savior (22:8–14).

A. *Promise.* Isaac was the son of promise. God had made a covenant with Abraham, telling him that all nations of the earth would be blessed through his descendants, but Abraham did not have any descendants. Abraham took this matter into his own hands. Since he did not see any way the promise could be fulfilled, he decided that he would help God work it out. Abraham had a son by the handmaiden Hagar, but he was not the son of promise.

Then God spoke when Abraham was ninety-nine years old and Sarah was ninety. God said, "I am going to give you a son." Miraculously, he did. Isaac was born.

Later God said, "Abraham, you must be willing to sacrifice your son." So Abraham took Isaac to Mount Moriah. Isaac, carrying a load of wood for a burnt offering on the altar, said, "Father, where is the lamb?" Abraham answered, "God will provide."

B. *The weight of sin.* Isaac carried the load of the sacrifice. All humankind is under the weight of sin. If we read this passage in light of our socialistic trends, we might judge God to be unjust in asking Abraham to sacrifice his son. But if we look at it from God's perspective, it is quite different. Isaac deserved to die, just as we all do. He was a sinner, and so are we, and the wages of sin is death. Isaac, on his way to his own sacrifice, is symbolic of the needs of humankind. He was under the load of sin—a sinner with questions and no answers, a sinner with sin and no forgiveness, a person with no hope even though the promise of God rested on his whole life.

C. *God's provision.* Abraham and Isaac went to the place God had designated, and Abraham built an altar. He tied his son and was ready to sacrifice him when God spoke. We see Isaac as a symbol of sinful humankind under the load of sin and without hope. But then God spoke and we do not see Isaac. We see the provision of God. For God supplied a ram with his horns caught in a bush, put there as a sacrifice in place of Isaac. God was ready to take the load of sin off the shoulders and out of the heart of Isaac. The ram was sacrificed in Isaac's place. Abraham's faith was demonstrated by his willingness to sacrifice his son, but the important thing is that a sufficient substitute had appeared by the grace of God.

This story reminds us of Jesus. We are carrying the burden of our guilt—not supposed guilt, not assumed guilt, but real guilt. We deserve the penalty of hell, but by grace God has sent a Lamb. That Lamb is Jesus, humbly born in Bethlehem's manger; sadly yet victoriously living among his own people who rejected him; and terribly yet gloriously dying on Calvary's cross for our sins.

D. *The victory.* Picture Abraham and Isaac coming down from Mount Moriah. Isaac is not carrying the load of sacrifice. The sacrifice has been made. Isaac is no longer asking, "Where is the lamb?" The lamb has been provided. Isaac has been saved. The Christ has come. The sacrifice has been made. The price has been paid on the cross of Calvary, and the resurrection has provided salvation for all who will accept. We are free from the guilt of sin because of the Lamb God has provided.

II. A seeking Savior (24).

Another story about Isaac reminds us about the seeking Savior. Abraham had left his relatives in Haran and gone to Canaan. Isaac needed a wife. The Canaanite women were not right for Isaac because their people worshiped idols. Isaac, as the son of promise, would be an ancestor of Jesus. So the right wife had to be found for him.

377

A. *The searching spirit.* Abraham sent his servant Eliezer back to Haran to find a bride for Isaac. Eliezer went to the home of Laban, the kinsman of Abraham and Sarah, where he obtained Laban's permission to take Rebekah to be Isaac's wife. Rebekah's mother did not want her daughter to leave, but finally the moment came when Rebekah was asked, "Will you go and be the bride of Isaac?" She said, "I will go."

B. *The joyous Christ.* A glorious meeting took place between Rebekah and Isaac. "And Isaac went out to meditate in the field at eventide: and he lifted up his eyes, and saw, and, behold, the camels were coming. And Rebekah lifted up her eyes, and when she saw Isaac, she lighted off the camel" (Gen. 24:63).

Why would God put a beautiful love story like this in the Bible? Because God is telling us about Jesus. He is telling us about the son of promise, Isaac, in search of a bride. Jesus also came to search for a bride. Jesus is the Son of God, and his bride is the church.

As Abraham sent out Eliezer, God sends out the Holy Spirit in search of the bride of Christ. What did Eliezer do? He went to Haran and told Rebekah about Isaac. The Christ has come, and the Holy Spirit of God moves around the world to tell people about the Christ. He gathers the church, the bride of Christ. God has always had a plan, and the plan is Jesus. If you leave out Jesus, you have left out everything. Jesus is the essence of God's grace. Jesus is the Savior who not only saved Isaac from death but also from guilt and from hell. And he saves us from death, guilt, and hell also.

C. *The willing bride.* Jesus is the one who sends forth his Holy Spirit in search of his bride. What a beautiful truth! Not only has God provided salvation, but he searches the earth for the souls of men and women, boys and girls who will give themselves to him and who will say as Rebekah said, "I will go."

Conclusion

The story of Jesus is an eternal story. It did not begin in a manger in Bethlehem; it began in the very being of God. It is a story that has been included in the purpose of God ever since he said, "Let there be light." It is a story that is ever expanding as God touches the lives of all people who will submit to him. The Christmas story is not written in the pretty decorations we place around our homes. It is not written as we exchange nice gifts. The Christmas story is written in our acceptance of Jesus as the Savior and Lord of our lives.

SUNDAY EVENING, DECEMBER 5

Title: Walk in the Light

Text: "For ye were sometimes darkness, but now are ye light in the Lord: walk as children of light" (**Eph. 5:8**).

Scripture Reading: Ephesians 5:3–15

Introduction

Have you ever walked in the night by the light of a flashlight? When I was a small boy, I remember walking at night with my father down lonely country roads with the light of a small flashlight. The light guided us away from holes in the road and obstacles along the way.

Paul wrote to believers who had been converted, most of them from paganism. They had lived in ways that were contrary to God's ways. Paul used the terms "light" and "darkness" to describe righteousness and unrighteousness. There is a strong contrast between light and darkness in Scripture, as seen in 1 John 1:6: "If we say that we have fellowship with him, and walk in darkness, we lie, and do not the truth."

Christians must walk in the light. One of the best ways to discover the way of light is to look at the way of darkness.

I. The pagan walks in darkness (5:3–8).

A. *The life of the pagan is perverted.* The sinner lives in moral decay. "But fornication, and all uncleanness, or covetousness, let it not be once named among you, as becometh saints" (v. 3).

 1. Three words describe their perversity: "fornication" (*porneia*), "uncleanness" (*akatharsia*), and "covetousness" (*pleonexia*). Immorality and impurity are sexual offenses. The pagans perverted God's ideal for sexual relations. God intended that sex be within the bounds of marriage. The world distorted this idea by abusive sexual practices, including sex with members of the same sex. Paul went so far as to say that such moral debauchery should not even be discussed.

 2. Paul mentioned other perversions. "Neither filthiness, nor foolish talking, nor jesting, which are not convenient: but rather giving of thanks" (v. 4). Paul grouped filthiness, foolish talking, and jesting together and said that they were inappropriate for believers.

B. *The future life of the pagan is a dreadful prospect.* "For this ye know, that no whoremonger, nor unclean person, nor covetous man, who is an idolater, hath any inheritance in the kingdom of Christ and of God. Let no man deceive you with vain words: for because of these things cometh the wrath of God upon the children of disobedience" (vv. 5–6). God will not allow people into his kingdom who have not repented and trusted the Lord. The wrath of God, not the kingdom of God, awaits those who practice pagan morals.

II. The Christian walks in the light (5:8–14).

A. *The Christian has a transformed life.* Paul contrasted the present lives of believers with their former lives. The transformation occurs at the point of relationship. "For the fruit of the Spirit is in all goodness and righteousness and truth" (v. 9). The essential features of the transformed life are "goodness and righteousness and truth." These qualities are the moral results of accepting the light of the gospel. Goodness describes the transformed character of a new believer. Righteousness describes the cleanliness of life that comes only through the indwelling of the Holy Spirit. Truth marks the harmonious relationship of the mind to God's will.

B. *The Christian has a tested life.* "Proving what is acceptable unto the Lord" (v. 10). The Christian tests all things by the light of Christian truth and acts accordingly. The Christian tests deeds as well as people. "And have no fellowship with the unfruitful works of darkness, but rather reprove them" (v. 11). Paul forbade Christian converts from having any part in the impure practices of the pagan world that surrounded them.

Paul closed his appeal to walk in the light with what may be a portion of an early Christian hymn. "Wherefore he saith, Awake thou that sleepest, and arise from the dead, and Christ shall give thee light" (v. 14).

Conclusion

When you accept Christ into your personal life, you begin the joyous journey of walking in the light. The Lord will guide you and lead you away from the dangers of darkness. Walk in the light.

WEDNESDAY EVENING, DECEMBER 8

Title: Parable of the Lost Son

Text: "This my son was dead, and is alive again" **(Luke 15:24)**.

Scripture Reading: Luke 15:11–24

Introduction

The chief message of this Scripture passage is unmistakable: the hunger of God for the wayward person and the hunger of the wayward person for God. The almighty God is doing all he can to bring the wayward home. At the same time, many wayward people are longing to be at home with the heavenly Father. We will consider this dilemma under four descriptions.

I. Rebellion.

Sin is rebellion against God.

A. *Rebellion has its origin in selfishness.* We notice in the Scripture passage that the essence of the prodigal's request was, "Give me what I want so I can go my own way." Rebellion is a refusal to comply with God's standards.

B. *Rebellion, in its progress, is dissipation.* Dissipation is satisfying one's own lust in one's own way. The prodigal wanted his inheritance so he could chase after his own desires. This describes a person's refusal to entrust his or her life to God.

II. The result of rebellion.

A. *In this passage, the result of rebellion is estrangement from the father.* The wayward son was separated from the love of his father. The love was there, but the son did not want to benefit from it. Love cannot be forced, nor can one's response to love. Both must be voluntary.

B. *In this passage, the result of rebellion is estrangement from the comforts of home.* For example, a good, affluent family may live in a fine, comfortable home. A son who could have the privilege of living in that home chooses to live in squalor. This describes a person's spiritual life when he or she rebels against the heavenly Father and lives in the mire of sin.

C. *In this passage, the result of rebellion is estrangement from the rights of home.* At one time the young man had all the rights and privileges of a son. He was a legal heir. In his rebellion he became a hired man living in a hog pen. The depth of his depravity is seen in that he asked to be a slave.

D. *In this passage, the result of rebellion is estrangement from the provisions of home.* The necessities of life are food, clothing, and shelter. The young man had none of these necessities during his rebellion.

III. The repentance of the rebellious son.

A. *Repentance is a change of mind.* When people repent, the evil they once loved they now hate. The company they once enjoyed they now shun. The God they once scorned they now embrace.

B. *There are four steps to repentance.*
  1. The first step is right thinking. What am I doing here?
  2. The second step is recognition. I see where I am because of what I have done.
  3. The third step is resolution. "I will arise and go to my father." I will turn from my sin.
  4. The fourth step is return.

IV. The reception of the rebellious son.

A. *The Scripture passage contains symbols of welcome.* The robe was a symbol of honor. The ring and shoes were symbols of freedom and complete forgiveness. The fatted calf was a symbol of joy and rejoicing. The whole parable is a symbol of God's welcome.

B. *In the reception, the very heart of God is revealed.* God is seen as a loving Father who longs for the wayward to come home. He is seen as a forgiving God who removes all that stands between a sinful man and a holy God. He is also seen as a rewarding God who showers mercy on those who come to him in repentance and faith.

Conclusion

By reading this parable, anyone can find out how to be saved. I hope you will take the parable's message seriously and come to the Savior right now.

SUNDAY MORNING, DECEMBER 12

Title: The Word Became Flesh

Text: "The Word was made flesh, and dwelt among us, (and we beheld his glory, the glory as of the only begotten of the Father), full of grace and truth" (**John 1:14**).

Scripture Reading: John 1:1–5, 14; 1 John 1:1–3

Hymns: "Joy to the World," Watts
        "Hark! The Herald Angels Sing," Wesley
        "Gentle Mary Laid Her Child," Cook

Offertory Prayer: Dear Father, thank you for sending your Son to this world for us. We know that we are undeserving of him. Thank you that he came to a humble manger and to a humble people. May he who so humbly came gloriously live in our hearts. In the name of Jesus. Amen.

Introduction

The Gospels speak in different ways about Jesus' birth.

    A. *Matthew lists the genealogy of Joseph.* He was interested in the legal and the Jewish aspects of Jesus' birth.
    B. *Luke, who apparently had many conversations with Mary and with others, told of the visit of the angelic choir.* He spoke of the manger and listed the genealogy of Jesus on Mary's side.
    C. *Mark did not even mention Jesus' birth.* But he does tell about Jesus' miraculous deeds.
    D. *John wrote his gospel from an entirely different perspective than did the other three.* He was the youngest of the apostles. He wrote his gospel, his three epistles, and Revelation when he was an old man. He did not give a chronological view of Jesus' life, but he reflected on Jesus' life in relationship to what had happened to him. It is not appropriate to simply say that John wrote philosophically about Jesus. He was more interested in Jesus religiously than historically. John was saying, "Let me tell you what has happened to me because I know Jesus."

I. Jesus as the Word.

When John called Jesus the Word, many believe he brought a new dimension to Christian theology. They say that John tried to unite an African philosophy and Christianity. I doubt that John even knew what the philosophers of Alexandria were saying. John wrote under inspiration, "I want to tell you about what I have experienced from God; I want to tell you about the Word, the *Logos* of God, one whose name is Jesus." He said, "In the beginning was the Word, and the Word was with God, and the Word was God" (John 1:1).

A. *Before Bethlehem.* Before Bethlehem, the Word existed because God is the Word. John believed that Jesus was the Son of God. In fact, there is no reason for Christian theology if Jesus is not the Son of God.

B. *The Word as authority.* There must be a basis for Jesus' authority. Why would John call Jesus the Word? Because he thought of God as absolute authority. He thought of God as the source of every existing thing. So he said, "In the beginning was the Word." God has always existed. John said, "And the Word was with God, and the Word was God." He was calling Jesus the Word; and he was saying, "Jesus was with God, and Jesus was God." John had a Trinitarian concept of God. He was saying, "There is one God; and while there is one God, Jesus, the Word is with God. The Spirit is with God; and he is God."

II. Jesus as the source.

"The same was in the beginning with God. All things were made by him; and without him was not any thing made that was made" (John 1:2–3). This God who is Christ is the source of all things. "All things were made by him." Our environment was made by him. Our lives were made by him. In fact, "without him was not any thing made that was made." Nothing is possible in this life without God. Without Jesus, people can create nothing. Without Jesus, people can accomplish nothing.

A. *The source of life.* Life comes from God, and thus all of life's meaning comes from God. Every activity of life comes from God. "Without him was not any thing made that was made." We are totally dependent on him. "In him was life; and the life was the light of men" (John 1:4). God did not come to the world as theory. People have always tried to explain the source of life in some natural way. People may explain life as coming from the sun, from fire, or from a process of evolution. People may actually admit they don't understand life, but they do know there must be a source.

B. *The source of light.*
 1. Tradition says that John ministered in the city of Ephesus, the ancient city built around the worship of Diana of the Ephesians. Diana is a form of the ancient Greek god Aphrodite. The Ephesians believed that the very unusual statue they had of Diana had been dropped out of heaven. There stood this gigantic stone statue of a virgin goddess; and a whole state bowed around her

and acclaimed her to be God, but she was dead—only a stone—nothing else. God sent his Son, and he is alive.

2. The life is the source of light for humanity. Listen to John. "In him was life; and the life was the light of men. And the light shineth in darkness; and the darkness comprehended it not" (John 1:4–5). What is the darkness? It is the darkness of our sin. It is the darkness of the despair in our lives. God says that even the darkness of sin and death cannot hold back the light. The world says, "We will snuff out the light of Jesus; it must not shine." God says, "The darkness cannot hold back the light of the living Son of God." Light comes to our souls to change us, to make us new creatures; and this light comes from Jesus.

III. Jesus as man.

John said, "And the Word was made flesh" (John 1:14). The Word was in the beginning. The Word was God. And the Word became flesh. God came in flesh in the manger of Bethlehem. It was God in the flesh who walked the streets of Nazareth. It was God in the flesh who touched blind eyes and deaf ears and healed them. It was God in the flesh who taught by the shore of Galilee. It was God in the flesh who faced controversy at Jerusalem with the religious powers. It was God in the flesh on the cross of Calvary, and it was God in the flesh who rose from the dead. "And the Word was made flesh . . . (and we beheld his glory, the glory as of the only begotten of the Father), full of grace and truth" (John 1:14).

A. *The glory of God.* Many people claim that Jesus is not the Son of God, saying that he is an example to be followed but no more. How wrong they are! He is not just an example. Any person can be an example. We see in Jesus the glory of the Father. We see him full of grace, full of unmerited favor, and full of truth. We see him, the Son of God, willing to die for us though we are sinners. We see him paying the price of our sin on Calvary's cross though we do not deserve it.

B. *The glory in humankind.* John testified that the glory of Christ is available to all (1 John 1:1–3). He told about his personal experience with Jesus as the Word of Life. He testified that he had seen Jesus with his eyes and had touched him with his hands. He is talking about his Christian experience. He is saying, "Christ was born! Christ came to the world, and he became the ultimate sacrifice for sin." But more importantly he is saying, "Christ came to me! I saw him, I touched him, and he changed my life!"

Conclusion

This is what Christmas means. It is not just a beautiful story, not just a nativity scene. It is not a star in the sky and certainly not one on top of your Christmas tree. It is Christ living in you.

"Why has God touched my life?" asked John. "To change it," he answers himself. But listen, for there is even more. "That which we have seen and heard declare we unto you, that ye also may have fellowship with us: and truly our fellowship is with the Father, and with his Son Jesus Christ" (1 John 1:3). With that John lifts the Christian experience entirely out of the realm of theory and puts it into the realm of practice. "In the beginning was the Word."

Is that all? Does the story end with a star and angels and shepherds and wise men? No, that is not all. There is more: Jesus' life, death, and resurrection. Is that all? No. Jesus is alive, and he comes to us one by one to call us to everlasting life and fellowship with him. The Christmas story is Jesus alive—and Jesus alive in you! Is he there? Has the star shone in your soul? The wise men followed it to Bethlehem. Wise men today come to the Christ and believe in him.

SUNDAY EVENING, DECEMBER 12

Title: Watch Your Walk

Text: "See then that ye walk circumspectly, not as fools, but as wise" **(Eph. 5:15)**.

Scripture Reading: Ephesians 5:15–20

Introduction

A husband and wife traveled to several different countries. In each place they visited, a tour guide helped them with their sightseeing. One line was repeated by all the tour guides: "Watch your step!" As the couple got off buses and went into various buildings and to other sights, their guide cautioned, "Watch your step!"

Paul was telling the Ephesians, "Watch your step as a believer!" "See then that ye walk circumspectly, not as fools, but as wise" (Eph. 5:15). Christians must be extremely careful about how they live in an unbelieving world. The word "circumspectly" here implies looking all around, paying attention to all circumstances, as one might do when passing through a dangerous place. Ephesians 5:15 could be translated, "Pay careful attention to the way you live."

I. Make use of all opportunities.

    A. *Seize every opportunity to do good.* "Redeeming the time, because the days are evil" (Eph. 5:16). The Greek word for "redeeming" is a market term that means "to buy out" or "to purchase completely." "Time" is the translation of a Greek word that came to mean something like opportunity. The expression "redeeming the time" means to make good use of every opportunity.

    B. *Opportunities redeem society.* "Redeeming the time, because the days are evil" (Eph. 5:16). Because the world is morally corrupt, we must seize every opportunity to redeem our evil society. No time should be lost.

II. Seek to understand God's will.

A. *The unwise person does not understand God's will.* "Wherefore be ye not unwise" (Eph. 5:17). The word "unwise" refers to being senseless. It means to be without reason or moral intelligence. Such a person does not think a matter through to its logical conclusion. The unwise ones were pagans who were unable to see through the immoral life to its end product.

B. *The wise person seeks to discern God's will.* "But understanding what the will of the Lord is" (Eph. 5:17). God seeks the best for all his creation. Thus the wise person wants to know his will.

III. Submit to the Holy Spirit's control.

A. *The Holy Spirit can control the believer's life.* "And be not drunk with wine, wherein is excess; but be filled with the Spirit" (Eph. 5:18). In contrast to the pagan conduct produced by drunkenness, Paul presents the kind of conduct produced by the Holy Spirit. The word "filled" was used in sailing. It referred to sails filled with the wind. When sails of a boat get filled with the wind, the boat can be controlled by the wind. Being filled with the Spirit describes a believer who submits to the control of the Holy Spirit and so becomes empowered to do God's perfect will.

B. *The Holy Spirit produces character in the believer's life.*

1. The Spirit produces joy. "Speaking to yourselves in psalms and hymns and spiritual songs, singing and making melody in your heart to the Lord" (Eph. 5:19). The Holy Spirit produces a genuine joy that comes from the heart. This joy is expressed outwardly in a number of ways.

2. The Spirit produces gratitude. "Giving thanks always for all things unto God and the Father in the name of our Lord Jesus Christ" (Eph. 5:20).

3. The Spirit produces mutual submission. "Submitting yourselves one to another in the fear of God" (Eph. 5:21). This is an attitude that is opposed to rudeness. It is the opposite of a stubborn insistence on one's rights. Paul expressed the same idea in Romans 12:10: "In honour preferring one another."

Conclusion

Go back to our *text:* "See then that ye walk circumspectly, not as fools, but as wise" (Eph. 5:15). Believers do need to be careful about how they live. The admonition "Watch your step!" should be remembered constantly.

WEDNESDAY EVENING, DECEMBER 15

Title: Parable of the Rich Man and Lazarus

Text: "If they hear not Moses and the prophets, neither will they be persuaded, though one rose from the dead" (**Luke 16:31**).

Scripture Reading: Luke 16:19–31

Introduction

Our Scripture reading for today is another passage that is treated as a parable even though it is not specifically stated that it is such. However, it is a passage that can probe the depths of one's soul. No other passage presents life after death as does this one. It is obvious that Jesus' intent is to encourage preparation for eternity. In this message we will consider three different eras of life.

I. Life on earth.

In the parable we find contrasting lifestyles.

    A. *The lifestyle of the rich man.*
1. Some truths about this man need to be emphasized. The rich man is not named. The Bible says, "There was a certain rich man." This is intended to show a type, not a particular person. The man was not condemned for being wicked, worldly, or rich. The only negative thing said about him is that he trusted in the wrong things for eternity. He is not even condemned for neglecting the poor man.
2. We can learn some lessons for modern living from this man's life. Material things are neither good nor bad as they are considered within themselves. The significant thing is how we depend on them. Another lesson is that the way we live in this life will determine where and how we live in the life after death.

    B. *The lifestyle of the poor man.*
1. Some truths about this man need to be emphasized. Poverty is not glorified. The Bible does not portray the poor life as good. The one thing that is pointed out as good about the man is that which he trusted for eternity.
2. We can learn some lessons for modern living from this man's life. We are never to substitute poverty for faith. All of us should make sure we are trusting Christ for eternal life.

II. Death.

    A. *The poor man died and was carried to Abraham's bosom by angels.* This is one of the greatest reasons for being a Christian. Only God's attending angel can be with a person in the hour of death.

    B. *The rich man died and was buried.* The horror here is that there was no angel. In all probability, there was an elaborate funeral.

C. *Everyone dies.* The point is, each of us should put our trust in Christ in order to have the assurance of an attending angel.

III. Life after death.

A. *The Bible says that the rich man was in torment.* Torment is the absence of all that is good and the presence of all that is bad.
B. *The Bible says that the poor man was carried to Abraham's bosom.* Abraham's bosom is a phrase used for eternal bliss, or heaven. Heaven is the absence of all that is bad and the presence of all that is good.

Conclusion

This is a parable that tells of one's eternal welfare. To ignore this message is eternal damnation, while to respond favorably is to have eternal life. I urge you to accept Jesus Christ as Lord and Savior of your life.

SUNDAY MORNING, DECEMBER 19

Title: Light and Wisdom from the Wise Men

Text: "When they saw the star, they rejoiced with exceeding great joy" (Matt. 2:10).

Scripture Reading: Matthew 2:1–10

Hymns: "O Come, All Ye Faithful," Oakeley
"Away in a Manger," Murray
"O Little Town of Bethlehem," Brooks

Offertory Prayer: Dear Lord, we are often blind to your leadership and deaf to our responsibilities as your children. Help us to follow the light of your leadership, and give us wisdom to use that revelation in our lives. May we apply in our daily lives the wisdom that comes from your Word and from the Holy Spirit. For the glory of Jesus. Amen.

Introduction

A. *There was a scurry in heaven.* A commotion was caused by the fact that the Christ was leaving heaven for his humiliation. Peter said in his first epistle that the time of the coming of Christ was a time unknown to any of the angels in heaven. Only God knew the appointed time. When the time came, even the angels of heaven participated in the things that God was now doing. God sent an angel to speak to Zechariah, Mary, and Joseph, and also to announce Jesus' birth to the shepherds. He even sent an angelic choir to the shepherds.

During this great commotion of heaven, God decided to speak to some Gentile men. We do not know much about these men, but many fables and myths have arisen about them. The Eastern church in the fourth century gave names to them and declared that there were three of them. The Bible does not tell us who they were. Doubtless they were students of the stars and probably some of the wisest men of their time. The Bible says they saw a star in the East, which they knew to be the star of Christ. Upon seeing that star, they became excited and made the journey to Jerusalem so they might inquire about the birth of the Messiah.

B. *If we do not get lost in the fables and myths, and if we stay with God's truth, we have a marvelous revelation.* Some theologians tell us that when Paul went on his first missionary journey, or when Peter went to share the gospel with Cornelius, the first Gentiles were converted to Christianity. Actually this is untrue. The first Gentiles to be converted were these wise men who came when Christ was born. They fell down before him and worshiped him. There are two lessons I would like for us to learn this morning. I would like for us to gather light from the star and wisdom from the wise men.

I. The light of the star.

A. *The star was an unusual creation.* It may have been a comet, as many have claimed. It may have been a special creation. Whatever it was, it revealed to the magi that the Jewish Messiah was born. God had told Israel to be ready for the coming of the Messiah. They were ready neither to receive him nor to share his message, so God revealed the coming of the Messiah through creation.

God never fails. If people do not do his will, he uses others.

B. *A leading light.* This star led to Christ. It told the wise men that the Christ had been born. Then they went to Jerusalem. They traveled through arid desert country. No doubt it was a difficult trip, but they would not be stopped. They inquired as to the place of the Messiah's birth. Ultimately they were taken to the scribes and told that the Christ would be born in Bethlehem. As they proceeded toward Bethlehem, the star appeared, leading the way to the Christ. We ought to be like that star, leading people to Christ, always showing the way to him.

The star attracted their attention. The Word of God taught them the exact details. The light led them to the Christ and stopped there. The light of every Christian needs to lead others to Christ. Do not lead people to church buildings or programs and leave them there; lead them to Christ. The star became a witness. It told those wise men that the Messiah was born. Then it led them to the Messiah. That is the kind of light the church must have in the world today.

II. The wisdom of the wise men.

Perhaps these men were teachers of science in Persia. They were not called kings; they were called magi, which means "wise ones."

A. *God's message in nature.* Many scientists conclude that perhaps the Christian message is not true because we have made so many myths about God rather than listening to God as he has spoken. God spoke loudly through nature to those ancient scientists. People may see God's handiwork in a tree or in the human body. Who could study either without recognizing that a divine Designer made them?

B. *God's message in his Word.* Paul said that God reveals himself in nature. He reveals himself in a general way in nature, but for details we must turn to God's Word. That is exactly what these wise men did. Let us be just as wise. When we look at the beauty of the sky, of the ocean, or of human life, let us recognize God's handiwork. Then let us turn to his Word and believe the exact details that God reveals to us about himself.

C. *The wise men persisted.* When the wise men saw the Messiah's star, they wanted to know him, so they traveled across the desert. They went through wild, rugged country filled not only with physical hardship but also with bands of robbers. They journeyed not on a jet airplane but on camels or by walking. They persisted in their search. They were not discouraged when they arrived at Jerusalem and found uninterested people. Many today are discouraged by lesser things in their search for Christ. The wise men did not become discouraged. In trying to learn about the Messiah, they could have said, "We will see if we like the scribes. Where did the scribes go to school? Are they friendly scribes? Are they good mixers? Do they stand at the door and shake hands when you come in, or do they not?" They did not say those things. They went eagerly to hear the message of God. They were tenacious in their search.

D. *The wise men rejoiced.* They knew that God was leading, and they rejoiced. Oh, my friends, if we could return to a rejoicing search for God! We come here to church like zombies. We come here to the house of God acting as if we do not want to hear God talk. Is God speaking to us out of his Word through his prophet? If he is, then we ought to rejoice as we come into the presence of God. That is what the wise men did. They rejoiced when they saw the star!

E. *The wise men worshiped.* They finally arrived at the house where Jesus was. Now with all of their persistence, with all of the revelation they had, they could have blown it right there. They came to the house where the young child was, and what did they do? They did not call a committee meeting. They did not send a telegram to their denominational headquarters to get permission. They entered the house. They came to Jesus. They did not hesitate; they immediately came to him and fell down before him and worshiped him. They had found the revelation of God.

Conclusion

The wise men worshiped the baby Jesus. Theirs was not curiosity gratified but devotion exercised. We also must worship the Savior, or we will never be saved by him. He has not come to put away our sins and then to leave us ungodly and self-willed. Oh, you who have never worshiped the Christ of God, may you be led to do so at once. He is God over all, blessed forever. Adore him. Was God ever seen in such a worshipful form before? Behold, he puts rainbows in the heavens, he rides upon the wings of the wind. He scatters flames of fire. He speaks, and his dreaded artillery shakes the hills. You worship in terror. Who would not adore the great and terrible Jehovah of the Old Testament?

But is it not much better to behold him here, allied to your nature, wrapped like your own children in swaddling clothes—tender, feeble, next to kin to your own self? Will you not worship God when he has thus come down to you and become your Brother born for your salvation? Here nature itself suggests worship. Oh, may grace produce it! Let us hasten to worship where shepherds and wise men and angels have led the way!

SUNDAY EVENING, DECEMBER 19

Title: Christianity Makes the Difference

Text: "Wives, submit yourselves unto your own husbands, as unto the Lord" **(Eph. 5:22)**.

"Husbands, love your wives, even as Christ also loved the church, and gave himself for it" **(Eph. 5:25)**.

"Children, obey your parents in the Lord: for this is right" **(Eph. 6:1)**.

"Servants, be obedient to them that are your masters according to the flesh, with fear and trembling, in singleness of your heart, as unto Christ" **(Eph. 6:5)**.

"And, ye masters, do the same things unto them, forbearing threatening: knowing that your Master also is in heaven; neither is there respect of persons with him" **(Eph. 6:9)**.

Scripture Reading: Ephesians 5:21–6:9

Introduction

When Jesus came to earth, he brought the reign of God. After Jesus' ascension, he sent his Holy Spirit. Christians began to spread the good news of Jesus Christ throughout the world. Wherever the gospel went, it made a difference in individual lives and in the community as a whole. Attitudes and actions in many areas of life were changed. Let us consider some strategic areas where Christianity made the difference.

I. Christianity affects marriages.

Paganism had affected marriages adversely. Little regard was given either to binding contracts or personal respect. Christianity made the difference in a marriage.

    A. *Christianity causes a wife to be regarded as a person.* "Wives, submit yourselves unto your own husbands, as unto the Lord. For the husband is the head of the wife, even as Christ is the head of the church: and he is the saviour of the body" (Eph. 5:22–23). It is important to notice that the broader application is of mutual submission to Christ (see v. 21). Otherwise, specific regulations tyrannically made a wife submit to her husband. As Christ protects and provides for the church, so the Christian husband regards his wife as an equal.

        This may not seem radical in the twenty-first century, but in the first century it was a revolutionary idea. Paul wanted the rights of womanhood to be protected because in the pagan world women were considered as property.

    B. *Christianity causes a husband to care for his wife.* "Husbands, love your wives, even as Christ also loved the church, and gave himself for it" (Eph. 5:25). Christ's devotion to the church is to be the example of the husband's devotion to his wife. The husband is to manifest the same kind of unselfish love toward his wife that Christ exercised toward the church.

II. Christianity affects families.

Paganism did little to safeguard family relationships. Responsibility was not stressed. Christianity brought amazing changes in family living.

    A. *Christianity brings responsibility to children.* "Children, obey your parents in the Lord: for this is right. Honour thy father and mother; (which is the first commandment with promise;) that it may be well with thee, and thou mayest live long on the earth" (Eph. 6:1–3). Paul stressed the obedience of children to their parents. The term "obey" means a readiness to hear, a willingness to heed counsel, to weigh words of advice, and to gladly shape one's course under the accepted guidance of more mature minds. In most cases, responsible obedience eventually leads to autonomous self-control.

    B. *Christianity brings responsibility to parents.* "And, ye fathers, provoke not your children to wrath: but bring them up in the nurture and admonition of the Lord" (Eph. 6:4). Parents have a twofold obligation to their children.

        1. They are to keep discipline in balance.

        2. They are to nurture and instruct their children.

III. Christianity affects labor.

The commercial world of Paul's day was a master/slave society. Paul provided the principles of survival in a slavery system. These were radical changes in the social lifestyle.

A. *Christianity encourages the recognition of authority.* "Servants, be obedient to them that are your masters according to the flesh, with fear and trembling, in singleness of your heart, as unto Christ" (Eph. 6:5). Christianity acknowledges that some people in the industrial world have a legal right to direct and control the activities of other people. Obedience to lawful masters must be rendered along with an eagerness to accomplish the task.

Furthermore, obedience is encouraged, not with hypocrisy or pretense, but with a sincere and undivided purpose. "Not with eyeservice, as menpleasers; but as the servants of Christ, doing the will of God from the heart" (Eph. 6:6).

Recognizing authority and obeying authority will lead to recognition and reward. "Knowing that whatsoever good thing any man doeth, the same shall he receive of the Lord, whether he be bond or free" (Eph. 6:8). The good things are known to the Lord. They are remembered by him and will receive full acknowledgment and recompense from him.

B. *Christianity causes a slave to be regarded as a person.* "And, ye masters, do the same things unto them, forbearing threatening: knowing that your Master also is in heaven; neither is there respect of persons with him" (Eph. 6:9). This command was radical. Slaves were regarded as little better than animals. It was in vogue to rule them by fear of punishment. Even in our day the business world often treats employees as "things." Christianity displaces this attitude by sympathy and by reverence for the divine Master, to whom both servants and masters must give an account.

Conclusion

Christianity makes a difference. If you open your life to Christ, he will make a difference in you. The best way to build a better society is to live Christlike lives and draw many to Christ.

WEDNESDAY EVENING, DECEMBER 22

Title: Parable of the Pharisee and the Publican

Text: "Every one who exalts himself will be humbled, but he who humbles himself will be exalted" (**Luke 18:14 RSV**).

Scripture Reading: Luke 18:9–14

Introduction

Attitude is what counts. If we have the right attitude, we can receive a blessing from this message. If we have a wrong attitude, we cannot receive any blessings. This parable has a twofold application. One is the spirit in which we pray, and the other is how to be saved. In this message the attitudes of the Pharisee and publican will be considered.

I. The attitude of the Pharisee.

    A. *This man had some remarkable qualities.*

        1. He did not do the things he was not supposed to do. He was not a wicked person outwardly. In his opinion, he had not violated the seventh commandment on adultery, the eighth on stealing, nor the ninth on trustworthiness. As his prayer continued, he probably informed the Lord of his many other virtues.

        2. He did do the things that were commendable. He fasted and tithed, both of which were commanded. He even went beyond these and did more.

    B. *Jesus said some interesting things about this man.* He was not declared right in the sight of God (v. 14). The reason was his attitude.

        1. His prayer was within himself. Notice verse 11. He "prayed thus with himself." He told himself what the grounds were on which he expected favors from God. It was not a silent prayer but an audible one. This man was his own god.

        2. He compared himself to others (v. 11). This is always dangerous. We are only to compare ourselves with God's ideal.

        3. He prayed in the spirit of self-sufficiency.

    C. *The attitude of the Pharisee is to be found in each person to a degree.* That is seen in attitudes toward each other and in the attitude toward the church.

II. The attitude of the publican (tax collector).

    A. *The Bible makes no reference to anything commendable in his life.* The title "publican" indicates the opposite of that which was commendable. The custom of his profession, and thus the reputation he bore, was that he stole and was dishonest.

    B. *Jesus said that this man was justified (v. 14).* Listeners are exhorted to take a lesson.

        1. His prayer was a real petition. He said, "God be merciful." God's mercy was this man's only hope.

        2. His prayer was personal and direct. He said, "God be merciful *to me*" (emphasis added). Each person must deal with his or her own sin.

        3. His prayer was humble. He admitted he was a sinner. He stood far off and would not look up. Guilty people always look down.

4. His prayer was from the heart. He beat his breast, a sure sign of emotional stress and deep remorse.

C. *Each person can derive some helpful lessons from this prayer.*

1. No one who is proud can pray. It has been said that the gate of heaven is so low that it is impossible to enter unless you are on your knees.

2. No one who despises others can pray. You cannot rightly lift yourself above others.

3. You really pray when you see yourself in relation to God.

Conclusion

Right now I want to ask you to examine your attitude. If it is not right, please ask God to come in and change it.

SUNDAY MORNING, DECEMBER 26

Title: The Time of Christmas

Text: "But when the fulness of the time was come, God sent forth his Son, made of a woman, made under the law" (**Gal. 4:4**).

Scripture Reading: Galatians 4:1–7

Hymns: "Thou Didst Leave Thy Throne?" Elliot

"It Came Upon the Midnight Clear," Sears

"Angels We Have Heard on High," Traditional

Offertory Prayer: Glorious God, most of us are quite busy these days, but we do not want to fail you. Time is a precious gift. Help us to realize that you gave us time. May we also realize that you appointed all time and all events. We praise you for what you have done in past time. We ask you to guide our lives in the precious moments of the present time. In the name of our Lord. Amen.

Introduction

As Paul reflected from a theological viewpoint on the birth of Christ, he said that until Christ came we were like children in a wealthy home. The child was the heir, but the child did not receive his inheritance. He was no different than a slave. He was under slave tutors who taught him. He was obedient to his father just as a slave would be obedient to his father, but he had a hope. He had a promise. The promise of those people of Old Testament times was the promise that the Messiah would come; so Paul, looking back on that event, which had just a short time before transpired, said, "But when the fulness of the time was come, God sent forth his Son." His Son changed our relationship. He came "that we might receive the adoption of sons. And because ye are sons, God hath sent forth the Spirit of his Son into your hearts, crying, Abba, Father. Wherefore thou art no more a servant, but a son; and if a son, then an heir of God through Christ" (Gal. 4:5–7). *Abba* is translated as "Father," but it really means "my Father." The significance of the birth of Christ cannot be fully known until Christ lives in your heart.

It is interesting that the evangelistic messages of the apostles recorded in Acts do not mention the birth of Jesus. Instead, they focus on his death and resurrection. Years later, however, under the Spirit of God, the apostles recorded the whole story of salvation. They wrote about the miraculous birth of Jesus. They told of one born of a virgin, born beyond the comprehension of human understanding. They told of God stepping into humanity to say to all people everywhere, "I am your Christ." They told of an angel choir, a shining star, a lowly manger, and shepherds who came to adore him, the humblest of all being the first to praise the King of Kings. They told of wise men from afar, educated men, who had come to praise him.

I. The fullness of the times.

A. *Historical significance.* The religion of the Greeks was dead. The religion of the Romans was already relegated to mythology. The religion of the Persians, though still in its ascendancy, had never satisfied the hearts of the people. So, suddenly, when people were in despair, when people were searching for reality, at that moment, God sent his Son.

B. *Spiritual significance.* Paul was suggesting that Christ came in the flesh to be God with us. Paul surely knew the story of the virgin birth. Doubtless he had heard of the wise men. He knew that Joseph had been told that Jesus was to be "God with us." When he said that Jesus was born to redeem, he believed that Christ had entered the world by God's miracle to deal with humankind's spiritual need. The greatest need humanity has is forgiveness of sins.

II. The spirit of the time.

A. *Not motifs but salvation.* If Christmas is only a time for decoration and festivity, its significance is lost.

1. Jesus came to be the Christ. If he is the power of heaven living in your heart, if he is God alive in you, then he is the Christ.

2. The Bible says, "All have sinned, and come short of the glory of God" (Rom. 3:23). "None is righteous, no, not one; no one understands, no one seeks for God . . . no one does good, not even one" (Rom. 3:10–12 RSV). That describes us naturally. We are not good people; we are sinners. We are not searchers for God; we retreat from him constantly. We are hopeless, but Jesus came to bring hope. Paul said of him, "God commendeth his love toward us, in that, while we were yet sinners, Christ died for us" (Rom. 5:8). Because nothing else could pay the price of our guilt, the Son paid it.

B. *Not despair but love.* Often people speak of the spirit of Christmas as though it is something to be caught while shopping. I heard someone say, "I went shopping and I caught the Christmas spirit." I recently went shopping with my wife, and people were in such a rush they shoved us and stepped on our feet. We stood in line for hours waiting to pay for our purchases. Furthermore, we spent more money than we meant to spend. If that's the Christmas spirit, I guess we're in trouble.

I think what most people mean when they say they want to catch the spirit of Christmas is that they want the warm feeling of love. They want to feel love for others, that inside warmth that says, "I want to give of myself to someone else." This is the kind of spirit that comes from God.

III. God's gift for the time.

A. *God's gift to us.* The real spirit of Christmas begins when we accept the best gift of all, the gift who was born in a manger, the Son of God. When we accept Jesus Christ, we accept the gift of salvation, the gift of forgiveness. But that is not all. We also receive the precious gift of the Holy Spirit, who comes to live within us and guide our steps.

B. *Our gift to God.* God wants us to give ourselves to him. How do we give ourselves in service to God? We must be willing to abandon self and let God use us in any way he chooses. Our service to God may simply be done by showing that the Holy Spirit is alive within us. If Christ is born in our hearts, God is our Father and the Holy Spirit is alive within us. Because of this, we will serve God by serving our brothers and sisters. "Whosoever will be great among you, let him be your minister; and whosoever will be chief among you, let him be your servant: even as the Son of man came not to be served but to serve" (Matt. 20:26–28).

Conclusion

If you really want the Spirit of Christ to live in you, and therefore the spirit of Christmas, you must be his servant; and you are his servant by giving yourself in service to others. Look again! "But when the fulness of the time was come, God sent forth his Son, made of a woman, made under the law, to redeem them that were under the law, that we might receive the adoption of sons. And because ye are sons, God hath sent forth the Spirit of his Son into your hearts" (Gal. 4:4–6). Where? In your hearts, so that out of your hearts you cry, "My Father," because he lives within you. If Christ is merely a nativity scene on your coffee table, he is dead. If the star of Christmas is only an ornament atop your tree, it has nothing to say. But if Christ lives in your heart, he has everything to say, because from your heart the living Christ causes you to cry out, "My Father!"

Sunday Evening, December 26

Title: Getting Ready for a Fight

Text: "Put on the whole armour of God, that ye may be able to stand against the wiles of the devil" **(Eph. 6:11)**.

Scripture Reading: Ephesians 6:10–20

Introduction

Getting ready for a championship boxing match requires a lot of work. Each boxer spends months and months in rigid training for the event. Promoters work hard to publicize and promote the fight. Millions of dollars, tremendous energy, and a multitude of hours go into preparation for the event.

Paul spoke of believers getting ready for a fight. He described the Christian life as one of continual conflict. Battle must be waged daily against the most relentless foe from whom there is no reprieve. Let us consider some ways we can get ready for our daily battle against the foe.

I. We need to know the enemy.

A. *The enemy is identified by name.* The enemy of believers is Satan, the great adversary, the slanderous accuser, the malignant foe of the followers of Christ. No believer needs to be deceived about his true identity.

B. *The enemy is identified by nature.* "Put on the whole armour of God, that ye may be able to stand against the wiles of the devil" (Eph. 6:11). Here "wiles" means schemes laid for spiritual disaster. Satan wages warfare with deception and crafty assaults.

II. We need to put on the equipment.

A. *We need the girdle of truth.* "Stand therefore, having your loins girt about with truth" (v. 14). Truth is seen in the person of Christ and in the relationships of Christians.

B. *We need the breastplate of righteousness.* "And having on the breastplate of righteousness" (Eph. 6:14). Righteousness denotes moral integrity. It protects us from the tricks of Satan. It helps us withstand a multitude of attacks and enter the conflict without fear.

C. *We need the shoes of peace.* "And your feet shod with the preparation of the gospel of peace" (Eph. 6:15). The Roman soldier wore strong sandals that protected his feet but also allowed him to stand in a slippery place. It is peace with God through our Lord Jesus Christ that enables us to stand firm in difficult places and to move swiftly in opposing the enemy.

398

D. *We need the shield of faith.* "Above all, taking the shield of faith, where-with ye shall be able to quench all the fiery darts of the wicked" (Eph. 6:16). The Roman soldier carried a huge door-like shield, usually made of wood and covered with leather. It protected him from the enemy's weapons. For believers, faith forms such a shield.

E. *We need the helmet of salvation.* "And take the helmet of salvation" (Eph. 6:17). The word "take" means to receive from God's hand something he has prepared for us. "Salvation" is such a gift.

III. We need to rely on another's resources.

A. *We have the resource of the Bible.* "And take the helmet of salvation, and the sword of the Spirit, which is the word of God" (Eph. 6:17). The sword of the Spirit is the one weapon of offense. The gospel message placed in the hands of the Christian warrior must be used with skill.

B. *We have the resource of prayer.* "Praying always with all prayer and suppli-cation in the Spirit, and watching thereunto with all perseverance and supplication for all saints" (Eph. 6:18). Praying in the Spirit describes the true character of prayer. It is offered under the guidance of the Spirit, in fellowship with the Spirit, and in dependence on the Spirit.

Soldiers fight more valiantly and more gallantly when they know they are not alone. The soldiers can remain in close, clear, personal communication with the commander. Also, around the Christian warrior stand countless others warriors who are ready to offer encour-agement and help.

Conclusion

Are you winning battles daily over the devil? If not, you need to get ready for a fight. Satan seeks to divert your attention away from the Lord. He opposes all the good that God wants to accomplish in your life. To meet the opposer, you need to put on the equipment God has for you. When you get your equipment in place, you can use the Word of God and prayer so that you will be a winner.

WEDNESDAY EVENING, DECEMBER 29

Title: Parable of the Wicked Husbandmen

Text: "What therefore shall the lord of the vineyard do unto them?" **(Luke 20:15).**

Scripture Reading: Luke 20:9–19

Introduction

The parable under consideration for this message is found in Matthew, Mark, and Luke. This being true, it is obvious that the Holy Spirit had some-thing he wanted the readers of the Bible to understand.

I. God is a compassionate God.

God is doing all he can for people, yet he still allows us freedom of choice.

A. *This truth is presented in the parable (20:9–16).*
   1. God is pictured placing confidence in humankind (v. 9). The verse "A certain man planted a vineyard, and let it forth to husbandmen," simply means the owner trusted the vineyard to someone else.
   2. God is pictured sending messengers (vv. 10–12). Three different messengers are mentioned. The number three in the Bible is a complete number. This means that God used his messengers to the fullest.
   3. God is pictured sending his only begotten Son (v. 13). The most compassionate and loving event in all history is that of sending Jesus Christ, the Son of God, to seek and save the lost.

B. *This truth is presented in the statement about the stone (vv. 17–18).*
   1. The stone referred to is Jesus. Stones have many purposes in buildings. They determine the positions of the walls and thus the shape of the whole building. A stone can be a keystone at the top and consummate the whole work. Or it can be the foundation stone, which determines the strength and durability of the building.
   2. Jesus is each of these to the human life.

II. To reject God's plea is a tragedy.

A. *This is portrayed in the parable by the rejection of the one whom God sends.* To reject God's servant is to reject God himself. To reject God's Son is to be destroyed.

B. *This is portrayed in the rejection of the stone.*
   1. An example is that of a trap to snare an animal. When an animal trips the trigger, the stone falls and the animal is crushed to death. When people reject Jesus Christ, their choice brings about their doom.
   2. Another example is that of a blind person stumbling and falling on a stone. This is the plight of those who are blind to the truth, with unbelief in their hearts, or with false beliefs. They are spiritually blind and fall into hopeless despair.

Conclusion

We have considered God's concern for people and his continual efforts to reach us. We have also been warned of the tragic consequences of rejecting Jesus Christ. It is my hope and prayer that you will not reject the Lord Jesus but accept him.

MISCELLANEOUS HELPS

MESSAGES ON THE LORD'S SUPPER

Title: Proclaiming Our Lord's Death

Text: "For as often as you eat this bread and drink the cup, you proclaim the Lord's death until he comes" **(1 Cor. 11:26 RSV).**

Scripture Reading: 1 Corinthians 11:23–26

Introduction

To properly observe the ordinance of the Lord's Supper, we need a spirit of solemnity and at the same time an attitude of joyful celebration. Memorializing an event as significant as the death of Jesus Christ should fill us with a spirit of awe and deepest reverence. Responding to the redemptive purpose in that event should cause us to celebrate the greatness of God's love for us. Let us seek an attitude of both solemnity and celebration as we consider this sacred experience before us.

Paul, quoting the Lord, declared that we are to partake of the bread and cup in remembrance of our Lord. As we do so, we are actually proclaiming the fact of his redemptive death on the cross. We need to do this for our own heart's good and for the salvation of others.

Let us consider why we should proclaim the death of our Lord as a great redemptive act that has significance for all people.

I. The death of Jesus reveals the awfulness of sin (I Cor. 15:3).

A. *The Scriptures declare that our sins were the reason for the death of Jesus Christ.* This may seem strange to a person of the twenty-first century who hears this for the first time.

B. *The angel told Joseph that the son who would be born of Mary would save his people from their sins (Matt. 1:21).* John the Baptist announced at the very beginning of Jesus' ministry, "Behold, the Lamb of God, who takes away the sin of the world!" (John 1:29 RSV). Peter, who had first resisted the thought that Jesus must die, later interpreted that death in terms of its substitutionary significance for us. "He himself bore our sins in his body on the tree, that we might die to sin and live to righteousness. By his wounds you have been healed. For you were straying like sheep, but have now returned to the Shepherd and Guardian of your souls" (1 Peter 2:24–25 RSV).

C. *At the cross we are confronted with the fact that each of us is a sinner in need of God's forgiveness.* This message is proclaimed as we partake of the Lord's Supper.

II. The death of Jesus reveals the greatness of God's love for sinners (John 3:16).

Paul declared to the Roman believers, "But God shows his love for us in that while we were yet sinners Christ died for us" (Rom. 5:8 RSV). Only with the help of the Holy Spirit can we begin to comprehend with all the saints what is the breadth and length and height and depth of the love of God that was revealed in Jesus Christ when he died on the cross for our sins.

In an age that dehumanizes the individual and discounts the value of a person, we come to Calvary to see how great God's love is for us. It was divine love that conceived the plan by which we could be saved. It was divine love that brought God's plan down to earth. It was divine love that carried out this plan of salvation on the cross. As we partake of the Lord's Supper, we are proclaiming the greatness of God's love for ourselves and others.

III. The death of Jesus reveals the value of a lost soul.

In the business world, the value of a person is often revealed by the price an employer is willing to pay for his or her services. In some parts of the world, human life is considered very cheap.

If you really want to know the value of a soul in God's eyes, you need to consider Calvary and see the great price that was paid for your redemption. Jesus came and gave his life as a ransom and to redeem us from the slavery of sin. It is here that God placed a price tag on the worth of the individual.

Do you have difficulty keeping a sense of personal value? Do you suffer from a sense of low self-esteem? Then go to Calvary and see the price that God has placed on you.

As we partake of the Lord's Supper, we proclaim in the death of Jesus Christ the value of a lost soul.

IV. In proclaiming Jesus' death, we announce the only way of salvation (Acts 4:12).

There was no other way to pay the price of sin. Only Jesus could unlock the door of heaven and let us in.

Our Lord died because the wages of sin is death. Either we must die for our own sins or we must accept the perfect substitute that God has offered us in Jesus Christ.

Conclusion

As we partake of the Lord's Supper, let us realize that in this proclamation of the death of Christ, we see the only way by which a lost and needy world can come to know the love of God and the way of salvation. Let us determine out of love for our Lord and out of concern for those around us that we will go forth to communicate God's love to those who have not yet come to experience it in Jesus Christ.

Title: When Jesus Gave Thanks

Text: "He took a cup, and when he had given thanks he gave it to them, saying, 'Drink of it, all of you; for this is my blood of the covenant, which is poured out for many for the forgiveness of sins'" **(Matt. 26:27–28 RSV)**.

Scripture Reading: Matthew 26:26–30

Introduction

On this most solemn occasion in the life of our Lord, he found it possible to be thankful to God. With the agony of the cross in the immediate future, he was able to offer thanks. Evidently our Lord had developed the habit of giving thanks in the midst of all things and at all times. As we observe the ordinance of the Lord's Supper, we have every reason to be thankful.

I. Did our Lord offer thanks for God's blessings in the past?

As Jesus contemplated dying on the cross, he offered thanks to God. Perhaps he was thanking God for the many provisions in his ministry up to this point. Perhaps he was thanking God for his redemptive purpose from the very dawn of beginning. Perhaps he was thanking God for the divine protection of his servants through the centuries. Perhaps he was thanking God for his abiding presence.

If our Lord could be thankful to God for the past, it follows that each of us can find many things for which to thank God. He has done so much for us. We can be thankful for the struggles and the sacrifices of those who are humanly responsible for the great spiritual heritage we enjoy today. We can be thankful for the prophets and the apostles, for the pioneer missionaries and our spiritual forefathers. Let us be grateful during this service for God's provisions in the past.

II. Did our Lord offer thanks for God's blessings in the present?

We can be certain that our Lord was living and laboring with an awareness of the abiding presence of the Father God. Twice the voice had come from heaven declaring, "This is my beloved Son in whom I am well pleased."

Our Lord had come on a mission that would involve teaching and healing and finally dying on a cross. He was so near to the completion of his mission that he felt thankful to God because of the joy of personal accomplishment.

Let us search for those things in our contemporary experience that can cause us to be thankful to God as we partake of these elements of the Lord's Supper.

What would our lives be like if we had never come to know Jesus Christ? Let us take an inventory and evaluate the differences that Christ has made to enrich and improve our total human experience. Let us be grateful for the friendships and the relationships that have been made possible by his life, death, and resurrection.

As we partake of these elements that symbolize Jesus' incarnation in human flesh and his sacrificial death on the cross, let us be thankful today.

III. Did our Lord offer thanks to God for the future?

With the agony awaiting him in Gethsemane and on Calvary, was our Lord anticipating the joy of returning to the Father? Was this an element in the thanksgiving that he offered to the Father as he held in his hands the symbols of his incarnation and sacrificial death on the cross? In the great intercessory prayer recorded in John 17, we hear our Lord saying, "And now I am no more in the world, but they are in the world, and I am coming to thee" (17:11 RSV).

Our Lord was thankful for what his life, his teachings, his ministry, his sacrificial and substitutionary death, and his glorious resurrection were going to mean to his followers. The writer of the book of Hebrews tells us that it was because of "the joy that was set before him" that he "endured the cross, despising the shame" (Heb. 12:2 RSV).

Our Lord was offering thanks because, through his coming death on the cross, it would be possible for the love of God to be revealed to a sinful race.

As we partake of the bread that symbolizes Jesus' coming to earth in human flesh, and as we drink the fruit of the vine that symbolizes his sacrificial death on the cross, let us rejoice and be grateful. Let us be thankful for what Jesus' death and resurrection have done for our past, our present, and our future.

Conclusion

Our Lord had the habit of being thankful. He gave verbal expression to God and to others of his inward attitude of gratitude.

As we participate in the Lord's Supper, let us be supremely thankful to him for what he has done for us in the past, what he is doing in the present, and what he is going to do in the future.

Title: Proclaiming the Lord's Death until He Comes

Text: "For as often as you can eat this bread and drink the cup, you proclaim the Lord's death until he comes" (**1 Cor. 11:26 RSV**).

Scripture Reading: 1 Corinthians 11:23–26

Introduction

Our Lord gave us a number of commands to obey until history comes to its consummation by his victorious return: He has commanded us to pray and to guard against temptation. He has commanded us to communicate the good news of salvation to the ends of the earth. And he has commanded us to love one another with the same kind of love he demonstrated toward us.

From time to time we are reminded of the greatness of God's love for us revealed in the suffering and death of the Messiah. As we partake of the bread, we are to remember with reverence and awe that God became a man and gave himself in the incarnation for us. As we partake of the fruit of the vine, we are to remember his sacrificial and substitutionary death and that it is by his blood that our sins are covered and forgiven.

By our observing this memorial supper, we are proclaiming our belief that one day Jesus Christ will return to the earth.

I. Jesus promised to return.

"And when I go and prepare a place for you, I will come again and take you to myself, that where I am you may be also" (John 14:3 RSV). Repeatedly our Lord promised to return. The greatest event yet in the future is the glorious return of Jesus Christ.

A. *Only when Jesus returns will we have complete and final victory over death and the grave (1 Cor. 15:51–57).*

B. *Only when Jesus returns will our salvation be complete (Heb. 9:27).* We can rejoice now in the assurance of salvation from the penalty of sin through faith in Jesus Christ. We can rejoice now in salvation from the power of sin in the present through the work of the Holy Spirit. We can rejoice in anticipation of salvation from the very presence of sin when Jesus Christ returns.

II. The angels announced that Jesus would return (Acts 1:10–11).

Following our Lord's victorious ascension back to the Father, the angelic messengers instructed his bewildered apostles to trust in his promises and to look forward to his triumphant return. As we partake of the elements of this supper, let us take heed to what the angels said. Let us look forward with joyful anticipation to the triumphant return of him who came to reveal God's love and mercy.

III. The apostles declared that Jesus would return.

Scriptural references to apostolic belief in Jesus' return are numerous.

A. *Peter believed in the glorious return of Jesus Christ.*

B. *Paul believed with all his heart that Jesus would return.*

C. *John received the great revelation on the Isle of Patmos that proclaims the triumph of Jesus Christ.* This glorious book contains in its final chapter three clear, definite, dogmatic promises of Jesus Christ to the effect that he would return (Rev. 22:7, 12, 20). Almost the last words of this tremendous book contain the prayer of the revelator. We hear him say, "Come, Lord Jesus!" (22:20).

Conclusion

As we partake of the bread, let us remember that God came in human flesh to reveal himself and his will for us in Jesus Christ. As we partake of

405

the fruit of the vine, let us be reminded that it was by the sacrificial death of Jesus Christ that a way was provided for us to receive the remission of our sins and the gift of eternal life.

As we partake, let us rejoice in the fact that we are a part of that chain of disciples, extending from the ministry of Jesus until his glorious return, who have the privilege of proclaiming his death until he comes.

MESSAGES FOR CHILDREN AND YOUNG PEOPLE

Title: The Savior Is Waiting

Text: "Behold, I stand at the door and knock; if any one hears my voice and opens the door, I will come in to him and eat with him, and he with me" **(Rev. 3:20 RSV).**

Introduction

The chorus "The Savior Is Waiting" by Ralph Carmichael was popular among young people when it was introduced throughout the world in the late 1950s. Carmichael's chorus contains a great truth regarding the Savior, who does not remain in some distant place unconcerned about the needs of individuals but who takes the initiative and always moves toward us rather than away from us. The first step always belongs to him. Why would the Savior want to come into your heart? Why would he be interested in you?

I. The Savior is waiting to come into your heart.

Christ can do very little for you as long as you keep him on the outside of your life. He wants to come into your life to bring the gift of forgiveness and the gift of new life. He wants to come into your life to make it complete as God meant for it to be from the beginning. He can only come in with your consent. He will not intrude. He will not be an unwelcome guest.

II. The Savior is waiting to do something to you.

Many of us think in terms of God doing various things *for* us, but he also wants to do something *to* us. Jesus Christ wants to give you the privilege of entering into the family of God by becoming one of God's children (John 1:12). He wants to make you a new creation (2 Cor. 5:17). He wants to give you a new nature that will cause you to love God and others. He wants to give you a new nature that will cause you to want to avoid sin and to love doing all that is right.

III. The Savior is waiting to do something for you.

All of us have various people who do things for us. Our parents do many things for us. Our teachers in school do many things for us. Our community does many things for us. But Jesus Christ can do things for us that no one else can. Only Jesus Christ could die for your sins. Only Jesus Christ could rise from the dead to give you assurance of eternal life. Only Jesus Christ can be the way to your acceptance in the family of God. The Savior is waiting to do something for you.

IV. The Savior is waiting to do something *with* you.

Maybe you have never even stopped to consider the fact that God needs you. He needs you as his servant and as a helper in your family. He needs you to be the salt of the earth and the light of the world in the place where God calls you. God needs you. He wants you. You can make the decision to let him have you, and he can do great things with you.

Conclusion

In the New Testament there is an account of a boy who presented his lunch to Jesus. Jesus accepted the five barley loaves and two fish. He blessed them and gave them to his apostles, and they distributed them to the multitude. Over five thousand people were nourished that day because a boy gave what he had to Jesus Christ.

Only eternity can reveal what Jesus Christ can do with you if you will let him come into your heart as Lord and Savior, Teacher, Guide, and Friend.

Title: I Love Thee

Text: "I love the LORD, because he has heard my voice and my supplications" **(Ps. 116:1 RSV)**.

"We love, because he first loved us" **(1 John 4:19 RSV)**.

Scripture Reading: Psalm 116:1–2, 8–17

Introduction

Have you ever noticed in a corner of your hymnbook near the title of a song the word "anonymous"? That means that the publisher does not know the author of the hymn that is printed on that page.

We do not know the author of a lovely chorus that goes as follows:

> I love Thee, I love Thee, I love Thee, my Lord;
> I love Thee, my Savior, I love Thee, my God;
> I love Thee, I love Thee, and that Thou dost know;
> But how much I love Thee my actions will show.

In the words of this poem, the unknown author declares his love for the Lord, and in the last line pledges that he will demonstrate his love for the Lord: "But how much I love Thee my actions will show."

This is just one of many hymns in which the writer was telling how he or she loved the Lord. In Psalm 116 we find the psalmist giving expression to his love for the Lord. He lists some of the reasons why he loves the Lord.

I. I love the Lord.

A. *God answers prayer (vv. 1–2).* If we have the privilege of living in a Christian home, we are taught to pray. We are also taught to pray when we go to Bible school and to the worship services at our church. It is by prayer that we confess our sins and ask God to forgive us. It is by prayer that we invite Jesus to become our Savior. It is by prayer that we ask God for help in our times of difficulty. It is by prayer that we ask God to help others. Those who have the habit of prayer can rejoice in the Father God who has promised to hear us even if he sometimes does not give us the things we ask for. The more you pray, the more love you will have for God.

B. *God delivers us from death.* "For thou hast delivered my soul from death" (116:8 RSV). The psalmist is not thinking of physical death so much as spiritual death. Spiritual death is the separation of the soul from God. God in his mercy has sent his Son to die on our behalf for our sins. He died for us that we might be saved from the death that sin always brings. The psalmist was rejoicing in the glad awareness of having eternal life. He loved the Lord because the Lord had saved him from death.

C. *God delivers us from bad decisions and the trouble that follows.* "For thou hast delivered my soul from death, my eyes from tears, my feet from stumbling" (116:8 RSV). God is interested in doing more than saving our souls from an eternity of separation from him. God comes into our lives to give us wisdom and direction so that we can avoid making choices that would put us on a collision course with disaster. When we invite Jesus to come into our hearts, he dwells there to help us become all that we are capable of being.

What are some of the personal reasons you have for loving the Lord? It is a good idea to write out a list of reasons why you love the Lord.

II. "But how much I love Thee my actions will show."

The unknown poet who wrote the words of the chorus mentioned earlier concluded the first stanza with this promise: "But how much I love Thee my actions will show." The psalmist had a similar attitude as he wrote Psalm 116. He asked, "What shall I return to the LORD for all his goodness to me?" (v. 12 NIV). What can we do for the Lord in return for all the good things he has done for us? The psalmist listed some of the ways in which he was determined to show his love for God.

A. *"I will walk before the LORD in the land of the living" (v. 9 RSV).* This probably means that the psalmist was determined that his conduct and behavior would be pleasing to the Lord. He would remind himself daily of the abiding presence of his great and wonderful God.

Do you walk before the Lord in the land of the living? Are you aware of his presence with you in the home? In the classroom? On the playground? While dating?

An awareness of the abiding presence of our Lord can help us control ourselves when we are tempted to do evil. It can also challenge us to do our best in times of difficulty.

B. *"I will lift up the cup of salvation and call on the name of the* LORD*" (v. 13 RSV).* The psalmist seems to be saying, "I will put forth an earnest effort to experience everything that God has planned for me."

C. *"I will . . . call on the name of the* LORD*" (v. 13 RSV).* The psalmist was determined to continue the habit of prayer. He needed to listen to God as well as talk to God.

D. *"I will pay my vows to the* LORD *in the presence of all his people" (v. 14 RSV).* In this statement the psalmist is saying, "I will keep my promises to God." God has made many promises to us, and we should make some promises to him. Promises should not be made lightly and without serious commitment to follow through.

E. *"I will offer to thee the sacrifice of thanksgiving" (v. 17 RSV).* The psalmist was determined to live a life characterized by gratitude and thanksgiving. Thankfulness is something we need to practice until it becomes a habit. Each of us should develop the habit of being thankful to God, our parents, our teachers, and others who play important roles in our lives.

Conclusion

"But how much I love Thee my actions will show." How can you express your love for God? Draw up a mental list and determine to express your love for the Lord in a meaningful way that will really let him know how much you love him.

Title: I Have Decided to Follow Jesus

Text: "And Jesus said to them, 'Follow me and I will make you become fishers of men.' And immediately they left their nets and followed him" **(Mark 1:17–18 RSV).**

Introduction

A folk melody from India contains words that describe the nature of the Christian life. The words of the chorus "I Have Decided to Follow Jesus" can put strength into our soul, serving as an inward restraint and as a means to self-discipline when we are tempted to stray.

I have decided to follow Jesus,
I have decided to follow Jesus,

I have decided to follow Jesus,
No turning back, no turning back.

The second stanza expresses determination.

Tho' no one join me, still I will follow,
Tho' no one join me, still I will follow,
Tho' no one join me, still I will follow,
No turning back, no turning back.

There are many ways in which we can decide to follow Jesus.

I. We can decide to follow him with faith in the Father.

From the very beginning, Jesus placed complete confidence in the Father God. He trusted him in the present. He trusted him for the future. Never was there a moment when he did not fully trust his Father.

Have you decided to follow Jesus by trusting in the Father God?

II. We can follow Jesus in a program of personal growth.

"And the child grew and became strong, filled with wisdom; and the favor of God was upon him" (Luke 2:40 RSV). We need proper food if we are to experience physical growth. We must nourish ourselves if we are to live healthy lives. Likewise, as the children of God in the Spirit, we must nourish our souls on the milk and the meat of God's Word. Not to do so is to starve (1 Peter 2:1–2).

III. We can follow Jesus in his personal and public worship habits.

"And he came to Nazareth, where he had been brought up; and he went to the synagogue, as his custom was, on the sabbath day" (Luke 4:16 RSV). It is interesting to note that our Lord found it appropriate to be regular in his attendance with the people of God for Bible study, prayer, and praise. Those who deprive themselves of this good habit are impoverishing themselves of that which comes only through a creative experience with God's people. Each person is required to attend school until he or she reaches a certain age. There is no law requiring you to go the church of your choice. But to be a follower of Jesus means that you will want to do this.

IV. We can follow Jesus in the matter of private prayer.

"In these days he went out into the hills to pray; and all night he continued in prayer to God" (Luke 6:12 RSV). This particular incident in the life of Jesus preceded the momentous decision of selecting his apostles. We must not assume that Jesus regularly spent an entire night in prayer, but we can be certain that he had the habit of prayer and did not break it.

Have you developed the habit of talking with God? Have you developed the habit of listening to God? Are you aware that you can let Bible study be the listening side of the prayer experience? One of the finest habits Jesus had, and that you can have, is the habit of daily prayer.

V. We can follow Jesus in rendering service to others.

Matthew tells us, "The Son of man came not to be served but to serve" (Matt. 20:28 RSV). Jesus defined his reason for existence in terms of serving God and ministering to the needs of others. If you will truly follow Jesus, you must be a servant in your family, in your community, and to the world. Jesus believed that greatness expresses itself in service to others rather than in seeking to control and use others.

What are your goals in life? What are your ambitions? What are your ideals?

Conclusion

Have you decided to follow Jesus? This is not a question to be taken lightly. It is not a decision to be made without serious thought. It involves deliberate choice and continuous self-discipline.

Following Jesus could lead to a cross. Following Jesus always leads to a crown. When we decide to follow Jesus, it means we decide to follow him throughout all of life and ultimately to heaven itself.

> I have decided to follow Jesus,
> I have decided to follow Jesus,
> I have decided to follow Jesus,
> No turning back, no turning back.

FUNERAL MEDITATIONS

Title: The Resurrection of the Dead

Text: "So is it with the resurrection of the dead. What is sown is perishable, what is raised is imperishable" **(1 Cor. 15:42 RSV)**.

Scripture Reading: 1 Corinthians 15:35–57

Introduction

From the dawn of human history, people have been mystified by the fact of death. Death came about as a result of human sin. People fear death because they are sinners. People are afraid to die because of guilt and a feeling of failure.

We can only speculate as to whether or not physical death was a part of the good plan of the Creator God from the beginning. Perhaps it was. If it was a part of his plan, then it is sin that puts the sting in death and causes people to be afraid of it.

Throughout the centuries people have asked the question that was verbalized by Job: "If a man die, shall he live again?" (Job 14:14). There was no authentic answer to that question until the resurrection of Jesus Christ took place. On the basis of the firm fact of a miraculous resurrection, Christians came to believe that death was not the end and that the grave was not the goal of human destiny. Jesus affirmed, "Because I live, you will live also" (John 14:19 RSV).

Our present belief in immortality is based not on the Greek concept of humankind's natural immortality but rather on the Christian teaching of a resurrection. In Paul's letter to the Corinthians, he encourages his readers to trust in the wisdom and power of God as they face the questions, "How are the dead raised? With what kind of body do they come?" (1 Cor. 15:35 RSV).

I. The wisdom of God.

"But God gives it a body as he has chosen, and to each kind of seed its own body" (1 Cor. 15:38 RSV). Some things must be left to the wisdom of God.

    A. *The wisdom of God illustrated in biological life.*
        1. A person has a body that is perfectly adapted for human need.
        2. The animals of the fields have bodies adapted to their habitat.
        3. The birds of the air have bodies perfectly adapted to their habitat.
        4. The fish of the sea have bodies perfectly adapted to their habitat.
    B. *The wisdom of God illustrated by astronomy.* Comparing our earthly habitat with the heavenly bodies is somewhat like comparing apples with oranges. The sun has its own unique glory. We are told that it is a continuous series of hydrogen explosions. If it were farther away from the earth, we might freeze. If it were closer to the earth, we might scorch. The moon has its own unique glory in that it reflects the sun's light. Even the stars differ in splendor. The apostle Paul declared, "So will it be with the resurrection of the dead. The body that is sown is perishable, it is raised imperishable; it is sown in dishonor, it is raised in glory; it is sown in weakness, it is raised in power; it is sown a natural body, it is raised a spiritual body" (1 Cor. 15:42–44 NIV).

II. The power of God.

The person of faith will trust in God's wisdom, goodness, and power in all circumstances.

    A. *God has the power to create plant life.* Each plant has a body perfectly adapted for its fruit. The same God who has the power to create plants gives us a body that is proper for eternal habitation.
    B. *God has the power to give each human a body.* He gives the animals their bodies, the birds their bodies, and the fish their bodies. This same God will give us a body perfectly adapted for living in heaven.

C. *God can create a sun, a moon, the earth, and the stars.* This same God can prepare for his children a habitat that will be perfectly adaptable for his purposes and our needs.

Conclusion

The apostle concludes, "It is sown a physical body, it is raised a spiritual body" (15:44 RSV). Only by faith in the goodness, wisdom, and power of God can we face the question "How are the dead raised and with what body do they come?" Let us trust in him who so loved us that he was willing to die for us. Let us trust in him who was so powerful that he could lay down his life and take it up again. Let us be comforted in our time of sorrow by the God who is the God of all comfort and the Father of all mercies (2 Cor. 1:3–4).

Title: A Very Present Help in Trouble

Text: "God is our refuge and strength, a very present help in trouble" (**Ps. 46:1 RSV**).

Scripture Reading: Psalm 46:1–7

Introduction

The pathway of life is strewn with difficult times, beginning with the difficult experience of birth. Starting school is a trying experience for a child. Having a child leave home to go away to college is difficult for parents. At times securing a job can be a tough experience. For some there are many disappointments along life's pathway.

The death of a loved one is always a painful time in which those who remain stand in need of help. When grief comes we need the support of friends, family, and the family of God found in the church. Most of all we need God's help.

The psalmist found in God the strength he needed for his time of trouble.

I. God is our refuge.

In the days of the psalmist, people needed a refuge in the time of storm and in the time of danger when enemies approached. Often they would build a refuge in the form of a tower on the top of the highest hill accessible. In this place of refuge they sought safety. Today God is the refuge to whom believers can go when threatened by the storms of grief.

II. God is our strength.

We can receive strength from our friends, our family, and even from financial resources. But the greatest strength that can meet the deepest needs of our lives when grief comes is that which can be found only in the Lord. He can give us the strength to adjust to new and difficult circumstances. He can give us the strength to look back and be grateful. He can give us the strength to look forward with hope.

III. God is our helper.

God will help us through his Holy Scriptures as we claim his precious promises. And the Holy Spirit will come alongside us to serve as our Comforter.

Conclusion

God will give you the help you need for the future. He will help you with your burdens, and he will help you with your decisions. Let us always remember that "God is our refuge and strength, a very present help in trouble."

Title: The House of the Lord

Text: "And I shall dwell in the house of the LORD for ever" **(Ps. 23:6 RSV)**.

Scripture Reading: Psalm 23

Introduction

In this beautiful psalm from the Old Testament, the inspired writer gives voice to his faith. At the end of his earthly pilgrimage, he will have the privilege of dwelling in the house of the Lord forever. This is a remarkable expression of confidence in the greatness and goodness of God in view of the fact that the psalmist lived on the other side of the resurrection of Jesus Christ.

I. "In my Father's house are many rooms" (John 14:2 RSV).

When Jesus announced that he would soon depart from his apostles, they were filled with despair. They were grieved at the thought of no longer being with him. He sought to comfort them and to encourage them by speaking of the Father's house to which he would go and to which they would someday come through faith in him as Savior. He spoke of the spaciousness of his Father's house, a prepared place for a prepared people. And he spoke words of assurance concerning his desire that they all be with him in his Father's house.

II. Paul spoke of a house "eternal in the heavens" (2 Cor.5:1).

Throughout the ages, people have been aware of the advance of age and of the deterioration of the powers of the human body. This has been a continual source of distress to men and women.

Paul, who had received divine revelations from God concerning the resurrection of the saints (1 Cor. 15) and the resurrection of Christ, spoke of the home beyond this home in terms of "a building from God, a house not made with hands, eternal in the heavens" (2 Cor. 5:1 RSV). Paul assured us in these words that God did not prepare us merely to live an earthly existence.

Instead, he prepared us that we might live with God for eternity in a house not made with hands. As an indication of this divine desire and this divine design, God has already given us the Holy Spirit. He is a resident in our hearts as a guarantee of our ultimate redemption from death and the grave (2 Cor. 5:5; Eph. 1:13–14).

III. John the revelator spoke of the Father's house in terms of a new heaven, a new earth, and a holy city (Rev. 21:1–5).

In some respects the Bible is a record of God's effort to restore sinful humankind to the garden from which they were cast out. Redemption is God's program of delivering humanity from the tyranny and waste that sin brought into human existence. In this passage of Scripture, we discover that what humankind lost because of sin is regained through faith in Jesus Christ at the consummation of history when the redeemed return to God's paradise.

In the house not made with hands, there will be no more tears of sadness and no more death to separate us from our loved ones. There will be no more pain that disrupts life, for the former things will have passed away.

Conclusion

Let us thank God today for being the God and Father of our Lord Jesus Christ who loves us and who has provided for us a house not made with hands, but which is eternal in the heavens.

Heaven is a wonderful place that we will reach if we are prepared. Have you prepared yourself not only for life, but for death, by receiving Jesus Christ as Lord and Savior? Only through him is there any hope for forgiveness that will give you a position of acceptance in the presence of a holy God. Only through faith in him can you experience a spiritual birth that will give you a nature that will enable you to enjoy heaven when you get there.

Before our Lord began his public ministry, he worked in a carpenter shop. After his ascension back to the Father, he began making intercession for us. But he is also in the process of preparing a place for those who love him.

In times of sorrow like this, we perceive in a fresh and wonderful way how good God is and how wonderful his provisions are for us.

(Note to pastor: Close with a prayer thanking God for his many provisions for us.)

WEDDINGS

Title: The Sacredness of Marriage

Text: "So God created man in his own image, in the image of God he created him; male and female he created them. And God blessed them, and God said to them, 'Be fruitful and multiply, and fill the earth and subdue it; and have dominion over the fish of the sea and over the birds of the air and over every living thing that moves upon the earth'" (**Gen. 1:27–28 RSV**).

Introduction

In the very first chapter of the Bible, we find it recorded that as God created man and woman, he also ordained that they should live together as husband and wife. Marriage is therefore a part of the divine plan for us.

Holy and happy is the hour when two devoted hearts are bound by the ties of matrimony. Marriage is an institution of divine appointment and is commended as honorable among all people. Marriage is God's first institution for the welfare of the race. In the quiet bowers of Eden, before the forbidden tree had yielded its fateful fruit or the tempter had touched the world, God saw that it was not good for the man to be alone. He made a helpmate suitable for him and established the rite of marriage while heavenly hosts witnessed the wonderful scene in reverence.

The contract of marriage was sanctioned and honored by the presence and power of Jesus at the marriage in Cana of Galilee and marked the beginning of his wondrous works. It is declared by the apostle Paul to be honorable among all people. So it is ordained that a man will leave his father and mother and be united to his wife, and the two will become one flesh, united in hopes and aims and sentiments till death alone will part them.

If you then, _____ (groom), and _____ (bride), after careful consideration, and in the fear of God, have deliberately chosen each other as partners in this holy estate, and know of no just cause why you should not be so united, in token thereof will you please join your right hands.

Groom's vow

_____, will you take this woman to be your wedded wife, to live together after God's ordinance in the holy estate of matrimony? Will you love her, comfort her, honor her, and keep her in sickness and in health, and forsaking all others be to her in all things a true and faithful husband?

Answer: I will.

Bride's vow

_____, will you take this man to be your wedded husband, to live together after God's ordinance in the holy estate of matrimony? Will you love him, comfort him, honor him, and keep him in sickness and in health, and forsaking all others be to him in all things a true and faithful wife?

Answer: I will.

Vows to each other

I, _____ (groom), take thee, _____ (bride), to be my wedded wife, to have and to hold from this day forward, in prosperity or adversity, in sickness or in health, to love and to cherish till death do us part, according to God's holy ordinance.

I, _____ (bride), take thee, _____ (groom), to be my wedded husband, to have and to hold from this day forward, in prosperity or adversity, in sickness or in health, to love and to cherish till death do us part, according to God's holy ordinance.

Then are you each given to the other for richer or poorer, for better or worse, in sickness and in health, till death alone will part you.

Presentation of rings

From time immemorial the ring has been used to seal important covenants. The golden band, most prized of jewelry, has come to its loftiest prestige in the symbolic significance that it vouches at the marriage altar. Its untarnishable material is of the purest gold. Even so may your love for each other be pure and may it grow brighter and brighter with each passing day. The ring is a circle, thus having no end. Even so may there be no end to the happiness and success that come to you as you unite your lives together.

Do you, _____ (groom), give this ring to your wedded wife as a token of your love for her?

Answer: I do.

Will you, _____ (bride), receive this ring as a token of your wedded husband's love for you, and will you wear it as a token of your love for him?

Answer: I will.

Do you, _____ (bride), give this ring to your wedded husband as a token of your love for him?

Answer: I do.

Will you, _____ (groom), receive this ring as a token of your wedded wife's love for you, and will you wear it as a token of your love for her?

Answer: I will.

Having pledged your love for each other in the sight of God and these assembled witnesses, and having sealed your solemn marital vows by giving and receiving these rings, acting in the authority vested in me as a minister of the gospel by this state, and looking to heaven for divine sanction, I now pronounce you husband and wife.

Therefore, what God has joined together, let no man separate.

(Prayer)

Title: Let Us Invite Jesus to This Wedding

Text: On the third day there was a marriage at Cana in Galilee, and the mother of Jesus was there; Jesus also was invited to the marriage, with his disciples. **(John 2:1–2 RSV)**

Introduction

We would like to think that every time the people of God come together for worship, the living Christ blesses them with his presence. He made a promise that "where two or three are gathered in my name, there am I in the midst of them" (Matt. 18:20 RSV). In view of the fact that Jesus attended a wedding in Cana of Galilee, we should have no hesitation at inviting him to this wedding so that we might be blessed with his presence.

On this high and holy occasion, when two devoted hearts are bound together by the ties of Christian matrimony, we should rejoice in the glad consciousness that this is a part of God's good plan. Marriage is more than just a human arrangement. Christian marriage should be something infinitely more than a legal contract between two individuals, for marriage is a divine institution that was born in the heart of God and designed to produce the highest possible human happiness.

Since marriage is a divine institution, we should look to the Scriptures for guidance and help if we would achieve the highest possible success in this most important of human relationships. One of the most beautiful passages dealing with the mutual responsibilities of husbands and wives is found in the apostle Paul's letter to the Ephesians.

(The minister should now read Ephesians 5:21–33.)

I would call your attention to the fact that in the first verse of this passage both the husband and wife are encouraged to recognize the absolute lordship of Christ in the marriage relationship. Marriage should not be entered into lightly or without inward assurance that the union of your two lives is according to the will of the Savior. This verse implies that God is to have first place and that we are responsible to him for the manner in which we relate ourselves to our companion in marriage.

This passage of Scripture compares the relationship of the husband and the wife to the mystical relationship that exists between Christ and his church. The passage emphasizes the mutual responsibilities within the marriage relationship rather than the rights and privileges of the relationship.

This passage contains a command to the husband to love his wife in a twofold manner. First of all, the husband is commanded to love his wife "even as Christ also loved the church, and gave himself for it" (Eph. 5:25). This is sacrificial love that places the welfare of the wife before the husband's own welfare. The second command to the husband is that he is to love his wife even as he loves his own body (Eph. 5:28). By a combination of sacrificial love and self-love, the husband is to devote himself to the welfare of his wife.

This passage contains two commands to the wife also. Verse 22 encourages the wife to recognize her husband as the head of the household. Verse 33 exhorts the wife to "reverence her husband." Nothing is said about the wife loving her husband, though it is implied. Genuine and abiding love is based on respect. We can safely assume that it is God's purpose for the husband to so conduct himself as to merit the reverence and respect of his wife and that the wife so conduct herself as to merit the respect of her husband.

Vows to each other

(The minister should now use the vows of his choice.)

Presentation of rings

(The minister should now receive the rings.)

From time immemorial the ring has been used on important occasions. In ages gone by, the official seal of the empire was often worn as a signet on the hand of the reigning monarch and was used to authenticate documents of state. But the golden circlet has reached its loftiest prestige in the symbolic significance that it vouches at the marriage altar.

(The minister should hold the rings up before the bride and groom.) The wedding rings are objects of great beauty. This is true because the ring is made of a precious metal that will not tarnish with the passing of time. At one time this ring was but crude ore in the depths of the earth. Someone discovered it, mined it, and refined it. Master craftsmanship turned the metal into an exquisite ring. Today you bring to your marriage the raw materials of character, unselfishness, love, kindness, honesty, and courtesy. If you combine these materials with master craftsmanship and combined effort, you will discover that even as there is no end to the ring, there will be no end to the happiness and joy you can experience together as husband and wife. Give to your Lord first place in your thoughts and in your affections. Give to your companion a place second only to your Lord. Place your personal welfare on a lower rung of the ladder and you will discover that as the ring does not tarnish, so your relationship as husband and wife will be more beautiful and precious with the passing of each year.

As a permanent reminder of the vows that you have made and entered into on this holy occasion, you will now give and receive these rings as a solemn seal to be known by all.

(The minister should present the wife's ring to the husband and wait while he places it on her finger. Then the minister should present the husband's ring to the wife and wait while she places it on his finger.)

In a moment of high and holy dedication, you have solemnized your marriage vows. Acting in the authority vested in me as a minister of the gospel by this state, I take great joy in pronouncing you husband and wife. Therefore, what God has joined together, let no one separate.

(The minister should now offer a prayer of benediction.)

(The minister should address the groom.) You may now claim your bride with a kiss.

Title: A Simple Ceremony for a Home Wedding

Text: "For this reason a man shall leave his father and mother and be joined to his wife, and the two shall become one" **(Eph. 5:31 RSV).**

Introduction

In the Scriptures we are taught in both the Old and New Testaments that we are to worship God alone. We must not permit a person, a cause, or a thing to usurp the place that belongs to God in our hearts and lives. We are to give our first loyalty to our God rather than to our government or to any human institution or relationship. First place belongs to God.

After we have made the decision to worship the Lord God, the relationship of husband and wife is to have priority over all other human relationships. From the beginning it was said, "Therefore a man leaves his father and his mother and cleaves to his wife, and they become one flesh" (Gen. 2:24 RSV). After marriage the husband is to have first place in the love and loyalty of his wife, and the wife is to have first place in the love and loyalty of her husband.

Our Savior honored and approved the contract of marriage by his presence at a wedding in Cana of Galilee. It was at this marriage feast that he performed his first miracle. This miracle manifested his glory (John 2:1–11).

The writer of the book of Hebrews declared that marriage is accepted as an honorable relationship among all people (Heb. 13:4).

(If the bride wishes to be "given" in marriage, the minister should now ask, "Who gives this woman to this man in marriage?")

If you then, _____ (groom), and _____ (bride), after careful consideration, and in the fear of God, have deliberately chosen each other as partners in this holy estate, and know of no just cause why you should not be so united, in token thereof will you please join your right hands.

Groom's vow

_____, in taking this woman to be your lawful and wedded wife, do you promise before God and these assembled witnesses to love her and honor her and cherish her in sickness and in health, and forsaking all others be to her in all things a true and faithful husband until death alone shall part you?

Answer: I will.

Bride's vow

_____, in taking this man to be your lawful and wedded husband, do you promise before God and these assembled witnesses to love him and honor him and cherish him in sickness and in health, and forsaking all others be to him in all things a true and faithful wife until death alone shall part you?

Answer: I will.

Then are you each given to the other for richer or poorer, for better or worse, in sickness and in health, till death alone will part you.

Presentation of rings

(The minister should receive the rings and hold them up before the bride and groom.)

The wedding ring is a perfect circle, thus having no end. As such it symbolizes our hopes and prayers that there will be no end to the happiness and joy you experience as husband and wife.

Do you, _____ (groom), give this ring to your wedded wife as a token of your love for her?

Answer: I do.

Will you, _____ (bride), receive this ring as a token of your wedded husband's love for you, and will you wear it as a token of your love for him?

Answer: I will.

_____ (groom), will you now place the ring on your bride's finger.

Do you, _____ (bride), give this ring to your wedded husband as a token of your love for him?

Answer: I do.

Will you, _____ (groom), receive this ring as a token of your wedded wife's love for you, and will you wear it as a token of your love for her?

Answer: I will.

_____ (bride), will you now place the ring on your groom's finger.

Here in the presence of your relatives and friends, and in the eyes of God, you have made vows to each other binding on you by the laws of this state and by the laws of God. You have sealed these solemn and sacred vows by the giving and receiving of rings. Acting in the authority vested in me as a minister of the gospel by this state, I take great joy in pronouncing you husband and wife.

(The minister should now offer a prayer of benediction.)

(The minister should address the groom.) You may now claim your bride with a kiss.

(The minister may wish to have the couple turn and face the guests.) May I introduce to you Mr. and Mrs. _____.

Sentence Sermonettes

TRUSTING IN GOD

Remember! Wherever God guides you, he will also provide for you.

For the Christian, death is a gateway into the nearer presence of God.

You will live as long as God lives—either in heaven or in hell.

Reach up as far as you can, and God will reach down the rest of the way.

God gives the best to those who leave the choice to him.

God's tomorrow is a day of gladness.

When Satan rocks your boat, Jesus is your best anchor.

No matter how deep the suffering, God's love goes deeper still.

The death of Jesus was—and is—life for the world.

Sometimes the Lord calms the storms; other times he lets the storms rage and calms his child.

The message from God's heart to your heart is "Give me your heart."

What really matters is what happens *in* us, not *to* us.

It is not the greatness of your faith that moves mountains, but your faith in the greatness of God.

LIVING THE CHRISTIAN LIFE

God's grace toward us should make us gracious toward others.

The world crowns success, but God crowns faithfulness.

If Christ is the center of your life, the people on the circumference will know it.

The Spirit of God should be the power in your sails.

The same Bible that says, "Believe," also says, "Behave."

If you think, you will thank.

A smile is a curve that can set a lot of things straight.

Thanksgiving is good, but thanks *living* is better.

The flowers of kindness never fade.

Pity stands and stares. Compassion sees and serves.

We do not stay still spiritually. We either go forward or backward.

Faith in God, like love, must be renewed every day.

Forgiveness saves the expense of anger, the cost of hatred, and the waste of energy.

You may give without loving, but you cannot love without giving.

Today is yours; use it kindly.

Faith opens the door to the heart of God.

DEVELOPING CHARACTER

Bad companions ruin good character.

No one succeeds until he or she turns dreams into action.

Never rest till the good is better and the better is best.

The flowers of tomorrow are in the seeds of today.

People cannot change truth, but truth can change people.

What you are is God's gift to you—what you make of yourself is your gift to God.

Experience is a great teacher, but if you can accept advice, the tuition is much cheaper.

Patience is idling your motor when you feel like stripping your gears.

He who has a sharp tongue soon cuts his own throat.

It is easier to learn truth than to unlearn error.

Just when you think tomorrow will never come, it is yesterday.

How you feel tomorrow depends on what you do today.

You are young only once, but you can be immature forever.

The only difference between stumbling blocks and stepping-stones is the way we use them.

Swallowing your pride occasionally will never give you indigestion.

The road to improvement should always be under construction.

Subject Index

Index of Scripture Texts

CPSIA information can be obtained
at www.ICGtesting.com
Printed in the USA
LVHW091257110722
723204LV00005B/38